Praise for the work

"The best book on the real history of MMA that I've seen...This book really is so great I couldn't put it down."

—*Wrestling Observer* on *Total MMA*

"If the history of MMA was taught as a college course, *Total MMA* would be the official textbook used for the class."

—Sam Caplan, former Bellator matchmaker

"An incredible resource for any fan . . . the book is a treasure trove of MMA stories, people and history."

—*Chicago Sun-Times* on *The MMA Encyclopedia*

"Highly recommended."

—WWE Hall of Famer Jim Ross on *Total MMA*

Copyright © 2020 by Jonathan Snowden

All rights reserved.

Cover Photograph by Ryan Loco
Art by James Frazier

A Hybrid Shoot book
Published by Hybrid Shoot
www.hybridshoot.com

Names: Snowden, Jonathan, author.
Title: Shamrock: The World's Most Dangerous Man
Description: First edition. | Alabama: Hybrid Shoot, 2020.

CONTENTS

Chapter One: A Dangerous Place 5

Chapter Two: Shamrock 17

Chapter Three: Wrestling with the Future 37

Chapter Four: Shooting 62

Chapter Five: Pancrase 84

Chapter Six: The Birth of Ultimate Fighting 99

Chapter Seven: UFC 3 and the Lion's Den 119

Chapter Eight: The King 139

Chapter Nine: Champion at Last 158

Chapter Ten: A Disastrous Dance 180

Chapter Eleven: Final Fight 198

Chapter Twelve: Getting RAW 212

Chapter Thirteen: World's Most Dangerous Man 236

Chapter Fourteen: Working Into a Shoot 257

Chapter Fifteen: Fighting for Pride 283

Chapter Sixteen: Holding Grudges 303

Chapter Seventeen: A Living Death 321

Chapter Eighteen: TUF Enough 346

Chapter Nineteen: Miami Madness 372

Chapter Twenty: World Tour of Sadness 393

Chapter Twenty-One: Final Fight (Redux) 411

Acknowledgements

CHAPTER ONE

A Dangerous Place

The five-year-old is surrounded by jeering, distorted faces, the kicks coming to his defenseless ribs as he tries in vain to protect his face with both arms. He's already learned a hard lesson about what happens when one of your arms slips from a careful shell, blood streaming from his lip a reminder in case his memory falters.

This is Ken Shamrock[1]'s first memory. For a long time, he wanted it to be his last, preferring to die in the ring than live a normal, ordinary existence. Whether he stills wants this, deep in his heart, isn't especially clear.

His rescue happened in a flash, his brother Richie, all of seven, darting into the frame he'd created with his arms, throwing a brick, then yanking his little brother, the third of three ragtag Kilpatrick boys, onto his feet.

"Run," he screamed, as the chase was on. Richie's brick had hit a girl in the face and the mob, already frothing, was truly out for blood now. These white kids didn't belong in their neighborhood, in their alleyway, in their school. They needed to be taught respect. They needed to pay.

---

[1] Kenneth Wayne Kilpatrick was born on February 11, 1964, in Macon, GA, to Dianne and Richard Kilpatrick, the third of three boys. At 18, he took the name of his foster father, a man named Bob Shamrock. I'll refer to him as "Ken Shamrock" throughout for the sake of clarity.

"We started running," Shamrock says.[2] "I don't know how we got through them all, but we did. One girl was chasing us with blood pouring down her face. I remember, the blood was pouring down, but the girl kept coming. Coming after me."

It was a miracle that they'd made it home, but no surprise there was no adult supervision there to help. There rarely was. His parents had split up when he was an infant. Perhaps because of the incessant rumors that each of the three Kilpatrick kids had a different[3] father, maybe because the one who was actually married to his mother was little more than a kid himself.

Either way, home was no sanctuary, not in this neighborhood, not with no adult there to try to restore calm or sanity. Childhood is a time when your personality begins to form, when you become who you are going to be. Ken Shamrock, the world's most dangerous man, was truly born here in Savannah, Georgia, surrounded by a mob, scared, helpless and looking for an escape hatch and a chance to breathe.

"We ran around locking all the doors and windows," Shamrock remembers. "They were throwing clay pots at the door. I stood on the counter in the kitchen to hold the window shut. Someone was trying to climb in. A kid broke the window and I fell down and cut my feet up in the glass."

He remembers running to his mom's bedroom and hiding under the bed. The door was open a crack and he could see all the way down the hall to the front door, shaking and shaking as feet thundered against it, the mob including grown-ups now, enraged by the young girl, the brick and the blood.

He closed his eyes and time passed. When he opened them, unfortunately, his problems hadn't disappeared.

"I saw this police officer come up with my mother," he says. "They were reaching past the police officer trying to grab her. I heard the police officer say 'calm down folks.' Someone reached over his shoulder and hit my mother and then craziness broke out. And I closed my eyes again. That's the last thing I remember."

---

[2] Interviews that use "says" were conducted specifically for this book. You'll also come across interviews that use "said." Those were either conducted by me for past projects or come from other media sources.

[3] "Robbie was the milkman's, Richie's dad was a soldier who never came back. I am Richard Kilpatrick's," Shamrock says, though he admits that's little more than family scuttlebutt.

Richard Kilpatrick had seemed like an exciting catch for a 16-year-old girl living with her parents near Hunter Airbase in Savannah. He'd always been good with the ladies. He had two things going for him—an easy patter and way with the women and a 1949 yellow Studebaker. He was a fast boy with a fast car, one he used to make the pocket cash that kept him in the good times.

"It had a Thunderbird engine in it. I had a hollow out in the trunk where you kept the moonshine," Kilpatrick says. "I picked it up in Douglas and took it back to Savannah Beach. People just liked shine better than they liked regular liquor. Plus they didn't tax it, so it was cheaper."

By the time he met Dianne, he had traded it in on a sharp set of dress blues. The two married when he was 17, newly enlisted in the Air Force after a run in with the law, and she was just 16. They tied the knot at the Airbase, then enjoyed the Bridal Suite at the DeSoto Hotel in town where Richard's father worked as the maintenance manager.

Their oldest son Richie was born shortly after. And the two tried—they really tried.

"I was too young. And I think she was too. I was too wild. But there's no changing it," he says. "But she was good looking and I didn't like to sleep alone."

Ken was born in Kilpatrick's last year in the Air Force. Before then, things went fairly well. They had moved away from his Savannah stomping grounds and were stationed nearby at Warner Robins Airbase. The military imposes some level of discipline on a man's life, and Kilpatrick was forced to curb what would become his rambling ways. When he left, for a job selling shoes in town and eventually throughout the South, things went bad quickly.

"I did a lot of gambling," Kilpatrick says. "I did a lot of running around with women. I was on the go all the time. I was at the bar every night. I was just wild. You couldn't get me to stay home. She didn't mind too much when she thought I was just out drinkin'. Once she found out I was running around with women, then we had problems."

As the fights escalated, the two went their own way. Dianne moved back to Savannah, to a bad neighborhood in Garden City and worked at "the Other End," at the time one of just a handful of drinking establishments on River Street in Savannah, now a popular tourist strip. Richard was busy out selling shoes and himself, to every woman who would have him.

"I was a womanizer," Kilpatrick says. "No use denying it. I'd stop by when I could to see the boys, but no, I couldn't say I was raising them."

Early memories come to Shamrock in a kaleidoscope of images, fragments that are as vivid as they are incomplete. There is the man, cornering him and his mom in an alley, very black and very naked except for the white underwear on his head. That one ends in another foot race to the front door.

There's the time he locked everyone out of his classroom at school after punching his teacher in the stomach. The teacher had picked him up by the earlobe and was dragging him to the principal, blood again streaming down his face. Life had taught him nothing but the instinct to fight and to run, in that order.

Mostly he remembers the beatings. In the bathroom at school, in the yard at recess, on the way home—wherever he and his brothers went, violence followed.

"I know why I got jumped," Shamrock says. "It was because of the color of my skin. We were these white kids stuck in the middle of an African American neighborhood."

What he doesn't remember is a single happy memory. The closest he can come is sitting in the backseat of the car and clowning on other drivers when they stopped at a traffic light. Birthday parties and play dates were things people on television did. They weren't a part of his existence.

"I don't remember being hugged or spending any time together with my mother," he says. "At all. Nothing. Zero."

Occasionally his dad would come around. Sometimes that was nice. Sometimes he just made things worse, throwing off the balance they were trying to maintain in a neighborhood where they never really belonged.

"There were a couple of boys that came to the house and said they were going to knock the door down," Kilpatrick remembers. "Well, I just happened to be there, and I told them I would beat their little asses. They said 'Im going to go get my daddy.' I said 'Well, go get 'em.'

"He came by knocking and I told him 'if you don't get off my porch, I'll whip your dumbass too.' He decided to get off my porch. It might have been because of that baseball bat in my hand. I can't say."

Eventually, though, Kilpatrick would leave, not to be seen for weeks. The boys, however, had to live in the chaos he'd wrought.

It was a hard way to live, especially for three kids often left to their own devices for even the most basic necessities. His brother Richie recalls scrounging in dumpsters and vacant lots for the things his parents couldn't provide.

"We'd look for food, look for toys. Anything we could find," he says.[4] "We learned to fend for ourselves. Survival was in our blood from a very young age."

Diane Kilpatrick was a waitress, a go-go dancer, or a prostitute, depending on what day you ask and Shamrock's mood.[5] It could be a combination of all three in truth. What she was, for sure, was a very young woman with three very young kids and a deadbeat ex-husband who eventually only came by to steal, borrow or beg money. She did what she had to in order to survive the crappy hand she'd been dealt.

"If she was there, she was usually with somebody," Shamrock says. "She would have people watch us. And me and my brothers were molested. You rarely hear about a woman taking advantage of a little boy and if you do, people laugh it off. But we were just kids, under 10. And this woman was forcing us to do sexual things with her. And doing things to each other. My oldest brother doing stuff to me.

"It messes your mind up. Your thought process, the way you think about women is messed up. I was having sex at nine and ten years old because I'd experienced that on a regular basis. I had seen so much already."

When Shamrock was five, Dianne finally left Richard Kilpatrick and snuck off like a thief in the night with an Army aviator named Bob Nance. Kilpatrick had met Dianne's new beau and the two had

---

[4] Before he fell victim to a stroke, Richie talked with author Richard Hanner for Shamrock's first book, *Inside the Lion's Den*.

[5] His past now belongs to Shamrock alone. His mother passed away in 1984, his brother Richie suffered a stroke and communicates only with difficulty, and his brother Robbie is serving a life sentence in a California prison after a third strike.

exchanged words when Nance tried to discipline the boys in front of him. To avoid an ugly scene, Dianne worked out a solution to clear any roadblocks in front of her.

"She had me thrown in jail for non-support before she left," Kilpatrick says. "I was not a real good person at that time. She knew I'd cause trouble if she tried to leave and take the boys[6]."

The makeshift new family drove for days across the country to Nance's hometown of Napa, California, offering Dianne and the boys a new start, a new home and a new adventure.

"We thought it was going to be great," Shamrock says. "White picket fence, food on the table, we have a daddy now. I had never known my biological father. Can you imagine?"

That first night at Nance's parents house, Shamrock got the first inkling that things wouldn't be the panacea he had hoped for. Nance's parents got into a vicious, physical fight, one everyone pretended hadn't happened the next morning. The suburbs, it seemed were no less violent than the streets had been—they just hid it better.

Nance was a Vietnam veteran, a member of the 162nd Assault Helicopter Company known as the "Vultures." He'd flown more than 1500 combat hours in a Huey. He was a hard man and unaccustomed to working with children. Likewise, Shamrock and his brothers weren't used to having someone attempt to parent them in any meaningful way. It was a disastrous combination from the start.

The boys wanted nothing more than to explore their new environment, check out the neighborhood and meet other kids. Instead, Nance put them to work, with long days spent weeding, raking and doing chores of all kinds.

"We never did things right," Shamrock remembers. "And he would scream at us. Then he would restrict us. Send us to our room. Things got really frustrating real quick."

Acclimating to their unfamiliar school was just as difficult. The "Nance boys" were outsiders, new kids with weird Southern accents and a world-weary swagger that no one in Napa could recognize or relate to. Very early on, a local tough named Bruce Hansen challenged Ken to a fight after school. Instead, Shamrock immediately belted him and put the boots to him. It was a shocking display of violence to the Napa kids. To Shamrock, it was just a day in the life, a matter-of-fact

---

[6] Kilpatrick wouldn't see his children again for almost 50 years.

survival strategy.

"We had grown up with no discipline," he says. "We raised ourselves. I walk into this middle class school in a predominately white neighborhood with a street thug attitude.

"I couldn't understand the thought process and they didn't understand me. Where I come from, you don't tell people what you're going to do. You don't say 'meet me over here.' You can get shot or stabbed or jumped. You don't plan a fight. In Georgia I didn't fit in because of my race but I fit in culturally. Here, I was in a place where I fit in racially, but I didn't really fit in."

The boys felt just as isolated at home where they never quite fit into Nance's regimented household. He tried to instill discipline, to involve them in sports, to be a father. Shamrock, in particular, excelled at sports and Nance helped push him in that direction.

"I remember one time we were at a golf course and he put me on his lap and tried to talk to me," Shamrock says. "Someone must have said something to him about his parenting and he tried to explain why he was doing what he was doing. Because he cared about me.

"It was almost like he wanted to but couldn't really connect with me. He didn't know how. I look at it now and I see that he was trying. But he was raised that way. The same thing had happened to him."

No matter how much Nance tried, he just didn't know how to raise three children, especially three bad kids who were already out of control. His short temper meant his anger would escalate from yelling to physical violence in the blink of an eye.

"As soon as I'd leave, they'd go back to raising hell," Nance said. "So I'd come home and beat the crap out of them again."

The beatings were numerous, whether with belt or open hand. Once, Shamrock remembers, he had been sent to bed without finishing his dinner after he'd tried to hide his peas under the table. In the middle of the night, he'd snuck into the kitchen and eaten a plate of cookies. The next morning, Nance lined the three boys up and demanded a confession.

"He acted like somebody had been killed," Shamrock says, still remembering the screams. "'Who ate the cookies!' The veins were just bulging in his neck. We don't say anything, me or my brothers. Because there's already a power struggle going on between us and him and this guy ain't going to break us.

"He knows it was me. Everyone knows. But he brings us into the bedroom and he asks again 'Who did it? One of you is going to tell me.' My brothers are glaring at me, but I ain't saying. He bends us over and wales on us with his belt. He's thinking the peer pressure from my brothers is going to break me."

It was an extended beating and eventually Nance sent Richie and Robbie out of the room. Now it was just him and Ken, a stubborn ten-year-old, running and ducking and diving around the room as Nance swung the belt wildly, all pretense of control long vanished. Then, finally, his step-father managed to grab a hold of him.

"He grabbed the end of the belt and starts hitting me with the actual belt buckle," Shamrock says. "He's hitting me in the head, in the body, in the groin area, the ankles. He's hitting me as hard as he can and finally I drop to the ground and he really beats me. He lost his temper.

"I checked out. I looked out the window into this white light. I could still feel it, it hurt, but it wasn't reaching all the way in. It wasn't in my soul. I just felt it on the outside."

It wasn't too long before both of Shamrock's brothers ran away for the first time[7], leaving him as the sole focus of all of Nance's anger and attention. His mother, almost pathologically afraid of conflict, would pretend not to notice the violent chaos swirling all around her.

"It was like being trapped in a world where you can't smile," Shamrock says. "You can't cry. You never feel comfortable. My only peace was sleep. I'd sleep so long I'd wet the bed rather than get up. I'd soil my pants when I was playing outside rather than have to come in the house."

Nance had no idea what to do with this unexpected display of weakness from his tough young charge. This was, to him, even worse than the recalcitrance and misbehavior. He bought a sheet that would shock Ken at night when he wet the bed and would attempt to embarrass him publicly in an attempt to shame him out of the habit.

"One time he stripped me down and made me go out into the front yard where all the other kids are playing," Shamrock says. "I'm completely naked. He makes me clean out my drawers in front of all the other kids.

"They all saw me. Now, kids will make fun of anything. But not this. This was hard for those kids. They didn't even make fun of me. It was too uncomfortable."

For Ken, it was the last straw. A week later, he too was in the streets.

---

[7] "There was a time I hated Bob Nance," Robbie told Hanner. "I think I ran away from home just to get away from him."

Home for a 10-year-old Ken Shamrock became the back of an abandoned car. He spent his days behind a 7-11 near Puebla Vista Elementary, the school he was *supposed* to be attending. Sometimes he would show up—to relieve kids of their lunch money.

"I was lost," he says. "I had no idea what the world was about besides taking things from people. Anything else was just an opportunity for someone to take advantage of you. We didn't know what a soft side was."

He was getting an advanced education in street urchin studies, learning how to remove the putty from a window frame, remove the glass pane, and take whatever he could carry.

"As crazy as it sounds," he says, "it was more peaceful than living at Bob Nance's house. On the street, I slept peacefully."

Things went on like this for some time until a group of kids descended on his turf from a different neighborhood, their eyes on his meager stash, including a stuffed animal he slept with at night.

His most precious possession, however, was a lock-knife, five inches of steel he wasn't afraid to wave around menacingly. But it wasn't enough to scare the other kids off. He took aim at one of his would-be robbers, with a trash can lid, but ended up with a steak knife in his arm, right down to the bone and blood spurting everywhere.

"I woke up in a hospital," Shamrock says. "The police had been called and they finger printed me and of course my fingerprints ended up being associated with all these robberies. My file was thick. That's when I became a ward of the state, living in juvenile hall. From that time on until I was 18 years old."

The system, like with many kids, didn't work out for a young Ken Shamrock. At juvenile hall, where he spent six months after recovering in the hospital, he was one of the youngest kids, constantly defending himself with a mop he was assigned for floor cleaning.

"Even though I was 10 years old, nobody was going to punk me," he says. "They'd have to kill me. I wasn't nobody's bitch."

Every day was a battle for survival. Some nights too. One night someone grabbed him and tried to stuff his head into the toilet and drown him. When the guards came, he told them he had slipped.

"I didn't snitch," Shamrock says. "That earned me some respect. After that I was okay in there. I would still have to fight, still got my butt kicked. But I wasn't a target all the time."

At his first foster home in St. Helena, near his stomping grounds in Napa, he clashed with the local sheriff who had taken him in and was using him as unpaid manual labor while his own son sat and watched.

"He's screaming 'I told you to be out there digging.'

"I was like 'what about him?'

'I told *you* to be out there.'

'I ain't going to do it if he ain't. I'm not your slave.'

'We're Indian here. The way we do things if you don't work, you don't eat.'

'Well, I guess I'm not going to eat.'

'You can either go out there and work, or I'm going to call someone to come take you away.'

'Call 'em.'

"And away I went, right back to juvenile hall."

If that was the life he'd wanted, he could have stayed with Bob Nance. He was shuttled from group home to foster home, sometimes lasting a few months, sometimes wearing out his welcome almost immediately.

"Every time I went somewhere it was a lie," he says. "We were just numbers, a piece of meat they got paid for storing. Nobody cared if we lived or died, just so long as we didn't bother them. We didn't matter. And kids can sense that stuff. Eventually, no matter where they put me, I wasn't staying."

At one house the kids were all smoking dope and wearing these ancient World War II gas masks[8]. There were, he was told, no rules there. But something told him, as promising as this sounded, there was more for him out there than a driftless life of easy drugs—not that he was above escaping his life from time to time, especially when he would get some time with his mom and Bob Nance and his brothers were around.

"There was this hopped up Vega in the neighborhood with these big tires and fancy stereo," Shamrock remembers. "This guy said he'd give us some lines[9] and we could party all night if I'd go get the stereo and the rims. So we went in and just trashed that car. Then we partied all

---

[8] Soldiers started smoking marijuana or hashish using their military issued gas masks during the Vietnam War, then brought the practice back with them into the civilian world.

[9] He's referring to cocaine, the drug of choice in the late 1970s.

night. We didn't miss a beat. We didn't know any better."

On one trip home, his mother hugged him. This wouldn't be unusual for most people. For Shamrock it was a revelation. She had started going to church and wanted him to come with her. So, he did, mostly because to do otherwise was to be left home alone with Bob Nance.

"I remember feeling the Holy Spirit," he says. "I was not looking for it. I just felt it. I didn't know what love was. I didn't know what peace was. I didn't know what it was to be calm. But I felt it. "

It was a strong enough experience that he sought out a pastor afterwards. He didn't know what was going on, but it was a feeling he was interested in exploring. But his street instincts kicked in instead. Contentment was not an emotion that he could trust.

"I was worried about sounding gay when telling the youth pastor about what I'd felt," Shamrock says. "And I was worried that he would feel like he had a license to do something. I didn't know any other kind of world."

Instead, he went right back into the system, yo-yo'ing from home to home, running away, getting caught stealing or fighting, or for vagrancy and tossed right back into juvenile hall to start the cycle over again.

By the time he was 13 years old, the system's patience with Ken Shamrock was wearing thin. Eventually, he was told, they'd stop placing him in group homes and send him to the California Youth Authority instead.

If juvenile hall is kids' jail, CYA is their prison, complete with gangs, fights, chain fences and a complete separation from the outside world. At the time, Shamrock says the prospect didn't frighten him. Today, he realizes he would have never emerged into regular society again.

"Sometimes it's worse than actual prison, because when you're that young, everyone has something to prove," he says. "In men's prison, it can be more relaxed, because they've been around and just want to do their time.[10] It sucks enough without making it worse. Once you go in, you're kind of a criminal. It's like an education in how to be a criminal and you come out only knowing other criminals."

---

[10] "That's why my brother Frank opted to go to prison instead of the California Youth Authority with punk kids trying to prove themselves," Shamrock says, getting ahead of our story. "He would have done harder time there than in regular prison."

There was, one social worker told him, one more chance for him that didn't involve CYA. She showed him pictures, of a beautiful home, of a horse in a stable, of kids playing at pool tables.

"I remember looking at it thinking 'bullshit.' It was a mansion," he says. "Everyone had lied before. They tell you what you need to hear."

Despite his reservations, Shamrock found himself packed in a car with a social worker, a kid by the name of Jeff Ainsworth who had tried to drown him in the toilet during his first stay in juvie and a third boy who wouldn't stop eye-balling him over an ancient beef with his older brother Richie[11].

It was a two-hour drive to Susanville, California, and the rest of his life.

---

[11] "My brother Richie had a lot of beefs," Shamrock says. "He used to collect for drug dealers. He's go and knock on the door and put a gun to a guy's head. One guy wouldn't pay. Richie wasn't very big, so he sat a bat next to the door....breaks the guy's shins. Puts a beating on him. That's how psycho my brother was."

CHAPTER TWO
Shamrock

* * *

Ken Shamrock had never seen a place quite like it. On television or in the movies, sure. But not in real life. If he'd passed a house like this in the car, staring up the hill at a golf course life he'd never know, he wouldn't have dared dream that one day he'd be living there.

The ceilings at the Shamrock Boys Ranch were 15-20 feet high, chandeliers hanging, covered the entire way to the floor with magnificent draperies. There was an enormous metal table with giant cast iron chairs, each place immaculately set with the kind of pewter goblets someone might drink out of in a period piece. There was a grand piano in one room and a fireplace in another. Out back there was a collection of bodybuilding equipment and two Arabian horses.

Most of all, it was the kids that shocked Shamrock. They were watching a giant big screen television, bugging the cook Elizabeth for a snack and, this was the weird part, smiling. It was like he was watching a foreign language film without the subtitles—none of this fit with how Ken had come to see the world.

"I saw these kids running around," he says. "They were like me, but they were playing, wrestling, playing pool. I couldn't figure it out. They weren't punching each other out or fighting. Something seemed wrong to me. Of course, there wasn't. There was something right. I just hadn't ever experienced it."

There was a standard protocol for checking into these kinds of group homes. Ken had done it all before. The adults would talk, mostly about him being a violent head case, while the kids would tell him what would get you a beating and what offenses would lead to being shipped back to juvie. But Shamrock Boys Ranch was different. Bob Shamrock came over to talk. Not to the social worker. To him. To Ken.

"Where I come from you aren't open," Ken says. "You're very closed off. Because you don't trust anyone. So, none of us accepted anything, even though we wanted to. We were very reserved.

"I remember thinking to myself 'why's he talking to us? I've got nothing to say to him and he's got nothing to say to me.' "

Bob Shamrock pulled out a file. It belonged to Ken and it was thick. But he didn't seem particularly concerned.

"This is who you used to be," Bob said. "You have a new start. You can change your outcome. I'm here to help you do that. I don't care what you did. I care about what you're going to do."

Bob and Dee Dee Shamrock had met on a blind date. Her best friend was her college roommate. The roommate's boyfriend's best friend was Bob Shamrock. They practically had to be forced into this first encounter, Dee Dee shy and Bob hard to pin down between church, community work and his job at his father's fabrication shop. But it was an instant, chemical romance.

"We fell in love right away," Dee Dee remembers. "It was my first week of college and we were married that following June."

Bob had always been a gregarious man, good with kids and an active mentor for youths at the church. But the two couldn't have kids of their own. At least, that's what doctors said—and in the age before in vitro treatments were common, there wasn't much more to be done.

The two felt a hole there, where kids would normally be, but had a happy relationship full of travel and adventure. Bob was just fun to be around, a people person who commanded attention and could liven up any room but equally sensitive to people's desires, often knowing just what someone needed to brighten up a gloomy day.

That's what led him to invite some local foster kids in Anza, California, to their home for Thanksgiving one year, a decision that changed the Shamrocks' lives forever.

Soon after, he was quitting his job with his father and opening up a group home in 1968. He went to work for the local school district driving a bus. She drove a mobile library to rural communities. Both had the summer off to spend with their new boys. What had been a nice gesture at Thanksgiving time had turned into a mission.

"All of them were troubled in some way or another," Dee Dee says. "You had to look past that. We, what we tried to do is see what they were good at and then invest in that part of their lives and not so much point out their past or their faults."

In 1973, they moved their operation to the small town of Susanville, California, where they found the perfect house at the perfect price. Renting with an option to buy so they could escape a crippling down payment, the couple moved into a 6400-square-foot house with 14 bedrooms, seven baths, and room for up to 25 wards of the state.

Near a golf course and Emerson Lake, and far enough away from what passed for "town" that they wouldn't constantly tempt trouble, the Shamrock Boys Ranch became the salvation for hundreds of boys over the years. Over the years, the couple had seen and heard it all—

and it was hard to put one over on them.

"When he sat down, I kind of went to shine him and do my bit," Frank Shamrock[12], who also lived for a time at the ranch, remembers. "And he just cut me off after about four words and said, 'you can stop right there and shut the hell up.' I'd never had anyone call me on my shit and bust my nuts like that."

By the time Ken arrived, the pattern of daily life there had been long established. The boys were expected to contribute to the running of the house. They all had chores and were expected to do them. A C-average was the standard in school and sports were highly encouraged. They would respect each other, the counselors and Bob and Dee Dee.

Acquiescence was rewarded with things typically unheard of in other group homes—an allowance, free reign of the house, stylish new clothes and shoes and even a trip into Reno, Nevada, in one of Bob's classic cars.

Punishments were meted out with some degree of patience. Shamrock preferred counseling to simply giving up on a boy and sending him back into the system. He knew his home was often the last stop before CYA, so he wasn't going to see a kid locked away because he got caught drinking a beer or getting into a scuffle in town. Those, he believed, were the kinds of trouble all kids got into—why expect that these kids wouldn't, well, be kids?

"We didn't get any angels," Bob said in a 2007 interview. "These weren't boys who were going to be perfect all the time. They all needed some help or they wouldn't have been with us."

A big part of Bob Shamrock's plan for his extended brood was simply treating kids like kids. In a lot of other facilities, the boys were little more than numbers, each one worth a certain dollar amount every month.[13] At the Shamrock Boys Ranch, the kids were more than just temporary residents in an institutional system. They were encouraged to think of the Ranch as if it was their home.

"The kids weren't used to be able to just come in and go and get something to eat," Jerry Ann Mambourg, a neighbor and close friend of the family says.[14] "Just like a normal kid after school. They could go

---

[12] Then known as Frank Juarez, he would later be adopted by Bob and become MMA superstar Frank Shamrock.

[13] In 1980 the monthly rate per kid was $863 according to a local newspaper report.

[14] The Mambourg's daughter Tonya became Ken's second wife in 2004.

into the refrigerator and get something to eat. That's not a fact in most group homes."

While the Shamrocks helped hundreds of kids become functioning adults, capable of being turned loose on the civilian population, his Boys Ranch, no matter how crisply the linen napkins were folded, still had a hint of *Lord of the Flies* to it.

"Pillow fights, brawls, all for one, one for all," Dave Cranney, whose time overlapped with Ken's at the Shamrock Boys Ranch says. "Jumping on each other and wrestling. There was many a time when you'd hear people screaming. But when Bob came in, alls he had to do was raise his voice. You'd see a bunch of rough boys toe the line real quick. He would just give you a look."

The Ranch was almost divided into two worlds. First, there was Dee Dee's world, a world of church services, songs around the piano and nightly dinners where kids who had never been asked 'hey, how was your day?' saw real life people spend time listening and sharing their own experiences.

"What we wanted to model in front of them was a normal life," she says. "We wanted it to look and feel like in a normal household. We didn't really have what you would call a game plan. We lived our lives as we would normally and shared in front of them who we were."

The whole house gathered for the nightly meal—no exceptions unless you were participating in an official school activity. Getting that many rambunctious kids settled down and seated at the same time in the same place was a logistical challenge. But, to Bob, the experience was integral to running the home because it gave him a chance to connect with each boy nightly.

"We sat at a giant table. There were pewter cups and bowls, very ornate and fancy," Frank Shamrock says. "It was very fine dining like. Everybody had to have nice manners. It was an education for us, how you act at the table. It was a process. Part of it was you didn't talk out of line. You didn't pick on granny. You didn't curse.

"You didn't do the stuff you're not supposed to do, and if you got asked more than once or twice, Bob would throw a spoon at you. If you talked during prayer or did stuff you shouldn't have been doing, he would instantly adjust you. But in the funniest way. He was funny."

There was another world at Shamrock Boys Ranch, too. Here, force was sometimes required to establish primacy or prove a point. Many of the kids, Bob believed, didn't respect anything but violence or power—at least in the beginning. While he was intent on changing that mindset, he and the counselors, often former college athletes, had to sometimes speak with a kid in the only language he understood.

"I remember him getting up and hitting one of the guys there right straight in the nose and there was blood everywhere," Rick Radosevich, who was Ken's roommate at the Boys Ranch and beyond says. "The kid was being out of line and being disrespectful when Bob was talking, so Bob got up and punched the kid in the face.

"I can remember there were four or five or six times where he knocked Kenny to the ground and shoved soap down in Kenny's mouth for cussing or back talking him."

Violence was used as a problem solving mechanism among the boys as well. They were expected to work through their own issues. If that wasn't possible, it was time to knuckle up, either in the backyard or the huge front room with couches that wrapped around the wall and left plenty of room to slug it out.

"If you had a disagreement at the house, you would put the gloves on and go three rounds," Cranney says. "It solved a lot of issues in the house. Bob would say, 'Oh, you're having an argument? Get the gloves.' The guys would either say, 'Okay,' or, 'No, never mind.' Shake on it. It was always a good deterrent to any more conflict. Either there was conflict resolution with your fists or you had to talk it out."

Grievances sometimes involved more than two individuals. When that happened, a bunkhouse meeting was called, a fearsome proposition for even the most hardened resident of the Ranch. The "bunkhouse" was a converted stand-alone garage that had eight bedrooms and a lawless reputation. It was outside the rules and grownup control of the main house, a world of its own, one filled with the constant thump of wrestling matches and general chaos. A bunkhouse meeting, often called when one of the boys had something stolen from him, almost always devolved into violence.

Shamrock remembers his first bunkhouse meeting vividly. He was one of three new kids, only there about three weeks, when one of the older boys had some money stolen out of his room. Shamrock had a sense for when violence was imminent and was ready for trouble, back against the wall to avoid getting jumped, when one of the other kids admitted to the crime.

"He says, 'What are you gonna do about it?' And it was like slow motion man," Ken says. "Scott, who was sitting down on his bed, in one single motion, rolled over, stood up, and hit him right in the jaw.

And it shattered his jaw. I mean, blood went everywhere. He had to have his jaw wired shut. That was my first experience there. And I was like, 'I ain't taking no money. I ain't gonna steal no silverware, I ain't stealing the goblets.' I mean, it set the tone."

The lingering threat of violence was a constant presence at the Ranch. But with that risk came the kind of rewards that just didn't exist at other group homes. Dee Dee made it a point to buy each boy new clothes, the kind of stuff other kids were wearing in school and not the cast-offs from Goodwill many of the kids were accustomed to.

They also made a point of integrating the boys into the community. The local paper is filled with "Thank you" messages to Bob and the boys for their participation in various volunteer programs and charity works. Trips to Reno were one of the carrots that influenced good behavior every bit as much as any stick.

"If you did your chores, you got an allowance," Cranney says. "If you didn't, you got a deduction. You got an allowance at the end of the month if you did the right thing and then you could take your girlfriend out to the movie or whatever. You had to be responsible. You learn behavior has consequences."

Shamrock was thrust right into the heart of this world almost immediately. Bob had identified him as a kid with real potential, in part Dee Dee believes, because he always gravitated towards the athletic and rambunctious kids.

"Ken was like the baby, but he wasn't the baby," Bob said. "He was the man very quickly. After a short while he kind of took over leadership of the house. He was ready to fight at the drop of the hat. But the other side of the coin was, he had a certain amount of character that a lot of these other kids did not have. He had a real sense of what was right and what was wrong."

Ken had never met anyone quite like Bob, who was quick with a laugh and a hug but sometimes harsh and violent when circumstances called for it.

"He immediately put me in charge of the red room[15]," Shamrock

---

[15] Rooms at the Shamrock Boys Ranch were named for the color of the paint on the walls.

says. "And I didn't have very good bedside manners. When this kid didn't vacuum the room like he was supposed to, I beat him up. My dad heard about it. And asked, 'So, you beat him up, huh?' That was all he really said. There was no punishment."

A few weeks later, it was Ken's turn to vacuum the room and he was late getting to it. Bob sprung into action, his opportunity to teach his newest ward a lesson finally at hand.

"He walked up, he shoved me in the closet and beat me up," Ken says. "Not like punching, but just physically grabbing and banging me around. He threw me into the closet, grabbed me back out, threw me into the closet again. He threw me on the bed. He goes, 'That's what it feels like.' What can you say? It was pretty clear. I couldn't even be mad."

The home was filled with alpha individuals, from Bob and the instructors right down to a 13-year-old Ken, many of them used to surviving in a very cruel world. But, even among this group, Ken stood out, constantly asserting his dominance over his surroundings.

"When I first met Ken for the first time, he basically wrestled me to the ground and told me he's going to make a man out of me," Radosevich says. "Kenny took me under his wing and he did exactly what he said, he made a man out of me. He was probably the toughest 13-year-old you'd ever run into.

"I wrestled with Kenny every day. He'd grab me and just take me to the floor and make you wrestle. A lot of the times there was blood all over and he would just keep going. He didn't care if he was bleeding or if you were. He wouldn't let you up even if your face was cut, nose bleeding, broken nose, he kept going."

Bob and Dee Dee looked to help kids explore their areas of interest. For some, that might be music and art. Others wanted to become writers or learn how to work on cars. But most, overflowing with anger and testosterone, needed a way to unleash some of their pent up energy. For them, the Shamrocks provided an outlet in athletics.

"Ken was really rough around the edges when he got there," family friend Don Mambourg says. "He had no respect for authority. But I think each of us saw the potential in him. It was just a matter of getting Ken to recognize what his potential was and bringing it out. And that's what Bob was so good at. He knew what Ken needed was a way to get his aggression out."

Sports matter in America. A lot of ills can be overlooked and problems overcome when a young man shows the first inkling of ability on the field of play. For much of his life, Ken Shamrock was ignored, cast out and left to his own devices to make his way in the world.

Then someone put a ball in his hand and everything changed. Or, more accurately, they put a football in someone else's hands and turned Shamrock loose to chase him down. That's when all the behaviors that had gotten him locked behind bars and then tossed from a variety of group and foster homes were suddenly traits that moved his life in a positive direction.

"I went from being the outcast and rebel to becoming someone people wanted to be around," Shamrock says. "People wanted to help me. Girls were interested. At the home I was becoming a favorite. Things changed so quick. All of the sudden my life, it meant something. I woke up one morning and I had a family, I had a mom and dad. I had friends. I wasn't running from the cops. I had never had that before. My world was good."

His introduction to the team got off to a shaky start when he showed up for practice the first day with metal baseball cleats, clacking down to the stadium while some of the upperclassmen just looked at him and shook their heads. But his aggression and anger[16] made him a natural, albeit one who posed a bit of risk to his own teammates at first.

"They had to tame him," teammate Billy Burke remembers. "He was hurting so many people during practice that they gave him a pad to hit people with instead of using his body to make a tackle. Because he was freaking knocking people out on our own team. It was like, you need to slow down here."

His biggest challenge was getting onto the field in the first place. Bob Shamrock required straight C's across the board in order to participate in athletics and Ken hadn't ever regularly attended school for any extended period of time. In his freshman year of high school he struggled to read, could only do single column addition and friends recall having to help teach him to read a clock. He was placed in special ed classes and raced to catch up with his peers.

The year had changed his life. For the first time, Ken saw a future and understood what it felt like to be nurtured and loved. Then he was allowed to return home to his mom and Bob Nance in Napa, free from

---

[16] His sheer power stood out. At 14 and just 160 pounds, teammates remember he was bench pressing 315 pounds.

all the rules and restrictions of Shamrock's Ranch. But, having seen a different way to approach life, he couldn't go back to his old one.

"I called him and said, 'Hey, can I come back?' And he said, 'Yeah, absolutely, if you wanna come back.'

"I remember fighting with my biological mother about it, saying, 'Here, I'm just gonna get in trouble.' She had her problems with it, but she let me go."

Back in Susanville with Bob, Ken picked back up at school without missing a beat. Life at the Ranch was good, too. He was a favorite of the counselors and always part of the group that would drive with the counselors into Reno on the weekends to go to dance clubs geared towards teenagers, decked out in Angel suits and silk shirts with an oversized lapel and a purple and green "Shamrock" jacket to complete the ensemble.

"We'd walk into a place and you would see the look of 'uh oh' on the other guys' faces," Cranney says. "Sure enough, it wouldn't take very long before we'd take the girls from them.

"There was nothing they could do about it because they'd have a group of two or three and we'd have eighteen. Even if you didn't get along with a guy, if somebody messed with a Shamrock, it was on like Donkey Kong. Eighteen guys came out of the woodwork."

Adjusting to a more typical teenage life wasn't always easy for Ken. Sometimes he wouldn't be able to control his rage and was quick to lash out. In his sophomore year he hospitalized a senior in a fight, knocking him down and putting his steel-toed boots to his head. Only a passionate intervention by Bob with the principal saved Ken from an expulsion he probably deserved.

"Sometimes he'd get so angry, he would just see black and have tunnel vision," Burke says. "He would just stare a hole right through you. I could talk him down when he would need to be talked down off the ledge. He was almost like a shark, when it rolls its eyes back in its head before it bites. That's where he would go in his head and it was like 'holy cow.'"

Ken was slowly integrating into the community when the wheels came off the bus all at once at the end of his sophomore year of high school—that's when Bob and Dee Dee Shamrock, his perfect example of an American marriage, split up. It was a blow to all the kids at the ranch, especially Ken, who had finally found the family he was searching for. They had even talked about adopting him[17], though his mom wouldn't allow it.

"It was like my heart had just been ripped out," Ken says. "Where are we going to go? I'm thinking the house is going to close and I'm going to be right back where I started. After all of this. And there's no way to direct my anger. I can't rip anybody's throat out. Who is there to blame? So, all my anger is directed towards Dee Dee.[18]"

For Dee Dee, it was a relationship with no future. She believed it wasn't even a marriage anymore. Instead, they were little more than two people who ran a group home together. While their friends expressed shock, she had been warned that the decision to devote their lives to foster kids often ended with relationships in tatters.

"I began to feel pushed out," she says. "I was no longer of any consequence or important and I felt like I wasn't needed anymore. It seemed that even the things that I wanted to share with Bob, just the two of us for anniversaries and the things that I would write him in cards, the intimate things that were just for us, he had to share in front of the boys. He had to read everything to them. I don't know why, but it humiliated me.

"We had, it got to the point where we had nothing. Our relationship had deteriorated and there's nothing just for us as a married couple anymore. It seemed like I kind of had to wait my turn if I wanted to be with him and share him with the boys."

There were whispers of other issues impacting their relationship as well. Rumors abounded of Dee Dee having a relationship with one of the older boys—and of Bob being caught in compromising positions with one of the male counselors.

"He used to go to the bathhouses in San Francisco," Ken says. "(Dee Dee) found the receipts. She tried to talk to him about it and he'd say 'just be a good Christian wife.' So there was a lot of weird stuff going on."

Many close to him believe Bob was a closeted homosexual who

---

[17] The Shamrocks also looked into adopting Dave Cranney, who ran away instead. They may have been desperately looking for a way to save their relationship.

[18] The two wouldn't speak for 30 years but have since reconciled and Dee Dee is an active member of the extended Shamrock family.

never managed to come out to the world. He gravitated towards physical, muscular young men, almost collecting them some thought, first at the Boys Ranch and later the various incarnations of the Lion's Den.

"Bob always had his favorite boy toys," one Lion's Den fighter says. "He only liked young, white, good looking kids. He took a special interest in them."

After Dee Dee left, things changed dramatically between Ken and Bob. He was no longer one among many at the Ranch. He was Bob's chosen one and their relationship became almost codependent at times, partners in a way and not just father and son.

"When Bob and Dee Dee got divorced, Bob put all that emotional energy into Ken," Shamrock's wife Tonya says[19]. "It was like Bob needed Ken as his almost significant other. Bob needed that emotional support from Ken because he lost it from Dee Dee. And he put too much on Ken."

"It really changed the environment from me being a happy kid, to me being a fearful kid," Shamrock told the Stone Cold Steve Austin podcast. " I didn't know where I was going to end up. And it turned me from being a son into being a person that would support him, someone he could lean on. And I was not capable of that. I didn't have the ability to do that. But I tried."

The additional emotional baggage made it harder for Ken to keep his anger, always close to the surface, from boiling over. When it did, it could be ugly. Bob brought in a psychologist to visit with Ken each week, but the young man shut him out too.

"I just couldn't handle all of it," Shamrock says. "How much more do you want to take from me? Why does the world want to bury me in the ground? It was a really scary time and I was spiraling out of control."

Eventually a sense of calm spread through the entire Boys Ranch. The boys had been sent home for two weeks while officials sorted through the mess of the Shamrock's personal life. Everyone assumed that the

---

[19] Tonya and her family were also his neighbors growing up. They had foster kids in their own home and a solid friendship with the Shamrocks.

facility would close and the boys would be distributed throughout the system, again left to their own devices. Instead, Bob Shamrock was willing to go at it alone and the Ranch continued without really missing a beat.

It was an opportunity for the kids to have a new life. But not everyone could be saved. Many didn't want to be. Sometimes success in life comes down to opportunities—other times it's all about choices. The Kilpatricks are a perfect example. In his junior year of high school, Ken's older brother Robbie got the same chance he had, the opportunity to turn his circumstances around and invent a new life for himself at the Ranch. But unlike his younger sibling, he couldn't figure out a way to leave his past behind.

In very short order, Robbie had gotten busted for drugs, tried to stab a kid at the home and gotten into a brutal fight with one of the counselors.

"When it was over, Robbie walked out," Ken says. "The counselor, this big old white guy, didn't. He'd beat the guy up. The door had a hole in it and I looked through it and the guy was lying on the floor.

"Robbie got kicked out. He had a chance. He screwed up a lot. There wasn't anything I could do to help him."

Brief experiences with Robbie offered Ken's new friends in Susanville a glimpse at his old life. While rough and tumble in its own small town way, it was still a relatively clean-cut place with small-town problems and temptations. Robbie Kilpatrick's world, the same world Ken came from, was different, more vibrant in many ways but potentially perilous.

"When we were juniors in high school Ken says 'Hey, my brother is getting out of prison, let's go to Napa and get him.' Here comes this guy, probably maybe 5'8" but just huge, muscle on muscle," Burke says. "And then they just started arguing about whether the pig iron in the fucking prison counts as real weights. Who could bench more and did the prison weight count. They're getting ready to go to blows over it.

"That night, they had a get out of prison party for his brother. Holy shit. Motorcycles, drugs, guns, fights and I never seen anybody doing cocaine and shit. I'm sitting there thinking 'someone can freaking die in here' and I was right in his back pocket. I was like, 'if shit goes down, I'm hiding behind you and we're out of here.'"

Athletics, and even the controlled boxing matches at the Ranch, weren't always enough to satiate Ken's bloodlust. Other kids at school, however, were mostly off-limits, especially after the incident his sophomore year. Instead, when he needed to get the edge off, Ken would find his way to the local Susanville bar scene, trouble on his mind.

"Ken liked to fight so he would go down to the TNA[20] when he was riled up and need to let off some steam," Burke says. "He would fight the adults coming out when we were in high school, because he knew he couldn't get in trouble. So he would just beat the shit out of grown men coming out, picking fights. Now a days, someone would have just shot him."

Ken and his friends had other ways to let loose beyond fist fights and football. It was the early 1980s and drinking was a core activity for most high school kids. There was an arcade parlor in town that would let the kids stay after closing and they would play video games and drink all night long.

Driving was sometimes in the mix, too; the punishment usually a ride back home in the back of a police car rather than any kind of serious trouble, no harm, no foul. Ken white knuckled his way to Shamrock's ranch on the outskirts of town in a 1973 SS Chevelle Bob had bought him many weekend nights—but one night, things went spectacularly awry.

"There was a turn we all called 'the 30 miles-per-hour turn.' Well, before we get to it, Kenny speeds up to 95," Radosevich remembers. "Right in the middle of the turn he tapped the brakes and the car did a spin, and we wound up like 15 feet from somebody's front door."

The car didn't quite hit the house, but it did knock over a bunch of fencing on its way into the front yard. A couple of pieces of barbed wire had pierced the bottom of the vehicle and almost impaled a kid in the back seat and horses were running wild. Laughing like a madman, Ken decided to leave the car where it sat and walk the rest of the way home. Police picked him up halfway there and a furious fight with Bob ensued.

"Kenny and Bob had more than a couple falling outs[21]," Radosevich says. "Kenny would threaten to leave the ranch behind and Bob would

---

[20] Not to be confused with Total Nonstop Action, the wrestling promotion Ken would later headline.

[21] "Sometimes Bob just told him to go, get out," Burke confirms. "He'd come and live at my house for a couple days. My parents brought him in and treated him like their own."

get really upset."

While he had a girlfriend at school, and friends would swear he wasn't into hard drugs beyond the ubiquitous alcohol, at the Boys Ranch things were different. Shamrock was already running through women at a ridiculous rate and fueling long nights of shenanigans with lines of cocaine.

"Kenny was a partier," one Shamrock Boys Ranch resident remembers. "Big time drinker and doing stuff like cocaine. He wasn't much of a pot smoker, but he liked the cocaine.

"Kenny had enough friends where mostly they'd offer him the alcohol or the drugs, and that's how he pretty much supported his habit through other people just giving it to him, you know, because of who he was."

By his senior year of high school, the future was looking bright. In February of 1982, shortly after his 18th birthday, he was officially adopted by Bob Shamrock. Ken Nance left his past behind in name as well as deed, becoming Ken Wayne Shamrock.

He had been approached by some smaller colleges about athletic scholarships and was having surprising success on the wrestling mats, competitive against some of California's best scholastic grapplers despite being a newcomer to the sport.

He was training for a run in the regional tournament when disaster struck. Two mats hadn't been taped together properly and slipped when the smaller Shamrock was attempting a fireman's carry on a heavyweight. The other wrestler landed right on Ken's head, the resulting crack drawing every eye in the room.

"Kenny can take a lot of pain and never show it," Radosevich, who was also on the wrestling team says. "But he was in tears, just about in tears, and I knew it was bad because for him to show emotion as far as pain, that didn't happen with Kenny."

An ambulance came for him and the news got worse when they got to the hospital. He was transported to Redding, about two hours away, and placed in a special contraption that had a hole for his head and a set of mirrors that allowed him to watch television.

A doctor eventually came in for a conversation that sent Shamrock spinning:

* * *

'I've got some bad news, I've got some good news. Let's get the bad news out of the way. You broke your neck. The good news is we can fix it.'

'Okay," Shamrock said. "How long until I can play football again?'

'I think your athletic days are done. You broke your neck. You won't be able to play contact sports again.'

'Just take me out back and shoot me. I don't know what else to do. What else am I supposed to do?'

Ken was despondent by the time Bob arrived with some words that turned everything around.

"It sounds bad now," Bob Shamrock said. "But you've got to trust in the Lord. Think about now. About getting out of this hospital. About getting yourself back to normal again. Then we'll work from there. It's too much to take in and deal with all at once. Let's just take it one step at a time. First we'll take care of right now."

Shamrock had to take some lumps upon his return. He'd been the alpha male, at school and at home and returned from Redding with a giant halo on his head, attached by four enormous bolts. He got in a fight almost immediately when someone called him "heavy metal," unaccustomed to being the butt of the joke. His girlfriend broke up with him and Bob had to shave him while he recovered.

He wore the halo for nine months—but the injury didn't slow him down for long.

"Within a couple of weeks he was running around playing football with it on," Radosevich remembers. "He was knocking people over, beating people up with it on. Lifting weights in the weight room. Nothing stopped him from anything. He just went full bore like it wasn't even there."

Even when the halo came off, it took some time for Ken to become Ken again. He challenged Mike Anderson, a fellow senior at the Boys Ranch to a foot race into town, just to prove to himself he could.

"We took off and ran. The whole house was watching," Shamrock remembers. "I couldn't even make it into town. He lapped me. As he came by, he didn't even say anything to me. I was too pathetic for him to even gloat.

"It took me all day. It was night time before I got back, but I wouldn't quit. Bob hugged me when I got back but depression set in because I just wasn't the same person I had been. It was humiliating. I'd been stripped of everything."

Time doesn't always heal all wounds. But, in this case, it did. Time and anabolics worked miracles. Shamrock had slipped to 130 pounds in the aftermath of his injury but built himself up to 225 pounds two years later. Soon he was back in Redding, this time as a football player at Shasta College.

The bulked up Shamrock was a defensive lineman and a good one, earning second-team All Division III as a sophomore. He worked nights at a bar called Doc's, bouncing drunks and fighting out back for money[22], two things that fit right into his skillset and temperament.

"He wound up getting fired from there," Radosevich, who had come to Redding as his roommate, says. "Some guy threw ice on him and put his hands on Kenny, and that was a no-no. He had picked the guy up, body slammed him and broke the guy's jaw."

Shamrock, despite being undersized, had the athletic ability for a Division I team to take a flyer on him. What he lacked was the grades or SAT scores to qualify for a four-year school. He soon found himself drifting, his path in life not entirely clear after years devoted almost exclusively to sports. After another argument with Bob[23], he'd run off in a tricked out Camaro Bob had bought for him, driving his brother Richie down the 101 to Texas.

Bob called the car in stolen to teach Ken a lesson, a decision that turned into a disaster when the two young men hit a roadblock near Saint Helena. The car was full of cocaine, broken into quarter bags and stuffed into cassette tapes. When police ran the car and saw it was reported stolen, they approached with guns drawn.

"I've got no shirt on and they tell me to get on the ground," Shamrock says. "I told him 'It's freaking hot' and he yelled 'Get on the ground.'

"Richie, he doesn't care man. They tell him to get on the ground and he says no. Meanwhile I'm down there burning. They rushed him and put him on the ground anyway."

The two were in the Salinas County Jail when Bob came to retrieve

---

[22] It was here that Ken entered his first tough man contest, earning the nickname "One Punch" Shamrock.
[23] At one point the two had a serious blowup when Bob asked Ken to move into his room, claiming the Boy's Ranch needed the extra space.

his car. He'd expected to be able to explain away the misunderstanding, leaving Ken with a lesson learned. Instead, thanks to the drugs, it was a bit more complicated.

"He said 'That's not your drugs and I know it Kenny. I know you.' But my brother would have gone to prison because he had a record," Shamrock says. "For me, it was going to be probation. So I copped to it."

Probation or not, the plea would have left Ken unable to work in the group home with Bob, who still saw a bright future for his young son. So, the three men concocted a plan. Richie signed a confession with a notary, then took off to Texas as planned. Ken, was free to go—the only problem was where?

His athletic career seemingly over, there was no place that felt like the right fit. He gave the Marine Corps a try and was a standout in basic training, where he maxed out his physical training scores and was the platoon guide, an honor reserved for the most promising young Devil Dogs. But, when they found out about his broken neck in a medical examination, his career was over before it started. Two weeks later, he was right back where he started.

"I felt so humiliated," he says. "Here I was, put in with the people who quit on themselves. All because I had a medical issue.

"I did everything right. There I was again. My dad picked me up. I felt useless. Absolutely useless."

Shamrock soon found himself drifting again, bouncing in Reno, Nevada, at the Premier Club, one of the roughest night spots in a rough western town. It gave him the opportunity to fight regularly, within the bounds of what the law allowed, and he was a natural, amazing other bouncers with his balance, speed and calm under pressure.

When he wasn't on duty, Shamrock ran completely wild. On Sunday evenings he and friends would wait at local bars for Rugby leagues to let out, challenging men, surrounded by their friends and lubed with alcohol, to fights for money. They rarely lost.

Other nights were lost to debauchery, drugs and women. Shamrock didn't have a car of his own and would ride on the back of his friend Remi Bruyninga's motorcycle. The two men felt like they owned the town, fueled by a potentially lethal brew of testosterone and cocaine.

"One night we're all partying, we're doing coke, we're drinking, we're acting the fool and we're chasing women," Bruyninga says. "It was the '80s. That's all I can say. It was late in the night and we ran out of cocaine and he goes, 'I want to get some more.' I say, 'Dude, we got no money.'

"And he says, "Well let's go to the coke dealer's house." So we go over there, the guy opens the door, Ken blasts him with a punch and runs his head into the drywall and yells to me, 'Grab all the blow.' And I did. Needless to say, we had more cocaine then."

Life continued like that for months, a blur of women and drug-aided shenanigans. Bob Shamrock, not far away in Susanville, would come to visit frequently, helping temper the young man's reckless abandon. But it would take a run-in with Trevor Molini, a former Brigham Young football player who had recently been expelled from school, to truly bring life back into focus.

Molini, a local football star with NFL prospects before becoming addicted to the pain killer Percodan, showed up at the club with several friends. He was no stranger there and no one was surprised to see him searching out trouble on a Sunday night.

Shamrock attempted to intervene, putting his hand on the football players's shoulder and offering to buy him a drink, a standard bouncer trick to calm down an escalating confrontation. But, he says, Molini wasn't in the mood to be calmed down.

"He knocked my hand off and said 'I will rip your head off and shit down your neck.' I looked at him and said 'Well, now you have to leave.'"

Shamrock grabbed Molini in a bulldog choke and pulled him out the door where his friends tried to corral him and keep him out of further trouble.

"He swings on two of them, then he comes running for me," Shamrock says. "I duck under it and just nailed him. His head hits the ground and there's just blood everywhere. I remember a girl screaming 'You killed him!' And I thought 'Shit.' Because maybe I had. It was a weird scene. We all thought I had just killed this guy."

Molini ended up in the Washoe Medical Center with a blood clot on the brain and a broken nose. Judge Mills Lane[24] called it mutual

---

[24] Lane was also a famous boxing referee at the time and no stranger to mutual combat.

combat. There were no criminal charges.

The civil lawsuit was a different matter. The Premier Club filed for bankruptcy and Shamrock was hit with a $935,000 judgement after failing to hire an attorney or answer the lawsuit filed against him.

"Later on I declared bankruptcy," he says. "And it was gone."

A few weeks later, Shamrock met Tina Ramirez at ladies night. He was in Chippendales gear, pouring champagne and handing out roses. She was taken in by his long hair, mustache and nice chest. He liked her smile, shiny dark hair and bubbly personality.

They were married on May 21, 1988, in Chula Vista, California. Their first son, Ryan, was born a little more than six months later. Serious about being the kind of father he never had, Shamrock took a job as a youth counselor, painting houses on the weekend for extra money. On a whim, he entered the 1988 Olympic wrestling trials that were held in Reno that year and acquitted himself well in defeat.

But Bob Shamrock still dreamed big dreams for his adopted son and saw a future in wrestling—just not the wrestling of singlets and half-nelsons. His son's future, he believed, was in the World Wrestling Federation. And the long journey there could begin just a few hours down the road in Sacramento.

CHAPTER THREE
Wrestling with the Future

* * *

-Mooresville, North Carolina
1989

The fight before the fight didn't take long at all. An open hand smack was all it took to drop the loud mouth who wasn't sure about betting big money on Ken Shamrock beating all comers at a biker bar down the road.[25]

Ken was game for it. Sure, it was two in the morning and his young son was asleep upstairs. But his wife was in San Diego, his father was in bed and Lord knows they needed the money. The pro wrestling business, once the lifeblood of the Carolinas, was struggling. If he was lucky, Shamrock might bring home $200 a month.

Five hundred bucks to follow his big old hillbilly neighbor out to the middle of nowhere for a fist fight?

'There's a dude at this bar down the road saying he could take you," his neighbor said. "I told him there was no way cause you were a tough man champion and a wrestler. He said those guys were all wimps and didn't know how to fight worth a damn. Five hundred bucks."

"For 500 bucks? And if I win, it's all mine?"

"Yeah, I'll cover you. I just want you to shut this guy up."

"500 bucks?"

"Yeah."

"Let me get my shoes."

Shoes on, Shamrock stood a little more than six feet tall and weighed 225 pounds, pro wrestling big and strong enough to bench press 600 pounds. But, apparently, not big enough or mean looking enough for his neighbor's buddy, who had something to say.

Hopping out of the truck, the man was already high but not high enough to prevent second thoughts from creeping in. This pretty boy was going to whoop a biker?

"He don't look like much to me," the friend said, putting $40 on the hood of the truck.

"What?" Shamrock asked. "Fight you? For 40 bucks?'

"Put your money where your mouth is," the skeptic responded.

One slap later the man was running off down the street and Shamrock was in the passenger seat of the truck, already $40 richer.

---

[25] Shamrock calls these bar fights "squatting."

The bar was closed, but there were seven trucks in the lot, formed in a circle with lights on, illuminating North Carolina's version of the Roman Coliseum, a gravel parking lot littered with bottles and used condoms, the detritus of a night well spent.

His neighbor plopped two things onto the hood of his truck—$750 and a pistol.

"That's my insurance," he said. For the first time, Shamrock wondered just what he had gotten himself into.

"Dude," he said. "You sure you want to do this?'

"You're gonna kick his ass right?"

"I'm pretty sure I can," Shamrock responded. "But I'm not sure we'll get out of here with our money."

That's when his opponent, at least 6'3", close to 300 pounds, came sauntering into the circle, barrel chest puffed out, looking to intimidate. Instead, it galvanized Shamrock, who loved fighting big guys, the bigger the better.

"Big guy, no question," Shamrock remembers. "I looked at the dude and said 'Let's do this.'"

The two stood staring at each other for what felt like an eternity. Shamrock refused to look away but also refused to make the first move. With a big guy, he thought, it was better to react to what they did and take advantage of his speed and athletic edge. And, so, the seconds ticked away as the two men stared.

"It seemed like forever," Shamrock says, "but it was probably five or ten seconds."

That's when the man let out a war cry and came barreling forward with a haymaker straight out of the movies. For Shamrock, it was like things were happening in slow motion, the man almost comically slow, big and burly but hardly the finely conditioned specimen of a man he'd become. He ducked, then unleashed a right and left that dropped the man into a sitting position, gushing blood from his forehead.

"He looked up at me with eyes that were glowing through the blood and goes 'this is going to be a long night for you brother,'" Shamrock says. "I thought 'am I missing something here?' He's the one on the ground with blood everywhere."

Powered by liquid courage at the very least, the big man charged again. This time Shamrock grabbed him in a body lock and grasped his hands tight around his waist.

"I suplex him over my head and onto his head," Shamrock says.

"And he's out cold. Not moving at all. I walk over to the guys and grab my money, put it in my pocket and hop in the truck."

"Let's get out of here," he said. "I don't want to stick around."

"Ain't nobody gonna mess with us," his neighbor replied, firing three shots into the air. The crowd scattered and Shamrock pounded on the dashboard, yelling at his friend to get the hell out of there.

"Ah, nobody's gonna care out here," the neighbor said with a nonchalance Shamrock didn't feel. "The cops aren't fixing to come all the way out here."

"Maybe not," Shamrock said. "But I'm not worried about the cops. I'm worried about the guys whose money we just took and who you shot at. They might shoot us."

"Drive!"

Buzz Sawyer was once one of the most promising young stars in professional wrestling. Starting as a teenager in 1979, he quickly impressed with his strong amateur background, barrel-chested physique and surprising athleticism.

He took wild bumps and gave even better interviews, so intense on the microphone that it was easy to overlook that much of what he said was completely nonsensical, the kind of cocaine fueled ravings wrestling fans would become accustomed to in the powder-filled 1980s. Sawyer was more than just talk though—he had a rough, realistic style and one of the very best powerslams in the entire sport, whipping his opponent through the air so quickly that disaster seemed imminent. Just two years into his career, the *Wrestling Observer*'s Dave Meltzer was already calling him one of the best workers in the business.

By the following year he established himself as the industry's top heel, headlining a series of matches against Tommy Rich that culminated in 1983's "the Last Battle of Atlanta" a long lost holy grail bout for enthusiasts and wrestlers alike.[26] Short, compact and already prematurely balding in his early twenties, Sawyer was the perfect foil for Rich, a pretty boy crowd-favorite with flowing blonde hair and an easy smile. When Sawyer busted him open, as he often did, the blood

---

[26] The match was discovered by a WWE Network producer in 2016 on a tape labelled simply "Omni Live Events." There was, among the hardcore fan set, much rejoicing.

would paint Rich's blonde hair red, a compelling visual both on television and in newsstand wrestling magazines that pandered in that brand of grotesquerie.

"It was a fight every night," Rich says. "He had a bad personality. He was rough. I just went in there and threw it back at him...That was Buzz. He was what he was. He didn't really have a nice word to say about anyone or anything. That was his personality."

The two packed 10,000 people into the Omni in Atlanta for an enclosed cage match that saw Sawyer's manager Paul Ellering in a second, almost birdcage style cage, hanging from the ceiling. The two beat each other silly to finally pour water on a fiery feud that had been raging for almost two years. It was the apex of the old Georgia territory and one of the swan songs for old school wrestling. That same year Vince McMahon had taken the WWF national and the wrestling business would undergo a seismic shift.[27]

Sawyer, like many of the wrestlers of this era, couldn't control what people in the industry called "his demons." By that they mean drugs and alcohol, the fuel that powered the performers from town to town as they actively destroyed their bodies in pursuit of a few dollars and that oh-so-satisfying roar from the crowd.

Some could handle that grind, the constant pressure of performing and the constant aches and pains that come from taking bodyslams, slaps and pratfalls night after night. Others wilted from the strain. Sawyer wilted, his body breaking down from the abuse. Just a few years after making magic with Rich in Atlanta, he was a well known problem child promoters knew they couldn't trust with anything important. No longer part of the main event picture, Sawyer started to supplement his declining income by opening up training "schools" in many of the territories he wrestled in.

Breaking into the wrestling industry has always been difficult. The business is part boys club, part secret society, part carny sideshow, part simulated fight. To get in, typically, someone has to vouch for you and your ability to do the work and fit in. That can require both plenty of money and a willingness to accept an awful lot of abuse.

Prospective grapplers were put through rigorous physical conditioning programs, then often beaten bloody and put into tortuous submission holds. Unless you knew one of the "boys" as wrestlers call

---

[27] Sawyer was one of the first wrestlers McMahon poached from his competitors. He was also one of the first fired.

themselves, a wrestling school's main purpose was to get the applicants to quit. Part of that was a necessary thinning of the herd. The business was tough, physically and mentally, so it made sense to cull the weak. But taking people's money up front, beating them up, then encouraging them to quit was also a pretty good grift for your garden variety blackhearted sociopath. And wrestling wasn't lacking in those. Sawyer, belligerent to begin with and often just as focused on his next fix as he was his next match, was among the worst.

At most wrestling schools, at least, there was a light at the end of the tunnel. If you put in the work, ate crap for awhile and showed potential, there was a chance when it was all over to get into the ring, even if it was just as enhancement talent at a local show. That wasn't always true with Buzz Sawyer, who would often take people's money, then disappear to the next town to grift a new set of willing marks.

Mark Calloway, later famous as the Undertaker in WWE, was one of Sawyer's victims when Sawyer was wrestling in the southwest. Desperate for a shot, Calloway borrowed $2000 from his brother, joining nine other interested wrestlers willing to pay Sawyer for his time and expertise. But after just a few days of training, Sawyer was nowhere to be found. Calloway later discovered Buzz had disappeared to California, leaving behind life lessons if not the wrestling ones he'd promised.

"It may not sound like big money now," Calloway told author Gary Michael Capetta. "But when you don't have steady work, and there's nothing in the bank, a couple of grand is like a couple of million."

It's unfortunate, then, that when Bob Shamrock looked for a place for Ken to learn the tricks of the wrestling trade, he stumbled across Sawyer instead of one of the more reputable schools on the West Coast. Bob was still convinced that his adopted son was destined for some kind of greatness. And, while the perfect competitive sport hadn't yet reared its head, he was convinced that Ken's physicality and magnetism could turn heads in the right environment. A lifelong wrestling fan, Bob became convinced Ken's future was in the professional ring.

In 1988, he and Ken made several long drives to Sacramento to work with Buzz, by then all but blackballed in North America and working the Japanese circuit a few times a year. There, they found a shell of a man who held his makeshift classes at a local gym with mats haphazardly tossed on the ground or out on the grass in the park.

In declining health, it was tough for Sawyer to fully take advantage of the prospective wrestlers he was trying to profit from and then discourage from pursuing wrestling further. That's where Ken came in.

"I wasn't learning much about pro wrestling," Shamrock says. "In fact, I never once got in a wrestling ring. Buzz would have people come in and pay him $700 to a thousand bucks to try out. He'd take us down to a gym, and there'd be some mats on the floor and Buzz would have me wrestle with them and make them quit.

"That's what he wanted. I'd go in and basically beat these guys up and he would take their money as a try out fee. I did that for three or four months. But he never got me a match and I never really learned anything about pro wrestling. I didn't learn anything from Buzz except beating people up and taking their money."

The trip to Sacramento from Reno was six hours round trip. With little to show for each excursion, short gas money, time, and Buzz's fee, the Shamrocks grew frustrated and began to suspect they were being swindled.

In November of 1988 the situation came to a head. Tina gave birth to the couple's first son Ryan at St. Mary's Hospital in Reno that month, a development that both thrilled and frightened Shamrock. He'd always wanted to be a father, to be the kind of role model he'd never had. But he also suddenly felt the pressure to provide for a new family. Working in a group home and a stalled wrestling career weren't going to be enough to support his growing clan the way he wanted to.

Bob started searching for another school to learn the tricks of the trade and eventually found one. The problem? It was clear across the country in Mooresville, North Carolina, a sleepy small town on the outskirts of Charlotte.

It would have been hard to recognize Nelson Royal if you saw pictures of him the first time he came to the Carolinas. By 1988 he was a grizzled veteran of ring wars, a cowboy-hat-wearing good old boy feuding with a new generation of light heavyweight stars. But back in 1964 he was "Sir" Nelson Royal, a fancy-pants British caricature in top hat and tails, teaming with "The Viking" Bob Morse.

The two were an unlikely pair of foreign invaders—Royal was actually born in Kentucky and Morse was an Army veteran and former sheriff from the state of Missouri. Either way, the fans bought it, and in the world of professional wrestling that's really all that mattered.

The two feuded with popular babyfaces like the Scott brothers but eventually parted ways. Morse, famed in the business as a skirt chaser and hard drinker, didn't mesh with Royal, a family man who settled in to a decade-long run as one of the region's top heroes.

"Royal was influenced heavily by Lou Thesz and was a junior heavyweight in the same mold," wrestling historian Mike Mooneyham, who has covered the sport for years in the region, says. "He had a realistic, hard-hitting style and took pride in the scars and injuries that sometimes made it tough for him to get up in the morning. He loved the days when wrestling was wrestling and wore those wounds as a badge of honor."

The Carolinas were a tag team territory and Royal came to specialize in that form of wrestling. He teamed with many of the region's top stars like Paul Jones and Johnny Weaver but found his best success with "Tex" McKenzie. The two presented a memorable visual, with McKenzie, who stood nearly seven feet, towering over his diminutive partner, who was charitably listed at 5'9".

In the late 1980s, Royal opened up a wrestling school in Mooresville. He owned a popular Western store on the outskirts of town complete with a barn and horses. The property extended quite a ways into the woodline and included an old metal shop and a single-wide trailer. They put a ring in the middle of the metal shop and, as quick as that, were in business.

His partner in the venture was Gene Anderson, one half of the leading team in the opposite locker room during Royal's prime. Known as the Minnesota Wrecking Crew, Ole and Gene Anderson were brutal heels who terrorized Mid-Atlantic Wrestling for a generation.[28] The two were hard-hitting and realistic wrestlers capable of giving as well as they got from the likes of Johnny Valentine and Wahoo McDaniel.

In a business of tough guys, both real and illusory, the Andersons had a reputation. Gene, balding and sporting a pot belly, could inspire terror. Even after a stroke forced him into a desk job, Anderson still found ways to impose his will on the other boys in the locker room.

"(Gene) had incredible grip strength. He would come up to guys and just grip him on the elbow," wrestling manager Jim Cornette

---

[28] Although really from Minnesota, the two men were not actually brothers. None of the fictional Anderson wrestling family, including their "cousin" Ric Flair, were blood relatives.

remembers. "He knew where to get it. He would have the Barbarian down on his knees saying 'Please Gene, please Gene.' And Gene would say 'tell me you're a faggot.'"

The two also seemed to take pleasure in torturing prospective wrestlers who were looking to get their foot in the door. As Ole Anderson wrote in his biography *Inside Out*, he would often tease his victims before rendering them unconscious with what the wrestlers called a "sugar hold," a modified choke:

> Once I applied the sugar hold, I would really work it. The most effective thing I did with it was to take a mark to the edge of passing out, then bring him back. In other words, as he started to go under, I'd ease up on the pressure and let him relax for a second. Just as he began to take a quick breath, I'd clamp down on the hold and push him forward again. It's the most miserable feeling you could ever have because you get panicky. The worst thing about it is, you can't do a thing about it. You can kick or do whatever you want to do, but you just can't do anything to get out of it.

Gene retired from the ring after a stroke in 1981 but stayed around the fringes of the business, working for promoters around the southeast. Unlike Sawyer, the two operated a real company, sending enhancement talent to a newly national Jim Crockett Promotions. Like Sawyer, they employed a tough guy, in this case future UFC fighter John Latu (John Savage), to weed out the weak.

"A lot of people came from all over the country." Latu says. "They worked them out for an hour, then put me in there with them to demolish the guys. That's just the way they did it back then. They wanted to see how bad these guys wanted to make it in pro wrestling. Most didn't."

Shamrock, with his chiseled body and cheek bones was an obvious keeper. Because of his experience with Sawyer, he was ready for any potential funny business, but no one in Mooresville tried him. They were too busy wiping away the dollar signs in their eyes.

"They saw right away that he was going to be one of our guys," Latu says. "He had charisma, he had the athletic ability and he had the perfect look they wanted. Ken came in with a high level of amateur skill and it wasn't hard for him to transition to pro wrestling. The moves came easily for him. He was a hell of an athlete and picked things up pretty quick."

WCW's national expansion had left an opening in the southeast, where fans were used to a steady stream of wrestling. With WCW in Chicago or on the west coast when they would have previously been in Orangeburg, South Carolina, or Charlotte, the opportunity seemed ripe for someone else to run what used to be the Mid Atlantic territory.

Royal looked to fill that gap with his newly formed Atlantic Coast Wrestling. But with most of the region's top stars busy wrestling on Superstation WTBS, he was going to need talent—and quickly. That meant Shamrock was put on the fast track for quick success, something he was hungry for.

"Even though I hadn't really done anything like this before, it just seemed to come naturally," he says. "Nelson saw it. Gene Anderson saw it. Everybody who saw me wrestle saw there was potential there. Six months later I was wrestling Nelson in the ring. We put together a pretty good match.

"They would tell me things like 'loosen up that hold' or 'make sure you keep your head up so they can see your reaction. If your head is down, they don't know what you're going through.' Advice like that really helped me communicate with the fans."

Royal was in his early 50's and called all of the young men at his school "son." He always made time to help people sort through their problems, both in and out of the ring. Anderson, despite his fearsome reputation, had also mellowed with time.

The two were a good pair when it came to teaching the intricacies of the business. Together, they had decades of experience and had seen almost everything there is to see in wrestling, wisdom they spent hours passing on to their students in sessions that could last up to five hours at a time.

"They'd stop the match or stop the workout process and explain things," Tommy Angel, who was Shamrock's main training partner in those days, says. "What Nelson and Gene poured into him was the psychology of it and how to use his gift and strengths.

"It was really cool because they had two different perspectives but together taught us how to tell the complete story. I hear some guys that have gone to schools that don't teach you anything except how to bump. All that time spent just to say 'I learned how to fall.'"

Bob Shamrock came with his son to North Carolina and worked in a group home there. He also helped humanize Ken, who didn't always connect with new people easily.

"When he walked in, we thought, 'Who's this clown?' He's all jacked up but we thought he was just another cocky green guy," Angel says. "But once the façade crumbled, I go, 'Oh, you're just one of us.'

"He was always very confident, almost arrogant on the surface. I think a lot of that has to do with his upbringing. He was afraid of anyone being too close, just protecting himself. 'I'm tough. I'm not gonna show you who I really am.' But after hearing his story, it made a lot of sense to me. Bob was a sweet man and he told us. It was very helpful in sharing that."

With Tina often traveling as a flight attendant and spending a lot of her time in San Diego, Bob took care of baby Ryan during the day, leaving Ken time to train. It was something he did obsessively, almost single-mindedly.

"The commitment and dedication that this guy had and has is just second to none," Angel says. "He would push our workouts to a limit of just absolute collapse. He's an all in, 100 percent.

"When you're with him, you strive to be at that level because you feel what he's projecting. That's what Shamrock was able to do. You felt it when you're talking to him just that confidence. That was a very positive feeling."

In the ring, Shamrock developed very quickly. Shortly after his debut, he was already being featured on local television and Royal got him a spot in a dark match at a WWF event in Greensboro. Despite losing to the usually hapless Barry Horowitz, Shamrock impressed with his look and physical tools. Likewise, the young wrestler was thrilled to be part of a big time event that featured the likes of Dusty Rhodes, Ted DiBiase and Demolition. To him, it was a glimpse of what the future held.

Royal was able to secure one place on the WWF card and gave it to Shamrock, despite others in his camp having more ring time and experience. Wrestling was still deeply enmeshed in steroid culture at the time and Shamrock had the look that was required to make a splash on the national scene.

"It was an unwritten rule that Vince McMahon and Turner aren't gonna look at anybody unless you're a marketable package and look good," one wrestler says. "Those big, puffy bodies that wrestlers had in the early 80s had morphed into that chiseled body kinda look. So as young guys, we were trying to get as big and cut as we could just to differentiate ourselves. Ken had great genetics and Bob helped him afford access to better drugs even though we didn't make any money. Winstrol B and the Equipoise were the two steroids we liked, what we called cutting drugs. And if we had the money, we would obviously buy them."

Even in a business fueled by steroids and filled with enormous physical specimens, Shamrock stood out. He concedes his stunning look was chemically aided.

"When I first went to Nelson's, I wasn't doing anything," he says. "But I started seeing what the other guys were doing and how people were getting over based on what their bodies looked like. That's when I started to use.

"It was off and on because I just didn't have the money to constantly do it. I had to pick and choose. Plus, I was very careful about what I did do. I didn't take the stuff people used to get stronger. I was already strong. I loved to be lean and athletic looking. I didn't want to be big and strong but bloated looking."

In October 1989, looking the part of pro wrestler despite his lack of experience, he toured Japan for the first time, filling in for Dean Malenko to work 17 matches in a single month for All Japan Pro Wrestling. It was by far the most time he'd ever gotten to work on his craft in front of a live crowd and he acquitted himself well in the ring against some of the very best performers in the world.[29] He may have only secured a single victory on the tour, but the experience was vital to his growth.

"I was able to express the feeling you get when you really go after somebody but not really go after somebody," Shamrock says. " I had the same mentality, the same feelings I would have had if it was real. It just came natural to me. I tried to mimic what would happen if somebody really punched you in the stomach or the face. I tried to act out what I would do in those scenarios. And I kind of fell right into it."

While Royal clearly saw a bright future for Shamrock, it wouldn't be

---

[29] Shamrock shared the ring with both future champions Kenta Kobashi and Akira Taue, veterans like Dick Slater and Rusher Kimura and workers in their primes like Dan Kroffat and Joe Malenko. Keeping up was a minor triumph for someone so new to the sport.

in his Atlantic Coast Wrestling promotion. The show failed to connect with local fans and Royal couldn't afford to continue running it at a loss.

But the idea of wrestling in the Carolinas was still a good one, at least to those who had been a part of Jim Crocket's promotion in the glory years. George Scott[30] came in to give it a try and brought with him established talent like Ricky "The Dragon" Steamboat and Robert Fuller. The promising young wrestlers like Shamrock, now going by Vince Torelli, were relegated to the middle of the card while they learned the business from some of the industry's established players.

"These were actually pretty good shows for the time," Mooneyham says. "Scott was able to use his relationship with Steamboat to get him on a lot of shows just a year after his legendary matches with Ric Flair. And the promotion had a lot of young wrestlers who ended up making a name for themselves in the industry like the Nasty Boys, Chris Chavis, Ken, and the Pitbulls.

"Unfortunately, you just couldn't turn the clock back and make regional wrestling work anymore. Sometimes they'd have just 50 or 60 people in the audience. It was kind of sad."

Now called the National American Wrestling Association, the group crowned its first champion in an 18-man tournament on June 30, 1990. While Steamboat and Fuller met in the finals, Shamrock and Mark Fleming stole the show in an opening round draw.[31]

"George Scott told us to go out there and wrestle so that is what we did," Fleming says. "Probably more people talk to me about that match, even today, than any of my other matches. We did not have a lot of big spots and all that to remember. No we just went in there and wrestled. Him being a wrestler and me being a wrestler, it just happened. We just did what we knew how to do."

The legendary Lou Thesz, Fleming's mentor and trainer, was on hand to lend both his voice and credibility to the proceedings. On commentary, the man who once held the world championship for 2300

---

[30] Scott and his brother Sandy had been stars in the Mid Atlantic region as "the Flying Scotts." After his retirement in 1973, he became one of the sport's leading creative forces. He helped many wrestlers, including Steamboat, make a name in the industry and called in those favors to try to make NAWA work.

[31] Conveniently, the promotion ran nine opening round matches. Had the bout not gone to a draw, it's unclear what would have happened to the extra participant in the next round.

days, put men over huge for bringing wrestling back to its roots with legitimate holds and pinning combinations.

"I'll tell you, this is so thrilling," Thesz told the television audience at one point. "I'm getting transfixed."

But not even the approval of Thesz, one of wrestling's most iconic performers, could do much to make the NAWA work. The group, despite Thesz and Steamboat, only drew 150 people to the cavernous Winston-Salem Coliseum. A month later, without Steamboat, the crowd was just 80 in Lenoire, North Carolina, to see Fuller versus Ranger Ross. It was the final straw for Scott, who sold the territory, such as it was to Paul Jones and Fred Dusek, two other veterans of the region willing to give it a go.

"We were making gas money," Shamrock says. "There was a lot of talent there, but we weren't making an impact."

While he paid his dues on the road, Shamrock was an immediate hit in the clubs. The younger wrestlers would tail superstars like Flair to places like Plum Crazy when he was styling and profiling in town, then mirror what they saw when he wasn't. Carrying themselves like *they* were the stars didn't always go over well with the other guys in the bar. Hard words and even fisticuffs often followed. When there was trouble, Shamrock's presence was almost a guarantee

"Ken would challenge the guy and tell him, 'You're not enough,'" Angel says. "He'd ask 'you want any friends? I'll fight your friends too.' He'd take on two or three guys and take some good hits. But he wouldn't stop, he wouldn't quit, until he beat them all up."

Ken rarely started a fight, but he never walked away from one either. A veteran of the club scene, he quickly befriended the bouncers at the most popular joints and had a little leeway to solve his own issues.

"When we were at the bar, we stood out," Latu says. "Sometimes that meant people wanted to be with us and be our friends, but sometimes that means they want to try you. They'd want to fight and show off for their girlfriend or their buddies. We'd say 'for $50 or $100 you can see some action.' Then we'd go out to the parking lot and kick ass.

"And he liked big guys. If it was a smaller guy, he would be willing to laugh it off as a joke. But if the challenge came from a guy his size or bigger? There was no talking. He would destroy you."

Eventually, trouble didn't seem like a byproduct of a fun night out—too often it seemed like the point. Whether he was trying to pick up some extra cash in tough man tournaments or betting on the bouts or just looking to let off some steam, friends soon knew that spending time on the town with Ken was going to mean throwing hands at some point.

"We'd always just tell him, 'Man, tonight we'll just chill, let's get some girls and get back to the house.' And, man, as soon as he'd get in the club, you could see him sizing people up," Angel says. "There was alcohol, there was drugs, there was all types of crazy stuff, getting in fights with punks over girls. When it started getting pretty deep, that's when I started distancing myself because bad things happen late at night with drugs and alcohol."

The drug of choice in the 1980s for professional wrestlers was cocaine, a substance Shamrock was quite familiar with. Despite his new family and promises to Tina that he would change, Shamrock was soon once again on intimate terms with the powder. When he was indulging, he became hard to control.

"At the time, he liked to do a little something in his nose," Latu says. "And it would make him crazy. He was always a party guy, but when he did that, I had to be very close to him. Because he'd be looking for trouble.

"He'd ask me to come outside and have his backside and I'd know something was going to go down. He'd go outside and there was no talking. Anybody that stood in his way was going down. One guy, three guys, five guys. I've seen him smash a guy's head through the windshield of a car. I don't know how we made it without getting shot or stabbed."

His growing confidence outside the ring started to bleed into the locker room, something that didn't always sit well with veterans in the crew like "the Raging Bull" Manny Fernandez and Matt Borne.

"Ken was maybe a little too cocky," Latu says. "Some of the older guys thought he carried himself the wrong way for a green guy. In those days it was all about who you know and whose ass you kiss and Ken didn't do that."

Heat with the boys not withstanding, Shamrock continued to grow as a performer. Building his reputation as a scientific wrestler, Shamrock was bequeathed the nickname "Mr. Wrestling" by the original "Mr. Wrestling" himself Tim Woods. He had the looks and skillset to back it up, the kind of young talent that seemed destined for success.

Dean Malenko had also joined the territory that summer and stayed with Ken and Bob at their house in Mooresville. The two had some very technical matches much like the kind of bouts Shamrock had with Fleming. More importantly he showed Shamrock a video tape of shoot style wrestling that would change his life.

"These two guys were rolling around and kicking and punching and I was like 'Man, that is unbelievable. Where is this?' And he says 'Over in Japan, but my Dad has a place where they train over in Tampa,'" Shamrock says. "I said 'Dude, can you hook me up with that?' And he said 'Are you sure? This is not regular pro wrestling. This is heavy.' I go 'Sign me up. That looks interesting to me.'"

A month later he was in Tampa, working out with Masami "Sammy" Soranaka, son-in-law of Karl Gotch and the conduit for American talent looking to work with the UWF organization in Japan.

Inspired by Antonio Inoki's foray[32] into "legitimacy" and trained by a collection of grizzled men with a very particular set of skills, the wrestlers of the UWF were on a quest to prove that professional wrestling was indeed strong.[33]

Inoki, in the midst of a promotional war with "Giant" Baba in the 1970s, needed something special to vault ahead of his nemesis and former partner. He imported Gotch, a 1948 Olympian and real life tough guy, to help create a more realistic style of wrestling.

A product of the legendary Snake Pit in Wigan, England, Gotch trained Inoki in traditional catch wrestling holds and techniques. Inoki

---

[32] Inoki battled a series of legitimate martial artists over the years in an effort to establish professional wrestling as a serious sport. With the exception of a famous debacle against boxer Muhammad Ali, these bouts were all worked wrestling matches.

[33] After winning the heavyweight tournament at UFC-Ultimate Japan in 1997, shoot style wrestler Kazushi Sakuraba famously told the world "In fact, pro wrestling is strong." Somewhere, no doubt, Inoki was beaming.

and subsequent generations of New Japan wrestlers[34] learned both how to wrestle for real and how to incorporate these holds in their predetermined matches. The training was legendarily brutal.

"Part of that first year, a lot of that first year was what he termed toughening up," Gotch's protege Joe Malenko said. "It was a toughening up process. I'd be down in referee's position on all fours, he'd get across my back and he would cross face me and I literally had to just sit there and take it. He'd come across one side and then he'd swing back the other way.

"You've got these big freaking raw bones and I wasn't allowed to say anything. I wasn't allowed to squeal or move or flinch. I just had to sit there and take it. Many nights I went home, I couldn't even eat."

Catch wrestling, Malenko and many others discovered, was an incredibly effective fighting sport, a truth proven again and again as martial artists came to the dojo and attempted to embarrass the "fake" wrestlers.

"I remember all the stories from the old-school guys at New Japan about when they used to take out ads in the newspaper saying professional wrestling was the strongest of all martial arts," former UFC champion and wrestling historian Josh Barnett said. "And karate guys, judo guys would show up at their dojo saying 'we don't believe that. We think that's crap. And we're going to come in and beat you and show you otherwise.' Gotch or Inoki would tell Osamu Kido, 'go wrestle that dude and just tear him apart.' They never lost. They beat everybody up who showed up at their gym."

It was there, in these private battles, that the efficacy of catch wrestling techniques passed on by Gotch, known to the Japanese as the "God of Wrestling," was established, screams and frantic concessions the currency that purchased respect. It was these men and their progeny who created shoot style wrestling in the 1980s, and they took wrestling incredibly seriously.

The UWF revolution was a repudiation of the increasingly Americanized wrestling that no longer resembled a contest. It began subtly, with strikes that carried a little more weight and submission holds that would work in a real fight. Then subtleness was out the

---

[34] New Japan remains the dominant wrestling promotion in Japan. Despite many changes in style and presentation, the young wrestlers in their dojo are still trained in the Gotch style, learning legitimate holds and strategies before moving on to more stylized modern wrestling.

window, with the shoot style wrestlers openly challenging their peers from other companies, calling them little better than showmen, proclaiming that they were the only legitimate performers on the planet.

"The UWF was there to change the world," Japanese wrestling reporter Fumi Sato says. "They were going to make professional wrestling a real sport. Many wrestling fans in Japan in late 1980s and into the 90s shared this dream. (They believed) puroresu[35] would become a real major league professional sport by becoming real. It was kind of like waiting for the day to see UFOs and meet ET or something."

The actual matches were still predetermined and often still structured just like traditional wrestling bouts, with the competitors building momentum and working towards their signature moves. But the techniques were legitimate, the attitude punk rock, and the crowds enthusiastic.

For much of Japanese wrestling history, the underlying psychology of the bouts was fairly simple—the native wrestlers were the plucky good guys, overcoming long odds presented by larger, brutish foreigners. That paradigm shifted in the 1980s as the wrestling war between WWF and the remaining NWA territories led to a stricter control on talent flow.[36] It simply wasn't possible for a wrestler like Hulk Hogan, for example, to spend weeks out of every year in Japan wrestling for Inoki like he had earlier in the decade. Vince McMahon needed him for every possible date to spearhead their national expansion.

The end result was an explosion of matches between Japanese wrestlers, with native stars doing battle in the ring regularly and the few remaining foreigners of any real repute like Stan Hansen, Bruiser Brody or "Dr. Death" Steve Williams being lavished with huge

---

[35] Puroresu is shorthand in Japanese for pro wrestling, derived from their pronunciation of "professional wrestling" (purofesshonaru resuringu).

[36] For almost 50 years professional wrestling promoters had divided the United States into distinct territories, each with a single company running events. Any challenge to this system was dealt with collectively and brutally. Vincent Kennedy McMahon, powered by cable television and a network of syndication deals, challenged the existing structure and his WWF ultimately put every competitor out of business.

contracts for their services.[37] It also meant a newer, up-and-coming promotion like the UWF had no real access to established American or European talent at all, forcing them to create their own stars if they were going to have any traditional matches between native sons and a foreign menace.

Like Inoki before him, UWF headliner Akira Maeda attempted to build his reputation against foreign martial artists including Dick Vrij and Chris Doleman. But his most successful bouts were against fellow Japanese like Nobuhiko Takada. Meanwhile, rising stars like Masakatsu Funaki were setting a new standard of performance that outsiders found hard to match. The promotion imported American outsiders with combat sports credentials like former WWWF champion Bob Backlund, but it was very difficult for them to keep up with the grueling, intricate style of wrestling the UWF performers had created.

The Florida school, run by Soranaka and the Malenkos, was meant to solve that problem and had produced midcard talent like Bart Vale and Norman Smiley who were able to fill undercard slots and hold their own.

"It was a big adjustment in the beginning," Smiley said. "I was used to the basic highspots. There a highspot was two slaps to the face, a kick to the jaw and a suplex. It was very, very aggressive.

"It was amazing to me. Just like a doctor is able to cure a person, a wrestler can break bones. And it's scientifically done. It was like the Ultimate Fighting we see today. So many people consider it barbaric, but when you look at it in detail, it's a science."

Shamrock didn't have the science down yet when he arrived in Tampa for his tryout, but he had the conditioning to handle the Hindu squats and squats with men across his back that were part of the Gotch training system.

Sorananka asked Shamrock for 500 squats. This would break most men, helping him weed out those who wouldn't be able to make it through the training. Physical failure was okay. It was those who quit on themselves Sammy was looking to eliminate. Shamrock never did. He had the raw physicality required for the unique style of wrestling, not only knocking out the squats but then running over the other guys

---

[37] All three would bounce between Baba and Inoki's companies, creating a big splash each time they jumped ship. They were the last real renegades in an increasingly corporate business.

in the gym.

"I stomped everybody," he remembers. "No one there could handle me."

Smelling potential gold, Soranaka arranged for Shamrock to have another tryout, this time in Japan, where he'd audition for an opportunity to compete in the UWF. It all happened quickly, but the promotion was running major events monthly and needed bodies to fill the fight cards immediately.

"I got off the plane and went straight to the gym. After flying all that way," Shamrock says. "They tell me to warm up and I see Minoru Suzuki and Masakatsu Funaki over in the corner putting their gear on. And I realized 'That's the two guys I saw on Malenko's fight tape.' So I started getting a little bit nervous. What did I get myself into?"

After a brief warmup, Shamrock sparred with some of the young fighters, then with future Pancrase fighter Takaku Fuke. After acquitting himself well, Suzuki finally stepped onto the mat and the tryout truly began. Shamrock, whose confidence had grown as he manhandled the Japanese wrestlers placed in front of him, suddenly went from predator to prey.

"I got thumped. I got choked, armbarred, leglocked," he says. "The one thing I remember most, because it hurt the worst, was his heel hook. It was this excruciating pain in my knee and my ankle. And I couldn't move out of it the way he was locking up my leg and my hips.

"I remember thinking 'I've got to learn that one. I love that move.' "

After a thorough drubbing, Soranaka asked Shamrock if he wanted to call it a day. He shook his head no, not willing to quit so quickly on his dreams.

"He looked at me like I was crazy, so he brings in Funaki," Shamrock says. "Funaki does even worse things to me. He just beats the crap out of me...I literally had nothing left. They were beating me up, but I never quit trying. I felt like I wasn't doing good enough, like I was failing. I tried to push myself more and more because I wanted this. This was my chance and I felt like I was stinking the place up."

Thirty minutes later, Shamrock was laying on the mat, drenched in sweat, but still insisting he could continue.

"Sami laughed," Shamrock remembers. "He said 'No, no, we're finished.' I told him 'I can go more if you want me to.'

'We've seen enough.'

"I was like, damn, I just messed up. I got my butt kicked and I failed."

But Soranaka had been impressed. The Japanese weren't expecting him to come equipped with submission skills and wrestling mastery. They were in the business of teaching those things. They were looking for the things you couldn't teach.

"He told me, 'You did really good.' I said 'What do you mean? I just got my ass kicked.'

'Yeah. But we can teach you. You have the heart,'" Shamrock says. "I thought maybe he was just saying that to be polite. Two weeks later I got a call at home asking me to come over and compete."

Shamrock all but had his ticket to Japan in hand when things nearly went horribly wrong. In October of 1990 after a show in South Carolina, things got extremely ugly at Plum Crazy, the famed Charlotte night club. It was the last night on tour for the Nasty Boys, Brian Knobbs and Jerry Sags, and a physical altercation very nearly changed Shamrock's life forever.

Shamrock's run in with the Nasty Boys is one of the most often-discussed shoots in modern pro wrestling history. There are multiple versions of the story, each deviating in key details, but the one thing everyone agrees on this—the future UFC champion ended up in the hospital and Knobbs and Sags ended up in the WCW.

Things were already combustible with Shamrock and some of the other boys before his confrontation with Knobs and Sags. He carried himself like a star despite being a relative newcomer and that didn't go over well with either established talent or other young guys on the come up.

"He'd exude confidence. He had that swagger," Angel says. "That's just him and it rubbed some of those guys the wrong way, you could tell, but he wasn't trying, that's just who he is. Someone like Manny Fernandez was incredibly insecure, so he hated people like Ken. He'd go out of his way to talk down to Ken. And when you stood up to him, you realized he was just a coward in a large man's body."

Ken had also gotten a reputation for working stiff, landing the kind of thudding blows that made a match an ordeal for the man on the other side of the ring. Shamrock was more than willing to receive and not just hand out beatings, but not everyone wanted to work that style, leading to at least one fight in the locker room with Curtis "US Male"

Thompson.[38]

"I think Curtis took it as 'you're trying to hurt me so I'm gonna be stiff with you back.' That was just how Ken worked," Angel says. "Curtis took it as 'he's trying to stretch me, he's trying to hurt me.' Ego comes in. Curtis was similar to Ken and just jacked up on roids and always wanted to be the center of attention. Ken just happened to be the center of attention."

After what Shamrock had considered a good match, he came back to the locker room and was met by a punch from Thompson right in the face.

"He jumped up off his stool while everybody was standing around and hit me in the face with everything that he had," Shamrock says. "I just turned to him and said 'If you do that again, I'm going to light you up.' Everybody was stunned that I was still standing there staring him in the face after he'd sucker punched me as hard as he could. He came at me again and I grabbed him, threw him on the ground and held him down."

Robert Fuller,[39] a veteran wrestler who headed The Stud Stable of heels that included Thompson, separated the two.

"I was so scared of losing my job that I never threw a punch," Shamrock says. "I was afraid of getting kicked out and black balled, that nobody would use me because I was uncontrollable. Because, in the pro wrestling business, it's less important to be tough than it is to be someone who can work with other people and who other people can trust. I didn't want to mess that up."

Thompson charged him one more time and was wrestled down to the floor again. This time, Shamrock had had enough.

"After the third time I told him 'If you come at me again, I will hurt you. I've given you enough chances.' He must have seen something in my eyes and believed me," Shamrock says. "He didn't come at me

---

[38] In this "US Male" gimmick Thompson dressed up as a buff mailman. He would later be better known as Firebreaker Chip in WCW and would dress up as a fireman. Sadly, these kinds of vocational gimmicks are considered passe in modern wrestling.

[39] Fuller came from southern wrestling royalty. He and his brother Ron owned Continental Wrestling and ran the Alabama and Tennessee territory. He came to national fame in 1993 as Colonel Rob Parker, an homage to Elvis's manager Col. Tom Parker that was mostly lost on younger wrestling fans. Most assumed it was a Colonel Sanders rip off.

after that."

Tension was brewing within the promotion as crowds dwindled without Steamboat's regular presence and the boys battled for an increasingly slim portion of an increasingly shrinking pie. Adding alcohol into the mix certainly didn't help, nor did Shamrock's escalating desire to mix it up every time he went out.

The fight, as so many bar fights do, started with a girl. Or, more accurately, a man harassing a girl.

"I was seeing Johnny Weaver's[40] daughter Wendi and her roommate was messing around with Shamrock," Matt Borne, who would go on to wrestle as Doink the Clown, said. "...I'm sitting at the bar with Wendy and all of the sudden there's this big commotion at the front door. What happened was, Knobbs was grabbing this girl who was with Shamrock. She started crying to Ken, 'Ken, tell him to quit grabbing my tits.'"

"She was quite busty and (Knobbs) came over and poked this girl in the boob. The girl was a little bit embarrassed," Shamrock says. "We went on with the conversation, but they did it again and the girl tells them plainly to stop. And they said 'Come on, when you dress like that you know you want people to touch them.' I got between them, but the dark haired one actually went around me and grabbed her boobs.

"I grabbed him and said 'Enough. You guys stop. You can be arrested for this stuff. Stop it.' And they had a lot to say 'Oh, what are you going to do?' and 'If you can't take it, better get out of the club.' All this stupid stuff. They were drunk."

The Nasty Boys, in a shoot interview[41] with RF Video, confirm this part of the story.

"We went drinking and I got loaded. There were a couple of things said," Knobbs remembers. "I went up to him and gave him a mug and that really made him mad....we were friends. It was just a drunken night."

---

[40] Weaver was the biggest babyface wrestling star in the Carolinas for decades and the first wrestler to popularize the sleeper hold.

[41] The unofficial oral history of pro wrestling is contained in these shoots, recorded long form interviews that purport to share the real story not contained in television storylines. Often filled with tall tales, confirming their validity is a historian's nightmare.

"It happened because of a no good rat,[42]" Saggs added. "A rat should never come between the boys but he was kind of green. Even greener than we were."

A bouncer, well aware of Shamrock's reputation, quickly grabbed a hold of him in a tight bearhug after Knobbs pie-faced him and the tag team was escorted out of the bar. Knobbs, who fell in the parking lot on the way out of the club and hit his head, had to be dragged into his room at the Ramada Inn where the wrestlers all had a special rate.

Meanwhile, Shamrock stewed.

"As we talked about it, I got more and more angry," he says. "So, I went back to the hotel where they were staying, by myself, and kicked in their door. I knew they were in there, because I could hear them rustling around. But they wouldn't answer."

Once inside, Shamrock jumped on top of Knobbs who had passed out on the bed and started wailing away on him. It was the last thing he remembers.

"From what I was told, he (Saggs) hit me in the head from behind with a phone, and they were heavy phones," Shamrock says. "I went down and they started putting the boots to me. Smashed my eye socket, fractured my ribs and were going to throw me over the balcony. And we were on the third floor. Fuller came up and told them 'Don't do that, don't do that.'

"What made me the most angry was these guys knew me. And they were still able to do something like that. I couldn't ever come to terms with that in my mind. It wasn't like we hated each other. They were drunk and thought the rules didn't apply to them. It told me what kind of people they were."

"It was a bad fight and he ended up in the hospital," Saggs said. "I don't like talking about it because it was a heavy duty situation."

On television, they blamed Shamrock's black eyes and bruised face on an attack by Fuller's Stud Stable. At home, his wife Tina put the blame squarely on Shamrock, issuing what author Richard Hanner called "a tongue lashing" to her husband in his hospital bed:

> You are thoughtless and irresponsible, she said.
> You very nearly left your wife without a husband, she said.

---

[42] Called groupies in the music business, a "ring rat" is wrestling parlance for a woman who follows the wrestlers from town to town and offers sexual favors.

You very nearly left your son without a father, she said.

If you truly love your family, she said, you will stop fighting, you will learn, finally learn, to walk away from a fight.

Shamrock could not respond. But he heard the words. He knew his wife was right.

Shamrock, always a quick healer, defied doctors' expectations and was quickly back in the ring—in Japan for his UWF debut against Yoji Anjoh.[43] He may not have been able to keep his promise to stay out of fights for long, but for the time being at least, they would be confined to the ring.

---

[43] While his last name is commonly spelled "Anjo" in the English language press, his tights read "Anjoh." I'm going to take him at his word.

CHAPTER FOUR

Shooting

1991

The Dojo

The dojo was small, about the size of one of the bays where mechanics back home would work on your car. They packed a lot into the space though, just about everything a young man needed to master the art of professional wrestling.

There were mats, of course, along with free weights and some jump ropes, the basic training tools of the fighter's craft. But there was also a small kitchen, where a hearty stew[44] brewed all day, loaded with meat, rice and vegetables and designed to help small frames pack on big muscles.

Above were some cots where the young boys lived during the initial stages of their training. When he first came to Japan, often for weeks at a time, Ken Shamrock lived there too.

Just about the only thing missing was the bathroom—for that you had to go outside.

---

[44] The stew was called chanko and came to pro wrestling from the world of sumo. A combination of carbohydrate and protein loading, it is often packed with chicken, rice and any vegetable the chef can get his hands on.

"There was an outhouse," Shamrock says. "You were in this ultra-modern city and the gym had an outhouse. You had to go outside of the building. And the way the Japanese use the bathroom, you had to squat.

"I remember training so hard, for hours and then going out to use the restroom. Your legs were so freaking weak, you could barely hold yourself up. I remember putting my hands on the wall to brace myself so I wouldn't collapse to the floor in this outhouse. Eventually I figured out the angles so I could rest. It was the only rest you got."

The culture was different, beyond the hazing he'd seen on sports teams in America. The system in the dojo was hierarchical to the extreme. Fujiwara, the senior man, was at the tip top unless his own mentor, the legendary Gotch, was there.

"He (Gotch) was older then, a tough leathery old guy," Shamrock says. "He would come down and do squats with us when we warmed up. He was still very athletic for his age. Him and Fujiwara could still go. They were like machines.

"Then, during the day when Gotch was there, he would float around and correct people's technique by physically demonstrating the moves on them and showing them how it was done. He would correct a mistake by actually putting you in the move. There was nothing soft about that man."

If Gotch was at the top of the hierarchy, the young athletes living in the dojo with Shamrock, of course, were at the very bottom of the totem pole, a cross between whipping boy and servant. It wasn't an easy life, though his status as a foreigner and no-nonsense temperament spared the American newcomer many of the indignities the Japanese absorbed with a quiet stoicism.

"Guys like Suzuki would go up and slap and kick the young kids," Shamrock says. "And they couldn't do anything but stand there and take it. I didn't think it was right, but I was in their house."

The morning began early, with the young boys preparing the gym for the day, cleaning and mopping and setting out equipment for their elders to use when they arrived. Breakfast followed, an enormous bowl of the mystery soup which the young men would eat right there in a tiny nook in the dojo, huddled together for warmth in the winter and despite it in the summer. There was no air conditioning.

Exercises would follow, endless repetitions of squats, pushups and stretching, interspersed with drills focused on the techniques they'd learn that day. Hard, intense cardio, either a run or jump rope would follow.

After lunch, it would begin again, this time focused on punching and kicking combinations and mat drills. You'd work on setups, you'd work on techniques. Sometimes you would spar the same young men you would lay next to at night. It was an exhausting time, mentally and physically and Shamrock was often the only gaijin in the room. Until Funaki arrived mid-morning, he was almost always the only person who spoke English—or, more importantly in this scenario, didn't speak Japanese.

"I was confused a lot. Funaki spoke real good English, so when he was around he could translate and I was able to be understood. But the majority of the time, I would just watch what someone did and then I would do it. Luckily for me, I was one of those people who, if I saw it done once, I could do it.

"I was real close with Funaki. We trained together a lot and were very competitive. We spent a lot of time together. I taught him how to work out and get ripped and he taught me striking and grappling. We worked well together and became friends."

It wasn't long at all before Shamrock was too much for any but the most experienced fighters to handle in the gym. He was bigger, stronger and had a natural affinity for all things combat. Soon enough, they recognized his ambition and his commitment.

"After they saw I was serious, they rented me an apartment in Shin-Yokohama," Shamrock says. "The apartment had nothing in it. It was more like a hotel room. The place was so small, you rolled out of the bed and you'd hit your head on the toilet or the wall. It wasn't very big or very fancy, but it did the trick."

After struggling to find his footing in North Carolina and the world of American pro wrestling, Ken Shamrock finally felt like he was home.

By the time he entered the ring for the first time as a UWF fighter on October 25, 1990, at a sold out Osaka Jo Hall[45], Shamrock had long been smartened up to the wrestling business. But this was the largest

---

[45] The building is best known for its yearly performance of Beethoven's Ninth Symphony with a 10,000 person chorus. It seats between 15,000 and 16,000 for wrestling shows, like New Japan's yearly Dominion event.

crowd[46] he'd ever performed in front of by far, and he still wasn't quite sure what to expect in his first match under this ruleset. He wasn't even entirely sure why they were announcing him using his middle name.

"It was Masami's idea to switch his first name from Ken to Wayne," reporter Fumi Saito says. "He probably did not want people to associate Shamrock with the young American rookie who had toured with All Japan the year before."

While his first opponent, Yoji Anjoh,[47] was often chosen to wrestle the foreigners because of his command of the English language, the two did very little planning before the match.

"They told me 'don't knock anybody out on purpose or break anybody's arm, but go in there and go after one another,'" Shamrock says. "There was nothing planned. We fought each other without trying to knock each other out."

The match is a revelation. Even the best wrestlers often need some time to develop when they begin with a shoot style promotion. Wrestlers are used to protecting each other in the ring and taking care not to do much actual harm to their opponent who is actually their partner in the match. A UWF bout was different, half worked performance, half real fight.

"I prepared for it like I was going into a fight," Shamrock says. "This is basically a hard shoot. The end is predetermined. But anything in between, you better protect yourself. I was really following his lead. I followed what he was doing and tried to do what I knew how to do.

"The guys from Florida had warned me, especially with it being my first time, they might try to take advantage of you and really lay you out. You've got to give it right back to them. You've got to give it back to them or you won't get their respect.

"So, as he started getting heavier and heavier on his strikes, I got heavier and heavier on mine. There was a point when he hit me pretty

---

[46] The UWF drew a reported 15,000 fans to Osaka Castle Hall, one of four cards to break five figures for the white hot promotion in 1990. Akira Maeda beat Masakatsu Funaki in the main event.

[47] Anjoh is best known to mixed martial arts fans for his disastrous fight with jiu jitsu ace Rickson Gracie. The wrestler traveled to California, with the Japanese press in tow, to challenge Gracie at his dojo. While he expected to arrange an eventual bout with the fighter, instead he was mercilessly beaten on the spot.

solid and I was like 'alright.' And I went after him and hit him hard. He threw some things and it felt to me like he was trying to lay one in on me. So I gave it back to him as hard as he was giving it me."

Anjoh was a UWF mid-carder, winning 11 and losing 11 in the UWF's final two years. But he was an excellent performer and Shamrock more than held his own. He had never truly studied martial arts and was throwing kicks for the first time in the match. While sometimes awkward, he had a natural grace and a warrior's spirit. Fans roared their approval when he got up at nine after a particularly hard series of strikes from Anjoh and celebrated loudly when he turned things around moments later.

He'd entered the ring in tiny fluorescent pink Speedos to a few jeers. By the time he left, hand raised after a submission victory in just over 11 minutes, the crowd was cheering wildly and even chanting his name.

"When you're in the ring, you don't really know how good it is," Shamrock says. "People tell you things, but you don't know for sure. By the time I got on the plane to leave Japan, I had a pretty good idea that I had put together a pretty good match, better than they've seen before from a first timer."

Shamrock stayed in Japan after the match, something that would become a habit over the years, and joined the wrestlers in the dojo for training. He and Funaki would go on to become fast friends and training partners. They started out with a comical misunderstanding when Funaki attempted to rib the American about his outfit despite their cultural and linguistic barriers.

"I didn't think anything of the shorts," Shamrock says. "I had them made for American pro wrestling and that color was big at the time.[48] Funaki came up to me afterwards. I don't know if he was being serious about finding out what my (sexual) preference was.

"He goes 'You okama?' I go 'What?' And all the people around me start laughing. 'You a faggot? You gay?' I said 'Dude, be careful.'"

Although their relationship was formed partly due to necessity, as Funaki was often the only person around who spoke English, the two soon found they were kindred spirits, equally obsessed with getting better and better in the ring.

---

[48] WWF's Hart Foundation tag team wore pink and black at the time and were a major act for the country's leading promotion. Bret Hart, the technician of the team, would later help Shamrock prepare for his own WWF debut.

"The first time I met Shamrock, I thought that he was the first foreigner I'd met in a long time who really had guts," Funaki says. "When I was still in New Japan, around 17 or 18 years old, I'd train with Chris Benoit. He and Ken were similar. Very focused on their training, and dedicated to staying in Japan and working here long term. He learned a lot in a short time. I knew he'd be a top guy."

The two men would meet in the main event of the UWF's next show in December 1990, a lightning fast elevation for the American newcomer who had seriously impressed the brass in his debut. It was a fast-paced match that lasted almost 20 minutes. Although he didn't win, Shamrock showed he could perform at an elite level against a wrestler most had tabbed as the future standard-bearer for the style.

"They really saw the potential," Shamrock says. "It wasn't about me being a tough guy. It was the way I was being noticed by the fanbase. They saw money and dollar signs in marketing me. Japan was still built at the time on that clash between the Japanese and foreign fighters. They loved that battle. They saw me come, even without any experience, and compete right away."

Unfortunately, Shamrock's big opportunity came just as the UWF descended into chaos. Maeda, the promotion's marquee attraction, and Shinji Jin, his former assistant and the company's President, were in a fierce battle for the UWF's soul. Jin wanted to take a big sponsorship offer from Megane Super Optical owner Hachiro Tanaka, a wrestling enthusiast who had already attempted to buy the promotion outright.[49] Tanaka launched his new Super World Sports promotion in 1990 and had no patience with the idea of building slowly. He was looking to run a show in the Tokyo Dome in March 1991 and wanted UWF wrestlers to join him.

Maeda, who had built his reputation in staunch opposition to "fake" wrestling, didn't think the promotion should associate itself with a group like SWS, which was planning to co-promote with the WWF.[50] Jin believed, despite the promotion's success selling out a monthly event and subsequent VHS and laser disc releases, that the lack of a

---

[49] SWS first approached Keiji Mutoh, coming off a run in America as "the Great Muta" to be his headliner. The UWF's Maeda was his second choice before ultimately settling on former sumo wrestler Genichiro Tenryu.

[50] The SWS' Tokyo Dome debut featured the Legion of Doom going to a count out against Hulk Hogan and Tenryu. It was, essentially, Maeda's worst nightmare.

television deal meant the group required a certain flexibility. The dispute soon went public, with Maeda accusing Jin of financial malfeasance and Jin suspending his top attraction, who did not wrestle on the December show, which ended up being the UWF's final event.

"Jin basically stopped doing paper work for each and every show they were running," Saito says. "The UWF office at the time only had like five employees and they simply did not have time to sit down and do the book keeping for the previous shows. They were working on the next month's show.

"Everyone knew (UWF was) making money but they did not know how much. All the wrestlers believed UWF was making a lot of money, therefore their paycheck should be a lot higher than they were getting.

"I am sure Jin and his guys had a lot to hide… Maeda brought in an outside company to investigate the financials by then. The big split was about to happen."

In January of 1991, all the top talent met at Maeda's house to discuss their options. While everyone agreed that the company couldn't go on as it was, they couldn't agree on who should be the standard bearer of the new group they were proposing. Some wanted Maeda on top; others believed his understudy, Nobuhiko Takada, should assume the throne. There was also significant disagreement about their creative future.

"It was no secret that Maeda's ultimate goal was to make UWF a legitimate sport," Saito says. "For real. Some guys agreed. Some guys disagreed. Some thought the status quo was the best way.

"…On the subject of going into all-shoot legitimate competitive professional wrestling, each and every wrestler had his own perspectives and opinions. I don't think it was possible to come up with a solution where everybody could be happy."

When the tense meeting was over, the wrestlers parted ways. No one knows for sure what happened there that day. Some wouldn't speak again for decades. Only the aftermath is clear. Three groups emerged from the implosion of the UWF. Fujiwara launched first with Pro Wrestling Fujiwara Gumi, Maeda formed RINGS and Takada, Kazuo Yamazaki and Anjoh created UWF International.

Shamrock, lost to the nuances of the dispute thanks to a language and experience barrier, wasn't sure what was going on and worried that his big break might only last a couple of months.

"I get a call after my second match that the UWF was over," he says.

"I was like 'noooo!'

"I should have known something was going on. Maeda actually took me out to dinner and was nice to me. A couple of weeks later, they split. I think he was trying to feel out whether or not I would be interested in going with him. But I think he saw my allegiance was to Funaki and to Sami. I didn't really have an understanding of who was doing what behind the scenes. I only knew who was doing what for me. So, I just went in the direction the people that were handling me went."

Most of the young wrestlers went with Takada to form UWF International[51] where Shigeo Miyato[52] and Anjoh intended to recreate the 1970's version of New Japan Pro Wrestling they had grown up with. Feeling the committee approach on top wasn't working, they went with Takada as their version of Inoki, the dominant superstar the entire promotion would be built around. They recruited familiar foreign faces from the past like Lou Thesz and Billy Robinson to bolster the group's tough guy credentials and even made Thesz's old school version of the world championship the centerpiece of their promotion.

Both Funaki and Minoru Suzuki were in their early twenties at the time and overwhelmed by the breakup of the promotion they had so recently joined. Leaving New Japan, where both were tabbed for eventual stardom, was a difficult choice—having it backfire so spectacularly was devastating. Suzuki had made frantic and tearful phone calls after the decision to blow it all up was made. When their mentor Fujiwara offered a lifeline, they were quick to grab ahold.

"I really thought it was a shame that UWF went under," Funaki

---

[51] Although this group is commonly referred to as "UWFi" in the American wrestling press, Japanese fans and media generally call it UWF International or shorten the name to U-Inter.

"Nobody calls it UWFI in Japan," reporter Fumi Saito says. "That is just what Wrestling Observer decided to call it."

[52] Miyato was an opening match wrestler but a powerhouse behind the scenes.

"This guy didn't weigh but 200 pounds but he was a tough little dude," Mark Fleming says. "He was tough as freaking nails. He conducted the workouts at the dojo."

says. "Maeda decided to break it all up, and Fujiwara started PWFG. He invited me in, and I accepted. All the others went to Takada and U-Inter. If Fujiwara hadn't asked me on board, I probably would have gone with U-Inter, too."

Fujiwara's promotion didn't have a distinct identity the way the other UWF offshoots eventually did. Funaki, Fujiwara and Suzuki were less popular than their counterparts in RINGS and UWF International and their decision to almost immediately mix in with Megane Super's other wrestlers sent confusing signals about who and what they were. But the promotion also had income streams the others didn't, offering some leeway and time to figure it all out.

"(Fujiwara) was the only one who got Megane Super's money for the next three year period and pretty much ran his own shows," Saito says. "He had promised Megane Super people that he would get Funaki and Suzuki. That's how it worked out.

"Fujiwara was their original coach from their rookie years when they were still working for New Japan. He was an almost father-like figure to them at the time."

Funaki had left home when he was just 15 to pursue his wrestling dreams. His parents had divorced when he was 12 and, having grown up following the adventures of his favorite wrestlers Tiger Mask and Hulk Hogan on television, he believed wrestling was the best way to help his mother and sister with mounting money problems.

"She didn't want me to be a pro wrestler because it was much too dangerous a job for a boy," he remembers. "But I tried to persuade her. I told her 'If I had two lives, I would follow your orders this time and follow my dreams in the other. But I only have one life. So, please forgive me this time. I really want to be a pro wrestler."

He spent years in the dojo learning from Fujiwara, who focused almost entirely on the mechanics of actual grappling, not the showmanship more often featured during professional matches. It was an eye opening experience for a young athlete who didn't do any amateur wrestling in school but found he had an aptitude for it.

"We would spar together for an hour everyday, starting when I was 15 years old," Funaki says. "Just the two of us wrestling. For him, guts were more important than technique early in training, so I would be beaten down again and again.

"Afterwards he would allow me to ask him questions about the techniques and show me physically, for example, how to escape from a hold that had been troubling me. We did this every day before the matches after doing our physical conditioning."

By the time Pro Wrestling Fujiwara-Gumi[53] launched in March 1991, Funaki had turned into a very capable young grappler, both as a traditional professional wrestler and a shooter. With his model looks and increasingly chiseled physique, he had all the hallmarks of stardom—everything except an opponent capable of launching his career into the stratosphere. Fujiwara was too old and hadn't been positioned as a star in New Japan. He was a respected presence for certain but not a megastar. Suzuki, by contrast, was his peer and faced the same problems. The two together would have a hard time pulling each other where they needed to go.

Shamrock, perhaps, represented his best hope. He was also new—to the style, to Japan, to submission grappling. But the rules were different for foreigners and the new American exuded charisma and physical danger in a way that was hard to teach. Even better, he was picking things up incredibly quickly and was tough. In the hardest niche of a hard business, this mattered quite a bit.

"Back then, there were pretty much no foreign pro wrestlers who could handle themselves in a real fight," Funaki says. "At the same time, back then a promotion absolutely needed foreign talent to survive...We saw great potential with Ken."

Problems for the doomed promotion mounted almost immediately. At the promotion's debut show at Tokyo's Korakuen Hall, Suzuki had shown world class potential in a match with Shamrock, leading the neophyte to a 30-minute draw that never once felt dull.

"We just flowed," Shamrock remembers. "He was a really good amateur wrestler and he moved really well on the ground and we both had the stamina to go really hard for a full 30 minutes."

A month later, the young Japanese star was sent to an SWS show for the first time, and this time, things didn't go quite so smoothly. He got

---

[53] The word "Gumi" is most often used to refer to a Yakuza crime family. Fujiwara also referred to himself as "kumicho" which is the leader or Don of the group. Considering the close traditional ties between Japanese wrestling and the Yakuza, it's hard to know what to make of all this.

into a fight in the middle of a worked match with Apollo Sugawara, a career undercard wrestler who thought Suzuki was taking liberties with him. There was hair pulling and full force headbutts, but more than anything, there was circling and staring. Not only was it a stunning lack of professionalism, it wasn't even interesting.[54]

"I didn't come here to do that kind of crap," Suzuki screamed afterwards[55], rejecting what he called fake wrestling in the press.

"Soon after that, we didn't work with the SWS wrestlers anymore," Funaki says. "When we were on an SWS show, we wrestled each other. They decided it was better for everyone that way."

Shamrock didn't work any of the SWS shows, focusing his attention on both learning to shoot in training and pretending to shoot in the ring during real matches. After a triumphant debut for PWFG against Suzuki, Shamrock lost his second bout in the company to veteran Naoki Sano. That brought his record in shoot style matches to an even .500 with two wins and two losses. He was at a crossroads—either the promotion was going to try to launch him as the next big gaijin star or he was going to be just another guy in the middle of the card trying to scrape out a living.

He had clear potential, but a high profile Japanese promotion isn't normally a developmental league for young Americans. They needed a polished product and Shamrock still had some work to do. Worse, at least for Shamrock, PWFG was looking to bring in foreign athletes with bigger and shinier legitimate combat credentials. Shamrock's next opponent fit that bill and the match ended up changing the way he was viewed in Japan.

Duane Koslowski was a raw-boned, American wrestler, country-strong from South Dakota with the kind of swagger that can only come

---

[54] If you search using Japanese Kanji for the wrestlers' names, you can see a bootleg version of the match on YouTube. But you'd be better off with this brief summary.

[55] This anecdote comes from Chris Charlton's excellent book *Eggshells*, a history of professional wrestling at the Tokyo Dome.

from dominating other big farm kids on the Division III scene.[56] A former college wrestling standout Duane, and his twin brother Dennis,[57] had continued their grappling careers in the Greco-Roman ranks and both qualified for the 1988 Olympics in Seoul.

While he didn't ever medal on the world stage, having finished a close fourth at the World Championships in 1986, Koslowski still brought with him a pedigree Shamrock simply couldn't match. He'd been an American champion three times and a Pan American gold medalist. Shamrock had little more than a good look and a burgeoning reputation. In wrestling, especially in Japan where perception and a glimmer of reality was so important, that wasn't always enough.

Sami Soranaka, who did all the matchmaking alongside Fujiwara, hadn't decided who was going to go over in the match when he introduced the two men at the dojo where they'd spend a few days prior to the bout preparing.

"'Hey, this is Duane,'" he told Shamrock. "'You're going to fight him.'"

'Cool.'

"I didn't have any ego about winning or losing," Shamrock says. "I was a young wrestler and we weren't a group that was doing real shoots yet. No big deal."

But just because he would willingly do whatever they asked, it didn't mean Shamrock didn't have an opinion.

Sami put both men on the spot, asking them who should win. Shamrock chose himself. He had been there longer and understood the style. Koslowski, naturally, thought his superior wrestling credentials should win the day.

"I didn't want to argue," Shamrock remembers. "I told him 'Sami, whatever you want.'"

But, instead of choosing, Soranaka came up with a novel method of deciding who would win a predetermined wrestling match—the two would have a real bout to see who deserved it more.

'Why don't you guys shoot for it?'

---

[56] Koslowski won a Division III wrestling title at the University of Minnesota-Morris where he also played football. He was inducted into the Northern Sun Intercollegiate Conference Hall of Fame in 2001.

[57] Dennis would later join UWF International after his own amateur career ended. Wrestling at 100KG (220 pounds), he was significantly smaller than his brother, who competed at 130 KG (286 pounds)

'What?'

'You guys settle it now on the mat?'

'You mean like fight? For real?'

'Yeah.'

"I remember Duane was like 'What if I hurt him,'" Shamrock says. "I looked at him and said 'Don't worry. You won't hurt me. I'm a big boy. If I get beat up, I get beat up. Let's do this.'"

This had the entire dojo's attention now and Shamrock gave them quite a show. He shot in for a quick single leg and almost immediately dumped the bigger man on the mat. Within seconds the amateur wrestler was in a heel hook and conceding. The whole thing took less than a minute. But Koslowski wasn't willing to concede quite so easily.

"'Wait a minute. Wait a minute. Wait a minute. I wasn't ready.'"

"'What do you mean you weren't ready? You were looking right at me and he said 'Go!'"

"'Nobody has shot on me in forever. There are no leg shots in Greco Roman wrestling. I wasn't ready.'"

"Sami asked him, 'Well, you want to do it again?' I said, 'I don't mind. We'll do it again.'"

Seconds later, the very same scene replayed itself. Koslowski's upper body wrestling techniques were no match for a fighter who was quickly becoming very skilled in the submission game.

"I looked at him and said 'You want to do it again?'" Shamrock says. "This time he just shook his head no and then shook my hand. Sami did that because Duane came in with an attitude. He didn't want to put anyone over because he was the 'real deal.' He didn't realize that what we did was real too."

Shamrock won both matches, the one to prove a point and the one in front of an enthusiastic crowd of around 6000 fans in Tokyo. Muscles bulging and hair pulled back into a stylish ponytail, he looked every bit the superstar. In front of the fans, he allowed himself to fall victim to several huge suplexes and carried the newcomer to a solid match. But, like the contest in the practice room, it ended with a Shamrock leg lock, this time after a spectacular Northern Lights suplex.

The Koslowski incident soon became the standard modus operandi for some of PWFG's tough young veterans. If a wrestler came in from a martial arts background and had some qualms about losing a match with a 'fake wrestler' they were able to rather quickly show them the error of their ways much the way Inoki's wrestlers had a generation prior.

"Suzuki used to do it, but they stopped letting him shoot with new guys because he would hurt people if he thought they had an attitude," Shamrock says. "And that's not who we are. Guy comes in with an attitude, first of all, they're probably a little afraid. And they were probably really good at whatever it was they did—but this was different.

"So, you just had to go in and show them. It's a different world. We needed bodies, people to compete. It didn't make any sense to bring people in and hurt them and send them home. We wanted to teach them what we do, get them excited and encouraged about doing it. Not discouraged. But you also couldn't have them thinking they were above you. There was a fine line."

Shamrock finished the rest of the year undefeated, highlighted by another excellent technical bout with Suzuki in September[58] at Hakata Starlanes[59] and a match in November that went just over a minute with Kazuo Takahashi.[60] A young bull of a fighter, Takahashi was Shamrock's main sparring partner and in some ways a kindred spirit. He was having a hard time distinguishing between a hard blow that looked real and just straight up bludgeoning his opponents. He was also frustrated by losing every match in the ring despite his significant success in the dojo.

"It was like they were holding this wild stallion in the corrals and they couldn't let him out," Shamrock says. "When you did, he had a hard time not throwing off the rider. When me and him got in there, I told Funaki 'let him run.' Let us go at it.

"So Takahashi came up to me and said 'it's okay? We hit hard?' And I said, 'yeah dude, turn it loose. Let's have fun. Whatever happens happens.' We went in the ring with the understanding that we would go in there and knock the shit out of each other. May the best man win."

During the match, Takahashi got Shamrock up in the air for a big

---

[58] The Suzuki match took place just two days after the birth of Shamrock's second son Connor on September 26th.
[59] Hakata Starlanes was an enormous bowling facility in Kyushu that frequently housed pro wrestling events. It closed in March 2019, much to the dismay of Japanese fans.
[60] He went by the name Yoshiaki Takahashi in both Pancrase and the UFC and was an excellent fighter in the early days of the mixed martial arts experiment.

slam, but in the ensuing scramble, the American rearranged his face with a soccer kick to the eye. The swelling began almost immediately around his broken orbital bone, and though Takahashi was desperate to continue, the referee called a stop to the contest.

As brutal as the wrestling sometimes looked in the UWF and its offshoots, this was clearly something different, the level of violence escalated beyond what was safe or comfortable for some viewers. It also, if fans thought about it too hard, exposed the other matches PWFG was promoting as the real deal as something a little less than pure competition. But, in the heat of the moment, Shamrock felt entirely alive.

"I respected the way that he wanted to come in and fight. He wanted to earn everything. And if he wasn't good enough, then he wanted to know it through the fight.

"I enjoyed it. With a guy like him, I wasn't worried about him trying to sucker punch me in that situation. He'd knock the crap out of you but not on purpose, but because he's an intense person who wants it to be as real as you can make it."

Shamrock finished 1991 wrestling three matches at a television taping in December for South Atlantic Pro Wrestling, bouts which ended up being his final dates with the struggling group. He'd wrestled there sporadically between matches in Japan, taking on faded veterans like Wahoo McDaniel and rising stars like Chris Chavis[61] and even held their heavyweight title. One match with McDaniel drew just 55 people in Gastonia, North Carolina—and that wasn't even the worst crowd of the year for a promotion doing little more than gasping for air. His heart, and the bulk of his income, was now in Japan[62].

He opened the year 1992 with consecutive main event matches against Funaki, the two establishing their places as the top gaijin and top native star respectively. The first went to a 30-minute draw and ended with Funaki locked in a rear naked choke as the bell rang. For the second, they added an additional 30 minutes to the time limit and used 40 of them before Funaki finally ended the bout. These were long,

---

[61] Chavis would later perform as Tatanka in WWF. He partnered with Shamrock when both were babyfaces then feuded with him when Ken turned heel. Both men had the look and feel of people who would go places.

[62] He was voted the seventh most popular foreign wrestler by Weekly Pro Wrestling's fans. Considering the size and reach of his promotion, Shamrock was making a considerable mark.

realistic and grueling displays of grappling prowess, featuring back-and-forth ground exchanges that left Funaki drained. Shamrock, however, emerged fresh and energetic, apparently able to wrestle for as long as you needed him to.

"I pretty much blew Funaki up[63]," Shamrock says with a laugh. "He told me something I actually took and applied to my guys. He told me 'the greatest honor you could show me is one day I want you to be better than me. That's what every instructor wants for their students. Take my ceiling and make it your floor.' And it came a lot sooner than he thought. But I really took that to heart. That's a great attitude to have, especially when you're teaching other people."

In March, the promotion held a show in Miami that was originally supposed to feature Fujiwara against legendary boxer Roberto Duran. But a variety of issues[64] forced the pugilist to put the match off a month[65], not least of which were the 249 pounds[66] he carried on a frame that was built to box at lightweight. The show went on without him and the core PWFG wrestlers made the most of their time in the States, training with Gotch at his home and then attracting a surprisingly robust crowd of 2,800 to the James L. Knight Center. The show, according to the *Wrestling Observer*:

> attracted mainly a karate audience rather than a pro wrestling audience and was billed more as a kick boxing exhibition than pro wrestling. The show was hyped as U.S. vs. Japanese with the Japanese treated as heavy heels by the crowd, although Yoshiaki Fujiwara was the only one who worked anything

---

[63] Wrestling lingo for tiring someone out. Grappling on the mat, surprisingly, is an easy way to exhaust someone even if they are in great shape and Shamrock preferred to keep the action moving.

[64] The Wrestling Observer reported that tax issues with the IRS made the Panamanian Duran wary of competing on American soil.

[65] Duran would eventually face off with Funaki instead, in a weird match where the Japanese wrestler was limited to just eight seconds at a time on the mat. For an old, fat guy Duran could still move. Though he eventually submitted in the third round, he battered Funaki to the body throughout a very entertaining bout.

[66] The Observer's Dave Meltzer reported he weighed "about 249 pounds." I'm not sure how one arrives at such a specific approximation instead of bumping the speculative weight up to 250 pounds.

resembling a heel style.

The event was advertised as "Shootfighting" and not pro wrestling and was treated by fans like the bouts were legitimate contests. It was covered that way in publications like *Karate International* magazine, despite some exchanges that were pretty firmly planted in the world of wrestling.

Shamrock and Suzuki stole the show with their third PWFG match, another display of fierce striking and non-stop action when the bout hit the mat, something that really separated them from the other wrestlers in the group.

"They were trying to give Suzuki a reputation and name. Because he looked good and had some pizzazz to him," Shamrock says. "He was really slick on the ground. He was really smooth and looked good going into and out of his submissions."

Bart Vale, the local promoter and a midcard mainstay of the group, won the first championship in the promotion's history via count out, the first cheap finish PWFG had ever attempted. It was hard to watch at times[67], especially following the impressive athleticism of the Funaki/Suzuki/Shamrock triumvirate.

Fujiwara was 42 years old, but it was an old 42, one that had included two decades of professional wrestling and all the associated wear and tear that brought with it. Considering PWFG was attempting to present a more realistic sports-based brand of promotion, the pushback against old guys overstaying their welcome was going to be a natural part of the ethos.

This divide, between the young, strong, vibrant stars of the future and the faded glory of the past, would become starker as the year went on. Fujiwara had gone undefeated in 1991, putting himself over Funaki and going to a 30-minute draw with Suzuki.[68]

The wheels fell off for Fujiwara in a May match against former kickboxer Don Nakaya Nielsen at the Osaka Prefectural Gymnasium. Nielsen was famed for his mixed matches[69] in the 1980s, especially a

---

[67] The finishing sequence, an especially slow series of Kenpo Karate kicks, was particularly embarrassing.

[68] He never lost a bout to either of his proteges, despite obvious fan enthusiasm for a changing of the guard.

[69] Popularized by Inoki, these were pro wresting matches between established wrestlers and outsiders from legitimate martial arts disciplines.

legendary tilt with Akira Maeda often held up as the greatest of the many bouts between Japanese wrestling superstars and their martial arts counterparts. He had actually won a match with Fujiwara in New Japan back in 1988 and was expected to return the favor in front of over 4000 fans in the main event here.

Instead, Fujiwara was bloodied and staggered by a kick in just over a minute. His right eye was a mess and he was forced to lean heavily on the referee for support as a doctor came into the ring to stop the match. Rather than a triumph for pro wrestling as a fighting art, the ultimate point of these mixed matches, it was a major defeat. Funaki believed it to be an unfortunate accident. Shamrock, who had lost to Vale earlier in the night[70], thought it might have been a double cross of some kind. Either way, to protect the business, something had to be done.

The promotion booked Nielsen for a shoot match that October for a show in the Tokyo Dome, giving the locker room a chance to defend the group's honor.

"After Nielsen fought Mr. Fujiwara the company asked 'Anybody wants to fight with Nielsen?'" Funaki says, recalling Shamrock's quick acceptance of the bout. "Then Ken said 'I can fight with Nielsen.'"

Like that, the bout was set.

"It was supposed to be a work and this guy went in there and knocked the shit out of Fujiwara. Now I'm in there to represent one of the Japanese heroes—and I'm not even from that culture," Shamrock says. "Me and Takahashi, we were the only two on that card who fought real fights. That's when I knew the organization really thought highly of me and how quickly I was learning."

After years of training and bouts designed to look as real as possible, Shamrock was finally going to compete in a real fight. Funaki trained him for the encounter, and though he recognized the potential pitfalls and the possibility of being clobbered with a hard strike from a legitimate competitor, Shamrock felt no nerves as he stepped into the

---

[70] Vale would hilariously go on to claim this match was an actual fight and most mixed martial arts reporters had no way of verifying the truth. The bout was clearly a work and Shamrock remembers refusing to go down until Vale actually hit him with something believable. That took some time.

"I was like 'come on man. Hit me!' I wasn't going down if I couldn't even feel it," he says.

ring.

"When you find something that just feels right and you're really interested in, you think about it all the time," he says. "Even when you sleep. You get up and train for it and you're not afraid to do it all the time. It all falls into place for you. The harder you work, the more things seem to work out for you.

"More than anything, it was an actual fight. It was everything I had grown up doing and would get in trouble for. And here I was going to get paid and people were cheering and screaming for me to take some guy down to the ground and try to break his arm."

PWFG packed more than 40,000 fans into the Dome, though only 25,000 of them paid for the privilege, scuttling fears in the press that the show would be a bust. The PWFG regulars all took on foreign martial artists, and with the exception of Koslowski, all were successful. After all the build up and years of training, it was time for Shamrock to represent himself, his trainer and the promotion itself. In the end, the introduction and staredown took longer than the fight itself, which clocked in at just 45 seconds before a key lock did Nielsen in.

"He didn't know how to tap out. He had gloves on," Shamrock says. "He was screaming in my ear and the referee didn't stop it because he didn't know what he was doing either. He was a boxing and Muay Thai guy. He didn't know what to do or what a submission was.

"I'm hearing his arm snap and I'm looking up at the referee and he's not doing anything. This poor guy! There was no one there to help him because they didn't know what was happening. He was screaming and I just kept cranking it. Sorry buddy. That's not how it gets stopped."

After an initial takedown Shamrock had quickly maneuvered onto Nielsen's back only to see the kickboxer scramble desperately for the ropes. Shamrock ate a kick on his way in the second time, but once he secured a bodylock, Nielsen again found himself on the mat in the middle of the ring and out of his element.

"Ken," Funaki says, "fought the perfect fight that time."

Funaki's five-round draw with kickboxing star Maurice Smith was a personal disappointment, though the crowd seemed entertained. Shamrock and Takahashi's success in legitimate contests had given him a taste of what was possible. He'd wanted a similar bout with Smith, but the powers-that-be insisted on a worked finish. Worse, things seemed to be heading in the wrong direction. Fujiwara had wanted to bring in Tenryu from WAR to face him in the main event of the show. When the younger wrestlers balked, he backed down. But the writing was on the wall that the group couldn't be shielded from the wider wrestling world for long. Funaki's dreams for the promotion appeared they might go unrealized.

"Funaki's real reason for staying with Fujiwara and PWFG was because he thought he could implement what became the Pancrase Style," television producer and future Pancrase President Masami Ozaki said. "In the UWF he was constantly pushing for it with Maeda, 'I want UWF to be legit "MMA",' and was told 'wait about five years.'"

He'd been dreaming of a version of pro wrestling that was completely legitimate since he was just 17 years old. The waiting game, much to his dismay continued. Fujiwara, despite his reputation as a fierce shooter, just wasn't willing to buck tradition and try something new. This clash of worldviews came to a head after the promotion's December show in Niigata, Japan.

"PWFG was tied up with Megane Super, who had their own promotion with Tenryu," Funaki says. "Megane Super wanted PWFG and Tenryu's group to merge. Me and Suzuki were dead set against that."

Rather than return to the world of traditional wrestling, the two young stars quit PWFG with no notice. Many of the promotion's younger wrestlers came with them into the unknown. It had all happened so quickly that no one was really prepared, not just long term, but even for the next night. After leaving the dojo, some of the young boys were essentially homeless and forced to spend the night in Ozaki's production studio. The Japanese scene had three shoot style wrestling promotions already. To make their mark, Funaki and Suzuki would need a compelling idea—and came up with one in the form of Pancrase.

"Maeda was with RINGS, Takada had U-Inter and Fujiwara was still with PWFG. Then there's me with less name value than the others," Funaki says. "We were the fourth spinoff. We had to do something to separate ourselves. We had to do something new, and that meant going with real fights."

The original Pancrase crew featured seven Japanese athletes[71] and none of the foreigners who filled up the rest of the PWFG cards.

---

[71] Takaku "Yusuke" Fuke, Masakatsu Funaki, Katsuomi Inagaki, Kiuma Kunioku, Minoru Suzuki, Kazuo "Yoshiki" Takahashi and Ryushi Yanagisawa.

Shamrock stayed with the promotion for one more show, losing his final bout to Fujiwara in January 1993. It was a promotional decision that infuriated him, especially after the Nielsen fight at the Tokyo Dome.

"He wanted to go over on me," Shamrock says. "And I was like 'You had me go in there and fight somebody in the Dome who knocked the shit out of you because it was supposed to be a work and he took advantage of you and knocked you out.' I got in the ring to fight that same guy and I beat him up. And you're going to put me in the ring and you're going to beat me?

"It was like, are you trying to build yourself or are you trying to build this company? That's what really made Funaki, Suzuki and myself mad about what was going on there. They weren't doing what was good for the company. It was what was best for an individual."

There were rumors that Maeda was offering positions to the remaining PWFG wrestlers, including Shamrock, in his RINGS promotion. But, already unhappy with the direction of PWFG, he saw Maeda as potentially nothing more than a more popular version of Fujiwara, an older, out-of-shape star to do jobs for.

The timing was perfect for Funaki to make his pitch, flying to California where Shamrock returned with his family to convince the rising star to join them on this adventure. Funaki knew he was pitching something unique and unusual. But it was something Shamrock was more than ready to try.

"I thought back to me at 17, wanting to do a kind of pro wrestling where you don't cooperate, you don't willingly take bumps," Funaki said. "I talked to the other boys, and they were up for it, and then I called Shamrock.

"Shamrock and I had that conversation. 'I want to do a kind of pro wrestling where we don't cooperate with one another. You don't bump for people.' He goes 'is that really ok? I might knock you out.'

"'If that happens, it happens.'

"'Man, that's what I've always wanted to do.'"

Coming up with the idea was one thing, funding it something else entirely. Their rejection of SWS and then WAR made taking Megane Super money impossible. They went to Ozaki, but he was cash poor at the time and couldn't come up with the 30,000,000 yen they needed to launch properly.[72] If they wanted to do it on their terms, it would be up

---

[72] Approximately $270,000 in 1993 money.

to them to make it happen.

"Me, Suzuki and Fuke borrowed the money to put it together," Funaki says. "Ozaki lent us an office. Suzuki found a gym.

"The concept was pro wrestling for the 21st century. Everything was a real meritocracy, not political."

Hardcore fans were rabid about the concept and the group was featured on the cover of the country's wrestling magazines multiple times before ever holding their first show. Funaki, in a press conference announcing the group's formation, set the stage for the sport's next great evolution.

"I have no regrets about being here," Funaki said. "I had to separate from many people. Instead, I have gained partners who can be sympathetic to my ideals. They are really important to me.

"With the fighting style that we've been using, I decided to form a new team in order to keep that principle. We'll never give up. I think making this team long lasting is the most important thing. A new fight is beginning. Please pay attention to us. That's all."

CHAPTER FIVE

Pancrase

Scott Bessac fancied himself a tough guy, right up until the moment when life assured him he still had a lot to learn.

A former college football player who moonlighted as a semi-professional well into adulthood, he was the picture of working-class American masculinity, from his long hair and mustache to his motorcycle jacket. In a different era he surely would have had a pack of cigarettes rolled up in the sleeve of his white t-shirt.

Working for Shamrock's dad Bob at a group home in early 1993, Bessac had heard all about the legendary Ken Shamrock. No one who was around Bob for long didn't hear his glowing tales of his beloved adopted son and his exploits as a Japanese shoot fighter. When Bessac finally got a look at Shamrock in action performing a triangle choke, he wasn't entirely ready to buy in.

"He was a big dude, really cocky," Shamrock remembers. "He said 'Pfft, that looks like pro wrestling. That stuff ain't real.' I told him, 'I'm telling you dude, it works.'"

"'Put me in it,'" was Bessac's retort, not believing any of it at this point, sure it was just pro wrestling smoke and mirrors.

Hold firmly locked, Bessac starts to pick Ken up to slam his way out of the hold. It's the natural reaction, but Shamrock is expecting it. He's seen every big, strapping wrestler to set in the PWFG dojo try the same move— and he simply grabs Bessac's ankle, throwing him off balance and making picking Shamrock up next to impossible.

"He wakes up, confused and looks around," Shamrock says. "'What happened?' he asked.

'You passed out.'

'What do you mean?'

'I mean, I just choked you unconscious,'" Shamrock said. "'I'm telling you, it works.'"

"Do it again," a stubborn Bessac demanded.

"So I did it again," Shamrock says. "This time it was a rear naked. Again, I choked him out. After that, he never challenged me again. He knew it worked."

Bessac was desperate to learn just how Shamrock had pulled those moves off, but the wrestler was hesitant to take a student on. What did he know about training anyone anyway? But when Bessac's fingerprints finished going through the system, his criminal record disqualified him from working with the at-risk youth and Bob had to let him go. He was desperate—and so, in his own way was Ken.

With Pancrase on the horizon, he'd need to keep his skills sharp. The Japanese wrestlers who had been his trainers and mentors would now also be his opponents in a legitimate competition. He'd need to know more than just what they deigned to teach him to beat them at their own game. But finding a place to do that and people to learn from was proving tricky. Most martial arts were entirely geared towards their own forms of competition and their own rules, both the formally written ones and the unwritten cultural mores that defined how they were taught and practiced. None of them, it seemed to Shamrock, were built to survive first contact in confrontations outside their own sandbox.

"I tried to find a place to train and just couldn't do it," Shamrock remembers. "This was way before the UFC and there was nobody doing this kind of martial arts training. I got with wrestlers and did some wrestling to get in shape. I lifted. I did some striking on the bag, but I didn't spar—I didn't know how. I had never done anything except tough man competitions. Really raw training and focused on getting in good shape.

"I'd tell people 'I want to have you punch at me, and then I'll take you down.' They were like 'What?' You couldn't train. No one wanted to do it. And that's really how the Lion's Den got started."

Bessac, stuck in a rut, needed something, anything. Shamrock needed some live bodies to experiment on with some relatively dangerous martial arts techniques. The result was a good match—if

Bessac could survive a gauntlet similar to the one Shamrock himself had gone through to earn his own spot in the UWF, the Japanese-style buzzsaw that was part hazing, part test of your manhood.

"To be a Lion's Den fighter, you had to go 30 minutes straight, no rounds or anything, and you get choked out, knocked out and submitted over and over," Bessac says. "It was a wake up call that a guy who was way smaller than me like Ken could do that to me. He was heel hooking me, ankle cracking me so much, knee barring me so much. That was a trip. I didn't know anything about arm triangle chokes and all that kind of stuff. It was all brand new to me. I was pretty shocked. And I couldn't walk for almost two weeks. I had to crawl to my door. "

The initial training took place at the Twin Arbors Athletic Club in Lodi, California, where the men would pull out all the mats they could find onto a racquet ball court and go at it. Sometimes, when they couldn't get space, they'd train in Bob's backyard or in a vacant room at Ken's house.

"We put mats down there and we went at it," Shamrock says. "But that didn't last very long."

With a wife and two young sons at home, Shamrock needed a dedicated space. He rented a small building in Lodi and the first Lion's Den was born.

"I remember sitting there watching a video in my man cave about these lions," Shamrock says. "They would chase this prey into the pack. What was most interesting to me was watching how they'd attack their prey. They would jump on the back of the animal and drive their claws into their neck, almost like they were choking them. They were the king of the jungle. The fiercest killers. Like us."

The business model was one his father Bob helped devise—the Shamrocks would provide fighters a place to train, a place to live, even the best food and nutrition advice. In return, they'd manage their careers and take a cut of anything they brought in from fighting.

Conditions, initially, were Spartan, especially by modern standards.

" I couldn't afford a regular ring, so I got a Muay Thai ring which sat on the ground," Shamrock says. "You could grapple inside of it, but it was pretty hard. It was like cement under these tiny pads. It was pretty brutal."

The training, too, was rudimentary. Shamrock, perhaps used to training in an environment where a language barrier prevented much in the way of detailed instruction, demonstrated mostly by doing. In this case, that meant his students took an awful lot of butt whippings, especially in those early days.

"(Early Lion's Den student) Noah Inhofer always said Ken's way of teaching you how to get out of submission was either Ken would break it or you would tap," Bessac says. "You would learn how to get out of stuff just by getting out of stuff.

"Ken, he was pretty aggressive, and then it got passed down. It got passed down from me to Vernon, and then we trained guys like that, too. We were just 100 percent sparring and 100 percent rolling and so that's why we had so many guys that would come out great if they survived. A lot of them didn't last because they were just like, 'You guys are nuts. This is insane.'"

In March 1993, a month after his final PWFG associated event, a shootfighting show promoted by Vale in Miami, Shamrock met the student who would be with him the longest and become the first to earn his seal of approval and the right to fight under the Lion's Den banner.

Vernon "Tiger" White was a 21-year-old taekwondo student drifting through life, angry and somewhat directionless. It was a common story connecting the young men who came to the Lion's Den over the years —but Vernon was the first. He knew a counselor at a group home who recommended Bob Shamrock as someone he should talk to, someone who could help him find his way. More than twenty-five years later, he's still connected to the Shamrock clan.

"I talked to Bob on the phone," he says. "And then I talked to Ken on the phone and he invited me over to train. Basically, talking on the phone that day, I made a decision about how I would spend the rest of my life."

White showed up to his Lion's Den tryout on a bicycle, riding 30 long minutes to the gym. His attitude was bad, his willingness to fight better. He came looking to put a whooping on this confident clown offering advice on the phone. Many martial arts instructors, he believed, were more than happy to talk about fighting. Few could back it up. An experienced street fighter, he expected to run right over Shamrock. He ran into a brick wall instead.

"When I met him and I was like, 'All right, let's see what this guy can do,'" White says. "I'd fought guys his size before."

Shamrock, defying his expectations, was more than happy to demonstrate what he'd be teaching and what White might learn to do in time.

"Punching?" White asked.

"Kicking?" he confirmed.

Shamrock answered both questions in the affirmative.

"He goes 'Are you sure?' I go 'Yeah. Do what you want to do. I'm a big boy. If you last with me for around an hour, then we'll talk,'" Shamrock says. "He just kind of chuckled and said 'okay.' And then I beat him up for an hour."

Both men smile as they tell this story separately but nearly identically, a memory fused permanently in their brains, a meeting that changed two lives.

"He kicked everybody out of the gym," White says. "I had two black eyes. I think I cut the bridge of his nose. We were going at it. I was probably about 185 pounds but I was in it to win it. I'm like, 'I'm not going to let this dude push me around,' because that's the mentality that I had.

"I remember when he hit me. The first time, he hit me really hard. And I was thinking to myself, 'I got to get him back.' We're trading, going back and forth, and at first, he wasn't trying to put me down. He was just letting me know, 'You're not going to win.'"

It was the right attitude for the Lion's Den. The perfect one. Shamrock wasn't looking for someone who was already a master of the martial arts anymore than Sami Soranaka had been when Ken had his own trial by fire. He was looking for heart. And White had it.

"I'd take him down, smack him, then let him up and took him down again," Shamrock says. "I twisted him in a knot. I put a beating on him. And he kept getting up. He kept getting up. Ten or fifteen minutes in, he's already gassed to the gills. He can barely get off the mat. But I keep kicking him, I keep hitting him."

White's body wanted to quit. Perhaps it had. But his mind and pride wouldn't allow him to stop.

"I didn't get it through my head that it was an impossible fight," White says. "We're going back and forth, back and forth, back and forth, and then finally, he was like, 'All right, I'm done with you.'"

The take down rendered White helpless. There were no grappling solutions in taekwondo, at least the way White had learned it. Certainly nothing in his experience had prepared him for a 220 pound bodybuilder laying on top of him, twisting limbs this way and that, challenging him the whole time to just *try a little harder.*

'I'm sitting on him yelling 'Get up.'

'I can't.'

'Well, you better try. Because I ain't getting up until you do.'

"I let him up, then take him down again and smack him," Shamrock says. "Then I sit on him again. And he's practically crying. But he did it, on the mat for almost 45 minutes."

White remembers it all like it was yesterday.

"He kicked my butt for half an hour straight," he says. "And then I had to clean the gym and also do 500 push-ups, sit-ups, leg lifts, and squats. That was my introduction to becoming a young boy."

Ken wished the kid well when he was done, calling out 'I'll see you tomorrow.'

"I didn't think I'd see him again," Shamrock says. "But he showed up. He always showed up."

"I was just drawn to that," White says. "He was no-nonsense. He's 'let's get crap done.' He saw something in me that nobody else did. No one has ever kicked my butt as hard as he did. No one.

"It was like, 'I *need* to learn this.' Once I started learning it then I started to respect him even more because this is a guy who I know he knew in the back of his mind that everyone that came in there wanted his number one spot, but yet still, he kept us there, and he kept training us and kept teaching us. We were always so competitive with each other. We wanted to be Ken's top guy. Everybody in there was striving to be Ken's top guy."

Shamrock's interest in recruiting students and building a team of warriors was about more than just finding training partners to toss around. Pancrase, with just a small collection of Japanese talent, was in desperate need of fighters to fill out their cards. White was the first, debuting the very first event after just a few months of training and eventually, the top ranks of the promotion was stocked with half a dozen or more of Ken's fighters.

"For me to know Ken as I started Pancrase, he was absolutely crucial," Funaki says. "And for him to hop on the offer I made him, I'm just really grateful. At the time there was a real shortage of people that could operate in a shoot environment, so the fighters that Ken brought over were a huge help that I was really grateful for."

The Lion's Den soon outgrew Shamrock's garage and a racquetball court and moved to a warehouse near a car audio shop in Lodi. Even the Japanese talent showed up to the new facility, both to train with Ken and his new students and to work on developing the streamlined physiques they'd need for actual combat.

"All their bodies changed," Shamrock says. "When we did UWF

and then Fujiwara, they were a little puffy. Funaki and Suzuki came down to my place in Lodi and talked to me about my diet and training methods. And they ended up taking it and putting it into their system for all their fighters. They got really lean and learned how to be strong without carrying so much water weight."

By the time the promotion debuted, Funaki and Suzuki were hardly recognizable, trading their pro wrestling bodies for a different look. On September 21, 1993[73], the underdog promotion reinvented what wrestling could be, finding the future of the business firmly rooted in its past.

Wrestling has survived the ages in various forms, from the gentle Glima of Scandinavia, where opponents threw each other by their belts, to the rough and tumble grappling of the American frontier, where you could often pick out the grapplers by the scars covering their faces and even their missing eyeballs.

Pancrase landed somewhere in the middle of that spectrum, a brutal competition of potentially harmful techniques and holds that was also carefully regulated and controlled, both by the formal rules and an unwritten Gentleman's Code[74].

The rules mimicked those of traditional pro wrestling and were relatively simple. Submission holds were broken if a wrestler made it to the ropes (though it would cost them a point) and the referee would start a ten-count whenever a fighter was knocked down by a strike. Closed fist strikes to the head were illegal, both standing and on the ground. A concession in the middle of the ring or a knockout would end the match. Otherwise, the winner would be decided based on points scored.

The UWF worked in much the same way, as did its spinoffs like RINGS and UWFi, so in some ways, Pancrase was nothing new to hardcore wrestling fans. In others, it was almost impossibly different

---

[73] A few months earlier, Shamrock's third son, Sean, was born on June 15, 1993.
[74] While open hand striking to the head was technically legal while the fight was on the ground, it was largely frowned upon.

—while other promotions claimed to be legitimate contests, Pancrase really was.[75]

Mostly.

Probably[76].

It all began at Tokyo Bay NK Hall, an indoor arena at the Tokyo Disney Resort. It held 7000 people and 7000 souls were reportedly there[77], unsure what to expect but willing to pay upwards of $135 ($241.15 in 2020 money) to find out. The result surprised everyone, the fighters most of all.

Everything about Pancrase was different. It was designed to be. The designers, writers and even the camera people were asked in their introductory interviews if they were big fans of wrestling. Those who said yes were immediately weeded out. Ozaki wanted fresh eyes and fresh ideas, a show that looked and felt unique. Much of their initial budget was spent on a firm that came up with the promotion's iconic logo and slogan "Hybrid Wrestling." Pancrase exuded class and was meant to come across as a serious and legitimate sport.

Suzuki opened the initial show against Katsuomi Inagaki, a young boy who had come over from Fujiwara's group and was making his debut. Fans were used to seeing long opening bouts at shoot style events, sometimes even 20 or 30-minute draws. Instead, Suzuki finished the young fighter in under four minutes, setting the tone for what was to come.

"It only took three minutes. I thought it'd be over sooner," Suzuki said. "I couldn't finish it sooner because, well, he was defending and that's just how fights go.

"I was allowed to do the move called the choke sleeper...Any kind

---

[75] There was an amusing, ongoing debate in the pages of the Wrestling Observer letters section between future UFC matchmaker Joe Silva and Japanese reporter Tadeshi Tanaka about Pancrase's legitimacy. Silva was convinced much of Pancrase was a work and remains adamant in that belief today.

[76] "It sounds very markish to say Pancrase wrestling is real shooting, because groups that claim to be that all seem to be something less," Dave Meltzer wrote in the Observer. "But the reason Minoru Suzuki and Masakatsu Funaki formed the new group and quit Pro Wrestling Fujiwara-Gumi at least publicly was because they didn't want to have pre-planned winners. "

[77] This was the contemporary reportage. In a book detailing the promotion's first 15 years, former Pancrase President Masami Ozaki admits they only sold tickets for 70-80 percent of the building.

of choking the neck was okay. So I wanted to do it no matter what. I wanted to show off to the audience on the biggest stage possible.

"I'd been trying for the sleeper hold the whole time. 'Man, come on, let me get it! This sucks, I can't get it!' In the past, when I used my moves on weird foreigners, they panicked and were scared so they gave up. But this time he didn't. So that makes this *our* domain now. We've actually gone through this experience."

While Suzuki opened the show, Shamrock and Funaki would close it, bookending the experience[78] with the fighters fans were most familiar with. Shamrock walked to the ring with a purpose, his face a mix of concentration and scowl, clad in only a simple white Pancrase t-shirt and his tiny red Speedo trunks. Funaki was resplendent in a peach colored robe with a giant Pancrase logo stitched on the back and a matching head band.

Both men looked like human perfection, cut to shreds with wide shoulders and tiny waists. They wore kickpads extending to their knees, the famed Pancrase "gogo boots" designed to both protect their shins and prevent cuts should a blow land to the head, but little else.[79]

Funaki, Shamrock says, was tense before their bout. As he stared into his mentor's eyes, his own nostrils flaring in anticipation of finally unleashing all he had learned, he saw fear. Funaki was not only risking his reputation and health, like all fighters, but had invested everything he owned in the world in the promotion.

"People can lose before they ever step into the ring," Shamrock says. "Funaki put way too much into this. He was working on it behind the scenes. It takes a lot out of you. And when you're fighting at that caliber, against the best of the best, you've got to have your mind in it and nothing else. He should have just been a fighter."

Funaki was betting, not just on himself, but his vision for what wrestling should look and feel like. When the bell rang to begin the contest, he felt like he was in fog, watching from outside his body as the fight commenced.

"I felt far away. First of all, I wanted to strike with him but I felt like I wasn't in range for my punches to land," Funaki said. " So I thought

---

[78] That first show included both fighters who would become promotional stalwarts like Dutch kickboxer Bas Rutten and one-and-done fish out of water like American pro wrestling journeyman George Weingeroff.

[79] In the original Greek Pankration, the fighters competed in the nude. This was about as close as you could come.

I'd try kicking. When I kicked, he backed up so then my kicks wouldn't land either. That's kind of how it went."

After an exchange of blows, kicks, knees, vicious hand slaps and even a punch to the body from Shamrock, the American shot in after catching a Funaki kick and ended up behind his opponent.

"He tackled me suddenly," Funaki remembers. "Usually I'm relaxed there, but I ended up thinking, 'Oh no, what should I do now?' My opponent started attacking with various techniques and it took everything I had to fend him off."

With no striking on the ground and no pinfalls, there's little need to maintain control of the kind we're used to seeing in modern MMA. In a fight with fewer rules, missing a submission attempt can result in being pummeled. That risk doesn't exist in early Pancrase, giving the fighters freedom to go after any hold they see. The result is ground work that flows, with lots of movement and scrambles.

That's not to say it's a battle of finesse. Shamrock is downright mean at times, grinding his forearm into Funaki's face and trying to force a mistake.

"It makes them uncomfortable and makes them want to move," Shamrocks says. "And that's what I want. I don't want to move. I want them to move. If he moves, I can catch him. When he moves, I react.

"I think that was a reality check for Funaki. UWF and Fujiwara were a hard style of wrestling but it wasn't a fight. This was a lot harder than even we were used to."

Shamrock took a lot of time to think about what he was going to do, even attempting a full nelson before finally committing to a leg attack that leads them, inevitably, into the dreaded dueling leg locks position[80], eventually forcing a break when they found themselves near the ring ropes and at a bit of an impasse.

This time, Funaki shot for a takedown, but after a beautiful whizzer[81], Shamrock again found himself on top. Funaki attempted to bait him into an armbar attempt, hoping for a scramble that would reverse roles.

Instead, Shamrock used his size and superior position to maneuver into an arm triangle choke.

---

[80] Two fighters on their backs, both attempting to twist and mangle their opponent's ankle and knee, was a staple of early Pancrase fights.

[81] A "whizzer" is a defensive wrestling move involving using an overhook to control your opponent's body when they attempt a takedown.

"I was on the defensive most of the time," Funaki said. "While I was busy defending, I got stuck in a position. Usually I have more space and I can make it to the ropes...I remembered a time years ago I was in the same situation, getting choked out by a senior fighter at my gym, and I had to tap out. Before I knew it, I couldn't breathe. I tapped."

In a traditional shoot style match, this would be a false finish. Funaki would make the ropes and the bout would continue. But this was Pancrase and there would be no fairy tale ending for the leading man. Instead, Funaki tapped out and just like that, a rival for Pancrase primacy was created.

"My arms are so big, all I've got to do is flex. I don't squeeze or anything. I just flex," Shamrock says, flexing again 25 years later for emphasis. "I expected more. I expected more of a fight. And he just kind of laid there.

"Funaki was depressed. I felt bad. I knew I had a chance to beat him because of my strength and because my skillsets were improving. But I don't think he was at his best."

Shamrock celebrated wildly in the ring as Funaki lay on the mat, attended by two of the young boys, shellshocked by what had happened. The organization's matinee idol, the man who was to be their leading light, had not only lost his first fight, he hadn't even looked particularly competitive.

"I knew it was a fight, with a terribly unfortunate result," he said. "I was really on the defensive most of the fight. It was only six minutes, but it felt so long, like the last scene in a movie.

"After the fight ended, I went back to the gym office. I said to my colleagues there, 'I lost,' and it sunk in at that moment. I knew that I shouldn't have lost. It was the first time for me to feel all those things. It's like when a watch first starts ticking and then never stops moving in a circle. It felt like that.

"After that, I had a fight in Nagoya. Kobe. Then in Hakata, then Yokohama. Everything continued on. If you get held up on one thing, you can't move on. You should finish one, reflect on it, and decide what you can do for the next time."

Fans were used to shoot style wrestling matches, bouts designed to look real but ultimately just more realistic works, lasting 30 minutes with fighters struggling valiantly to escape submission holds and surviving knockdown after knockdown. But when the competition was legitimate things looked a little different. The five matches lasted just a little more 13 minutes—total.

While the Western press assumed this was a problem[82] and something that needed to be tweaked, it was actually an image the Pancrase brass enjoyed and cultivated. As Masami Ozaki writes in his book *The Truth: 15 Years of Pancrase*, they realized they had something special when Weekly Gong magazine called the group "Instant Death Wrestling." Most wrestling shows aimed to begin at 6:30 PM and last until after nine. At a Pancrase event, fans could count on being on their way home by 8 pm.

Fans even watched the shows differently than they watched even the UWF and other shoot style groups. The crowd was mostly silent, watching intently to the minutiae of each match, the only sound coming from cornermen shouting advice. While there is still much discussion about how much of early Pancrase was real competition, the people believed, even those with intimate connections to the wrestling business.

"It was *not* a mix of pro wrestling and shoot," Saito says. "Believe it or not, Pancrase's matches were all legitimate since the day one. There was no booker in the dressing room like you would expect in a pro wrestling shows. Trust me. More than a half of the guys who were in the dressing room at the time were not wrestling people. They were ex-amateur wrestlers, kickboxers from different styles and different gyms. They were not pro wrestlers."

As soon as VHS tapes arrived in America, the debate about Pancrase began, most of it conducted in the pages of Dave Meltzer's *Wrestling Observer* newsletter. Meltzer, who would go on to cover the UFC and other MMA groups, had a keen interest in shooting and watched the events with scrupulous eye for detail:

> The big question the tapes ask is whether the matches are genuine shoots or the tightest, most realistic works ever seen in the modern era of pro wrestling. Upon casual viewing, the matches look like they could be shoots and there are less holes in the style than UWFI or Rings. There are spots where there are openings look to be not taken advantage of, but that is the case in "real" boxing and martial arts matches

---

[82] "Nobody complained about the show length," Ozaki writes. "It made the fans feel these bouts were completely legitimate."

as well. The main events, that involved Wayne Shamrock on the first two shows did have spots where it looked as though Shamrock could have put his opponent away but held back, but Shamrock also used subtle maneuvers you wouldn't think guys would do in a working situation. Anyway, after talking with one of the top pro-style wrestlers who has a combat sports background and has also seen the tapes, his opinion was most of the matches were 90% real but the main events were closer to 60%, citing there would be more serious injuries in shooting events with kicking and kneeing the face and submissions being legal.

Less than a month later, the circus was back, this time at the Tsuyuhashi Sports Center in Nagoya. The first Pancrase show had dropped like a firebomb on Tokyo's hardcore wrestling scene. Every other shoot style group, after years of calling out their traditional wrestling rivals and masquerading as the real deal, was suddenly exposed as little more than a collection of charlatans. If the first Pancrase show was a work, it was a brilliant one, both establishing its own legitimacy and destroying that of their rivals in one fell swoop.

This show was much like the first. The same core talent was there, and once again, the action moved at a dizzying pace. The entire event, if you only count the time spent wrestling in the ring, was over in less than 23 minutes. Shamrock, once again, main-evented the show. But in keeping with their pure sports image, Funaki moved himself to the mid card.

The whole point of Pancrase was that a man earns his place. Everyone considered Funaki the top fighter going in. But that meant nothing, not here. He had to prove himself just like everyone else. He, Suzuki, Ozaki and Tokumu Sakamoto were the matchmakers and thought it was important that the booking be based on results and not perceived star power. And so, the face of the promotion found himself in the middle of the card with an awful lot resting on his shoulders. In retrospect, it doesn't pop on his resume as a big fight, but at the time, it felt very much like a must win.

"Everything was a real meritocracy," Funaki says. "Not political. At the very start we booked in terms of career seniority and experience, but after that, you won the main event on one show that meant you earned your focus on the next."

Shamrock's opponent, Takahashi, had earned his spot with a brutal knockout of George Weingeroff in the first show in 1:23. He was strong and willing and had spent a lot of time training with Shamrock at the dojo.

"I thought 'If I beat the man who beat Funaki, I would be the best!' I had confidence I would win," Takahashi said. "If I could only stave off his attacks, I could find an opening. I knew he was a power fighter but I thought 'I know a lot more techniques than him,' so I thought I'd be fine."

The bout was one of only three that year to last more than 10 minutes but doesn't feel like two men trying to fill time. They go after each other hard from the opening bell and it turns into a wild scrap by Pancrase standards. Shamrock swings wildly with a right hand, while Takahashi focuses on grabbing big takedowns—for good reason.

"I made a bet with Takahashi," Suzuki admitted with a devilish grin. "If he could lift him up and take three steps, I'd give him one thousand yen. I'd expect that in that ring Shamrock would be good at defending the takedowns, so I bet Takahashi wouldn't be able to do it. 'Will he really try it?!' I thought, while watching."

Shamrock, cut on the nose, forced several rope escapes and knocked his opponent down with a blow that caused an audible buzz in the mostly quiet crowd. Ten minutes into the fight Shamrock was still exploding into strikes, popping Takahashi with a right hand on top of the head that was probably the hardest blow of the bout. Knees followed—and not dainty ones. They were meant to end the fight, but Takahashi wasn't the kind of man who yielded easily.

"He didn't lose any of his power as the fight progressed," Takahashi said. "My stamina, on the other hand, was being used up. I used the rope escapes two or three times. Then I thought, 'This is kind of bad. But maybe I'll have a chance in the end.' But at about the third escape, I got worried."

While he eventually fell victim to a vicious heel hook, Takahashi did manage to secure three big slams, a moral and financial victory of sorts.

"I actually lifted him up three times," he said. "And during the third time I picked him up, even in the middle of the fight, I thought, 'Alright! I just made three thousand yen!'"

Immediately after the fight, Takahashi was in no mood to celebrate his windfall. Suzuki and Funaki both enter the ring to comfort him, as he was clearly in agony. They covered Takahashi with a bottle of water, though the medicinal value was unclear. Shamrock again closed the show with a celebration but had the decency to do so in a muted fashion. Takahashi was clearly not well.

Funaki translated a brief conversation between the two and they shook hands. But Suzuki gave Shamrock a look—one that meant everything. Takahashi was helped to the back, but Suzuki's eyes told us it wasn't an ending. It was a beginning.

This was both Shamrock and Pancrase's first great fight—but far from their last.

CHAPTER SIX

The Birth of Ultimate Fighting

McNichols Arena
   Denver, Colorado
   November 12, 1993

Ken Shamrock was in shock as he felt himself slipping away, his vision blurring as the harsh and scratchy cotton canvas of Royce Gracie's judogi slowly choked him into unconsciousness.

Tapping out was the first indignity. It was something he refused to allow his students to get away with at the Lion's Den—instead, if they got caught, they'd eventually go to sleep. But as the gi stretched across his neck, suddenly his hand was tapping the mat. One, two, three, four times before Gracie finally let go.

"I felt the choke so I reached up to pull it off and there was nothing to grab," Shamrock says. "It was like a rope on my neck and I couldn't grab anything. I grabbed, grabbed, grabbed, and then I just tapped.

"Even to this day, I don't tap for chokes. But for whatever reason, man, mentally I guess I knew there was no way I was getting this off and I just tapped."

The choke ended what was a bad 57 seconds for the Pancrase star. He'd seemingly had Gracie right where he wanted him, stuffing an early takedown attempt and then sitting back for one of the leg locks he had practiced so arduously in Japan.

He hadn't counted on the gi being a factor. But Gracie smartly wrapped it around Shamrock's right arm and held on for dear life. When Ken dropped back for an ankle lock, he inadvertently pulled Gracie right on top of him. In the ensuing scramble, Gracie had quickly grabbed a hold of the choke. It was over before it had truly begun.

Worse than the loss was the aftermath. The referee Helio Vigio, despite being a decorated student of Gracie's uncle Carlos, somehow didn't notice Shamrock's vigorous concession and stood there wondering why the action had stopped.

"He's staring at me and I'm on my knees looking up and the whole time I'm thinking, 'I just got choked,'" Shamrock says. "'I just lost.' And I couldn't understand how that could happen to me. I don't do this, I can't lose.

"Royce said 'You tapped. You tapped.' And I looked at the referee and nodded, because I did. I mean, I lost. There's no question I lost. I said, 'Yeah, I tapped.' And that just tore me up inside to have to say it. It's his job, not mine, to stop the fight. For me to have to not just lose, but say out loud that I lost—I was just like, 'Argh!'"

Shamrock was visibly discombobulated as announcer Brian Kilmeade attempted to interview him after the fight. He had been convinced right up until he tapped out that he was the best fighter in the world. The loss had shocked him to his core. Kilmeade verbalized what many were likely thinking—that Ken was the second-best fighter in the tournament. But Shamrock refused to disrespect the other finalist Gordeau and would only concede to being the third best on the evening.

"Right then I knew Ken would go far in this," referee "Big" John McCarthy writes in his memoir *Let's Get It On*. "I think Ken's sportsmanship helped the UFC in those early events. Spectators could relate to him and wanted to keep tuning in to see him."

Backstage, where a fierce argument with his father ensued, it took Shamrock some time to come to grips with his new reality. On camera Shamrock was humble in defeat. When the red light went off, however, he couldn't quite accept it. If he wasn't the best fighter in the world, who was he? It was as if his entire world had been shattered. Picking up the pieces wouldn't be easy.

The same was true in Lodi, California, where students at the Lion's Den were almost in denial that there was someone in the world capable of beating Shamrock in hand to hand combat. He was stronger, more athletic, meaner and more capable than anyone else in both their gym or in the Japanese prize ring. Scott Bessac believed the bout must have been rigged. After all, how else could you explain Shamrock tapping out from a choke applied by a skinny Brazilian with no discernible muscle tone?

Vernon White wasn't so sure.

"It did not cross my mind that he would lose," White says. "When I saw them on the mat, I thought he was going to pick Royce up and slam him like Zangief in Street Fighter.

"When he lost that first fight I was just like, 'Oh.' People thought it was fake and I'm like, 'Yeah, the look on Ken's face, this was not fake. This was real.'"

Gracie went on to win the finals against Gordeau in fairly easy fashion despite Gordeau taking a little nibble on his ear.[83] When his hand was raised for the third time that night, Gracie celebrated in the cage with his Olympic style medal, an extremely large novelty check for $50,000 and an even bigger smile, his first of the night.

For Shamrock, despair would soon give way to determination. Instead of the $50,000 he'd been counting on, he went home with just four grand. He had thought himself on top of the world. The loss had given him a wake up call and a clear mission.

"From that point on," he says, "I was obsessed with beating Royce Gracie."

Ken Shamrock laughed the first time he heard about the Ultimate Fighting Championship. His student Scott Bessac was the one who brought it to his attention. He'd seen an advertisement in the pages of *Black Belt* magazine and even gone so far as to call promoter Art Davie in search of more information.

"He was responding to the ad for himself and telling me about the Lion's Den," Davie remembers. "I had never heard of it. Pretty soon he decided it would be a better fit for his coach and trainer, a guy named

---

[83] Gordeau would later blatantly gouge the eyes of Yuki Nakai at an event in Japan, causing his opponent permanent damage. Things could have been much, much worse for Gracie but Gordeau thought twice about creating a serious incident.

Ken Wayne Shamrock. I loved the name. What a marquee name. And he looked like Captain America in red speedos."

Shamrock, perhaps wary of *Black Belt*'s propensity to feature esoteric martial artists of questionable validity, was rightly skeptical. Davie too scoffed at many of the traditional martial arts, describing their competitions as "playing touch and giggle." But Shamrock suspected something else entirely.

"I was like, 'Dude, this is wrestling,'" Shamrock says. "'This is not real. It's fake.' Scott goes, 'No, no. I talked to them. It's anything. Anything goes.' And I was like, 'Scott, it's wrestling.' Just to prove him wrong, I said I'd check it out. Really, come on? That's not happening. Street fight, you get arrested for it. That ain't happening, so in my mind, there's no chance."

Shamrock had his father reach out to Davie, who in turn looked into the Japanese scene and discovered Ken's fight with Neilson for Fujiwara-Gumi. Eventually the two men connected on the phone and Shamrock agreed to compete for the fledgling promotion.

"Ken was very doubtful about what we were doing," Davie says. "Up until Friday night November 12, I think he felt there was a possibility I was bullshitting him and that this was a partial work."

Because of his experience in Japan, Shamrock knew just how easy it could be to present a very hard style of wrestling as a shoot to the unsuspecting public. A month earlier Nobuhiko Takada's UWF-International had attempted that very feat on American pay-per-view ironically called "Shootfighting: It's Real.[84]"

What Shamrock didn't know was the story of the Gracie family, particularly Davie's partner Rorion whose life long goal was to spread his father's martial arts innovations to the public. He had fallen in love with the country on a visit in his teens and was intent on spreading Gracie Jiu Jitsu to his new home.

The family's style was a bastardized version of the judo they had been taught by a Kodokan black belt and professional wrestler named Mitsuyo Maeda at the dawn of the 20th century. Maeda was uniquely well-suited to teach a style of very practical grappling—he had mastered the Asian arts as a young man, then spent much of his adult life traveling the globe with a wrestling troupe, borrowing effective

---

[84] It was not real.

techniques from everyone he came across.[85]

The Gracies had taken this martial system and simplified it, removing what didn't work for them and concentrating on the intricate ground work and submissions that did. Generations of the family then perfected their craft in a series of challenge matches throughout Brazil, testing themselves against martial artists of all kinds in an effort to establish supremacy for their family's potent brew of grappling ingredients.

"In the beginning when my father and my uncles started this, even before UFC, it wasn't about proving who was toughest," Royce, who would go on to win three early UFC events, says. "It was more of a quest to find out which style of martial arts is the best. Other people say their style is the best; we say ours is the best. There's only one way to find out. No rules, no time limit, no gloves, no weight division. Let's jump in a cage and fight until somebody quits."

Rorion brought that ethos with him to Los Angeles, where a *Playboy* writer named Pat Jordan's article brought his story to Davie's attention. With Davie's help Gracie, who had mostly taught classes out of his own garage to a tight knit group of true believers, escalated things quickly. The goal was television, but they were met with firm 'no's' everywhere they went until a producer named Campbell McLaren rescued their "Gracies in Action" tape from the dust bin at Semaphore Entertainment Group (SEG) and it quickly became a sensation around the office.

"Was it really safe? Was it a sport?" SEG executive David Isaacs asks. "We're watching this tape with Rorion Gracie narrating, saying things like, 'This man has insulted the Gracie family,' and then some scrawny Gracie brother or one of the uncles beating the crap out of him. It was really compelling, and our gut instinct was 'Holy crap, this is really interesting stuff. How do we do it?'"

At first glimpse, SEG wasn't an obvious partner for Rorion and Davie. Headed by Bob Meyrowitz, who had made his name in radio syndication[86], the company had seen its greatest success televising concerts by bands like New Kids on the Block. But the timing was perfect for what Davie was then calling "War of the Worlds." SEG was

---

[85] Maeda's nickname was "the Count of Combat." That's pretty cool as far as nicknames go.
[86] "The King Biscuit Flower Hour" was a weekly radio show that featured live concert performances from the rock bands of the day.

actively looking to break into the sports space and considering things like Mexican wrestling and a demolition derby.[87] What would later be called "human cockfighting" was right up their alley—style versus style to determine martial arts supremacy.

"The question to me is is Tae Kwon Do better than Karate? You go into a Tae Kwon Do dojo and they say we are going to teach you to defend yourself against a 250 lbs man," Meyrowitz said. "He goes to punch you, here is what you do. He goes to strangle you, here is what you do. He is going to grab you, here is what you do.

"But they never say to you, 'now if the guy knows karate, here is what he might do. Or if he knows ju jitsu, this stuff will not work.' They do not talk about that. This is really what this is all about."

Shamrock didn't do much to prepare for that first event. It wasn't even especially clear what he should be doing to get ready for such a nebulous concept. Besides, he still wasn't convinced it would be real or even happen at all.

"He *kind* of trained for it," Bessac says. "I remember putting gloves on while he just had bare knuckles and him just letting me take shots at him."

For the most part, however, Shamrock just continued doing what he was already doing—training for Pancrase's very ambitious monthly schedule that had kicked off in September. His third fight with the promotion was in Japan, just four days before the initial Ultimate Fighting event. Despite how important it has become in retrospect, UFC was not his top priority; Pancrase and its regular five-figure paycheck was. This was how he fed his family and paid for the space where his fighters trained.

His opponent, Takaku Fuke, was one of Pancrase's founders and a talented submission artist. Fuke, and not the then unknown Gracie, was firmly at the forefront of Shamrock's mind in the weeks leading

---

[87] SEG was trying a lot of diverse content, looking for a hit. A month after UFC 1, they ran a show called the "Young Messiah Concert."

"Let's put it this way, Ultimate Fighting Championship is the way to go," SEG's Cheryl Simon said. "Christian music is not the way to go."

up to the bouts.

"We'd practiced together many times. He was very physically strong. He was huge," Fuke says. "I wanted to confuse and fluster him during the fight. Funaki and Takahashi had great fights with him (at the first two Pancrase events). I just wanted to have a fight as good or better than theirs and make it memorable."

Shamrock, however, didn't arrive in Kobe to make memories for the fans and said as much in the pre-fight press conference. The announcers sensed it too. "It feels like Shamrock came to Japan just to get the win," they said as he immediately made his way across the ring and dropped Fuke with a hard knee. A rear naked choke quickly followed and 44 seconds after the bell rang, Fuke was unconscious and it was all over.

"At first, it wasn't too tight. I felt like I could almost get his arm off. Just as I thought I could pull his arms off, I went out," Fuke remembers. "When I suddenly came to, I was laying face up and the fight was over. I opened my eyes and the bright overhead lights which illuminated the ring were blaring down on me. It was so bright. I was like, 'Huh? I'm supposed to be about to go fight now,' I thought, 'But I'm already in the ring and there's the ref and the doctor standing over me. Why is everybody here?'"

Hours later both fighters, as well as Funaki and Pancrase's in-house doctor, were on a plane to Denver and whatever awaited at the McNichols Arena, now just three nights away. The Japanese were worried about the impact of a potential loss on their business, where Shamrock was riding high as the top foreign star. Ken, by contrast, was almost calm.

"I still think something is up," Shamrock says. "You never hear about stuff like this outside of the movies. We get there, they have this press conference, there are very few press there and I see the competitors. 'This is it?' A lot of these guys looked like they just came off a bar stool. There were a few of them in pretty decent shape but nothing intimidating. I was pretty confident."

In theory the Ultimate Fighting Championship was simple. Eight martial artists from around the world would meet in a steel Octagon, the tournament winner walking away with a giant novelty check for $50,000, awarded to them for "being the best." There were no official rules to the contest, only a plea to stay away from groin shots, biting and eye gouges, infractions that would result in a fine but not disqualification.

But when the fighters met at the Executive Tower Inn the day before the bouts, what seemed straight forward turned out to be anything but.

Fighters had been promised they could use the accoutrements of their respective arts inside the cage. When push came to shove, however, that didn't end up being strictly true. Most contentious was the use of hand wraps. Rorion Gracie wanted to limit them to one inch above the knuckle, no doubt in a conscious effort to limit a striker's ability to throw a punch at full force without breaking their hand.[88]

"There is no fighter meeting in boxing or wrestling to figure out what the rules are," Isaacs says. "We were inventing some of this stuff as we went, to try and make sure everybody understood what they were getting into and how this was going to work. One of the challenges we always had was anything you do benefits one style and harms somebody else. We did the best we could but Rorion didn't have much patience for it."

The hand wrap discussion ended up turning into a hand wrap argument and almost a hand wrap fist fight when, after much back-and-forth, Gracie asked Zane Frasier, a karate fighter who had once beaten up Frank Dux of *Bloodsport* fame in a hotel lobby, if he'd run home to wrap his hands if someone insulted him on the street.

Voices rose and the two men had to be separated. When the dust cleared Frasier's hand wraps and kick pads were both gone. So, too, were Shamrock's wrestling boots. If he wanted the option to kick, he'd be forced to compete barefoot.

"There weren't supposed to be any rules," Shamrock says, still mulling over the event 25 years later. "But they come in and tell us what we can and cannot do and they take away things. It's like being on ice when you're used to shoes and the grip that you have with that. I didn't fight it too hard though. I figured 'it doesn't matter. I'm gonna beat everybody anyways 'cause I'm going to the ground.' That cockiness got me in trouble. I should have said no. Royce got to wear a

---

[88] Runner up Gerard Gordeau ended up breaking his hand in the very first bout with the first punch anyone landed in UFC competition.

gi. Another guy wore a glove. Everyone wore their uniform. But I didn't argue it. I said 'Whatever.'"

Shamrock's confidence was peaking after easily beating both his mentor Funaki and Takahashi, a young fighter he considered one of the toughest of the Japanese competitors, in the first two Pancrase events. And it was contagious. Before the bouts, Elaine McCarthy, who arranged the travel for all the competitors and their entourages, remembers Shamrock's wife Tina telling her that Ken would destroy everyone else in the tournament with ease.

"Ken arrived late," UFC 1 promoter Art Davie says. "And I asked him 'Are you sure you're ready for this?' He said 'Don't worry, nobody in this event can give me any trouble.' And he tells me 'I know one of these guys has never been in a professional fight. He's wearing his karate pajamas.' He was talking about Royce Gracie. He did not think anything of Royce or anybody in a gi. He thought that was clown stuff."

Jason DeLucia, an alternate at the event and future Lion's Den fighter, had actually fought Royce in a dojo challenge and tried to warn Shamrock about the Gracies' propensity for using chokes and armlocks.

"He told me," DeLucia says. "'Ain't no 175-pound karate guy going to choke me.' Those were his words."

Intellectually, Shamrock understood that the Gracies must be tough. They were the event's organizers, which should have been a sign that they had something up their sleeves. But it was those sleeves on their uniforms that threw him.

"In my mind, I was like 'he's walking around in his pajamas,'" Shamrock recalls. "So you think he's like a karate dojo guy or something. Those guys walk around with their gi and their black belt and it was always this reputation, ego thing. Nobody who did that was tough, at least in my experience. It was a rookie move on my part to look at something and not study it."

Rorion's choice of his 26-year-old brother Royce to represent his system of fighting was surprising to some. His brother Rickson was the family champion and would eventually become a star fighter in Japan. But merely winning the tournament wasn't Rorion's goal. For him, promoting his family's art wasn't a bonus—it was the entire point. That was where the unassuming Royce would be worth his 175 pounds in gold.

"My objective was to showcase the effectiveness of jiu-jitsu," he says.

"Royce was a very sweet guy. He actually came from Brazil to help me take care of my house and help my wife take care of the kids. Half the time babysitter, half the time UFC fighter. Maybe he needed a break from helping me change my kids' diapers. So he goes into the UFC, chokes everybody out and comes back and changes diapers again.

"... By putting someone like Royce in the cage, with a skinny body and totally physically unimpressive, we showed everybody that little guys can be tough too if they know Gracie jiu-jitsu. People say, 'If he can do it, I can do it.' That was the message we wanted to put across, and it worked out great."

In interviews, Royce claims to have remained calm throughout the lead up to UFC 1. But the pressure must have been enormous. He wasn't just representing himself and his art. This was a family affair and almost everyone close to him would be there watching as he put their collective reputation on the line. As Art Davie recalls in *Is This Legal?*, one of the journalists at the event caught a private moment between Rickson and Royce that served as a powerful reminder that the Gracies were still human:

> They knelt on the mat facing each other, and Royce just started crying inconsolably. Rickson then tightly embraced his brother, the way a father holds his sobbing child who has just awoken from a terrible nightmare...The crushing pressure of the moment was squarely on the shoulders of Royce.

Suddenly Royce, the brother of the promoter, the only man in the tournament who truly understood what he was getting into, found himself in the same position as the others. Sometimes, knowledge only makes the inevitable worse. Either way, the time for fretting was over. Posters plastered around town had promised extreme violence—and that's just what the crowd of close to 5000 fans got in the very first fight.

The first two fighters in the cage for the Ultimate Fighting Championship were sumo wrestler Teila Tuli and Dutch striker

Gerard Gordeau. Tuli had put an end to the rules meeting squabbling by slamming his own waiver down on the table and announcing "I came here to party. If you want to fight, I'll be there tomorrow night" before exiting the building.

His opponent was a veteran of the international scene who Shamrock had seen in Japan. That match had been a work with pro wrestling superstar Akira Maeda in the UWF, once again making him suspicious of the entire endeavor. Ken was backstage waiting for someone to come and tell him the finish when Gordeau sidestepped a charging Tuli and literally kicked his tooth into the crowd with a vicious blow. He followed up with an undefended punch right to the face. If there were doubts before the bout, none remained in its aftermath.

"The locker room went silent," Shamrock remembers. "It was something that you only see in movies or you see on the street. It was only quiet for one or two seconds, but it felt longer than that. Then people realized what had just happened and just went nuts. I'm jacked up now, like this is real. I'm smiling. I get to fight one guy, no gun, no knife, no weapons, one person. Like this is a dream. I fight on the street just for my pride, and now I'm gonna get paid to do it."

In the third fight of the night, Gracie stopped Art Jimmerson without doing, well, much of anything. Jimmerson was paid a large advance just to show up. The Gracies had been challenging boxers for almost 50 years at that point and Rorion thought it was important that the family representative dispatch one to silence naysayers from the get go. But Jimmerson had been listening to the backstage scuttlebutt and had seen some demonstrations of what Gracie jiu jitsu was capable of during the course of the week. He came out wearing a single boxing glove, perhaps to make tapping out just a little bit easier. A Gracie had finally beaten a boxer, though you could hardly call it a fight.

"I was like, 'He can't do that to me. There's just no way he can do that to me. I'm too strong,'" Shamrock says. "I wasn't anticipating how effective a gi could be. This was another rookie move on my part."

Before he could fight Gracie, Shamrock had to get past local sensation Pat Smith, billed as a ludicrous 250-0. As the two waited for their cue to walk out on live television, Smith and his entourage were mean-mugging Shamrock and his small group of friends and family.

"There was probably 10 or 12 guys we had to walk past that all had these red shirts on," Shamrock remembers. "He says, 'I'm gonna kill you.' He had all those guys around him, seriously like a gang. There was no security there and they're all in our faces."

Shamrock had two Japanese submission masters in his entourage, but it was his unassuming father Bob who stepped to his son's opponent.

"He looks at Pat and he says, 'He's gonna beat the hell out of you.' I was like, 'wow, wait a minute,'" Shamrock says. "Beating people up, that's my job."

Some men might have been shaken by the experience. For Shamrock, it was motivation. Tempers were hot in the ring, Shamrock's visage frozen with the grim determination of a professional prizefighter, Smith's with the wild eyes of a madman. As the two men crossed the cage towards each other, Shamrock realized for the first time just how much missing his wrestling boots was going to impact his game.

"I had never had a chance to feel what it would be like to not have shoes on in a fight," he says. "For years, going back to high school wrestling, I wore shoes when I did combat. Now they've taken my shoes away and I'm trying to take Patrick Smith down. And I'm having a problem. I went to shoot and there was no grip there. I wasn't slipping yet, but I knew that I didn't have any grip so I had to try to spin and heel trip him."

Once on the mat, Smith had little chance against the techniques Shamrock had been perfecting for several years in Japan. Before the bout, Smith had vowed he didn't feel pain. Afterwards, a still angry Shamrock wanted to check and see if that was still true.

"I remember putting the heel hook on him, didn't even have it really tight, but I knew I had it enough to hurt him," Shamrock says. "I heard this 'Ow!' and he screamed. After I jumped off him, I was still really amped up. I still wanted to fight. And I asked him, 'You felt that, didn't you?'"

There was a learning curve for the crowd, which jeered both men, thinking they had been witness to a fixed fight. Unfamiliar with ground work, and unable to see much of the action on the mat because most arenas in that era lacked a big screen to provide the television feed, they didn't understand what had happened.

Despite the grumbling in the audience, the victory set up a semifinal match that would help ignite one of the great feuds in MMA history—Shamrock vs. Gracie. On the surface, it was a mismatch: Shamrock looked like a Greek god sculpted from marble, and Gracie looked like the promoter's goofy little brother fooling around in a bathrobe.

"We had dealt with Rorion enough and seen them roll around enough that there was no doubt they knew what they were doing," Isaacs says. "At the same time, I hadn't seen them fight against anybody who really knew what they were doing. Ken had a wide ranging background and he looked mean. And he was built. If anybody was going to come in and toss Royce Gracie around like a rag doll, it was Ken Shamrock."

Fourteen minutes later, Shamrock was again on his way to the ring to find out just where he stood with his fellow grappler, stopped on his way into the restroom and summoned by a television producer to head back to the cage before he could make one of two planned wardrobe changes.

"I had three different shorts I was going to wear, one for each fight," Shamrock says. "Red, yellow and black. By the time I got back to the locker room, I didn't even have the chance to change."

The first semi-final between Gordeau and Kevin Rosier had lasted less than a minute. Destiny was calling.

Shamrock had been the Gracie family's staunchest competition—and they knew it. As the only other fighter in the tournament with a grappling background, Davie says Royce spent extra time preparing for him:

> (Rorion) did not tell me much about Royce's week of training in their Executive Tower Inn hotel suite, but Rorion did say that Rickson had special drills that he was putting Royce through, so as to be ready for Shamrock in case they fought.

Ken, by contrast, barely prepared for the event at all. He'd never studied Brazilian Jiu Jitsu or judo and had never rolled with anyone wearing a gi. Now focused on a rematch, he vowed never to make that mistake again.

To prepare for a Gracie rematch, Shamrock brought in some local judo players, but, like most contemporary judoka, their games were focused on throws and not on ground fighting and the experiment was a bit of a failure. Ken's next idea was to have White put on a gi on when they sparred at the Lion's Den. But, while that gave him some idea how to manipulate the material, White was no Gracie on the mat.

"Ken had me acting like Royce Gracie because I was the closest to his body style, but I was nowhere near his skill level," White concedes. "I just remember he'd be like, 'Well, Royce does this.' I'm like, 'Well, I don't want to do that.' I knew what Ken was going to do. He's going to have me lay there in the guard and try to freaking smash my face in."

Royce's performance at UFC 1 made Jiu Jitsu the hottest martial art on the planet in just a few months. Still, finding a world class trainer in the relatively new art wasn't easy in late 1993, especially one in California who would risk angering the Gracie machine by preparing Royce's rival. Shamrock took a road trip to roll with the only BJJ experts who would have him—the legendary Machado brothers, famous for their willingness to train all comers, even those competing with fellow Brazilians.

"Me and Funaki and Suzuki went to Los Angeles to train with them," Shamrock says. "They were catching us with the gi and it was impressive. We were excited to be there. I learned a lot. I was told not to go 100 percent. I put the gi on and just kind of rolled with them. We let them be the teachers. And, even if I had wanted to go hard at them, I didn't have a chance wearing the gi. I'd never studied it."

Things got testy when Funaki wanted to test what the Machados could do without the gi, thinking to bring them into Pancrase at some point. The grabbing of clothing, however, was apparently a hard habit to break. One of the Machados choked Funaki with his own t-shirt, leaving it ripped down the front. Words, but no blows, were exchanged and the Pancrase contingent found the experience valuable.

"It was hell," Funaki says simply. "It was my first time training in a gi. I got tapped out over and over again. But it was important to learn their techniques if Shamrock was going to fight Gracie again. Shamrock blamed his loss on a mistake. Watching the video, we saw it wasn't a mistake. There were so many techniques we didn't know."

Shamrock got valuable work with the gi from Gracie's own distant cousins and he once again felt confident things would be different this time.

And then it happened.

At the Lion's Den they sparred hard. So it was no surprise that White was throwing full power kicks at his head and Shamrock responding with hard palm strikes. White believes it was a kick that broke Shamrock's hand. Ken thinks it was a palm strike to Vernon's dome. While the genesis of the disaster isn't entirely clear, what happened in the aftermath was.

"I hit him with an open hand strike and it bent my hand back," Shamrock says. "My fingers actually went back and touched my wrist. The bones in the back of my hand spiraled and splintered and broke. I couldn't grip and couldn't hold on to anything."

For a moment the gym just stopped. Injuries are part of life for a fighter, but no one had ever heard Ken express any weakness, let alone cry out. No one was sure exactly how to respond.

"It was the first time that I ever heard Ken say, 'Ouch.' I never felt like so much dog crap in my life," White says. "I'm looking like, 'Oh, my god. This is my fault.' And he tells me, 'It's not your fault. I blocked wrong.' He was making excuses for my sake saying 'Don't feel bad. It's all right.'"

Shamrock actually considered for a time going forward with the tournament despite his injury. He had a lot invested in the opportunity, both psychologically and professionally. A month before the injury, concerned by their top fighter losing to Gracie at the first UFC, Pancrase officials had asked Shamrock to put over Suzuki in a match that January in Yokohama. Rather than compete in an actual bout, the two went into their match with a predetermined finish, a return to their shoot style roots.

"I felt almost obligated, because they gave me the opportunity," Shamrock says. "The guy didn't have a chance in hell against me in the ring. And I had to go and put him over. It pissed me off. Of all the guys. And they built him that way. Funaki could destroy him. I could destroy him.

"And yet we were made to go in and do certain things. That whole organization, not one time did they ask anyone else to put somebody over. No one had to do a worked fight—except me. I had to put him over. And that wasn't what that organization was supposed to be about. That's something that eats inside of me. Because I did it. But I wish I hadn't."

They had split three hard matches in PWF-G in 1992, two young stars just coming into their own in the wrestling ring. The potential was obvious for both, with Ken standing out as the top foreign star and Suzuki being groomed as the number two on the Japanese side behind Funaki.

But tension between the two had been thick for some time

backstage. Suzuki was known for his physical abuse of young wrestlers and trainees, a somewhat common paradigm in martial arts circles in Japan, where hazing was just a way of life.

"They used to treat them like crap, beating them up, make them wipe the sweat off our backs," Mark Fleming, Shamrock's old wrestling buddy from North Carolina[89] remembers. "But that's the way it was. They'd get a young boy in there and stretch him and make him scream and bust him in the face. That's how they made them tough and that was their training method."

This behavior, Shamrock felt, was different than the garden variety hazing that surrounded him when he trained in Japan. Suzuki took things to the extreme, going beyond the initial culture shock of life in the dojo. Eventually Shamrock just couldn't stand it anymore and felt he had to speak up.

"I heard he killed a kid in the gym[90]," Shamrock says. "No one talks about that. The kid was supposedly just standing there and he hit him in the head. He would do that all the time with young boys. He would just have them stand there and he'd smack them in the face. I just didn't have the stomach for that. I got pissed off and said 'you know what, don't do that in front of me anymore.' This was after I had started getting up there. We never saw eye to eye."

Suzuki, for his part had begun to feel differently about Shamrock too. In his mind, though competitors, the Pancrase founders were still all in this together, pro wrestling compatriots on the same journey into the unknown. "Teammates without being teammates," he says.

But at the second Pancrase event in October 1993, Shamrock had

---

[89] Fleming was a protege of Lou Thesz and wrestled in the Union Of Professional Wrestling Force International promotion, another spinoff of the UWF like Pancrase.

[90] While several of the foreign Pancrase fighters have heard this story, there is nothing documenting the incident.

"I can't confirm the trainee death in this particular case," reporter Fumi Saito says. "Pancrase did not make any announcement on this.

"It did happen at UWF, New Japan, World Japan, and other dojos over the years, and sometimes the company made an announcement. In some cases, they did not say a thing. It is very hard to confirm each and every case."

put Takahashi at real risk with a heel hook, looking to injure[91] and not just win in Suzuki's mind. The younger fighter had to be carried out of the ring as Shamrock celebrated a victory.

"In the final moments comes a do or die point. That heel hold was at a really extreme angle," Suzuki says. "My attitude towards Shamrock changed a bit. I thought 'Wow, that guy will go this far?'"

With that as the backdrop, the two were set to square off in what was the second real marquee match in Pancrase history in Suzuki's hometown of Yokohama. Suzuki came to the ring in tight black speedos and a black towel draped over his head like boxer Mike Tyson, cultivating his bad boy persona. Announced as "Wayne Shamrock," Ken came out to the roar of lions, clad in a bright yellow robe to accompany his yellow speedos. This extravagant ring wear was Funaki's influence, made at Ken's expense to maintain the perception that he was a main event star.

"Japanese fighters lost (to Shamrock) one after the other," Funaki says. "At the end, Suzuki was the last Japanese fighter to take on Shamrock in Pancrase. Suzuki pursued the fight also feeling this way. I could sense the power welling up inside Suzuki when the time came.[92]"

In the ring, Shamrock started fast with palm strikes and a solid knee in the corner, just wanting Suzuki to know, even though the fight was fixed in his favor, the Japanese wrestler would have to work for it.

"I was really angry about the situation. I didn't like it. He's not even in my league," Shamrock says. "I just didn't understand it. He was a good amateur wrestler and a real shooter… Why wouldn't you want to test yourself? If I was him, I would have wanted to really fight me. Just to see. We could have worked later. But I was in their country, it was their organization."

From the fast start, the match devolved into five minutes of positional changes, but little else of note. Perhaps wary of doing anything that looked less than real, Suzuki opted to do very little at all, even after Shamrock gave him the top position and opened up his guard to allow the possibility of leg lock attempts.

---

[91] Eventually Bas Rutten would break Takahashi's leg with the same hold. Sometimes it's better to tap out.

[92] None of the Japanese fighters ever conceded the existence of any worked or fixed fights in Pancrase. They spoke consistently about these bouts as if they were all legitimate contests.

"I basically gave him every opportunity to try something and he didn't," Shamrock says. "Everything was there for him to make it a good match, but he just didn't. We had a specific finish, but nothing was stopping us from going back and forth with submission attempts. But I couldn't initiate it. Because if I attack him—what if I get it? So, he needs to be the one attacking with me rolling in and out of holds and blocking."

After 7:37, the two landed in the classic Pancrase dueling leg lock position. Shamrock grabbed an Achilles hold, but was out-gunned when Suzuki secured a heel hold and forced a rope escape.

"The harder I held on, the more it prevented his escape," Suzuki says. "Even if he hurt my ligaments, it's not like my foot would fall off. I'd get up anyway. 'If you wanna break my leg,' I thought, 'Go ahead. I'll still beat you up.'"

Although it wasn't the scheduled finish, Shamrock couldn't continue and Suzuki celebrated like a mad man as the Lion's Den and Funaki hit the ring to help a furious Shamrock limp to the corner. He was thoroughly defeated and angry that Suzuki had held the submission a beat too long and put him at risk of serious injury.

"I didn't think he wouldn't stand up," Suzuki says. "I thought he'd stand and come at me. So I was planning how I'd go back to that position. When he came at me, I'd smash him. Then, he didn't get up. I was like, 'Huh? I won?!' I was so excited for two or three days. Then I started feeling like, what if I'd just injured a friend?

"In the following years, I started thinking it was no good to go so far with submissions. Long ago when I'd first started doing joint locks, I'd been learning from Fujiwara-san. Something he said suddenly came back to me. He said, 'It's a pro's duty to be able to apply joint locks without breaking anything.'

"I remember he said that. 'You win by making your opponent surrender. Anybody can break something. Making them surrender is the correct way of joint locks.' Aw crap, I thought, I hurt my opponent, didn't I? I did a bad thing, didn't I?"

Having put over one of their top stars in Suzuki, the Japanese were happy to send Shamrock back into the UFC to see if he could secure the win in a rematch with Gracie. Instead, the injury from the fight and a broken hand meant the second UFC would have to go forward without any Pancrase representation at all.

Shamrock considered entering the tournament despite his physical condition, only to be talked off that ledge by his father.

"He said 'listen, you've got everything in front of you,'" Shamrock recalls. "'Why go in there limited. In the first fight you made a mistake. You underestimated him. Don't make the same mistake twice. Go in there 100 percent.'"

But, though Bob successfully convinced his son not to enter the cage again without being in top condition, no one could keep him from the dojo, where he remained a terror even with the use of just one arm.

"He would still roll around with us, and I'd have scrapes and little, teeny cuts all over my face," Bessac says. "They came from him running his cast across my face over and over again. There was just no mercy."

Even though Shamrock couldn't compete, SEG executive McLaren had identified him as a potential star and the company flew him back to Denver for the event anyway. They put him in front of the media, taking advantage of the opportunity to build towards an eventual rematch with Gracie, who won the second tournament by beating Shamrock's old nemesis Pat Smith in the finals.

For Shamrock, it was also an opportunity to search out new talent for Pancrase, where he served as the North American talent scout. He and his father identified two potential fighters at the event, Sean Daugherty and Jason DeLucia, who would eventually join them at the Lion's Den. DeLucia, who had prepared for the possibility of fighting Shamrock at the event, was curious about how he matched up with the man who would soon become his sensei and the two worked out together backstage before the fights.

"I said, "You wanna see what I was gonna do," and he said, "Sure." So, I showed him what I was gonna try on him, and the amount of power that he exhibited was just mind-boggling to me," DeLucia says. "He just exploded through me, and when he was grabbing me, you know, he grabbed my legs, you could feel like he could just twist them off like a chicken bone. He would have just ripped me apart, limb from limb."

DeLucia would soon move from Boston to stay with Shamrock and his family at their home beginning his training at the Lion's Den as the team's first high profile recruit. Within a few weeks, he was booked in Japan for Pancrase, where he'd remain a mainstay for years. He also became an important cog at the Den. He took over for White as Shamrock's Royce Gracie proxy, sparring with Ken in preparation for what everyone felt would be an inevitable showdown.

"DeLucia was like, 'Well, you know. I fought Royce. Maybe I should be Ken's main training partner?' He may not have known what he was signing up for," White says. "I said, 'Sweet, Jason. You get in there and you take that punishment. I don't want it.'"

When the poster for UFC 3 came out, Shamrock stood face-to-face with Gracie like the two were going to be matched up like two boxers. It was the match the no-holds-barred community wanted to see more than any other—but things for Ken Shamrock were never quite that simple.

CHAPTER SEVEN
UFC 3 and the Lion's Den

* * *

The UFC continued forward, a strong showing on pay-per-view earning the promotion a second, then a third opportunity to present a battle of martial arts styles to an American public primed for that kind of ultra-violence. While Shamrock's heart may have been in the Octagon, his primary paycheck was still being generated in Japan.

Pancrase had started life as a revolution, returning professional wrestling to its roots—pure sport, or at least a reasonable facsimile of an actual athletic contest. By December of 1994, the promotion had held 12 cards in Japan, each in front of a capacity or near capacity crowd of enthusiastic fans.

The business was red hot and not just for the three UWF spinoffs. Wrestling generally was thriving, with acts both decidedly mainstream and incredibly niche finding their audiences in an aesthetic renaissance.

"More wrestling fans, actually, followed 90s version of New Japan with Keiji Muto, Shinya Hashimoto and Masahiro Chono," Fumi Saito says. "They also followed All Japan with Mitsuharu Misawa, Toshiaki Kawada, Akira Taue, and Kenta Kobashi, Atsushi Onita's FMW[93] and even women's wrestling groups. All at the same time. Wrestling fans wanted to watch everything."

About half the matches on any given card featured Ken and his growing stable of Lion's Den fighters. Jason DeLucia, splitting the rent with Ken on an apartment he eventually shared with Ken's foster brother Frank, worked diligently to incorporate Shamrock's philosophies and teachings into what had been a lifetime of martial studies.

"The training was intense," DeLucia says. "You're up every day and the first thing you're doing is you're hitting the gym and training weights very heavily. And then after that, you're doing conditioning, which was 500 of everything. And then we were wrestling and then sparring. It was a full day of work, beating the living piss out of ourselves.

"Ken didn't do the training with us. He waited 'til we were done training, and then he would come in. He sometimes had a savage streak and he would hurt you. He would damage you. It's the way he could be in the dojo. Depends on if he was pissed off that day. He

---

[93] Onita's wild Frontier Martial Arts Wrestling was a death match promotion that featured barbed wire and explosions. It was, arguably, the only wrestling in Japan more violent than Pancrase's subtle but stiff shooting style.

would do wacked out shit."

Shamrock doesn't disagree, admitting that he was angry, amped up and still felt like he had a lot to prove, not just to himself but to the wider world.

"I was on the warpath in life to make sure I didn't end up back where I'd started from. And no one was going to get in my way," Shamrock says. "I was out for vengeance. I wanted the lifestyle I'd seen other people enjoy. It was right there at my fingertips. I just had to go out there and take it. That was my mentality. And there was nobody who came into my gym or went into the ring against me in those days who didn't know I was for real."

Everyone associated with the Lion's Den has a story, either about getting beat up by Shamrock or watching him decimate some other poor sap. The Den was no place for the soft, either physically or mentally. There were no quarters given and little remorse for the awful things done there.

"Ken and I were both similar in we're violent," Scott Bessac, one of Shamrock's first students says. "We really like to hurt other people. I mean, I remember once we're lifting weights at Twin Arbors, and he's like, 'Bro, we got the best job in the world, man. We get to beat the shit out of people and don't get to go to prison for it.'

"And I'm like, 'I know, it's awesome right?'"

DeLucia never quite fit that mold. He was always an old-fashioned martial artist, even in a gym that disdained the traditional dojo. He began bowing to Shamrock and calling him "sir," bringing some institutional structure to what had previously been madcap violence. Still, despite an improving culture, just surviving the gym to make it to the ring was a major accomplishment. While DeLucia and the others were learning from Shamrock, they were also serving as his human punching bags. Somedays, that went better than others.

"He was looking for someone to spar one day before the Frank Lobman fight," DeLucia says. "I said, 'Ken, I don't have any of my stuff with me.' I didn't have a mouthpiece or anything. And he said, 'Don't worry about it. We're not gonna be going hard. We're not gonna be doing knees. We're not gonna be doing leg kicks. We're just gonna be doing light kickboxing.'

"And, the first thing he did in the ring was knee me straight in the mouth. And the second thing he did was punch me straight in the mouth and elevated me because he could bench press 605 pounds. I broke my teeth in the back, and I was like, 'Really?'

"That's the kind of shit that he used to do. And that's small. He used to abuse the other guys fairly regularly because that's the way he was."

On April 7, 1994, the Lion's Den got a new member—Shamrock's adopted brother Frank. Bob had recognized many of the same attributes in a young man named Frank Juarez that he had seen in Ken, staying in touch even after Frank, addicted to crank, had been sentenced to six years at the California Youth Authority for a string of robberies that ended when he was caught breaking into a Taco Bell through the drive-thru window. He ended up in adult prison instead of a youth facility so he could work to support his wife and young son.

When he got out, Bob Shamrock was there to help pick up the pieces. Swollen with prison muscles and weighing close to 210 pounds, Frank had dreams of being an entertainer. He wasn't sure exactly how to actualize that goal, especially since he lacked any real ability to sing, dance or act. He was good looking and muscular and charming so stripping came to mind immediately. But when Bob offered up the possibility of joining Ken on the fighting circuit instead, he was quick to jump on it. Two days after being released from prison, Frank was standing in front of Ken for his first introduction to the world of professional fighting—the infamous Lion's Den tryout.

Because of his UFC fame, there had been a stream of prospective fighters making their way to the gym, still in a tiny space behind a car audio shop at this point. Shamrock didn't always personally spar with them in the ring, relying on White, Bessac or one of his other students to test their mettle. But this time, he knew he would need to do it himself. Frank was like a wild stallion. Before you could train him to his full potential, he would need to be broken.

"My father said I had to do it," Shamrock says. "Frank didn't fight anybody but me. He was in good shape and had this long, flowing hair. I asked him, 'are you sure you want to do this?' And he said 'I've been in prison, I can handle anything.' He had this cocky attitude and my father said 'you're going to have to really lay into him because he thinks he's all that. When it's over, you better be sure he has your respect.'

"Well, my father knew people. So, I went in there and told him 'you better give me all you've got, because I'm going to come after you. I'm going to push you past the limits you think you can go to. Do you understand me?'"

After pushing Frank with squats and other bodyweight exercises, Shamrock had him step into the ring for the first time. Frank had been in some street fights and confrontations in the prison system. This was something different.

"Frank never played sports or anything," Bessac says. "He was more like the hackey sack kind of guy, and so it was a shock to Frank. He came out of prison with this long black hair and big muscles. He thought he was pretty tough. He didn't know Ken.

"Ken was pretty hard back then. Beat the shit out of everybody just like he beat the shit out of Frank. Everybody got the shit kicked out of them by Ken at one time or another."

Ken broke Frank's nose quickly with an open hand palm strike, then took him down and battered his body. In his book *Uncaged*, Frank described being tossed around, choked and brutally leg locked for the promised 20 minutes. But, as bad as it got, he never quit:

> We had gone the whole twenty minutes. I had passed the tryout. Ken walked out of the ring looking disgusted. I crawled out after him. Someone drove me to Ken's house and took me upstairs and put me in a bedroom. I passed out and slept for the next two days. When I finally came downstairs, I actually had to slide down the stairs on my ass because my legs wouldn't work. It would take two weeks of icing and heat on my knee to walk without a limp and another two weeks before I could take a full breath without the rib pain sending me to the other knee. That's the shape I was in when I started training at the Lion's Den.

"The thing Frank didn't realize is that I didn't do any less or any more than I would have done to any other cocky kid who walked in there to tryout," Shamrock says. "He got the same treatment everyone got, except he got it from me personally.

"I wasn't going to waste his time or mine, only to find out halfway through training them that they couldn't take it. I was going to find out in one day if they had what it took to be a fighter. We had to know right away that they were a bad ass and a tough individual."

Now living with DeLucia in Shamrock's home, Frank began what has become a life-long journey as a martial artist. At first, like many of what the Lion's Den called "young boys," he did little more than clean the gym and serve as a human punching bag for the more experienced fighters.

"Frank came into it with nothing, so, you know, it was extra hard in a way for Ken, " DeLucia says. "At least with me, I was already a martial artist with nearly 20 years experience. Frank came in with nothing. Ken had to start from the ground up, working with him. He got half of a fighter in me and got nothing in Frank. And he had to get us ready for opening day."

Ken, Frank says, was a better fighter than a teacher, demonstrating the moves ably on his students but not especially adept at explaining how or why they worked, though Ken says there was a method to his caveman madness.

"I knew the angles and I knew the direction in which they would turn to injure themselves," Shamrock says. "And I wouldn't let him go that way. I'd push them the other way, which is the way out. So I would force them in the right direction until they got it. I wouldn't tell them. I'd force them in the direction that they could get out. I wasn't much on talking."

This approach was frustrating for someone as analytical as Frank who wanted to understand why he was doing things, not just how to do them. But he learned quickly—which was good, because he would be in the ring for Pancrase after just eight months of training.

"I came out into a burgeoning sport where a bunch of idiots thought toughness was the baseline for being a professional athlete," Frank says.[94] "Having a 140 IQ, I was the only idiot bringing a notebook to Ken's sessions and within six months, I was beating the professional fighters because they were off flexing their muscles and their dicks and talking about how tough they were and I was studying martial arts because that was my journey."

After taking two months off thanks to the hand injury that kept him out of UFC 2, Shamrock rebounded with three wins against a single loss. His return fight, two weeks after jumping Frank into the Lion's Den family, had been a brutal domination of 21-year-old prospect Ryūshi Yanagisawa, finishing the bout with a heel hook that destroyed

---

[94] Frank eventually decided not to cooperate with this book in any substantive way. Whatever peace had been made between the two foster brothers doesn't appear to have been permanent.

the young fighter's knee and put him out for over a year with major surgery. The loss, the first legitimate setback of his professional fighting career in Japan came against Frank Lobman, a powerful puncher and champion striker who had once defeated the formidable Bas Rutten in a kickboxing match. It was contested under kickboxing rules, Lobman's specialty, allowing Shamrock to save face in defeat. If anything, a spirited performance only raised his stock with the fans.

Shamrock's next victim was Matt Hume in the middle of the card underneath DeLucia's Pancrase debut against Funaki. That was the pattern for Pancrase booking—a loss at the top of the card sent members of the big three down to the midcard, where they would quickly be rehabilitated against an often-overmatched opponent. Hume, who would go on to become a famous MMA coach and executive, was the overmatched foe on this day. It's become a controversial bout in online circles, both because of some very obvious pro wrestling elements[95] and Hume's coy comments about it.

It's the main example critics use to point to Pancrase being something less than legitimate. While that was true, using this particular bout as evidence he wasn't a capable fighter is galling for Shamrock, who says he was taking it easy on Hume, not to get a win he didn't deserve but as a kindness.

"There was nothing worked about that fight other than, going into it, Matt Hume did not have the skillset he needed to get in that ring and fight a guy like me," Shamrock says. "I told him before hand 'listen, we'll go in there, move around a little bit, you do what you do, I'll do what I do, but I'm not going to hurt you.' I was that much better than him. I'd rolled with him in the gym and knew what he had. I want the guy to go out and show well. He was nervous and afraid. I just wanted to make him feel at ease.

"None of what I did in that fight was planned beforehand. I just did it. He couldn't stop me. He talks like he talks now and it pisses me off. He knows the reality of that fight. He knows he was scared to get in the ring with me. I was a beast in those days. I went after people."

Ironically, the same card included another fight that may have featured a work gone wrong, this one better hidden from skeptics in

---

[95] The finish of the bout included a Northern Light Suplex and float over into a double wristlock. It was a stunning display of physical dexterity but also quite obviously straight out of professional wrestling.

the public. DeLucia, battered but not broken[96] after his brutal sparring with Shamrock in May, made his Pancrase debut against Funaki in the main event at the Amagasaki Gymnasium. With his handsome good looks and UFC pedigree[97], DeLucia was immediately targeted for stardom. The decision was made to launch him out of the gates with a big win—but not one quite as spectacular as what transpired. After a brief scramble on the ground, Funaki was caught in a kneebar and forced to tap out.

"The way that I heard it, he was supposed to carry me a certain distance through the fight, and when I caught him, he meant to be able to get the ropes, but he couldn't," DeLucia says. "Like, he goofed. He was supposed to put me over, but it wasn't supposed to happen that way.

"I can't say for sure. And it don't phase me either way, because all fighting has work in it. Like, all sports has work in it. Anybody says it doesn't, well, you can fool the fans. You can't fool the players."

Shamrock's other students didn't fare as well as their mentor or the UFC veteran. Bessac was submitted easily in each of his first four fights, his style and aesthetic barely resembling that of Shamrock and the other Den competitors. Vernon White, despite his best efforts, continued to struggle in the ring, losing seven of his first eight Pancrase fights before closing 1994 with several career-saving victories. A chemical boost, he believes, helped level what had previously been an uneven playing field.

"There were some guys that got really strong really fast, and I'm thinking to myself, 'Well, how is it that these guys are getting so much stronger than me so much faster?' I ended up taking some stuff," White says. "I wasn't gung-ho. I had watched videos on people having heart attacks taking steroids and stuff. So I was like 'two weeks on, two weeks off.'

---

[96] Except for a few teeth.
[97] DeLucia had won a bout at UFC II before losing to Royce Gracie by armbar.

"When I was done with UFC 2," he remembers, "I owed more in medical just because of my broken leg than I made for the fight."

"I just wanted to be able to be in there with anybody. I didn't want to fall by the wayside. Even the Japanese said, 'If you don't get stronger and better we can't use you.' To me, I'm like, 'Okay. Well, I'm going to do it.' Then I started winning more fights. After I started winning more fights I became more popular. It started to become fun after that."

Steroids were a reality, both in the sport generally and inside the Lion's Den. Shamrock was a user, enough so that training partners had a pretty good idea whether or not he was on a cycle when they rolled. The drug use belied his heroic public persona, but so did a lot of Shamrock's behavior when the news cameras shut down and the reporters turned their tape recorders off.

"Back then, he was cheating on Tina so much that he was always paranoid she would find out," Bessac says. "He was a big time into drugs and strippers and all different kinds of illegal substances that he was snorting. And ecstasy and steroids. He was out of control there for awhile."

While he embraced his new role as a father and publicly said all the right things almost every time, maintaining his marital vows to Tina was a trickier proposition for a fighter with growing fame and popularity.

"I was traveling all the time," Shamrock says. "I tried to bring her places, she just didn't want to go. I go to Japan, she didn't want to go to Japan. It just felt like I was growing apart from her. I go on the road and it was like I was in a separate life. It just got old after awhile.

"I'm on the road by myself all the time. I don't feel like I have a relationship with my wife and pretty girls are coming around all the time. I'm going to do what I'm going to do."

Twenty days after the Hume "fight," Ken stepped into the ring again, back in the main event, this time taking on an opponent that in retrospect would become the top name on his fighting resume.

Bas Rutten would eventually become a legend, winning both the King of Pancrase and UFC championships[98]. He was already on his

---

[98] The list of fighters who have accomplished this task is small: Ken, Frank Shamrock, Rutten and Josh Barnett.

way in the early days of Pancrase, announcing his presence with an emphatic knockout at the first event and offering fans the first look at another approach to mixed rules fighting. Every other top Pancrase fighter, and top UFC fighter for that matter, was a grappling specialist, able to control an opponent on the ground and manipulate joints and appendages en route to victory.

Rutten was something else entirely—an athletic striker who struck fear into the hearts of every one forced to step into the ring against him. More than that, he had a fun personality, a marketable look and spoke a smidgen of Japanese confidently if not perfectly. What he didn't have was a grappling background, making the higher level Pancrase fighters very difficult matchups. He could smash lesser lights with aggression and athleticism. But against the top guys, that wasn't going to be enough.

"In my third fight, when Funaki took me in a toehold, owe-wee. I couldn't wear shoes," Rutten said. "My ankle was swollen so badly. I didn't even know what a toehold was at that time. That was the whole reason for the boots, let's face it. The Japanese guys were very good on the ground. And they were less good with striking. So what did they do? They said 'Let's not wear gloves, let's open our hands.' It's good for grappling and chokes but not much good for anything else. 'And we'll wear shin protection so the impact of the kicks will be a lot less.' Plus the shoes were perfect for leglocks. Everything was adapted for their fighting style."

In some ways, however, the very things that made Rutten vulnerable early in his career also made his potential unlimited. He brought a much-needed element that Pancrase was otherwise missing, a sense of real, unadulterated violence. Most of the top Japanese fighters, and even Shamrock and his progeny to an extent, had the same pedigree. They were students of Gotch and the catch wrestling tradition of Wigan, England. They moved the same way, thought the same way and understood the same techniques and strategies.

At times this led to beautiful, fluid exchanges of wrestling holds, especially on the mat. But it could also look more like an intricate dance than an honest-to-God fight, each competitor taking his turn to lead. With Rutten, there was none of that. He threw his strikes with an energy and intention that left no doubt that he was in the pain business, gasps from the audience often following an especially vicious kick or knee. He was an obvious future star—if he could figure out the ground.

The promotion wasn't blind to this. They saw big potential too and wanted to fast track his rise to the main event scene. He'd lost that third fight against Funaki in January 1994, then run off three wins in a row, including a stoppage against Suzuki. It was a weird situation, as the top Pancrase performers doubled as the promotion's management. They wanted to compete and win, sure. But they also had an obligation to the promotion as a whole, creating an atmosphere where they would teach fighters who would eventually attempt to use that knowledge to beat them in the ring.

"After my second fight, Funaki and Suzuki invited me to have dinner with the both of them," Rutten said. "I thought that was going to be it. Because Chris Doleman[99] had told me 'Bas, they're probably going to ask you to work the fights.' I was totally prepared to say 'F-U.' We went to dinner and we ate and had a good time. They gave me a book from Fujiwara about submissions. And I said, 'Man, you are actually trying to make me stronger.' They laughed and that was it. So when I walked to get in the cab, I turned around and said 'I thought you guys were going to ask me to throw a fight.' And Funaki told me right to my face 'I would never ask you a thing like that.'

While Pancrase may not have asked Rutten to do anything untoward, they were less circumspect with the fighters who came from a pro wrestling background. Pancrase asked Shamrock to help continue to build their new star, though not explicitly to lose to him. That would come later and force a standoff that further damaged a strained relationship. He would do jobs for the top Japanese stars, though begrudgingly, but refused to put over other gaijin, who he viewed as more direct competition.

"I saw the writing on the wall that they were trying to groom him to take my place," he says. "Or, at the very least, provide some competition."

Shamrock did agree to carry Rutten and make the match look competitive, something he, Suzuki and Funaki occasionally did to make the cards more compelling and help keep some of the other fighters looking strong in the eyes of the fans. But extending a fight against a striker like Rutten was a dangerous proposition.

"Doing it with Bas was crazy," Shamrock says. "The guy was trying

---

[99] A RINGS fighter, Doleman had discovered Rutten doing marital arts comedy bits on late night television. While he wasn't fighting for real, Doleman saw what he called Rutten's "genetic potential."

to take my head off. He had no idea that I was carrying him and to this day he still doesn't believe it. Five minutes, six minutes go by and I'm thinking 'Hurry up!'"

Shamrock controlled the action, mostly on the mat, while Rutten took every opportunity he got to try to end the bout with one blow. When he found himself on the ground, his focus was mainly on survival.

"I said to my corner, 'He's got too much balance. His balance is very good. It's very difficult to get him off.' You can throw away a lot of energy if somebody has real good balance, and you constantly try to throw him off," Rutten said. "And if it doesn't work, you're going to run out of gas."

To the untrained eye, it looked like a classic battle between grappler and striker. Even Rutten, one of the participants, believed it was fully on the up-and-up. But rather than looking to win, Shamrock was instead trying to extend the bout and make everyone look good. The fight went more than 16 minutes, one of the longest in MMA history to that point, before Ken finally secured the rear-naked choke for the win.

"I tried to make the fight interesting, so it's fun for the fans," Shamrock says. "But I'm thinking to myself, 'I'm going to get killed here. He's going to catch me with a shot.' Luckily for me, I was able to get good enough to do those matches without putting myself at too much risk."

The fight worked out well for everyone. Rutten was able to look strong and gain confidence[100] and Shamrock's aura remained intact heading into a rematch with Funaki. The first time the two men met, in the first Pancrase event the previous September, Shamrock had pulled off the upset win leaving his trainer in a daze. This time the promotion would leave no doubt about the outcome.

"When we put Pancrase together, Funaki told me 'we want something real. We want to shoot. We want real fighting.' That's what it was all about," Shamrock says. "So, imagine my frustration when I was reaching for a goal and they changed their minds. They changed the landscape. And I had to adapt to it in order not to blow myself out of the water.

---

[100] "I was already very happy because he was the main guy right there," Rutten said. He's added a commentary track to each of his Pancrase fights and it's worth seeking these out on YouTube for a further look at the strange world of proto-MMA.

"That was something because I was going to a UFC fight. They wanted to protect the company. I was happy to do it for Funaki. We were friends and he was the only person who ever gave me a challenge in Pancrase. He had the ability to beat me if I made a mistake. At least he had a chance to beat me in a real fight. If there was one fight I'd like to have not done, it was the Suzuki fight. Suzuki had no business beating me."

There were several reasons to push Funaki back to the top of the promotion, not least of which was his upcoming bout with Suzuki, the first time the two Japanese superstars had ever met in competition.[101] Just as important was Shamrock's impending return to the UFC Octagon, presumably to meet Gracie again.

That fight was Shamrock's obsession, to the point he even asked to pull out of the Pancrase event to be as fresh as possible for the UFC tournament and he had suffered an injury, he believes celebrating a previous win in the ring, leaping off the ropes in joy, then feeling his knee give. Pancrase, however, decided it needed to keep its high profile main event—and had some ideas about how it should turn out.

While his participation in cage fighting was a net-positive for Pancrase at this point according to former Pancrase executive Osaki, giving the group a boost of credibility by proxy, having their top fighter potentially lose a second time was a risk they weren't willing to take. Positioning Funaki as the best fighter in the promotion alleviated that concern. Now a Shamrock win over Gracie would make a third match between the two even more palatable, while a loss left Funaki as a perceptional equal to Royce, two stars who had both beaten Shamrock.

Contemporary reporting suggests Funaki was unhappy with Shamrock's performance in the bout, thinking he didn't do enough to make fans believe it was an actual contest, let alone one he was trying to win and not just survive. The Wrestling Observer reported:

> After the match Funaki was visibly upset in the dressing room because Shamrock didn't do anything, as he apparently was resting himself up for the

---

[101] Even Funaki doesn't understand why the two were never matched against each other in Pro Wrestling Fujiwara-Gumi. It was typical for the UWF offshoots to pit top Japanese talent against each other, but that was one dream match that was years in the making.

Ultimate Fight Championship tournament on 9/9 in Charlotte since the show is built around him and Royce Gracie.

Footage from the bout tells a different story. It was an active fight, with Shamrock securing a quick takedown, then dropping for a leglock that allowed Funaki to reverse to top position. The finish was a relatively brutal choke, with Funaki crossfacing Shamrock and yanking aggressively at his head to clear space for his arm to sink beneath the chin for the finish. It was a dominant win for Funaki, no doubt, but not one characterized by a lack of action, as Shamrock both attacked and defended with apparent energy and verve.

There's no doubt, however, that his mind was on another bout, one that would take place just eight days later in Charlotte, his old stomping grounds. Funaki would be there as well, his main strategist and cornerman for what Shamrock hoped would be an opportunity to right all the wrongs of UFC 1.

"I went into this tournament with injuries[102]," he says. "Because there was no way I was backing out if Royce was going to be there."

The new sport was just starting to catch fire in the mainstream, with high profile stories in *The New York Times*, a spirited review on the Howard Stern show and, most of all, the release of VHS tapes that brought the spectacle right into the living room of anyone with a Blockbuster video card. MTV called it "the sports of the 90s." Wally Paige, the cantankerous Denver Post columnist, offered the opposite take.

"The most disgusting, horrifying thing I've ever seen," he told *Newsday*. "It's basically taking cock-fighting and putting it in human form.[103]"

Good or bad, they were talking. And Shamrock, even in defeat, emerged as one of the breakout stars of those early shows. While pre-

---

[102] A knee injury, specifically, was causing him trouble.
[103] Senator John McCain is often erroneously credited with first comparing UFC to human cockfighting.

fight commercials subtly positioned him as the heel to the smaller Gracie's babyface, he claims behind the scenes the Gracie family were doing everything they could to manipulate the outcome.

While the Pancrase fighter-owners did their best to build up their competition, the Gracies, who owned a piece of the UFC, did everything they could to make Royce's path to a third consecutive tournament victory as smooth as possible. Despite SEG putting the two men on the event poster like they were certain to square off at the show, Shamrock and Gracie actually found themselves on different sides of the ever-changing tournament brackets. If they were to meet, it would have to be in the finals of the eight-man tournament.

"They wanted the advantage. Like they've always done. They've done everything they could to push things in their advantage. They bounced around the brackets," Shamrock says. "No one knew who was fighting who until the day of the event. And that was because of me. They knew I'd be the toughest guy for Royce. They had it setup the way they thought would benefit Royce the best. They put me against one of America's top judo players in the first round."

Christophe Leininger *was* judo royalty of a sort. His father Maurice had been a champion in France in the 1950s, helping establish a thriving sport in the military there before moving to Phoenix, Arizona, to raise his children. Christophe was a three-time Olympic alternate and one of the few practitioners in his sport able to make martial arts a full-time gig. He'd trained extensively with Wellington "Megaton" Dias[104], a jiu jitsu black belt under Royler Gracie who had immigrated to Phoenix and Leininger felt like he understood the ground well enough to compete with anyone.

"Judo is like kabuki theatre," he told the Phoenix New Times. "It's not just banging heads. In a tournament, you experience every emotion: fear, courage, defeat, victory, pain, discipline. There's a conflict of personalities, villains and good guys, one man stalking another."

Shamrock, though he didn't yet know who he'd be facing when the video was filmed, certainly looked confident in the tape that rolled before his entrance to the cage. He'd wear a red Lion's Den robe to the Octagon but was pictured on camera working out in jeans and no shirt, telling the audience "I'm here in Ultimate Fighting Championship 3 to

---

[104] Today Megaton is best known as the father of female Jiu Jitsu ace and UFC contender Mackenzie Dern.

redeem my performance."

The UFC was still finding its way in 1994. The announcers, despite Gracie's success in the first two tournaments, didn't know the first thing about judo, wondering aloud why Leininger would want to wear his judogi in the cage. Shamrock, at least, was all too familiar with the power of the gi and aware that judo was a sister art of Brazilian jiu jitsu and included the same basic grappling techniques. He stuffed an early Leininger shot but remained wary of his opponent, defending an attempted triangle choke smartly and actually using the gi against the judo player[105].

Leininger was known as a bit of a rough-and-tumble character in the judo world. But nothing he'd experienced along the "gentle way" prepared him for a monster like Shamrock who had been preparing obsessively for another fighter with very similar tricks up his literal sleeves. Funaki credits training against fighters in a gi with Shamrock's success against an athlete with some of the same skillsets that made Gracie so successful. He wore shoes to the cage this time out as well, even though it made it technically illegal for him to throw any kicks. If nothing else, he was adaptable. Eventually, just as referee "Big" John McCarthy inexplicably screamed for him to work[106], Shamrock secured his hooks and, after a brief scramble, had his man pinned on the mat in half guard. Five hard punches ended things as Leininger eventually tapped out.

While Shamrock cruised against the toughest opponent on his side of the bracket, Gracie met his stiffest test yet in the form of Hawaiian street fighter Kimo Leopaldo. Now living in Huntington Beach, Kimo had escaped the street life where he'd been in the collection racket for drug dealers. He was intrigued at the idea of bringing some of the skills from his former life into his new one as a devout Christian and used the pay-per-view broadcast as an opportunity to spread his truth.

Not only did he come with his trainer Joe Son in tow as a pro

---

[105] Leininger would tell the press that he had been expecting a striker who would charge recklessly across the cage into his waiting arms. To be fair, that would have been the case for almost every UFC fighter of the era except Shamrock and Gracie.

[106] McCarthy, who for the first time was allowed to stop a fight when he deemed it necessary, seemed very keen on becoming part of the show. It was a savvy move, as he is still around 25 years later as a television commentator for Bellator.

wrestling style manager, he'd managed to bring a prop with him as well. Kimo emerged from the smoke and walked to the cage carrying an enormous wooden cross on his broad shoulders, "Jesus" the sole word tattooed on his midriff. UFC producers, trying to avoid what they felt would be the taint of professional wrestling, were totally unaware of the very pro wrestling entrance he had planned[107]:

> Kimo told Art Davie the large box he had shipped to the Arena was special training equipment. Officials were not amused when an enormous cross emerged just before he made his entrance to the Octagon.

Kimo continued to surprise once he got into the Octagon, using his size and pure ferocity to rough the smaller Gracie up in a way no one else had yet managed to pull off. It was a spirited bout that saw the fighters crash through the door of the Octagon in the first 20 seconds and both corners refusing to obey McCarthy's instructions throughout. Eventually, the technical wizard was forced to resort to hair pulling, grabbing a hold of Kimo's ponytail and using it to control him on the ground, leaving tufts of hair all over the mat.

"I fought Kimo at 250 lb[108] and with a pharmacy in his body," Gracie told *Fighters Only* in 2018. "Everybody told me he was strong, but he was super strong. He was probably the strongest guy I fought. I used the wrong strategy. I tried to match strength. It was wrong, but I got him in an armlock and I finished him."

Shamrock, who had changed into bright yellow trunks[109] in the back, once again preparing to wear three different outfits en route to victory, watched carefully on the monitors as Gracie struggled to the

---

[107] This anecdote, and many other great stories, courtesy of Clyde Gentry III's seminal *No Holds Barred: Evolution*. The book was a $29.95 paperback when first released and worth every penny to hardcore fans desperate for the true story of the birth of a sport.

[108] The UFC broadcast had him pegged at 240 pounds. Of course, it also claimed he had five percent body fat, which was clearly absurd. Equally absurd was the third-degree black belt he was awarded in an art he'd never studied a day in his life.

[109] His poor seconds, including Funaki, DeLucia and Bessac, were forced to wear a truly hideous yellow sweatshirt to match. A truly unfortunate sweatshirt.

back. His next opponent would offer an entirely different experience than the one he'd just finished with. That was the beauty of early no-holds-barred fighting—the sport hadn't yet become its own form of martial art and practitioners would often confront strategies and techniques they had never previously encountered.

Felix Lee Mitchell, a rock-solid prison guard from Nashville, Tennessee's Riverbend Maximum Security Institution by day and Shaolin Kung Fu specialist at night, wasn't going to be easy to intimidate. His day job brought him into regular contact with death row inmates. A cage fight for a $15,000 prize was unlikely to phase him.

The two had adjacent hotel rooms in the days leading up to the fight, though neither was apparently aware of that fact until later. Mitchell entered the night as an alternate, replacing Keith Hackney who had broken his hand in his own opening round shellacking of the giant Emmanuel Yarborough.[110]

Taking no chances, Shamrock shot a double leg from what seemed like miles across the cage, securing a body lock against the cage. Mitchell, to his credit, defended surprisingly well, at one point even landing two hard elbows to Ken's body. The crowd, despite his pre-fight positioning as the heroic Gracie's foil, begins chanting for Shamrock, but eventually their enthusiasm wanes in the desperately hot Grady Cole Center and the cheers turn to boos. The fight, likewise, devolves into tomfoolery, with both men grabbing at the other's trunks and Mitchell trying to remove Shamrock's protective cup, a scandalous tactic prevented only by Ken's ridiculously tight Speedos.

Shamrock eventually maneuvered his way into a choke and advanced to the finals, limping to the back with the help of his cornermen. The preliminaries were done—all that remained was Gracie.

"I had gone through two fights with a meniscus tear in my knee I'd had to shoot up before I got in the ring," he says. "It was excruciating anytime I tried for a takedown or bent my knee. Well, that shot was wearing off going into the last fight. I didn't care, because I was there

---

[110] Keith Hackney flew down to North Carolina with only the promise of front row tickets. He would have to earn his way into the cage as a last-minute replacement with a closed door fight just two days before the event. In front of Art Davie, Rorion Gracie and handful of others, he sparred Thomas Ramirez and was impressive enough to be fed to a monster.

for Royce."

A haggard Gracie walked slowly to the cage for his own semi-final bout against Canadian brawler Harold Howard.[111] It was almost 100 degrees in the building according to some estimates and the UFC made matters worse by packing the arena far beyond capacity. Royce claimed later that he had passed out in the back after the Kimo fight, tossed in a cold shower by his family and all but dragged to the cage to defend the family honor.

"I was completely dehydrated and had low blood sugar," Gracie told Kid Peligro.[112] "So when I got in the ring I got dizzy and everything turned black. Referee Big John McCarthy[113] came to me and asked 'are you ready?' I said 'Yes!' And I turned to my corner and said 'Guys, I can't see anything.'"

McCarthy came back to check on Gracie again and Royce again told his corner he couldn't see, signaling he wanted them to stop the fight.

"I turned to them and said, 'Guys, I am doing my job, you have to do yours. I can't see anything. What should I do?'"

After some deliberation, Rorion Gracie threw in the towel and Howard celebrated like he'd just won the lottery, soon joined in the cage by a bare-chested Kimo and an unfortunately equally shirtless Son, who took their own victory lap for Gracie's unexpected departure from the tournament. Backstage, already changed into his black trunks for the finals, Shamrock seethed.

"I don't understand it to this day when people talk about how tough Royce is," Shamrock says. "Skill wise? Absolutely. When it comes to toughness, unless things are set in his favor, he doesn't fight.

"He was exhausted. That's all. He was tired. So he goes into the ring and forfeited the fight, put on this extravagant show. Just because he was tired. He threw the towel in and still everybody wants to say 'he's

---

[111] Howard's wild-eyed pre-fight promo saw him remove his sunglasses and menace the world with both his mullet and his words. "We have a saying back home," he said in a thick accent. 'If you're coming on, come on." It remains one of the UFC's most iconic interviews 25 years later.

[112] Peligro's book *The Gracie Way* is a glowing family history. Peligro calls Rickson, Royler and Royce Gracie his three greatest friends and the book borders on hagiography at times.

[113] McCarthy was not only a Royce Gracie student, he actually trained with him in North Carolina up to two days before the fight. The Gracie family truly had their fingers in every aspect of each UFC event.

the greatest fighter of all time.' He's technically sound and has a good strategy. But don't you ever tell me this guy is tough."

Bob and UFC executives tried to get Shamrock to go out for the finals. Not only would he write his name into sports history as a tournament winner, he'd walk away with a much needed $60,000.

"I thought Ken was making a big mistake," Bob Shamrock said in a 2007 interview. "This was his chance to win the tournament that had escaped him at the first UFC. Then, when he met Gracie again eventually, it would be as equals. He wouldn't feel like he had so much to prove."

But without the promise of another shot at Gracie, Ken just couldn't muster up the interest.

"He has a big argument with Bob Shamrock, who says to him 'You're turning down a $60,000 payday.' That's $10,000 more than they paid Royce in the last event, but he don't want to come out," UFC matchmaker Art Davie remembers. "I used to say at the time, Ken Shamrock 'to be or not to be.' He was Hamlet in red Speedos. I never knew which Ken Shamrock was gonna show up."

What Ken couldn't articulate at the time was a feeling that few could understand. He was a prize fighter and definitely wanted the big check. But this fight was bigger than that, at least to him. He wasn't there for Harold Howard or anyone else. They were just obstacles on his way to revenge.

"I could have smoked them[114]," Shamrock says. "No problem. I knew it. But I wasn't there for the money. I wanted him. I think it makes a statement. And it was real. I wasn't there for the money. I wasn't there to win a tournament or to beat anybody else. I was there for Royce. Nothing else really mattered to me. And I stand by that.

"I wanted to be the best at this. Better than anybody. Me walking into that last fight and beating some guy from Canada doesn't get me any closer to my goal. That doesn't make me the best in the world. There was a guy who beat me. And the only way to fix that was to face him again."

---

[114] Howard ended up losing the finals to alternate Steve Jennum, a police officer from Nebraska.

CHAPTER EIGHT
The King

While Shamrock continued to stew about his loss to Gracie back in 1993, the business of fighting continued. Just a month after his decision to walk away from $60,000 at UFC 3, and days of the silent treatment from his father, Shamrock was back in the ring for Pancrase. By this point it was becoming rote. His fight with Takaku Fuke was his 30th trip to Japan for the purposes of competing in either pro wrestling or Pancrase and he'd fallen into a bit of a pattern starting five days before the fight.

"All the guys flown in from the U.S. usually traveled together," he says. "They were either training at my gym or I booked them to fight. We'd get there, we'd hit the hotel, check in and the next day we'd go to the dojo together to work out and then back to the hotel. That was an every day thing up until the fight."

Their base of operations was typically Shin Yokohama, where Funaki had set up a gym, though they'd sometimes work out of Tokyo where Suzuki had a separate facility. Each day the foreign fighters would be bussed from the hotel to the gym where they'd have two or three hours to work on their techniques and strategies without any of the Japanese fighters present. Then it was back to the hotel and what felt like an endless wait for the actual fight, the psychological battle almost as hard as the physical one at times.

"The day of the fight everybody would meet in the lobby and we'd jump on this bus at the hotel that would take us to the arena," Shamrock says. "We'd go down to the player's entrance and unload and head to our locker rooms. Once we were there we'd go out to the arena and the ring and get a feel for the entrance where we'd be walking in, get a feel for the ring, make sure everything is tight on it."

A Pancrase event was an all-day affair, culminating in a fight. Even at less than 100 percent, Fuke was no match for Shamrock and he made short work of him, leaving plenty of time to get to the back and watch Suzuki and Funaki square off for the first time ever. It was a spirited but obviously worked match that lasted just under two minutes, playing into Pancrase's reputation as "Instant Death Martial Arts."

Two months later, the promotion held a two-day, 16-man tournament to crown the first King of Pancrase. Negotiations had fallen through on a co-promotion with UFC to host a series of bouts between the Gracie family and Pancrase fighters at the Tokyo Dome. Pancrase, as it had throughout its history, would live or die on its own merits. Now that they had established *what* Pancrase was and how to succeed in this new world of shoot matches, it was time to determine who the best fighter in the world was.

Like UFC, and most professional sports for that matter, the mechanism for doing that was as simple as it gets. Pancrase held a series of qualifying bouts to find the 16 best fighters in the world and put them in a tournament. The winner, after surviving four bouts in just two days at Tokyo's Sumo Hall, would be crowned champion, given a title belt literally encrusted with jewels so valuable the promotion made them removable to avoid temptation and struggle to lift the kind of enormous trophy that pretty much only exists in the world of Japanese wrestling.

It was the most stacked tournament in the admittedly young history of what would eventually be called mixed martial arts. In addition to the two Pancrase stalwarts, the regulars from Shamrock's Lion's Den, and budding stars like Rutten and Matt Hume, the field included world class kickboxer Maurice Smith, Shooto fighter Manabu Yamada and the debut of future UFC champion Frank Shamrock.

After just a few months training at the Lion's Den, Ken had determined Frank was ready to make his professional debut. He had survived his initiation and several months living at Ken's house and training every day in the brutal world Ken had cultivated.

"Everybody was a tough guy and I was a young kid," Frank said in an interview for *Shooters*.[115] "It was tough. It was wild. I'm surprised I made it, because it wasn't a welcoming atmosphere where they wanted you to be successful. It was certainly not that...Ken was the king of the cavemen and we were all underneath him. We learned that way."

Although he had no real fighting experience, Frank was strong and smart and a natural. He took instruction well and had clear potential. Plus, there was no time to waste. Pancrase desperately needed fighters who, at the very least, looked the part. At a chiseled 185-pounds, Frank had the looks to make it. Everything else he could learn on the fly— and he was picking it up faster than anyone ever had.

"No one had ever learned as quickly as Frank did," Bob Shamrock said. "He was one of the best fighters in the Lion's Den after just a few

---

[115] My book *Shooters: The Toughest Men in Pro Wrestling* covers the proto-MMA scene in Japan fairly thoroughly, provide a broader overview of this fascinating time.

months but we were worried he didn't have the temperament for UFC. Ken decided to send him to Japan first so he could continue to learn. That's what we did with the more technical fighters and it worked well. The scrappier guys were pushed towards UFC instead."

Frank was shipped off to the same Yokohama dojo where Ken had learned the finer points of the Pancrase system, bowing to the same picture of Karl Gotch each morning and counting aloud to the same series of three hundred squats. Little changed in the dojo except the faces. Funaki, much like he had been for Ken, was quickly a lifeline for Frank, who wrote glowingly about him in *Uncaged*:

> He was, to me, the ideal of the martial artist, a charismatic leader with a brotherly tone. When teaching, Ken had been like an animal. Funaki was gentler. Ken would show you an armbar and almost break your arm doing it. Funaki would show you a new move and say, "This uses less energy" or "This will scare your opponent" or "This will make you confident." No one had talked to me like that. No one ever criticized me by saying, "That works but this works better."

While most fighters had to earn their way into the tournament, the Shamrock name and Ken's seal of approval went a long way. He made his debut in a first round match against Rutten, who had built up a 6-2 record and was quickly earning a reputation as a very dangerous man.

"Suzuki was the guy who told me how to beat Bas Rutten in my first fight. He said 'Bas knows nothing about wrestling.' And I said 'But I know nothing about wrestling either,'" Frank said. "But he said, 'You've trained with Ken, you at least know how to take someone down.' And he was right. I didn't know how to strike or do much of anything. But I knew how to take people down."

Frank was welcomed to the world of professional prize fighting with a snapping front kick to the nose but more than held his own, particularly on the mat where Rutten was still very much a work in progress.

"Frank was a cool guy," Rutten remembers. "We were talking to each other the whole time. When he had something close I would say 'nice attempt.' And he would do the same thing the other way around."

After 10 minutes, Frank was awarded a decision and a succinct "good job" from Ken. That was all it took for a star to be born in Tokyo. Ken was the next man up for the team, submitting Alex Cook in just over a minute.[116]

"Because the sport was so young, there weren't a lot of people who had everything they needed to compete," Shamrock says. "Knees in the clinch, kicks, punches to the body, grappling. There weren't many fighters educated in all these areas. So, going into it, I didn't think there was anyone who could challenge me besides the Japanese. I was pretty confident."

Eventually all four of the Lion's Den fighters advanced out of the first round, meaning half the quarter-finals consisted of the American contingent, one that was quickly establishing itself as the most formidable team in martial arts.

Their reward was another bout that same night. This time out, only Ken emerged unscathed. His opponent was Maurice Smith, a kickboxer who was legendary enough to earn a namedrop in the John Cusack film *Say Anything*[117], but experienced enough to realize how dangerous this new game could be.

"Maurice, before the fight, comes up to me and says 'Don't hurt me.' This was a world class kickboxer, one of the most bad ass standup fighters on the planet," Shamrock says. "I said 'if I get you down, I'm going to give you every opportunity to tap or get the ropes. I'm not going to just crank it.' He said 'fair enough.' And I said 'if you get me hurt, you better give me a chance to go down. Don't kick me in the face when I'm on the ground.'

"We were just kidding, but part of it was serious. I didn't want to break anything on him. I was going to give him time. It doesn't mean you have to quit. But I will give you the opportunity to tap. But once that opportunity passes, I will turn it. He appreciated that."

The imagined scenario actually transpired in the fight. Shamrock would shoot from ridiculously long distances to secure a takedown, then Smith would scramble to the ropes at the first sign of trouble. At one point Shamrock secured a heel hook, the same hold he'd used to

---

[116] Cook's corner encouraged him to move into the guard, saying "he's not going to do anything to you there." Seconds later, Shamrock was securing a heel hook and the win.

[117] Kickboxing was not, in fact, the sport of the future. But MMA was. They almost nailed it.

put multiple fighters out of action for months at a time. But instead of cranking it, he was true to his word—he allowed Smith to go to the ropes instead.

"He did try to fight out of it. I'll give him that," Shamrock says. "But once it got painful, he went for the rope escape and I didn't hurt him. After that, we became friends."

Smith, a 16-year veteran of the kickboxing scene, was intrigued by the tales of Shamrock's gym. Perhaps appalled might be a more apt description, especially after learning that the Lion's Den fighters sparred without any real protective equipment at all.

"He's all, 'What the hell are you talking about? No, dude, no! You gotta wear gear.' So we went out and got boxing gloves and then shin pads and headgear and everything," Bessac says. "When we first started we didn't know anything, so we went and got Kempo Gloves because Bruce Lee used them in *Return of the Dragon*. And we got the headgear that had metal face masks on them that were meant for fencing or something. But I was smashing in the metal face mask and it was tearing up people's faces, so we stopped using those. Maurice schooled us about using shin pads and head gear and it got easier on people."

White and DeLucia fell quickly, to Funaki and Suzuki respectively, but Frank had a great showing against Yamada, pushing the more experienced fighter to his limit before eventually conceding to a leg lock. But the younger Shamrock made his mark on the tournament with a succession of heel hook and toehold attempts that left Yamada doing his best to hide an injury going into day two and his semi-final match with Suzuki.

"I saw broken blood vessels," Yamada said. "The foot stiffened up. 'Oh no,' I thought. I couldn't move at all. I couldn't go in with a low kick. Well, we're both good at grappling, I thought, so it will have to be a battle on the ground...It was a tough situation, for both of us."

Suzuki too was injured, breaking his rib in his opening match with Hume. He'd wanted to keep it a secret, but he and Yamada were in the same locker room and he'd overheard Suzuki talking with the doctor. He considered dropping out of the tournament but was pressured by Pancrase executives to continue.

"I couldn't sleep, it hurt so much," Suzuki said. "I was surprised that it hurt so much it prevented me from sleeping. I got someone to go out in Shibuya again and again to buy me ice. I just kept laying it on my chest, constantly. I couldn't even doze. The pain was killing me!

"...I tried not to worry too much about a plan. I'd have to go out there and grab him and finish him somehow when I saw the opportunity. I thought nothing else. When the fight started, the pain kicked in something fierce. A little voice inside of me kept screaming, 'Oww oww oww it hurts it hurts!' It hurt so badly. I remember fighting through that."

Yamada won his fight by armbar after forcing several rope escapes. He passed Funaki in the hallway on his way back from the ring, moments before the Pancrase star's own semifinal match with Shamrock.

"We shook hands," Funaki said. "I thought that was that, but when he went into the back, he called over his shoulder, 'Funaki-san, I'll be waiting for you in the finals.' I heard his words and then it sunk in. After fighting Shamrock, I'll have Yamada waiting for me. This will be rough."

The upset was a big deal, both for Suzuki and the promotion. Shamrock believes they intended for the two to meet in the finals.[118] He was already planning to tell them to shove it when they asked him to take another loss, which he suspected they would.

"I wouldn't have done it. There was no way I was doing that again. That was going to be real," Shamrock says. "They knew there was no way I was putting him over. No way. And I believe that the only shot they had to capture the championship was Funaki beating me in the semi-finals. There's a lot of scenarios working, but when Suzuki lost, it felt like they were scrambling around shocked. There was a lot of confusion afterwards. I felt it."

Now, with his compatriot out of the mix, the pressure was firmly on Funaki's shoulders to win. Yamada had just joined the promotion in May after a mixed career in the Shooto[119] promotion. Him defeating

---

[118] "I believe that Yamada was supposed to put Suzuki over and chose not to," Shamrock says. "That's why they were shocked. Yamada was better than Suzuki and everybody knew it."

[119] Shooto was the first true mixed martial arts promotion in Japan. Founded by the original Tiger Mask, Satoru Sayama, it had focused a lot of energy and

Pancrase's top fighters would be a blow, not just to the individual athletes, but to their claim of supremacy.

"I stumbled out to the ring for my next match," Funaki says. "I saw Shamrock standing before me, his eyes staring down at the ground. And then we were fighting, somehow it felt like we were both forcing ourselves through the motions of punching and kicking, just trying to get through the fight.

"However, an MMA fighter has to fight despite that. I have to dispose of those feelings by myself. So I forced myself to fight Shamrock. But in that state of mind, I lost...I entered a state of gloominess. I wasn't sure how to pull myself out of it. I felt like I was stumbling around in a daze like a sleepwalker."

It was a competitive fight, but never one in which Shamrock looked threatened. He finished his former teacher in less than six minutes with an arm triangle, the same hold he used to win their first bout at the inaugural Pancrase show the previous year.

While Funaki pondered his various problems, both as an athlete and a promoter who had seen his two biggest drawing cards eliminated in the semi-finals, Shamrock continued forward towards glory. Now a single fight was all that remained before he could be crowned "King of Pancrase." But a year's worth of bumps, bruises and injuries suddenly weighed very heavy on him. The Yamada fight would be his twelfth of the year—and he was feeling each one.

"Funaki came to me and said 'You have to win this.' I know they didn't want a gaijin winning the first Pancrase title, but because Yamada was from Shooto and he'd just joined the organization, they needed me to win," Shamrock says. "He wasn't solid there yet. If he won the belt and went back to Shooto, there's a problem.

"I was like 'dude, I have a bad shoulder and bad knee. I'll do what I can. I'm banged up.' I felt a lot of pressure to win. In my mind going into it, I was concerned. I didn't think he could tap me out, but I didn't know if I'd be able to perform at a high enough level to win the fight."

Shamrock wore an angry look on his face as the referee checked his

---

attention on creating an athletic architecture for the new sport and not done much to garner mainstream attention or financial success.

boots before the bell rang to commence activities. Across the way, Yamada looked non-plussed. But a thousand thoughts were racing through his head as he prepared for the biggest fight of his career. He'd twice fought for middleweight glory in Shooto in much smaller gyms in front of modest crowds. There were 11,500 fans in the building to see *this* bout against a foreigner with seemingly every advantage.

"I was so happy and also terrified," Yamada said. "'He's like a demon,' I thought. That was my first impression.

"...In more ways than one, I felt my potential at its highest in a manner of speaking. I was at the top of my game... He was durable, physically powerful, and had a lot of fighting experience, so he probably wouldn't have many holes in his game. But this fight was about finding that hole in the other's game. Whoever found an opening first would win.

"To me this meant more than something to excite the fans. It was a fight for myself in which I wanted to shine. To be honest, I didn't think about the audience and entertaining them, in regards to this fight and this tournament."

For 30 minutes, Shamrock and Yamada repeated the same pattern. The Japanese fighter would get taken down by the larger American, then scramble for submissions while Shamrock mostly defended carefully, wary of his opponent's clever entries and slick attempts as he made Yamada carry his weight for much of the bout.

"He was unpredictable. That's why, instead of being the aggressor like I always was, I decided I was going to let him take charge and make the mistakes. I wasn't able to move in and out of submissions like I usually could because my knee[120] was really bothering me. But I was on top."

After 30 minutes, neither fighter had made a mistake. It was a strategic bout but never boring, mostly due to Yamada's constant activity on the mat. He refused to concede Shamrock's domination there and never gave up hope that he might pull out a submission win.

"This is leaving a bad impression, I knew," Yamada said. "My opponent was trying to pin my shoulders to the mat. I felt like I might be able to escape, using angles, or speed, or timing. What I had that Shamrock didn't was technique. What he had that I didn't was

---

[120] His partially torn meniscus was still troubling him. With a show scheduled every month, Pancrase fighters never had an opportunity to rest and recuperate.

power. We both had stamina."

A desperation dropkick by Yamada in the final minute grazed Shamrock's face but did no lasting harm. The fight ended much like it was contested throughout—with Shamrock in control on top. With no knockdowns and no rope escapes to determine the outcome, the first King of Pancrase was crowned by a panel of judges. The winner wasn't especially clear. Yamada had the crisper striking game, but every time Shamrock landed, he would knock his foe back a step.[121] On the mat, Yamada moved well but could never quite shake his persistent opponent.

"I was the cornerman for the fighter I lost to, Shamrock, and shouted out advice," Funaki said. "After the fight ended with Shamrock winning and I saw the belt strapped around Shamrock's waist, I thought, 'Man, this guy is pretty awesome. If I could just fight him one more time, I'd figure out how he fights and win.' He fought so hard. I thought, 'Those who fight hard end up getting the belt. Those who don't give it their all, lose.'

"I helped create Pancrase and was thrilled about it. Then a year later, I thought, 'It's really hard to run Pancrase!' I hadn't realized how much trouble it would be to keep the organization alive. Despite me bringing Pancrase to life, I had to deal with a lot of negative things surrounding it. 'I gave birth to a monster,' I thought."

As the announcer read his name, Shamrock looked on in disbelief, even asking "Me?" at one point before leaping into the air in a combination of joy and relief. He'd declared himself the top fighter on the Japanese circuit going back to UFC 1. Now, finally, he could back that claim up.

Shamrock had fought 12 times in 1994 for a total of 95:29.[122] On top of that, he was launching a fight team, training a new crop of fighters and responsible for main eventing promotions in two countries.

"After I won, I was ecstatic," Shamrock says. "Because going into it, I knew it was going to be a tough night. I had to pull out all the stops to beat this guy the way I was feeling. I knew I had fought the fight of my life, even though it wasn't action packed.

"That year took a toll on me. I knew I was at the forefront of doing

---

[121] "His kicks sucked, but if they landed, I felt them," Yamada said. "...When his low kick landed, 'wham!' I'd be propelled backwards."

[122] That's the equivalent of four five-round title fights in the contemporary UFC, only without any rest between fights.

something great. This was what I had been doing for years and it was important to me to capture the belt in Japan. I went to this organization to fight for real. And there I was, standing on top of the world as the best fighter on the planet."

On the same weekend Shamrock was writing his name into Pancrase history, Gracie won a tournament of his own at UFC 4 in Tulsa, Oklahoma. Recovering smartly from the UFC 3 debacle, he beat White Tiger Kenpo Karate specialist Keith Hackney[123] in the semi-finals, then spent more than 15 minutes underneath American wrestler Dan Severn before finally securing a triangle choke and the tournament championship. It was one of the most dramatic finishes the young sport had ever seen and re-established Gracie as the most compelling fighter in all of no-holds-barred fighting.

While Gracie came out of the event looking like roses, the UFC was taking a beating from outside forces. Gracie's win over Severn had sent the broadcast beyond the limits set by pay-per-view providers. Campbell McLaren made the call to let them fight to a finish rather than declare a draw and it was an expensive one. Many viewers had paid $19.95 for the pleasure of watching the tournament, only to have the show cut off before a winner was determined. Depending on their cable system, they were either offered a refund, half of their money back or an opportunity to watch a replay with the complete fight. It ended up costing the promotion close to $100,000 in total refunds.

The more important battle saw its first salvo launched in Oklahoma when Arizona Senator John McCain looked to shut the event down. Dave Meltzer, one of the first to regularly cover the UFC as part of a beat and not just a one-off feature, had the details in the Wrestling Observer:

> U.S. Senator John McCain, an Arizona Republican, made a lot of noise in the week prior to the event

---

[123] Hackney showed fleet feet, strong striking and a baseline level of skill on the ground. Of course, no one remembers that because his two highlights were dropping the enormous Emanuel Yarborough with an open-hand slap and punching Kimo's manager Joe Son repeatedly in the testicles.

trying to get the event nixed. Tulsa County officials, which at first had approved the event, spent the last week trying to cancel it due to both political and media pressure on them for agreeing to a bare-knuckle almost anything goes fight. However, since the promoters had a signed contract months earlier, the officials were unable to break the contract.

The Oklahoma boxing commission, which goes into effect on 1/1, claimed they would have shut the event down but it was taking place two weeks before they were empowered. The district attorney of Oklahoma, after being contacted by representatives of McCain, then attempted to find a bylaw allowing them to shut down the event and came up empty-handed.

McCain also attempted to get Viewers Choice, Request and the cable industry to not broadcast the event, thereby shutting it down in another form. Because of the strong advance buys on PPV, that avenue didn't work, although talk that somehow the event may not take place continued as late as the day of the event. All the competitors were encouraged to play down the brutality in pre and post show media interviews, which originally was one of the main selling points of the prior shows.

While UFC prepared for what would become the fight of its life, Shamrock had his own problems in Japan. For the first time, there was significant pushback from Pancrase about him working for UFC while representing their company as champion. It's not just that they didn't want him to lose a bout in another promotion—they also felt they needed the champion to help draw an audience in a crowded Japanese combat sports marketplace.

The tension played out in the ring, where Shamrock destroyed the knee of newcomer Leon Dijk, a student of Bas Rutten's, with a vicious inside heel hook. The young fighter would miss six months of action while recovering. That was terrible for him, of course, but perfect for the storyline Pancrase had in mind next.

Immediately before he was seen on camera coaching Dijk against the new champion, Rutten had flattened Yamada, the man who had just pushed Shamrock to the limit the previous month, in just 65 seconds. He would be next in line for a title shot, one the promotion hoped desperately he would win. To Pancrase, that was the perfect solution. Shamrock could go and fight Gracie again for UFC and Rutten could take over as the promotion's top foreign fighter. There was only one problem—this time Shamrock wasn't ready to do business.

"Ken was like 'No way, I'm not losing to Bas.' Bas[124] and Ken got along fine," Bessac said. "But that was a no go."

With the easy way out the window, Funaki took his chances with the hard way, bringing Rutten in to train him personally for the impending battle. After all, who knew Shamrock better than the man who had taught him for years, fought with him tooth-and-nail and even cornered him for his most important fights?

"They worked with him for quite some time," Shamrock says. "I don't think they realized, when I fought him the first time, that I could have submitted him any time I wanted. I think they thought I had a hard time with him.

"They believed he would beat me and carry the torch after that. And they could send me away to UFC. Well, when we fought, I took him right down and submitted him. They were pretty much in shock. I don't think they realized how good I was getting. Because they never really let me go full speed."

The entire fight lasted just 1:01 and ended with one of the most beautiful sequences in MMA history, a top-down camera positioned on the ceiling of the Yokohama Cultural Gymnasium catching Shamrock elegantly swinging his leg around Rutten's head en route to a kneebar that forced a submission.

"[Funaki] was a great guy," Rutten said. "And he tried to help me with my fight with Ken. But when he tried to show me how to defend the kneebar, he should have told me 'Listen, don't let him step over your hip.' There are many ways to get in the right position for it. But Funaki only showed me one way to defend. And we worked on it for three weeks. Then when I fought Ken Shamrock he threw his leg over my head. He did it a different way and I thought 'Hmm.'"

The win sent Shamrock into UFC 5 on April 7, 1995, as the King of Pancrase, putting the company's reputation on the line against a man

---

[124] Ken confirmed this story: "The second time I fought Bas, they wanted me to put him over. I said no."

who had previously beaten him and just submitted UWFi wrestler Dan Severn in a classic bout that was pushed as a big deal in the Japanese press. That promotion hadn't wanted Severn to compete in UFC, but his performance saw him emerge as a bigger star than ever, even in defeat. Though Pancrase had tried their best to take the title from Shamrock, and even though they had an event the very next day in Nagoya he would have to miss, they begrudgingly allowed Shamrock to fight for the third time in the Octagon. But cracks were beginning to form in their relationship.

"I was kind of moving away from Pancrase, but I had so many fighters there and I didn't want to muddy the waters and mess it up for them," Shamrock says. "So I tried to bow out by moving towards the UFC, because I felt like I had a future there. I wanted to test myself in a different way. It would have been easy to stay there. I was a champion there, already a legend. A lot of people would have been content with that. Me, that just wasn't who I was. I was 31 years old and I wanted to test myself. So I took what I believe was a step up, from the Pancrase world to the no-holds-barred world and the UFC.

"It's like an infection. If you don't treat it, it keeps getting worse and worse. Well, we never talked about it. We never tried to fix the problems. They felt that me fighting in the UFC was hurting their organization. And when I wouldn't leave, it kept getting worse and worse. I made it clear to them, 'I'm not your puppet. I work for you, and in my contract, I'm allowed to do anything as long as it isn't in Japan.' My contract stated that, and they didn't like it. But I went ahead and did what I thought was the best for me."

UFC 5 was back in Charlotte, home of Shamrock's disappointing UFC 3 experience , though this time upgraded to the larger Independence Arena. There was some discussion about running an immediate rematch between Severn and Gracie and putting Shamrock back through the tournament grind for a shot at the winner. When Shamrock balked, and Severn agreed to do another tournament in exchange for a guaranteed title shot if he won, SEG decided to once again roll the dice on Shamrock and Gracie.

"Bob Meyrowitz, who was the head of the company, was very anxious to do that fight because to him it looked like a boxing matchup," Campbell McLaren said. "It was a guy that you knew with credentials against the current champion. It was programmable.

"We had the Gracies, but we needed a foil. And that was Ken Shamrock. A lot of the stories that were there were real and weren't some marketing guys idea. Ken Shamrock was a street kid from a very rough and tumble background. And the Gracies, even though it's a fighting family, are all about family. You had Ken who was kind of a street orphan versus this whole clan and it was pretty compelling stuff. He was the gunslinger, the cold professional, and the Gracies were kind of pure."

The metaphor played out during the ring walks—Gracie came out in the "Gracie train," his entire fighting family walking with him in step. Shamrock, with the rest of the Lion's Den in Japan for their own fights the next day, was alone except his adopted father Bob. When the doors closed, of course, both men would be left to their own devices. Moral support could only go so far.

Still wary of Gracie's submission credentials, especially after his come-from-behind win over Severn and Shamrock's own close calls against Yamada, Shamrock and the Den devised a cautious gameplay that minimized risk to the point it was almost non-existent.

"My strategy was to go in, not over-pursue, control and beat the body. Stay in his guard and wear him down," Shamrock says. "I didn't care if it took two or three hours. I was going to wear him down until he couldn't keep his legs up anymore. And then I'm going to have my way with him."

While Severn had established himself as one of the sport's leading stars[125] in just a single appearance thanks to his successful showing at UFC 4, the event was built around Ken and Royce, a rematch fans had been craving for almost two years at this point. The poster resembled the kind you would see advertising a boxing match—dominated by images of Gracie and Shamrock staring into each other's eyes, UFC champion against the "World Shootfighting" champion.

"They talked so much about this fight being the little guy against the big guy," Bob Shamrock said. "They were trying to make it seem like there was a huge weight difference between the two. There wasn't. By

---

[125] The loss had even benefited his wrestling career. Not only would he get a better push in the UWFi, he won the NWA World Championship against Chris Candido a month before the show and would carry the pro wrestling title into the cage for each match.

the second fight Royce weighed 190[126] pounds and Ken was all the way down to 205 pounds."

Controversy reared its head, as it seemed to do before almost every UFC event in these early years, when Shamrock found out just a day before the event that there was a 30-minute time limit for his Superfight with Gracie.

"The only way this guy had a chance of surviving with me was with a time limit," Shamrock says. "I couldn't roll with him and out-position him for submission. That I knew. But I could wear him down and beat on him with my strength and leverage. And they took that away."

Though he blames the Gracie family for this change[127] to this day, it was actually a response to the previous event running over time. For the first time since UFC 1, tournament matches had to fit in a 20-minute window and the Superfight was also bound by time constraints. Going long had cost the UFC money and, just as importantly, credibility with pay-per-view providers, a precious resource with McCain continuing his attack on the event.

"The political pressure associated with no-holds-barred fighting has been absolutely ridiculous," referee John McCarthy said in a contemporary interview with the *New Full Contact*. "You have a bunch of politicians out there who look at us and see an easy target. They feel that they will be politically correct by attacking us. They get their names in the media and show how against "violence" they are. The funny thing is most of the people who come out against us have never even taken the time to watch one of our shows."

The UFC continued to gain steam in the mainstream, for both good and ill. There was a major feature in *Details*, a popular men's magazine, that focused on Shamrock and his compelling backstory. The same week the magazine hit the stands, the promotion was spotlighted on NBC's "Dateline," a popular primetime show with a significant audience that saw SEG boss Meyrowitz caught in several

---

[126] The official UFC tale of the tape listed Gracie at 180 pounds and Shamrock at 205 pounds. Royce was 29 and Shamrock 31 years of age.

[127] "You were always fighting against the odds because the Gracies were trying to maneuver themselves into situations that were best for them," he says. "They weren't trying to make the fights fair. They were there to promote Gracie Jiu Jitsu and themselves. And they did a hell of a job."

lies[128] and McCain make the case against the sport, which he would repeat to North Carolina Governor Jim Hunt in an attempt to get the show cancelled.

Ironically, the problem with UFC 5 was a lack of violence, especially in the not-so-super "Superfight." Clad in tiny black Speedos and black Asics wrestling shoes, Shamrock was true to his word, taking Gracie down and then essentially sitting in his guard for the entire 30 minutes.

"I wouldn't call him a good grappler," Gracie would tell *Hook n' Shoot*'s Jeff Osborne. "He knows how to play the game. That's different. He can grapple against somebody that doesn't know. Once he gets somebody that knows, he's in trouble."

While the jiu jitsu player attempted to use his gi for a variety of chokes or just to hold Shamrock in place, the wrestler had put the year and a half between fights to good use. He understood what Gracie was trying to accomplish and, though perhaps not ready to counter him move-for-move, had the skill level to negate everything his opponent wanted to do.

"All I did was follow his hips," Shamrock says. "Whenever he stopped trying to do submissions, I could feel it. Thats when I would raise up and beat on his body."

While McCarthy was empowered to stop a fight if one of the competitors was in danger, he didn't yet have the authority to break them out of a stalemate. And so the boos rained down, certainly at a greater frequency than the blows Shamrock would only occasionally unleash. It was a battle of tiny blows, Shamrock's short knees to the rear end and headbutts against Gracie's heel kicks to the kidney and light punches and slaps to the side of the head.

"Ken was too cautious," Bob said. "I was yelling at him throughout the fight, even cursing him. I wanted him to be more active. It was a very frustrating fight because he needed to be more aggressive but he had too much respect for Gracie's submissions."

While the announcers tried to sell the snoozer as an epic battle of attrition and a subtle chess match for the ages, McCarthy may have been the only one having fun, as he writes in *Let's Get it On*:

---

[128] In one memorable sequence, Meyrowitz told an NBC reporter that SEG's cameras had caught Teila Tuli's mouthpiece, not his tooth, flying through the air at UFC 1. The next cut was to Tuli himself, confessing it was indeed his tooth that ended up as a souvenir that night.

* * *

I was able to laugh in the middle of it all when Bob Shamrock, Ken's feisty adoptive father, finally grew frustrated with his son's tactics and yelled, "Well, if you're just going to lay there with him, you might as well start kissing him."

The always stoic Royce looked at the elder Shamrock and then at Ken and said, "Please don't do that."

The 30-minute match went 31:06 before matchmaker Art Davie signaled McCarthy to stand them up. Chaos reigned, with the television announcers just as confused as everyone else about what was happening.

"There was no overtime discussed. It was supposed to be a draw," Shamrock says. "Which was a really bad rule. Who comes up with a time limit but no judges? Somebody who is afraid they are going to lose. Then they didn't want it decided that way.

"Rorion Gracie comes out of the crowd. Out of the crowd. And he yells 'five more minutes.' I kid you not. This is completely illegal. But I was good with it. Royce didn't want five more minutes. I was wearing him down and he could feel it."

The most telling moment of the fight came in that final five minute stanza, a hard right hand from Shamrock that immediately created an ugly mouse under Gracie's right eye. Unfortunately for the crowd, just as the action picked up, Gracie immediately shot for a takedown. Shamrock countered with a whizzer, and the two ended the seemingly endless match in much the way they started. There was no official winner[129] and the two men embraced as the crowd mercilessly booed one of the least eventful sporting contests anyone could recall.

"You just got the feeling that his head wasn't right," former UFC President David Isaacs says of Shamrock. "Over and over. We heard the way people talked about what he was doing at the gym, but it didn't always translate to the Octagon. He just couldn't put it into the right gear when he needed to.

"He had so much potential. And don't get me wrong, some of it was

---

[129] The UFC had commissioned Joe Marshall to design a title belt for the first time at a cost of $1650. Since there was no winner, the belt had no home—Art Davie eventually absconded with it and sold the belt to a collector.

reached. But you always felt he could have done more. He could have been the guy. He had the skills, he had the looks, he had the toughness. And we built that up. But the reality is, he did not achieve what he probably should have."

While he was in Nagoya to fight John Renfroe in Pancrase and not present in Charlotte for Shamrock's fight, DeLucia had some sympathy for the pressure his sensei was under.

"The burden on Ken was many fold," DeLucia says. "One of which was his body had already been through the ringer, many times over, from all the years of pro-wrestling...You're looking at the potential of fighting for 30 minutes, straight. That's a lot of conditioning.

"...He also had to carry the banner. He was the guy that had to carry the banner, carry the belt, and, in Japan especially, the pressure that put on him."

His father, once again, was despondent. While the pay-per-view would set a new company record, SEG executives were afraid the boring fight would hurt them long term. Only Shamrock, though he didn't end up with his hand raised, seemed happy by the result.

"It felt like a victory to me," he says. "I considered us to be 1-1 after that. I had been fighting against the odds and they were in control of everything, from the tournament brackets, to the time limit, to what you were going to wear. I was sitting in his wheelhouse. I sat in his guard for 36 minutes and pounded on him. And he's telling me that I didn't want to fight? Well, if I'm sitting in your wheelhouse, what more do you want from me? I was on the ground grappling with you.

"I wanted to be the world's best fighter. Not boxer. Not wrestler. Not karate guy. Fighter. In the whole world. And I was."

CHAPTER NINE

Champion at Last

Shamrock returned to Japan from UFC 5 without a Superfight championship belt around his waist. That would have been the best case scenario. Of course, it could have been much worse. The middle ground was certainly better than nothing—Shamrock and Gracie were plastered all over the Japanese wrestling press[130], with Gracie's swollen, bloody eye telling a clear story that didn't require a single word.

All the same, he'd missed a Pancrase event to participate in the UFC[131] and already had a match scheduled for July with other appearances an almost certainty. There was just no way that he could fully participate in either group as the frontman and champion. Something had to give.

When he arrived in May for his bout with Minoru Suzuki, Pancrase officials shuttled him to the Prince Hotel near Shinagawa train station where they met in a private room at the top of the building on the 39th floor.

---

[130] The fight was the lead story in both Weekly Pro Wrestling and Weekly Gong magazines. Japanese wrestling fans, clearly, had caught UFC fever.

[131] The Pancrase President also missed his own event to watch Shamrock fight, one of busloads of Japanese fight fans who made the trip to watch the Superfight.

"Two executives came in, along with Suzuki and Funaki," Shamrock says. "And they were begging me. 'Suzuki is not feeling good and just had his wisdom teeth pulled. Please, Mr. Shamrock. He win. It's good for us. You beat everyone.'

"He had no problems with it and no shame. He was even selling the toothache. They were trying to give Suzuki a reputation and name. Because he looked good and had some pizzazz to him."

Something about losing to Suzuki felt different than dropping a match to Funaki the previous year had. Not only did he dislike Suzuki personally, they had a fundamental philosophical difference when it came to the martial arts. Suzuki believed the techniques he'd learned from Gotch could win the day against any opponent. Shamrock, who had seen a broad new world of martial arts strategies developing around the world in response to the UFC, disagreed.

"He was too close minded," Shamrock says. "His mentality was that he could wrestle everybody and take them down. Well, he couldn't touch me. He couldn't touch Funaki. Once Takahashi came into his own, he beat the hell out of Suzuki. Eventually they didn't get along. Because Takahashi was of the mindset that you have to grow. If you didn't, the sport was going to pass you by.

"Suzuki would have arguments with Takahashi and others about the striking. He didn't think he needed to learn it. Takahashi and him got in a fight one time about it at a bar. And Takahashi beat the crap out of him."

Shamrock was boiling on the inside at what he thought was an audacious request but remained calm. This, after all, was their company. Like it or not, he'd opened the door by agreeing to make previous concessions. But having had a taste of the pure combat UFC offered, it was hard to take a step backwards into the murky world of Japanese wrestling.

"They asked me to do some things I didn't agree with, exactly the thing I believed we were working against," he says. "But when it happened, I realized where I was at, who I was doing it for, and I did what I thought was the right thing at the time. I made it clear to them, 'I'm not doing it again.' That was it."

The match was quick, as the works often appeared to be in Pancrase, with Suzuki winning with a kneebar in a little over two minutes. Unlike his first fight with Suzuki, it's an aggressive loss for Shamrock. He defended takedowns with an extra dose of physicality and, at one point, secured an armbar and just kind of let it go, presumably to show that he could.

"Nobody entered Pancrase during the time Ken was fighting there that could ever beat Ken," DeLucia says. "Nobody there at that time could touch him. Ken was the only one that they had to ask to lose. Not a single person there could beat him. So if you saw anything else, you didn't see the truth."

It was a dominant performance until the end, including a knee against the ropes that knocked Suzuki for a loop and caused brief panic in the ring.

"I gave him a knee to the head because of what he did in the first fight, when I actually gave him my leg and he yanked on it and hurt me," Shamrock says. "I gave him a receipt for that and I had to hold him down because I'd actually knocked his ass silly. I wanted him to know he wasn't getting away with it this time and if he pulled anything, I was going to kill him.

"I ended up having to hold him there until he came to his senses. I basically put my knee on his belly and asked him 'you alright' until he could answer me. Then we went through the match and he did what he was supposed to do. But I just felt dirty."

Suzuki became the second King of Pancrase, only to quickly drop the belt to Bas Rutten that September.[132] Rutten and Frank Shamrock would become the leading foreigners in the promotion while Ken took a step back and focused on the UFC.

Shamrock and the Lion's Den seemed to acquire stray cats at every UFC event. Guy Mezger, a karate standout from Dallas who had won undercard alternate fights at UFC 4 and again in Charlotte, had hit it off with Bob at UFC 3 and eventually had a chance to connect with Ken.

"When I first met him his knee was all jacked and he had this big ice pack on his knee," Mezger remembers. "Bob introduced us and I sort of asked him some questions. He was real nice but he said, 'Yeah, I'd

---

[132] This was the outcome Pancrase was looking for prior to Shamrock's second fight with Gracie earlier in the year. A week later, Shamrock would fight Oleg Taktarov for the UFC Superfight title and was unavailable for the Pancrase event, highlighting the issue for the Japanese promotion pretty clearly.

love to talk to you but first I want to dance with my wife.' I liked that."

What followed was a career-long partnership that benefited both men immensely. Mezger was able to take advantage of Shamrock's submission knowledge and contacts in Japan, where he became a Pancrase champion, and Ken got access to Mezger's accumulated wisdom from more than 60 karate and kickboxing fights, a stable of new training partners in Dallas and someone who could function more as a peer than a subordinate.

"I had a lot of striking experience and had been a high school All-American wrestler and judo player. That's a lot of experience," Mezger says. "I brought a lot to the table. And one thing about Ken, even though he has very specific ideas about how things should be done, he's always been open for instruction."

DeLucia, who had come from the more structured world of traditional martial arts, welcomed the addition of fighters like Mezger to the Lion's Den family, even though they would likely be competing for the same opportunities and spots.

"Guy had his own, very functional stable of professional martial artists," DeLucia says. "So, between the two, if you put them together, that really was the Lion's Den. We had Frank, Vernon, myself and Scott. For each of us, Guy had a fighter who was an equal. Guy's participation in the Lion's Den brought a whole different dynamic. His participation was more important than people realize."

Maurice Smith was also a presence at the Lion's Den in those days, making good on his promise to teach the striking game to Shamrock and his students. Smith, whose kickboxing career went back to 1980, had been in the ring with legends like Don "The Dragon" Wilson and Peter Aerts. He was the kind of athlete that just didn't exist in the new, wild west world of no-holds-barred fighting. The Lion's Den, collectively, soaked up his knowledge greedily.

"More than anything the level of professionalism he brought into the gym was important," Shamrock says. "You've got to remember, there wasn't anything professional about mixed martial arts. There was nowhere to look to see how things were supposed to be done. Maurice came from professional kickboxing and was seasoned. To have him around, with that kind of background, was tremendous for the guys in the gym. To see what it was to be a professional athlete. To see how he carried himself. It was great to have Maurice entangled with our team and the young guys.

"Being able to rub up against him showed them that this was a business. It's not just about being tough. Yeah, you're going to get all the girls and make a big pay day. All those things you dream about when you're young. But once you do that for a couple of years, you look at it and think 'okay, it's time to grow up.' This is a business and we need to treat it as such."

The UFC was undergoing a facelift of its own—just 12 days after watching Royce go to a decision against Shamrock, Rorion Gracie sold his stake in the UFC to SEG[133]. In some ways it was a declaration of victory. The family had created a global phenomenon and put their own martial system on a tier above the traditional Eastern arts that had become ubiquitous around the world. Reading between the lines, it was also a concession—the days of familial domination were over. Their art, strategies and tactics now belonged to the world.

Royce wouldn't fight again for five years and Rorion, whose vision and drive helped breathe life into the UFC concept, would never again promote a mixed martial arts event. It would be years before Shamrock would have an opportunity at revenge. In the meantime, there was the looming presence of Dan Severn to deal with.

Although never played up on the actual UFC broadcast, among hardcore fans, the two men's pro wrestling connections were of great interest. Not only were they active in competing shoot style promotions in Japan, as Dave Meltzer excitedly pointed out in the *Wrestling Observer*, they were both world champions:

> When was the last time two recognized world champions in pro wrestling met in a legit shoot? 70 years? Maybe 100 years? Suffice to say it was long enough ago that nobody alive could vouch for it ever happening. Certainly there have been double-crosses in world title matches in the old days and non-cooperation, but two people going in without a predetermined finish?
>
> It will take place on 7/14. UFC has Ken Wayne Shamrock (Pancrase) vs. Dan Severn (NWA) in its superfight from Casper, WY.

Severn had burst onto the UFC scene with his standout performance

---

[133] This wasn't widely known at the time. The official story for Royce missing UFC 6 was that he was on his honeymoon.

against Gracie at UFC 4. No one, including Shamrock, had managed to give Royce so much trouble—and Severn did it with almost no training and very real concerns about whether or not participating in this new sport was moral or ethical.

"I struggled with my conscience more than I did with my opponent," Severn said. "Even when I did throw strikes, you can see it's half-heartedly. Yes, I tapped out. But did I lose to another man? Or did I have to tap because I was unwilling to do what I needed to do in order to win? That fight still haunts me, even today."

Some UFC executives privately agreed with Severn's self assessment. In some ways, he was a precursor to today's UFC fighter, a former collegiate wrestler who had the tools to compete in this new sport but didn't have the kind of natural aggression that drove so many of the UFC's early participants.

"A lot of the early fighters were tough guys who fought a lot outside the cage. Like Ken. And he would tell you that about himself," former UFC President David Isaacs says. "He was absolutely game and he meant business. Ken was very intense and you knew he was a guy who fought regularly and enjoyed it. Dan Severn was the exact opposite. I would bet Dan has never been in a fist fight in his adult life outside of competition. Dan is not that kind of guy."

If he wasn't that kind of guy, Severn was at least smart enough to pretend he was, making "the Beast" persona his new calling card, pulling extravagant faces after each win. Whether he was trying to convince the audience or himself is a question only he could truly answer. But by the next event, Severn was at least able to do what needed to be done without compunction, wrecking Oleg Taktarov's face en route to winning the UFC 5 tournament.

With that win under his belt Severn, it seemed, wasn't especially thrilled to be facing off with Shamrock instead of confronting Gracie in a rematch of their UFC 4 classic.

"To me a Superfight should pit a champion against another champion," Severn said. "And Ken Shamrock had never been a champion in the UFC. He'd never even been a finalist."

In his book, *The Realest Guy in the Room*, he went even further, not just disparaging Shamrock's accomplishments, but calling them into question:

> Just because UFC had some 'roiled up freak who looked good in a pair of trunks, they thought they

had something marketable. They were impressed by Ken because he had the body of a chemically-enhanced athlete, which he was.

The fact that Ken had been the King of Pancrase in Japan didn't mean anything to me, because everyone in Japanese wrestling circles knew what the deal was with Pancrase; Pancrase's fights were fake.

In his book, Severn further claims he took Shamrock lightly, working a pro wrestling match with Tajiri just two days before flying to Wyoming for their UFC 6 showdown. In reality, it appears he actually took a full three weeks off prior to his fight and the Tajiri bout he mentioned actually occurred the previous month.

Shamrock, too, was fresh and ready for the bout, having skipped Pancrase's June event in favor of training for Severn. He and his team had identified a weakness in Severn's game and had drilled relentlessly to take advantage of it.

"Ken and I went out to Wyoming ten days early to get used to the altitude," Bessac says. "I was training exclusively with Ken to beat Dan Severn. I would do exactly what Dan Severn did when he shot in and that's why Ken damn near popped his head off. Dan did just exactly what we expected him to do."

Before the fight, things nearly got out of hand between the two competitors. Not only was there an unflattering flyer disparaging Shamrock floating around the fighter hotel that had Ken's blood up but Severn actually got up and walked out of the press conference while he was speaking.

"He walked out during the press conference because no one was asking him any questions," Shamrock says. "He didn't seem to understand that was because he wasn't very good at engaging with the media. He'd have one word answers to questions. He was just really flat with no personality[134], so they were more interested in what I had to say."

That left Shamrock to trade banter with Severn's matronly pro wrestling manager Phyllis Lee.

"I was just going to beat him," Shamrock told Lee. "Now I'm going

---

[134] Severn may not have been a dynamic interview, but his incredible mustache did a lot of his talking for him.

to hurt him."

Before the fight, Lee had looked to secure every advantage for her client, even reaching out discretely to some Lion's Den fighters to see if anyone would be willing to jump ship.

"She tried to get me before Ken and Dan had their fight," White says. "I think she wanted me to give her and Dan some of Ken's secrets for when they fought. I was like, 'man, please.'

"He was stronger than Dan, hanging out with bodybuilders. We didn't have the same size or strength so he made us get stronger so it would be more realistic and he brought a bunch of bodybuilders in to help us."

Shamrock too had put on significant weight before the fight, topping out at 220 pounds in an attempt to be able to match Severn strength for strength in the clinch. While he was upset that Severn had accused him of steroid use, the truth was, they had been part of his life since high school. Bob Shamrock was a bit of an amateur authority and Ken surrounded himself with strong men and medical experts[135].

"You can't be on all the time," he says. "You just can't. It will just tear you down. Cycles are key. People talk about it, but most people, once they go on, they never come off. They've got this ego thing when their shirt doesn't fit quite as snug anymore. It's because they don't train as hard. If you go in there and you train hard, even when you're not on something, you're going to do fine. You may not feel like it, because it messes with you mentally. But you're good.

"Working with a doctor was key, because even when I wasn't on anything, they would give me medicine to push my testosterone levels back into the normal range. So I don't need to always be on something and can still train hard and don't lose that much size."

To Shamrock, this bout was very different than his first Superfight. With Gracie he had no qualms about admitting to himself that he could lose if he didn't perform perfectly. He had learned the hard way that Gracie jiu jitsu warranted that kind of respect. With Severn, he just couldn't see how he could fall short.

"People talked about how he was favored," Shamrock says. "But in my mind I just thought 'how's he going to beat me?' Is he going to take me down? And I'm going to lay there and let him beat on me?

"I had submission skills. I was stronger than he was. I'm a decent

---

[135] While Shamrock is coy about the specifics of his steroid use, those in this circle believe he was using heavily in the lead up to this fight.

wrestler—not as good as he is, but my submission skills are a lot more valuable and better than his. So I'm thinking to myself 'how is this guy going to beat me?'"

Acclimated, ready and strong, Shamrock felt confident enough to both wear purple Speedos into the Octagon and to spend some time at play in the days before the fight.

"Ken wasn't answering his phone for two days," Frank Shamrock remembers. "So (Tina) was flying out a day early. We get the call and are like 'oh, shit!' There was some stripper chick that Ken picked up at the night club the night before and we were fucking lowering her out the window while one of the boys was rushing to the front to distract Tina."

While the Lion's Den was able to remove the other woman from the room, the detritus left over from a night of passion was harder to hide.

"Tina came and knocked on the door and Ken wouldn't let her in because he had no clothes on," Bessac says. "Then, when she walked in the door there was a pink gym bag laying on the floor. She was like, 'Who the fuck's bag is that?' And he was like, 'Oh, that's my bag.'

"There was a lot of that and I heard all about it because Tina and my wife Simone were friends. We would get sick of it, because Tina would call our house at like six in the morning, drinking Tequila and being like, 'I just caught Ken cheating again.' It got really out of control."

The interpersonal drama didn't appear to impact Shamrock in the ring. Introduced as the Pancrase champion despite the Suzuki loss, he came to the cage in a beautiful purple Pancrase robe to go along with his trunks, with Bob, his brother Frank, mentor Funaki and leg lock specialist Gokor Chivichyan by his side.

He outwrestled Severn early, shooting for a takedown of his own and then lowering his base as the two jockeyed for position. Severn's 40-pound weight advantage seemed immaterial. When he shot in for his predictable single-leg, Ken went for the kill—and missed.

Cursing himself, he backed up to the fence, wary of being in open space with a wrestler of Severn's caliber. He hoped that Severn hadn't noticed he was being set up for a guillotine choke and would be foolish enough to try it again. In a game where a single mistake could be deadly, Shamrock was hoping one of the best in the world would make two in a row.

"I wanted him to come after me, like he'd done in all his other fights," Shamrock says. "That was the gameplan, to get him to shoot. Because he kept his head down and he did it every time.

"It was actually a shocker that he did it again. After I had come so close to getting it, he did it *again*. I thought I had missed my shot."

Gifted a second chance, this time Shamrock didn't miss. He grabbed a perfect guillotine, leaving the supposed sportsman little choice but the kind of desperation punch to the family jewels you'd expect from a street fighter like Tank Abbott, not a former Olympic hopeful like Severn.

"He hit me right in the nuts," Shamrock says. "That was his last punch though, because he was going out. The choke was in good and I've got big biceps so I cut off his oxygen."

Severn dropped to his butt and tapped out. After John McCarthy helped the two men separate, they embraced and shook hands, the bad blood gone, at least for a few months.

"I didn't mean any disrespect," Severn told him.

"No worries, brother," Shamrock responded.

It was easy to be magnanimous. After ending each of his three previous Octagon nights in disappointment, the fourth time was finally the charm. Ken Shamrock was UFC Superfight champion at last.

Shamrock's continued success kept prospective fighters migrating from all around the country to the Lion's Den, to learn from the master himself.

"When Ken and Royce fought at UFC 5, I was over at Pete Williams' house. We watched that fight. That night, I decided Ken was my hero," Jerry Bohlander remembers. "I called the gym and talked to Bob, who encouraged me to come down to Lodi for a class. Once I found out Ken was having classes, I said, 'Well, shit. I got to go do it.'

"I don't want to call it a primitive training facility, but we had basically like a body shop, if you were to walk into a body shop for a car. Back in the day, it wasn't some nice, dojo-type mat where it absorbs all the impact. It was just some frigging carpet padding over the concrete with a canvas over it and a ring around it."

It was a different time, before the internet had taken off, so many of them found the gym in the Yellow Pages. Either that or the persistent and brave would track down the Shamrock entourage at a UFC event. The first person they talked to, more often than not, was Bob Shamrock.

"Bob was unbelievable and was without question the reason why I got the invite to tryout—and why I pursued a spot on the team," former Lion's Den young boy Matt Rocca says. "He was an incredibly giving man and had a take no BS attitude when it came to discipline.

"Whether that was dealing with (Ken's young kids) Ryan, Connor and Sean, or even the fighters living with him. He was respected and loved by all the guys. Bob was a huge car guy and had a bunch of classic cars. Back then he used to drive an old restored Rolls Royce."

While Bob's comforting presence served as a gateway to the gym, once there, a prospective fighter would come nose-to-nose with the unsmiling faces of the Lion's Den fighters. Their goal wasn't strictly to locate potential talent. Because of the way the gym operated, with Ken providing his fighters room and board in exchange for a 15 percent share of their fight purses, the tryout was more about eliminating people from consideration than finding them.

"They would work you until you thought you were dying," Lion's Den fighter Pete Williams says. "There were times we were just so exhausted and that's what the trial was about. It doesn't test your martial ability. Ken could care less about that. It was more like, "Are you gonna quit?" It's sucking beyond suck and it's just nuts. Are you gonna stand up or are you just gonna fucking lay there? That was his litmus test of your character."

Part Marine boot camp, with the Lion's Den fighters serving as particularly ripped Drill Instructors, part gang initiation, it was designed, first and foremost to identify toughness. That, above all else, was what Ken saw as the defining attribute of the prototypical Lion's Den fighter.

"You're talking about individuals with a very different mentality than most people. It was like back in the gladiator days," Shamrock says. "That didn't exist anymore, but there were still the kind of people out there with that machismo. They were still in the world, but there was no way for them to express it unless they could run a 4.4 forty yard dash and strap on a football helmet. In boxing, you needed high level coordination and speed. This was an opportunity for people who were gladiators at heart. There was finally a place for you again."

The tryout would begin outside, whether in the blazing heat or winter chill, with an insane workout featuring hundreds of squats, pushups, stair runs, and burpees, Lion's Den fighters right there in your face if you began to flag. This eliminated many, who eagerly came all the way to Lodi, California, before building a baseline level of fitness. Then it's back to the gym to face a professional fighter in the ring at the Lion's Den.

"The initiations that happened in the dojo in the first couple years were guys basically getting Rodney King beat downs, " DeLucia says. "If you did that today, people would be going to jail, you know? That kind of thing doesn't exist anymore and rightfully so.

"The first time I met Tra Telligman I said, 'Wow, what happened to your chest?[136]' Without missing a beat, straightest face he could put on, he goes, 'When Ken initiated me he got me down on the mat, and he stomped my chest.' And as soon as he said it, I didn't miss a beat, 'That motherfucker,' like I was pissed off. They all bust out laughing. But they were laughing more because it was easy to believe."

While Ken stepped back from this part of the process, fearing potential liability and lawsuits, his students happily filled the void, twisting limbs and applying chokes with aplomb.

"His motto was 'win or you die trying.' And it was a literal thing," Lion's Den fighter Mikey Burnett said. "I'd never been choked unconscious. And the first day I was there, I got choked unconscious twice. I thought he was going to have to call home and tell them he'd killed me."

Making it through the tryouts was just the beginning of a fighter's journey. From there, you officially became a "young boy," first living in the pool house at Ken's ranch in Clements, California, or later at Bob's house when his latest Boy's home shutdown. Based on the Japanese system, the young boys were in charge of cooking, cleaning and every other menial task imaginable.

"Most guys didn't stay. I was a young boy for about a year and a half," Burnett said. "They had tryouts every three or four months and I'd be really happy thinking I wouldn't have to do this shit

---

[136] Telligman lost his right pectoral muscle in a car accident as a baby.

anymore. But then we'd get these new fighters in and the guys would just torture them.

"If you lived in the house, it was open game. You knew it was going to be hell, at least until you proved your worth. Until you got into that clique with Jerry, Pete, and Frank, life was not good."

The toughest part of living in the house was the constant threat of being choked unconscious when you least expected it. Ostensibly to develop the instinctive responses required to defend a rear naked choke in a fight, it turned into little more than hazing. Eventually, fighters established a rule that you couldn't choke someone out more than three times a day—at the house.

"That's how guys got good at choke defense," Rocca says. "Guys would randomly throw chokes on you. And if you didn't defend it, you went to sleep. Period. To this day, if someone touches me from behind, I tuck my neck and raise my shoulders."

There was a low key sense of danger lingering at all times. Some people were built to handle it. Others eventually cracked under the unrelenting pressure, sometimes slinking out in the middle of the night never to be seen again. The Lion's Den was out in Napa wine country and Burnett would look at the white crosses holding up grapevines and imagine they were grave markers for all the departed young boys he'd known.

"Frankie choked somebody out that was on the phone," he remembered. "And they had a BB gun out pointing it at the kid when he woke up. The guy was out of his mind when he woke up and obviously he left shortly after that.

"They'd decide to leave and I'd beg them 'please don't go.' I think they tried to run everybody off. Because if you wouldn't go, they figured you were tough and crazy enough that you were going to be a good fighter."

And then there was life in the gym, crazier if you can imagine, than the house itself. Prospective fighters were immediately thrown into the fire with gruff, aggressive professionals, a combustible mix that didn't always go well for the newcomer. It was also a place to settle any accumulated grievances from the house. Didn't like something your roommate was doing? You could let him know on the mats every day until your point was clear.

"Ken's like, 'All right. You're gonna be my fucking minions. I'm gonna pay for your house and all that and teach you how to fight, but you just do whatever the fuck I say,'" Williams says. "And Ken definitely tested that willingness to stay. That was his style, the shock and awe. Even fighting or whatever, just test your fucking will to even be there. And if you left, he felt, 'Well, okay, you're gonna crumble when it gets tough. I only want people here who are ready to die.'"

Shamrock himself didn't always show up for fight practice, although he was almost always present for physical drills and weight lifting sessions at a commercial gym in the morning. When he did show up, everyone knew it was going to be an awful day.

"It would be a head fuck. Sometimes he'd show up an hour late, just when we'd thought we'd gotten away. We'd be finishing our training and then here comes Ken. We're like, "Fuck.' We all dreaded it when he showed up," Williams says. "We knew the normal intensity of our workouts is gonna go up a huge degree because Ken's just gonna make us do a bunch of crazy shit. And someone's probably gonna take an ass whooping, either from Ken himself or he's gonna make each of us beat the shit out of each other."

The worst beatings were delivered to fighters who broke the rules, didn't show an appropriate level of effort, or angered Ken in some way. The most frequent victim was Vernon White, at one point victim of a beatdown that became legendary among fellow fighters.

"Vern was a noted pussy hound," Williams says. "To the highest degree. So we're lifting weights, and every time it's Vern's set, he is over across the gym talking to some girl. Ken, oh you saw him snap, kind of. He didn't do anything there at the regular gym. He was just like, 'All right.'"

That afternoon at the team's MMA practice, Vernon came in with his girlfriend and her young son. Ken told him to take the kid to the other room and get his gloves on. That perked up every ear in the gym, all very mindful of their mentor's mood at all times.

"Everyone was just like, "Oh, shit. There are some major warning signs here.' Whenever Ken tells you to put the gloves on, you're fucked. And he made the kid leave the room which he didn't normally do," Williams says. "Ken just proceeds to lay an ass beating of epic proportions on Vern. To where Vern is just trying to survive. He's just like, "Ahhh." Making noises you want no man to. It made us uncomfortable. And we had seen some shit."

Shamrock beat on White mercilessly.

"I remember Vernon trying to crawl out of the ring," Bessac says, "and Ken just dragging him back by the leg."

Again and again he tried to escape the ring, thinking he could save himself, looking for a respite or at least a restart. No such luck.

"Ken just proceeded to try and smash Vern's head into the cement ground and into the pole of the ring, the metal pole," a Lion's Den fighter says. "It was pretty raw. So raw that one of the young boys we just called 'Young Ken' said, 'You know what? I'm out.' He's like, 'This ain't for me, I'm flying home tomorrow.' Just like that. Just another day at the Lion's Den."

While White is sure some of it was intended to impart a lesson, other times he thinks Shamrock was just letting off steam from a relationship with his wife that was increasingly fraught.

"If you said 'Hey, Ken. How you doing today?' and he wouldn't say nothing back? Or you heard his car peal into the parking lot? There were those telltale signs that it was going to be a bad day for us," White says. "When he'd pull into the parking lot squealing his tires it's like, 'Oh, crap. Here we go.'

"They were going back and forth trying to get back at each other, and the only people that were truly suffering were the fighters and the kids. While this crap was going on, all of us fighters were like, 'Fuck, man. Do we really want to be here anymore? Is this worth it?'

"Some of us couldn't walk after training was over. Then Ken was like, 'Hey, well, you need to talk to Tina.' Because you guys have marital problems, that's why I'm getting this shit?'"

Some days Shamrock would call a young fighter over to the mats and proceed to torture him with submissions, screams resonating through the building as the others attempted to ignore the suffering.

"Young boys had to go through a thing called callousing," Rocca says. "That's where Ken would apply submissions and take it to the verge of injury. But he would not finish the hold. You had to fight the pain and try to escape. You learn there is no such thing as quitting."

Ken wanted his fighters to understand how far you could take a hold, or how far someone could take it on *you*, before you would have to tap out. The idea, he says, was to make fighters less afraid of the pain that would come from a submission hold, even one that wasn't fully locked in. Others, however, believed he just liked to hurt people.

"I remember Pete going through it," Bohlander says. "And he's screaming and crying and just yelling. I'm just like, 'Oh, my God. This is fucking terrible. I know my turn is next. Oh my God, oh my God, oh my God. This is going to be terrible.' He's making Pete just squirrel and scream.

"Then it's my turn. He's putting Achilles locks and toe holds and heel hooks. Not injuring me, not damaging me, but hurting me like a motherfucker. I'm holding out and it seemed like an eternity. It was probably five minutes, but it seemed like it was 100, 200, 300 minutes. Finally, after holding it in for as long as I could, I just start screaming bloody murder."

Other times, he would show up to the gym and demand a fight, forcing these young men who lived, played and trained together 24 hours a day to engage in brutal bareknuckle combat.

"We walk in one day and Ken says, 'Strip down to your shorts, shirt, and whatever the fuck you're going to train in,'" Bohlander says. "'You guys are fighting.' Me and Frank. By fighting, he meant *fighting*. It wasn't certain rules sparring. It was, 'You guys are going in there and you are fighting like you're in the UFC.'

"We'd walk in and we'd just start throwing down. Thirty minutes later, Ken would call it. That was including bare fist punches, no shin pads kicking, headbutts. If we chose to wear mouth pieces, we wore mouth pieces. If not, oh well. You'd just go in there and you'd try to kick the shit out of each other."

No one was ever really sure what to expect on any given day at the gym. Burnett believes that was intentional, all part of Shamrock's demented master plan to harden his fighters, body, mind and soul.

"Ken was probably the biggest mindtrip," he said. "It was all mental. He would come in in the morning, sometimes 4:30 or 5:00 in the morning, and wake you up by whispering 'I'm going to kill you tonight.' And sometimes he would show up that night and tear into you and sometimes he would show up and not even look at you.

"He just totally screwed with your head until you got to the point that there was no fear of death after leaving the guy's place because they would tell you they were going to kill you as they were choking you out. You learn not to fear, but that's a dangerous thing. I don't think any of the guys feared any repercussions in life at all."

The idea, according to Shamrock, was to make sure that the fighters' experiences in the gym were worse than anything they might face in an actual prizefight. To that end, all agree, he was successful. Training at the Lion's Den was way worse than any fight.

"Ken did not want us to ever accept defeat, to ever be beta,"

Bohlander says. "One day in training, I was about a month after my tryout. Frank grabbed some sort of submission on me. I ended up tapping out. Ken saw what anybody with a trained eye would have seen. I didn't have to tap. I gave it up. Ken takes me to the side and said 'Why the fuck did you tap out to that?' I said, 'Well, he had the submission.' He said, 'No.'

"The only time in my life I'd ever been bitch slapped. Ken bitch slapped me. It was a backhand, just straight across my face. He said, 'What the fuck's the matter with you? You just gave up. He didn't have it yet you quit.' That imprinted on me. I've never tapped out without truly needing to since then. I've never just given up."

Five days a week, they'd train all day then continue scrapping in the house at night. Bed time was a strict 10 P.M. Although for the first few months, guys would typically fall asleep long before that, exhausted from the kind of physical toll most people never experience.

"They had to come live in the fighters house and they had to be there for a year," Shamrock says. "I don't have to worry about girlfriends or worry about parents or worry about outside influences getting in the way of my training with these guys. They had to be at the house and they had to train there and they had to give me their full attention."

On the weekend, they'd attempt to let their hair down, on their own from Friday night until Sunday at 6 P.M. when they were expected back at the fighter house—but there just wasn't much to do in Lodi. Shamrock kept his training camp there for a reason, despite offers to move to larger media centers to further his career.

"We watched *Tommy Boy* and *Black Sheep* about a million times," Rocca says. "When we were bored we'd either hang out at the Walmart in Lodi or go to the Jackpot gas station to get out of the house. There wasn't much to do in Lodi.

"You'd see fighters getting wild at UFC after parties back then. In my eyes, it was because it was really the only chance to cut loose. If we weren't at events, we were training and resting. It wasn't beaches and bikinis. It was driving past pungent vineyards to and from training sessions."

Even their off time was spent in competition, either shirtless *Top Gun* style volleyball games that would draw admiring female eyes at the park or simply trying to outdo each other in various physical challenges.

"On the weekend, our day off, we'd go to the lake and swim and do what was called 'Dinosaur Training.' It was the old strongmen stuff," Williams says. "So we'd be out there just lifting huge rocks and logs and shit. Just doing shit that you do when you're living out in the middle of nowhere and have nothing else to do but train, smoke weed, and, you know, lift shit."

Bohlander echoes a sentiment I heard from several Lion's Den fighters—they were willing to die on the quest towards greatness.

"We were just a bunch of fucking primitive fucking cavemen," he says. "We would push each other. I mean, one of our goals early on, I remember we would talk about it—if we could train so hard that we died. If we could've worked out so hard that we physically died, we would have. That was the mindset."

Eight days after winning the UFC championship, Ken was back in Pancrase, relegated to the opening match against Larry Papadopoulos, a Brazilian jiu jitsu player who had lost three of his first four Pancrase fights. Those included losses to both Bessac and White, perennial Pancrase job guys, a clear sign of his comparative lack of competitive ability. That card position and opponent was a clear sign of Ken's fading star, if not with the fans, with Pancrase executives.

Meanwhile, in the UFC offices in Manhattan, Shamrock's victory over Severn was an event worth celebrating. He was the man they wanted as the face of the company, a good-looking fighter who could turn on the charm with the press when called upon.

"We were believers in stars. Ken didn't position himself as Captain America. We did," UFC President David Isaacs says. "We were trying to make these fights interesting and create personalities where we saw possibility. Ken fit that mold. We spent a lot of time building Ken and hoping he would win, ready with the next thing if he did and it didn't ever work out quite right multiple times."

Case in point was his first defense of the UFC Superfight championship.[137] Oleg Taktarov had beaten Tank Abbott to win both

---

[137] UFC 7 was on September 8, 1995, just a week after a big Pancrase event at Sumo Hall. Pancrase allowed Shamrock to skip the event in exchange for securing a date for Taktarov to fight in the Pancrase ring in 1996. Bob Shamrock brokered the deal.

the tournament at UFC 6 and a title shot. On the surface, it was an easy opportunity for Shamrock to get an exciting, dynamic win and help push memories of his dreadful fight with Gracie further into the back of people's minds.

Taktarov was a Russian sambo specialist with a murky past, each story about his Army exploits more amazing than the last, all of them as impossible to confirm as they were wild. He had met Guy Mezger in Dallas and through Guy come into the Lion's Den family.

"He lived in our fighters house," Bob Shamrock remembered. "He was a tough guy but refused to follow our conditioning program or diet. At one point I got frustrated with him eating junk food, so I bought him a turkey. He was supposed to cook it and eat it over the course of the week.

"Instead, one day I came in and found the kitchen covered in flies and maggots. He was taking the turkey, cutting slices off it raw whenever he was hungry, and popping them in the microwave."[138]

Shamrock and Taktarov had trained together plenty at the Lion's Den and Ken had always gotten the better of their sparring sessions. At one point, Taktarov, covered in his own blood, escaped to the bathroom to regain his composure. He was in there, those in attendance remember, for nearly an hour.

Bohlander, though technically still a young boy, was put to immediate use as a sparring partner after some unexpected success against Ken on the mats.

"Ken decided to use me as a training tool. I was supposed to take him down," he says. "He was going to punch and kick on me. That's the way that it went back then. So I shoot in, I grab him, I launch him, and dump him on his back. He's like, 'Holy shit.' He literally told me, 'Nobody's ever done that to me, except maybe Suzuki.'

"Of course, he stopped my second takedown with a frigging hip block from hell. It felt like I was hitting a brick wall. Then he dropped an elbow into the middle of my back. It hurt for like a month afterward. But you kept training through it. And I got one on Ken, which didn't happen a lot."

The actual fight wasn't nearly so impressive. Shamrock just couldn't take it seriously and marital problems had him seeking substances to dull the edge.

---

[138] This story was first reported in Erich Kraus's book *Brawl*. It was so impossible, I asked Shamrock to confirm it—and he did.

Shamrock

"Here I was, I had this big fight and I was out partying the night before[139]," Shamrock says. "I think about how much talent I had and wasted. A lot of my career, I was only fighting to half my potential. It just seemed like it came too easy. There were times I just didn't want to train."

Though Taktarov lived up to his pre-fight promise to never tap out, he was beaten bloody by Shamrock, who added a headbutt to his developing ground-and-pound game.

"I think this time was tougher because Oleg was stronger," Shamrock told the press after the fight. "Oleg is more dangerous with leg submissions. Gracie only has chokes and armbars and he can't beat me with either of them. Oleg knows leglocks, kneelocks and his punches hurt me. Gracie couldn't hurt me. When Oleg hits me, I feel it. When Gracie hit me, it was like a fly[140]."

The truth was a little more complicated. Shamrock had signed Taktarov to fight in Pancrase on a big money deal and didn't want to jeopardize that pay day by doing the Russian any permanent harm.

"I could have destroyed Oleg[141]," Shamrock says. "But I knew, if I put him in a submission he wouldn't tap. I'd have broken his leg. And I didn't want to hurt him—he was going to fight for me in Japan. I was going to make money on him. It's business. I want him to be able to fight.

"So, my plan was just to knock him out. But what I didn't realize was just how tough Oleg was. I did pretty much beat the hell out of him. But he just wouldn't stay out. I hit him twice in that fight, open handed so I didn't hurt my hand, and saw his eyes roll back in his head. Then, as soon as I hit him again, he'd wake back up."

In the prelims, Scott Bessac made his UFC debut, but the bonds

---

[139] Ken, according to one Lion's Den fighter, was still high on ecstasy during the fight. The team used to watch the tape and try to spot the times his eyes would dart around crazily.

[140] The bad blood between Shamrock and Gracie continued in the months after their fight, especially after Gracie wrote a column in *Black Belt* magazine calling Shamrock's UFC 5 strategy "disgraceful."

[141] Taktarov had his own thoughts about the fight, crediting Shamrock's victory to PED use: "It was hard to grapple with Ken Shamrock because he used steroids. It was especially noticeable when he couldn't make it through 12 minutes on a practice, but before the fight with me, he became much stronger, and at the bout made it for 30 minutes. At that time, I realized that I can't compete with guys on steroids."

between student and teacher were stretched almost to a breaking point. He and Ken had gotten into a fierce argument about fight strategy that ended with Shamrock calling him into the ring and delivering a beatdown that left Bessac dazed.

"He beat the shit out of me and ended up giving me a concussion," Bessac says. "I went home and my ex wife was folding clothes on the bed in the bedroom and I went to put my hand on the doorway to talk to her. Turns out I was actually three feet from the door and fell flat on my face.

"She called Ken all pissed off and yelling at him and he had no emotion at all. He was just like, 'Oh, just take him to the hospital, he's got a concussion.' He was pretty hard."

After his next fight, Bessac, Shamrock's earliest student, left the gym never to return. Many of the earliest Lion's Den members had been pushed beyond their limits and were ready to move on. Of course, with Shamrock's success, there were dozens making their way to Lodi for the mere chance of meeting a burgeoning legend. That couldn't help but change a man, and the people around him were starting to notice.

"Pre-UFC 6, Ken was really nice, really humble, a really good guy. Couldn't say a bad thing about him," one Lion's Den associate says. "And then, after he beat Dan Severn, that's when we could see that he's got an ego going. I mean he was always still courteous to us, courteous and nice to us. But we could see that he was a totally different guy. The vibe was just different. Instead of coming over and saying hi, he wanted you to court him and seek an audience with the big UFC star."

As the UFC grew, so did Shamrock's fame. At events, he would be mobbed by fans, looking to connect with one of the sport's top champions. His fighters, though part of the show, served almost as bodyguards, just trying to keep the madness at bay.

"UFC used to be kind of like a rock concert. I mean, Ken was kind of a rockstar," Bohlander says. "Wherever we'd go, he was the star. There's more times than I can count that I was mean mugging people down, just to get them out of the way. Just opening up a way for him to walk. It was kind of amazing."

Though the fight was technically a draw, there was no doubt who the better man had been. Still, for UFC executives, it was a disappointing performance. First, the show had run over on time again, costing the promotion $650,000 and infuriating cable systems around the country. While a 23-minute power outage in the building hurt, Shamrock's seemingly never-ending 33-minute fight hadn't helped. The crowd chanting "We want Tank" in honor of new favorite Abbott was also a clear sign that Shamrock wasn't delivering exactly what the UFC needed.

"We were trying to take Ken and turn him into a bankable star," Isaacs says. "There was a little bit of frustration because all the components were there and it just didn't come together the way we wanted, or the way he wanted or the way the audience wanted.

"He was saying 'he's a training partner, I didn't want to hurt him.' Meanwhile, he's killing people in the gym. You hear all these horror stories coming out of the Lion's Den of him injuring people.

"We wanted him to be our Mike Tyson. Ken had a lot of things going for him that would have made him an even bigger star than he was."

CHAPTER TEN

A Disastrous Dance

The UFC's performance in Buffalo had been a mixed bag. The live crowd was the biggest in company history but the pay-per-view numbers took a step backward from the record-setting shows earlier in the year. Worse was the continued attack from Senator John McCain. This time, instead of merely contacting officials in New York, he sent a letter to every U.S. state and territory calling for the sport to be shut down.

McCain continued to make the rounds on television as well, appearing on CBS' "Eye on Sports" to make his case that the UFC didn't belong in a civilized society.

"It's not a sport," he said. "It's a bloodletting that appeals to the basest instincts in our psyche that in my opinion has no place in the United States."

Elbow surgery forced Shamrock to pull out of a November fight with Funaki in Pancrase. Instead, he was enlisted in the fight to save the sport from local politicians under pressure from McCain to stop the UFC from appearing in their city.

"I thought he was good when McCain was attacking the sport," Isaacs says. "We needed one of our top fighters to represent the sport and Royce wasn't going to be the one doing that. It fell to Ken and he could speak knowledgeably and clearly. He helped us a lot with that stuff. We were all doing whatever we could and Ken was willing to help."

Mayor Wellington Webb of Denver took advantage of an opportunity for some national press, making appearances on both "Good Morning America" and "The Today Show" to combat a sport he later admitted he had never even seen.

"My constituents elected me to do something about violence," he said. "This type of event desensitizes people to violence."

As officials in Denver waged a fierce battle to keep the UFC out of the city, Bob Meyrowitz agreed to pull the card from the National Western Stock Show Events Center and move it to the much smaller Mammoth Events Center. The next day, he and Shamrock joined host Larry King on CNN for a head-to-head debate with McCain and Nevada State Athletic Commissioner Marc Ratner[142].

"We'll look at a frightening new fad that might be coming to your town," King said, only to have Shamrock and Meyrowitz systematically dismantle every argument thrown at them by the sport's opponents.

"He could do a decent interview," UFC matchmaker Art Davie says. "He looked like a million bucks. He was the face of the UFC and we were very happy with that. Remember that Royce's English wasn't super great, so Ken was often used in that role.

"He was everything that Milius[143] once said to me about Captain America. He looked like the best of the best. You couldn't invent Ken Shamrock. He appeared to us like a gift from God."

When it was over, Shamrock was greeted by SEG brass like a conquering hero. The press had a version of "the cage fighter" they wanted to portray, and Shamrock's calm self-assurance had belied the caveman image they had been expecting.

"Why do you do this?" King, in his trademark suspenders and a purple shirt, asked incredulously at one point.

Ken, in a grey sport coat over a black t-shirt, kept his cool. "Well, it's a sport, you know. It's chance where you can go in and test your ability against someone else's ability."

Shamrock, however, understood this was no fair fight. It didn't matter if they could out-debate critics. The other side had the

---

[142] Ratner, here a vocal critic of cage fighting, would ironically later go on to work for the UFC.

[143] Movie director John Milius was an early supporter of the UFC and helped provide creative direction for the early events. He is best known for writing *Dirty Harry* and *Apocalypse Now* and directing *Conan the Barbarian*.

overwhelming power of the government behind them, a force no chokehold or leg lock could possibly stop.

"When it was over, everyone told me 'you destroyed him,'" Shamrock says. "But even though we were right, even though we 'won' the debate, we actually poured gasoline on the fire. Because we didn't have the power to stop someone like John McCain and now we were in his sights. Right, wrong or indifferent, it didn't matter. There were too many people in his pocket, too many powerful people to fight."

Shamrock closed 1995 in Japan, fighting on the midcard of a Pancrase event in Sapporo, one of five Lion's Den fighters competing at the event. Compared to the previous year, it was a light schedule with just eight prize fights. But the near-monthly grind of Pancrase was taking its toll on everyone associated with the promotion.

"We'd all be hurt all the time," Bessac says. "And in Japan, they'd shoot you up before your fights. It was called Carbocaine[144]. It's like Lidocaine but it doesn't last as long. We'd all sit there and doctors would shoot you up wherever you need to be shot."

Despite the grind, trips to Japan had become highlights for all the athletes involved, a chance to compete, make a few thousand dollars and really let loose with your friends when it was all over. The crew adopted Bas Rutten and other English speakers stuck as strangers in a strange land and made the most of their burgeoning celebrity.

"We just lived large," Mezger says. "It was just a lot of fun. You got to live like a rock star for a while. I had a different life over in Japan. I had girlfriends in Japan, you know what I mean? So it was like I had two lives going on, one in Japan and one in the United States. Pancrase was very, very popular. Very popular. And so to be honest with you, we lived like Gods over there. It was a lot of fun."

After the events the fighters would hit the town, often the Roppongi district in Tokyo. Not only were the fighters high on adrenaline and fame, they were often loaded with money, which some would spend recklessly.

---

[144] Carbocaine is often used to numb an area for surgery. It's a pretty serious drug.

"You got to understand they paid cash," Mezger says. "You're fighting 10 times a year, well that's 150 thousand dollars tax free. That's not a bad living. Stacks of cash. They would put it in these green folders. Instead of manila folders they had these green folders with the Pancrase logo on it. You'd have your stack of cash in there."

Sometimes sponsors, who were basically mega-fans would take them to expensive restaurants for steaks that cost $250 an ounce. Sometimes they would hit the clubs or have a celebrity encounter.

"We would party to meet people from Australia, Brazil, I mean we met girls from all over the world there," White says. "It was crazy. They would find out we were fighters and next thing you know we're partying in the hotels, just crazy stuff happening.

"I remember being at a rave in Japan. They bring us up on stage on the third floor. We start doing crowd diving. It's me, Bas Rutten, Frank, Jason, Guy Mezger. We're crowd diving and picking up little Japanese dudes and girls and throwing them out in the crowd. People are catching them. There was a sea of people on this floor. They're jumping up and down. You can feel the whole floor literally rocking because these people are jumping up and down."

The debauchery was almost unchecked, in part because of their fearsome reputations. No matter what they were doing, people were loathe to ask them to stop. When the Japanese fighters joined them, things were often particularly wild.

"After a few beers, Suzuki would stick toothpicks in the young boys head," Bessac says. "Then he'd light them on fire."

Anyone getting aggressive with the fighters would quickly be clued in on just who they were messing with.

"If trouble came it'd be so funny," Mezger says. "People would be going, 'No, no, no, no, no. You don't want to start trouble, they're Pancrase.' As if we like werewolves or something. It was funny. They literally got backed down because we were 'Pancrase.'"

Rutten, a notorious drinker and all-around good time guy, was everyone's favorite. It didn't matter if they had just finished having him knock the crap out them—everyone in the Lion's Den loved having Bas around, especially Frank.

"One time Frank and Bas got in a pissing match over which one could climb the best," Mezger remembers. "They started climbing up the side of an apartment building. Then Bas started slipping and Frank jumped over onto a balcony and pulled him up. It was amazing. Then they knock on the guy's door and run out the guy's front door and down the stairs. Because they weren't about to try to climb back down."

While all the fighters enjoyed some degree of notoriety, there was no doubt who the big dog was. Only one of them was featured on magazine covers and television specials. The Lion's Den were fighter famous. Ken was something different entirely.

"Ken was a *big* star," DeLucia says. "You know, walking through an airport the customs agents wouldn't even care if he was there on a tourist visa. They'd be like, "Yeah, yeah, fine!" They'd circle him and go, 'Hey, can we have a picture with you?' He was a *star*. Whereas, you know, I could be walking with him, and they'd be like, 'Hey, who's that?'"

While Ken was slowly drifting away from Pancrase, his fighters remained a key part of the show, especially Frank, who was dipping his toes in the main event scene despite being less serious about his career than he would become later as a long-time UFC champion.

"It was really unique and I had never experienced anything like celebrity. All of it was new to me. And I experimented with everything, tried to do everything," Frank said in an interview for *Total MMA*. "I smoked for the first year of my fighting career. In Japan, Lucky Strike was our biggest sponsor so you get free cigarettes. It never dawned on me. The Japanese all smoked. It never dawned on me that I needed a bigger commitment to be a great fighter."

Frank was enjoying his time in Japan—perhaps, he writes in *Uncaged*, a little too much:

> In the beginning, I was very serious about training. I wouldn't do anything before a fight. But after a while it got to where I'd even go over to Japan a little early —not for any extra training, but so I could start partying with my girlfriend in Japan. I had always smoked pot but I started smoking hash a lot in those days, mainly because it was the only hard drug that you could buy in the Japanese subways.

Despite his sometimes less than rigorous training habits, Frank thrived in Japan, going 6-2-1 in 1995 against the top fighters in the promotion. He beat both Funaki and Suzuki and went to a split decision with Rutten in a loss.

Former training partner Scott Bessac dismisses some of Frank's success as "work," suggesting the bouts weren't legitimate. Promoters, he believes, saw Frank's potential as a drawing card and took the steps necessary to establish him as a star. In *Uncaged*, Frank conceded that could be true. The fact is, you could be involved in a Pancrase bout and have no idea what kind of machinations were working behind the scenes to benefit you.

"I don't know if I was just too young, or didn't need to know, but no one ever shared anything with me. I had a feeling … there were always secret meetings and whatnot, but I never knew anything about it," Frank said. "No one ever asked me to end it a certain way. I do know that it went on, but I was never approached or had any experience with it.

"I believe some of the fights that I fought with the upper-echelon guys[145], they may have let me win or had some sort of ending in mind. But I always fought my heart out and fought as hard as I could and gave as much as I could."

Regardless of how he got there, on January 28, 1996, less than two years after beginning his professional career, Frank found himself in the main event of a Pancrase show in Yokohama. His opponent was Suzuki. The prize, an interim King of Pancrase title belt. But he wasn't entering the bout at 100 percent, thanks to a brutal session with Ken days earlier.

"One of the most intense moments I ever witnessed was the night before we left for Frank's title fight," DeLucia says. "Ken took Frank into the gym. He says 'Come on, Frank. We gotta go callus up.' So he took him in the ring, and with bare fists, he beat his ribs and broke a lot of his ribs. Not a couple, not one, a lot. He just pounded him in the body until he broke his ribs.

"So, fast forward a few days later. We're in Japan, the night before the fight. And, Frank says, 'Jason, I need some help.' He was in pain. We're in his bedroom. I got him laid on his bed, and his ribs had already started to callus so the calcium deposits were all over the break. And Frank and I were setting his ribs.

"Can you imagine that? Me and Frank are putting his ribs back together like one of those models you get that doesn't use glue. 'Click-clack, click-clack.' We set his ribs that night and he fought the next day. And won."

---

[145] In his book, Frank pinpointed fights with Funaki and Suzuki as potential fixes in his favor.

Underneath Frank's main event title win, Ken struggled with Yoshiki Takahashi in what would turn out to be his final Pancrase fight. He'd helped arrange a four-event PPV deal between the Japanese promotion and SEG, which owned UFC, but was eventually let go after an extended contract battle that ended up in court.

"Unfortunately, it was really down to money," Funaki recalls. "And that's something Pancrase couldn't compete with UFC on. I think, as well, that Ken wanted to fight closer to home in America."

The Pancrase fight was less than three weeks from his upcoming Superfight with Kimo on February 16, 1996, but unlike his bouts with Dan Severn and Oleg Taktarov, Shamrock didn't ask for a break to train exclusively for the UFC. Actions, as they say, speak much louder than words and choosing to fight in Pancrase instead of train spoke volumes about Shamrock's respect for Kimo's skillset and ability to beat him.

Confident in his own preparations, Shamrock turned his attention to his students. SEG had offered him one slot for his team in an upcoming "David vs. Goliath" tournament and he had a tough decision to make. His initial inclination was to give the opportunity to Bohlander. Frank, DeLucia and Mezger, his seniors in the gym, were occupied in Japan. Plus, Jerry had acquitted himself well in his fighting debut a couple of months before and Shamrock just liked the kid. He saw something of himself in the young man, who at first turned down a chance to join the Lion's Den because he was working to support his disabled mother. Shamrock offered him a loan that allowed Bohlander to pursue his dreams.

But as much as Shamrock admired the young fighter, *giving* something to a fighter wasn't the Lion's Den way. If Bohlander wanted a shot at the UFC, he'd have to earn it the old-fashioned way—by fighting for it.

"One day, out of the blue we walk into the gym and he said, 'You and Pete (Williams) are going to fight for it,'" Bohlander says. "Pete and I were high school friends. We both looked at each other and kind of like, 'Oh, Jesus.'"

"It was strange," Williams remembers. "It was just us three in the gym. Me, Jerry and Ken. I was just like, 'What?'

"And I think he sensed our hesitation. He's like, 'If I don't feel you guys are fighting to your potential, I'm gonna beat the shit out of both of you.'

"So we're like, 'Oh, fuck. Okay.' So, we did this fight in the gym. And yeah, Jerry ended up getting a heel hook on me."

The fight was initially stressful for both young competitors. But eventually, the combat instinct Shamrock had carefully instilled in both kicked in and they had a heated back and forth battle with serious professional consequences.

"You know what? It wasn't really that much different than what we'd been doing except, all the sudden, there was something at stake," Bohlander says. "We both had to earn it. If he hadn't told us that we were going to fight for it, we probably wouldn't have fought as hard. But he said, 'You guys are going to go for it,' and all the sudden, it was, 'Okay, we're going to kill each other.'"

While primitive in a way compared to modern mixed martial arts training, Shamrock was a master motivator. His fighters, after just a few months with him, were generally capable of competing with top fighters, on mindset alone.

"There were guys in there that did a little bit of high school wrestling like Jerry, and they're fighting at a world class level very quickly," Mezger says. "I don't think other coaches would have been able to get that much in the short amount of time. Ken could get these guys to perform, to believe in themselves. They were beating world class guys when they didn't really have world class skills because of the way Ken could get them going.

"He had a matter of fact kind of way of talking about stuff. He could say 'Yeah, we're going to move Mt. Everest three feet over today.' And because he's Ken Shamrock, the way he'd state it so matter-of-factly, you'd just believe it was true. He always had that way about getting the guys to really believe in themselves and they did, they really outdid themselves."

The event was held in San Juan, Puerto Rico, but if UFC officials thought moving away from the continental United States would eliminate the political pressure they were now facing before every show, they were sorely mistaken. The island had gone UFC crazy—market research showed they bought UFC pay-per-views at three times the average rate and UFC VHS tapes were among the most popular rentals in all of Puerto Rico. But popular acceptance did little to stop politicians with a purpose and the UFC had to sweat out a legal battle before finally getting the go-ahead to run the show.

Bohlander shined in his UFC debut, beating the enormous Scott Ferrozzo in what many thought was the best fight of the night. Giving up around 150 pounds to a man wearing a giant yellow smock that read 'FEAR ME' in all caps, Bohlander overcame the odds and a huge size disadvantage to secure a guillotine choke and his first UFC win. John McCarthy ended up stopping his semi-final fight with Gary Goodridge but not before Bohlander again put on a display of both technique and moxie.

Shamrock, as expected, cruised past Kimo[146] with a kneebar, controlling all but a few seconds of the bout. Kimo was spirited but out-gunned physically and technically by the Lion's Den leader. Shamrock appeared in an issue of *People Magazine* the next week and was becoming the UFC's first real break out star.

Sitting at Shamrock's table at the after-party were both Funaki and Pancrase President Masami Ozaki. It wasn't purely a social event, as the three men had plenty of business to discuss.

At the end of April the term of Shamrock's Pancrase fight contract expired. This being the world of combat sports, of course, things weren't nearly that simple—while his one year deal had run out, according to Pancrase he still owed them three fights. Shamrock believed that his UFC fights, where he represented Pancrase on the international stage should count against his total. Pancrase only wanted to consider bouts in their ring and in Japan against his deal.

The relationship, already fraught due to Ken's frustration about being asked to put over other fighters and Pancrase's frustration with Ken's decision to prioritize the UFC over them, had continued to deteriorate. Oleg Taktarov finally had his agreed upon fight in Pancrase in 1996, an arrangement made so the Japanese promotion would free Shamrock up for their 1995 UFC Superfight. But Taktarov angered Pancrase officials by making what appeared to be only a half-hearted effort to win and Shamrock bore the brunt of the backlash.

"I love Oleg, but for his only fight in Pancrase, they paid him a ton more money than they paid Ken," DeLucia says. "I couldn't believe it. It's like, really? And he shows up and he fought like shit. Ken was livid. And I don't blame him. It's like a slap in the face."

Complicating matters further was a second contract that named

---

[146] Kimo came to the Octagon with a sign depicting a bloody Jesus on the cross. It read (sic) "If I'm Ok And Your Ok, Then Explain This!" Kimo was, without a doubt, an enigmatic fellow.

Shamrock the North American talent agent for Pancrase, supposedly in charge of selecting and booking the American talent. When Pancrase President Masami Ozaki began signing fighters without Ken's input at all, a rocky relationship reached the breaking point.

Shamrock also spent less and less time in the gym. He'd often disappear for a week or more at a time. When he did show up, however, he was still Ken Shamrock, ruler of the roost.

"Ken was never there," Bohlander says. "I know Frank says he was training us, but we spent a shit ton of time training one another. We would develop our own training programs and beat each other up. Then Ken would come back and he was kind of our measuring stick. Ken would come back and then we'd roll with him and we would get put in our place. Basically, for lack of a better word, he'd whoop our ass."

No one knew where he'd been and no one asked. Ominous signs were everywhere. Tina told the *Philadelphia Inquirer* she was happy to have Ken participating in such a violent sport, citing his violent nature.

"I'd rather have him get his frustrations out before he gets home," she said. "Than have him take them out inside the house."

Drugs were also becoming a bigger and bigger part of his life, the party sometimes just as important as the fight. It was an issue that had always lingered. Now, with money and fame and access to anything he wanted, saying "no" wasn't a particular priority.

"I think he just let it get to his head," Bessac says. "Which I can't blame him, really, for it because it kind of got to all our heads. It just kinda got out of control."

The UFC generally was a wild scene, with drugs, steroids, strippers and booze a constant, not just at the often out-of-control after parties that followed each event, but for many fighters as part of their regular life. Even among a class of people inured to such behavior, Shamrock stood out. Rumors of his exploits were everywhere, from his prodigious drinking to the time he slept with a Dallas Cowboys cheerleader.

"Ken was a heavy partier," one UFC employee says. "He played hard. He fought hard. The 500 free squats. I mean, everything Ken did was pretty extreme. There was heavy use of the best vodka, of dope, cannabis, cocaine, and nobody fucked more girls in my humble opinion than Ken Shamrock.

"I would run into people later who said, 'did you know he fucked this other guy's wife?' I would say, 'wait a minute, stop. Say that to me again, which guy's wife?' The stories of Ken Shamrock were legendary. For the fighters at that point, the partying was fierce. Ken was a party animal and if he's told you that there were sex, drugs and rock and roll and broads, he ain't lying."

Bohlander says he went a long time missing most of the signs, until another Lion's Den member simply told him 'you know Ken's a drug addict, right? He's a crackhead.' Like most of the other guys, the things he'd personally seen made it easy for the puzzle pieces to fall into place.

"Ken was the one who introduced me to cocaine," Bohlander says. "That was in Hawaii. I was young, impressionable, whatever, blah, blah, blah. You know what? I got one of the best lays in my life from it.

"I'm a young, 20-year-old guy, fucking hanging out with a super hard-ass guy and fucking a 30-some-odd-year-old fucking stripper. Snorting coke. It was frigging crazy.

"Ken had his problems. He had his addiction. The fact that he had those issues, and he was able to be as successful as he was with those issues is fucking amazing."

As life at the Lion's Den got wilder and meaner, the UFC's relationship with cable and pay-per-view providers also began to crumble. McCain continued his assault on the sport on any television outlet that would have him, his rhetoric like a powerful blow in its own right.

"We don't let roosters engage in cockfights," he said in one interview. "We don't allow human beings to go out the street and engage in this kind of activity. We call it disturbing the peace."

The bad optics coming out of UFC 8 couldn't have helped. The David vs. Goliath concept was a cool idea—but visuals like an enormous Goodridge brutally knocking out a much smaller Paul Herrera with a series of vicious, undefended elbows gave opponents an even stronger case that no-holds-barred was little more than bloodsport. The UFC's early marketing, essentially exaggerating and playing up the inherent violence, had eventually backfired, allowing news anchors like ABC's Charles Gibson to read off the promotion's own rules stating "each match will run until there is a designated winner by means of knockout, surrender, doctor's intervention, or death," in a comically grave tone, playing up the idea of dead bodies piling up on the floor of the Octagon.

"You had cable throwing us under the bus," McLaren said. "You had an America that was a little squeamish. You had McCain who found a perfect thing. No one stood up and said 'No, we must have more violence on TV.' McCain found the perfect thing to come out against. Illegal immigration, that's a pretty tough subject. Abortions, that's a pretty tough subject. You've got to be careful how you answer questions about those things. But if you stand up and say 'We shouldn't have people beating each other to death on TV,' pretty much everyone agrees with you."

Before the next UFC, more than 15 percent of potential homes no longer had the option to purchase the event—the cable companies simply weren't going to offer it.

"It was a very cheap way for the cable companies to portray themselves as anti-violence," Carol Klenfner, spokeswoman for UFC's parent company, SEG told *Slate*. "It did not cost them much and it made them look good in Washington."

This was a particularly devastating blow because the cable systems that banned the sport from their airwaves included those in Canada, a traditionally strong market for UFC. Meanwhile, as pay-per-view was sent into a deathspin, every live event faced a robust legal challenge.

"Almost everywhere we went we ended up in court," Shamrock says. "We'd get a license to do a one-time show in a building somewhere and then politicians would come in and try to get it banned. SEG was spending a lot of money on lawyers. A lot of money. They drained UFC. They were always in court. "

In the midst of all this drama came a fourth UFC Superfight, this time a rematch with Dan Severn. Between their two bouts Severn had re-established himself as a major player in the sport, dispatching all comers at the UFC's Ultimate Ultimate 95 tournament in Denver. It was the deepest, best tournament the UFC had ever put together to that point and Severn was barely tested, completely outclassing "Tank" Abbott in the semi-finals and steam-rolling an overmatched Oleg Taktarov to take home a then UFC record $150,000 pay day.

Shamrock's life was a blur in the month leading up to the fight. Trying to make things right with Tina, and to be the father he never had, he had rededicated himself to his family and was coaching t-ball.

He also had a major role in the straight-to-Blockbuster movie *Champions*[147] and a dizzying array of media appearances. Severn, though present in his mind, didn't loom there.

To prepare, Shamrock brought in bodybuilder Dan Freeman to help him bulk up and former University of Nebraska wrestler Mike Radnov to simulate Severn's size and power. Radnov may have done too good a job. Thirteen days before the fight, the wrestler broke Shamrock's nose while trying to wiggle free from a kneebar.

"I had a cracked rib and a fractured nose and a bad meniscus in my knee," Shamrock says. "I was actually going to back out of the fight, but there was a lot riding on it. In those days you just kind of got used to fighting with a bunch of injuries. When you're fighting ten times a year, that's just how it is."

The political battle between UFC and the McCain-led political forces reached a fever pitch in Michigan. The afternoon of the fight, they still didn't know if there would be an event at all. Local officials, citing a law prohibiting prize fighting from all the way back in 1869, attempted to get the UFC banned from Cobo Arena, where Severn hoped to get his win back against Shamrock in front of a home-state crowd. The case was tossed from state court to the federal system and back down to the state over the course of a month, landing, finally, on the desk of Wayne County Circuit Judge Arthur Lombard. He only had one day free to hear arguments—the day before the show.

After hearing arguments from both the UFC as well as the opposition, Judge Lombard made his ruling the afternoon of the show at 2:30 P.M.[148] The show could go on, he said, but only if closed fist punching and headbutts were outlawed. Bob Meyrowitz quickly agreed, and the UFC was back in business for one more night.

"I appreciate that the judge is looking for the safety of the fighters and trying to make the event better." Meyrowitz told the press. "And we've always said that's what we're trying to do as well."

Referee John McCarthy, as he wrote in his book *Let's Get it On*, was shocked and confused. How could you have the UFC without punches? They were, like in most combat sports, the heart of the

---

[147] Here Shamrock really stretched his acting muscles, playing a vicious cage fighting champion.

[148] Some reports say the decision was made as late as 4:30 P.M., but most seem to agree no one knew for sure there was going to *be* a UFC 9 until the afternoon of the show.

enterprise:

> Outside the courthouse I grabbed Meyrowitz. "How the fuck are we not going to have any punching in this?"
>
> "I didn't say there wasn't going to be any punching," Meyrowitz cooly answered. "I just said I'd make it illegal. When they punch, you're going to tell them, 'that's illegal.' And you're going to have to fine them eventually. When they have to pay that fine, only God knows."

Semantic language games were not Shamrock's strong suit and he was furious when he heard the news. Not only did he have kids at home he had to set an example for, the last thing he wanted to do was get arrested and find himself unable to work with the young men at Bob's group home. And going to jail didn't feel like an idle threat or distant possibility, not in the political climate of 1996.

"I was going to knock Dan out, ground and pound him because I couldn't use my knee," Shamrock says. "Well, they took the striking away. They came and told us that if we were to strike, we would get fined. Now this is the UFC, saying 'we will collect at our leisure. Wink, wink.' Which meant go ahead and strike. We're not gonna do anything and hopefully they're not going to arrest you if you do.

"Two to three weeks prior to that, these guys did a show over in Canada and they *were* arrested. They were told not to do it and if they did, they'd get arrested. Well, they did it. And they got arrested. I didn't want to risk that and I didn't want to be a bad example.[149]"

If Shamrock did break the rules, it wouldn't be a low profile decision. Lacking any television deal or many reporters on the UFC beat, the promotion was about as media friendly as you could be—and everyone wanted to spend time with Shamrock.

"During that week, *Sports Illustrated* was in town and they were interviewing only one guy, Ken Wayne Shamrock," UFC matchmaker Art Davie says. "CNN was there. Everyone was interested in Ken's story. His adopted father runs a Father Flanagan type of home for kids. He has the look, the image. Kids will naturally look up to him as a role

---

[149] Canadian officials had indeed briefly jailed some of the participants at an Extreme Fighting event the month before.

model. It's a great story.

"He decided, with the ruling of the judge, he doesn't want to punch because it would ruin his image. He's a role model for kids. He'd have to tell the guys from *Sports Illustrated* that he was going to do the expedient thing and not the right thing."

Shamrock refused to leave his hotel room for the Arena, insisting he wasn't going to do the show. Once he made up his mind, Shamrock was a hard man to budge. Tina couldn't move him at all and decided to enlist the help of UFC brass, who left the event site just hours before the show was supposed to start to try and rescue their main event.

"We were up in the hotel room," UFC President David Isaacs remembers. "Ken was about to explode about these rules the judge had imposed. We didn't have any system established that said, if you broke the rules, what the penalty would be. Essentially nothing. We talked about that and Ken was adamant, adamant, that he was not going to break those rules. And when I say adamant, I mean he was screaming and there was a vein popping out of his forehead. He looked like he might jump over the table. He was incensed."

The conversation was intense, to the point of being out of control. It was the world against Ken and Ken didn't show any signs of being convinced.

"At one point he was crying in his hotel room," Davie says. "Bob Shamrock wasn't talking to him. He was angry. They were having another one of those knock down things that would last three months. It was a love hate relationship. You know there seemed to be a lot of tension between them.

"In fact, being in the room with those two men where you'd be the third person always made you feel that you had to kind of be careful what you said and where you were going to go with this because there was a possibility you could say something that would trip the trigger for one or both of them. It was a very complicated relationship."

Eventually, Meyrowitz and Isaacs laid it bare, telling Shamrock 'if you don't fight, you might personally kill this sport.' As they left, no one knew for sure if Shamrock would decide to come to the Arena or not.

"He just wasn't going to break the rules and hit Dan," Isaacs says. "Yet, if they had gotten in an argument at the bar after the fight, Ken would have happily punched Dan in the face. But in the public eye, he was not going to be someone who intentionally broke the rules. I respected that in some ways. But there was part of me that was like 'after all the things you've done in your life, this is the one place you're drawing a line? Really?'"

In the end, Shamrock showed up and stepped into Octagon—but it might be stretching the truth to say there was a fight. Competitors earlier in the night were happy to violate the UFC's new "rules" against closed fist punching and no one in the crowd knew that anything was amiss. The announcers on television also failed to mention the legal drama and never explained why Shamrock might not be throwing any punches.

"These are the greatest fighters in the world," color commentator Don "The Dragon" Wilson said. "But they aren't fighting."

The bout was a disaster. Shamrock threw the occasional open-handed blow and Severn was content to circle to his right for minutes at a time. He wasn't opposed to throwing punches but chose not to. The crowd booed early and often, eventually even throwing things into the cage.

"It *was* boring," Ken concedes. "The most boring fight ever in UFC history. He danced around the outside and never shot on me. I was waiting for him to shoot on me to try to at least stay in top position and look for a submission and try to catch a submission. I knew it had to be set up for me because it'd be hard for me to move around with my knee and I couldn't set anything up with strikes."

Ever the sportsman, Severn told the *Detroit Free Press*, "It was a chess match. People want you to go toe-to-toe. My nose is a little crooked, but it's still mine. All original material. I like having it where it is."

Today, Severn has doubled down on his chess match claims. He will tell anyone willing to listen that it was all a brilliant scheme on his part to throw Shamrock off his game:

> I was going to force Ken Shamrock to make the first move, and if he didn't, I would just continue to circle him for a long, long time. I prepared myself for the fact the crowd would be irritated about the way the fight was going if Ken didn't initiate any action, but I wouldn't allow it to affect me.

The crowd chanted everything from "Bullshit" to "Red Wings," which seemed fine to the announcers because the fighters themselves weren't giving them anything to holler about. At one point, referee McCarthy actually separated them and screamed in Severn's face "You came here to fight, so fucking fight." That moved Severn to attempt a couple of shots, which ended with Shamrock in the mount. At one point Severn reversed position briefly and landed a few punches, one of which cut Shamrock's eye.[150] It was the closest to interesting the bout would be in a 30-minute slog ironically referred to as "The Dance in Detroit."

The *Detroit Free Press*, like many publications that took the time to watch the event before opining, didn't quite know what to make of UFC:

> It might have been the strangest sporting spectacle presented in Detroit. The combatants are remarkably skilled and conditioned athletes with extreme proficiency in a variety of martial arts.
>
> But at times, the bouts had the appearance of barroom brawls—fought by sober men who should know better.

Severn eventually took a split decision win, but it was hard to call anyone a winner after that kind of disaster. While the show drew more than 11,000[151] people to the Cobo Arena, most of them left mad.

The lackluster show, in conjunction with the UFC continuing to lose cable systems, led to a drop of more than 30 percent for UFC 10. Detroit police chief Isaiah McKinnon left the show early, convinced the participants were in violation of the law. He recommended the prosecutor's office request a copy of the tape for possible criminal action, though nothing ever came of it. Shamrock and the others, though disappointed, weren't going to jail on this night. No one had been seriously hurt, except UFC officials feared, the future of the sport.

"At the end of the day, and it's not Ken's fault, that fight was a blow to the growth of the sport at the time," Isaacs says. "Because it was so terrible. We didn't know it was going to be *that* bad. I had seen Pancrase fights that were pretty good, pretty brutal without any closed

---

[150] Shamrock believes he was cut by the seam of one of Severn's open-hand gloves, then a new innovation just becoming a staple of UFC action.

[151] There are attendance reports ranging from "over 9000" to 12,000. With no definitive source, this estimate is as good as any.

fist punches. But, at the end of the day, this had been imposed on us. This was the best we could do in court."

CHAPTER ELEVEN
Final Fight

Four days after the Severn debacle, Shamrock appeared as part of a CBS television special called "The World's Most Dangerous." The show featured the world's most dangerous drugs, most dangerous job and most dangerous man. That was Shamrock and the moniker stuck. "One Punch" Ken Shamrock was going to be a hard sell at that point anyway, especially after so many long fights that were left with no definitive winner.

While Shamrock's personal brand was only getting stronger, the UFC was struggling mightily in the wake of his terrible fight with Severn and an even worse battle with cable companies. Their next event was down 32 percent, partly because of cable companies pulling them off the air and partly because fans didn't feel they were guaranteed a good time.

It was a number that pushed the company dangerously close to losing money on each show—and that was before factoring in the now regular legal battles that had to be fought every time out. That meant booking expensive stars like Severn and Shamrock into Superfights was out the window. UFC chose to focus on the tournament, a move that cut their fighter pay in half and kept Meyrowitz's head just barely above water.

"We cut costs and we cut costs dramatically," former UFC President David Isaacs said. "We pared down everything we could...We fought a lot of battles in court and I spent a lot of time making deals with fighters that just sucked. It's not fun to have to pay guys less money than you want to and than they want.

"I remember one time I made (former UFC welterweight champion) Pat Miletich take a bus. That's the kind of numbers we were dealing with. We couldn't afford to fly people. We cut down the number of days people were there onsite, we cut down our own staff, we cut back our marketing. There was a point when we made a good deal of money at this and then we kind of spent it all with lobbying, lawsuits, and sustaining the events as best we could."

Shamrock had even worse problems in Japan, where negotiations with Pancrase were falling apart. His knee injury had required surgery, forcing him to miss a scheduled bout in June. He made an appearance at the event on crutches and met with fans, partially assuaging the Japanese promotion. But the relationship was too far gone. By mid-1996 Pancrase had even banned Ken from cornering his fighters, thinking he provided an unfair advantage.

"Frank was a remote controlled robot fighter controlled by Ken when he beat many of the top fighters because of Ken's strategic advice," reporter Tadashi Tanaka wrote. "You could actually hear Ken's voice from ringside and a bi-lingual ringside fan could enjoy the match twice as much."

Without Ken's presence, Frank struggled in his final Pancrase fights, losing three of his last four including a fight with Bas Rutten for the King of Pancrase title the day before Ken's fight with Dan Severn. It was a bout that infuriated Ken when he saw the tapes, driving the brothers further apart.

"When he fought Bas, that's when I was gone," Ken says. "And he didn't train. And then, he made those faces, sticking his tongue out at Bas. That really made me angry because that's not what we do. The fight was caving in on him. And so, he wanted to cover it up with shenanigans. He didn't want to face the fact that you were gonna get beat.

"And that's the truth of it, that he knew he was gonna lose. So he started putting on this show. And I called him out on it. I said, 'Dude, don't ever do that again.' He said, 'What are you talking about?' I said, 'When you're sticking your tongue and doing that face to him, what does that mean?' He said, 'I was just letting him know he wasn't hurting me.'

"'Well, that's the opposite, because when you did that, people knew he was hurting you. Everybody knew that you were losing the fight.

And that's why you did it. That makes you look ridiculous, makes the Lion's Den look ridiculous.' And of course, he didn't like that. But I'm saying, 'Dude, you do that again, man I'm gonna...'

"That's stuff that we didn't do. We went in there, and we fought. And we fought with toughness. And desire. And if we lost, we were respectful. Before the fight, after the fight, building a fight, I'm fine. But during the fight, you go in, you take care of business."

As a legal battle loomed, Pancrase made an offer for one final fight —a bout with his brother Frank in December. The Lion's Den turned it down, leaving the Japanese flustered and out of ideas. Eventually there was no turning back. Pancrase officially cut ties with Shamrock after the summer, both as a fighter, a talent scout and a manager.

"They wanted me to stop fighting and just be with Pancrase," he says. "I was building their reputation worldwide. They were getting more popular because I was competing in UFC. They even got onto American pay-per-view with me as the commentator. They were competing with these pro wrestling groups and were able to say 'our guy is a real champion. One of the top fighters in the world.' It didn't make sense to me."

Not only was Shamrock banished from the group but his fighters as well. Frank's contract wasn't renewed at the end of the year and Vernon White was cut outright.

Mezger, by then developing a name in his own right, was allowed to stay on. He'd won a tournament in April to become the number one contender, then dispatched Suzuki with relative ease the next month. He talked about it with Ken and they agreed he would start dealing with the Japanese on his own.

"I was a top guy at the time, a top contender. So they weren't going to make me disappear," he says. "And I wasn't a Shamrock. But they made Frank disappear. They made Vernon disappear."

But, while allowed to stay on, he believes his association with Shamrock made him a target for the rest of his tenure there.

"I mean nobody fought that many top 10 guys," Mezger says. "They were just trying to wear me out. The only guy I hadn't beat was Funaki, who they figured was the only guy who could beat me at that point. I'd beaten everybody else kind of pretty handily. And then I just beat him. I beat the next two contenders after that too and then I went back to the USA."

Only one Lion's Den fighter survived the bloodletting completely unscathed. Jason DeLucia had become a key part of the Pancrase inner circle and was intimately involved in the complicated process of moving chosen favorites up and down the card by losing select bouts on purpose.[152] He was committed to the organization and liked the style better than the more brutal and physical UFC. He had joined the Den after UFC 2 but left the fold and took Ken's spot as the North American talent coordinator.

"It was like *The Godfather*," DeLucia says. "When he took me over there the first few times he would tell me exactly how my career was gonna go. He said, 'They're gonna bring you in, and they're gonna squeeze me out. Then they're gonna put you in my place. They're your best friend when they want something, and then when they're done with you, they don't wanna know you. All of a sudden, it's the coldest shoulder you've ever felt.' And, you know, everything that he told me actually happened."

DeLucia consulted an attorney about getting out of his contract with Ken and was advised he could just walk away, that the contract wouldn't hold up in any court in the world.

"Rather than do that, I called Bob Shamrock, and I came to an agreement with him and bought the contract out, outright," DeLucia says. "These were Bob's words to me, from Ken: 'You're fucking us over. We're gonna fuck you over.[153]' Really? After I just bought myself out? I'm the only fighter who honorably bought my contract out."

For Shamrock, it was a brutal year. While earning a good living in the realm of $500,000 a year, he and his family were spending money as fast as he got it[154]. Worse he'd invested a lot of it back into the gym, counting on UFC's continued rise and his ability to groom fighters for top positions. He'd bet on UFC over Pancrase and lost both in the process. UFC was declining and appeared on death's door. Pancrase had slammed the door shut. As an athlete, Shamrock had never given much thought to the future, always figuring there was another fight around the corner. Now it kept him up nights. To survive, he started looking at a variety of options, including pro wrestling.

---

[152] "When it happened, it would be because we were pushing a guy," DeLucia says. "Quite honestly, I would do it."

[153] There is also a he said/he said/ she said triangle between Delucia, Shamrock and his wife Tina. It's probably a web best left untangled.

[154] "I remember, back when cell phones were expensive, Tina running up a $10,000 cell phone bill," one Lion's Den member recalls. "They were terrible with money."

"I got injured," Shamrock says. "I blew my knee out and had surgery on it. I had been fighting on it for awhile, but it was affecting my abilities. I couldn't fight, I had to back off. That's when it started setting in. Because the bills kept coming. There was a $20,000 a month bill for all the things that I had going. And when I wasn't fighting, that's when I realized 'wow, wait a minute.' If I stop fighting within a few years, I'm not going to have anything left.

"Bad financing, bad management. I mean, a lot of things went wrong. Myself too, I was part of the problem. My dad was rolling in and having fun, my wife was out buying Fendi shoes and all these other expensive things. And even though I wasn't managing the money, whenever I wanted something it was there. It was really a bad group of people to be handling that much money. We did not take care of it properly."

While negotiating simultaneously with New Japan Pro Wrestling[155] and WWF, Shamrock signed on for his first UFC tournament since UFC 3 way back in 1994. Attempts to run without Shamrock had seen diminishing returns, and after ten months, the promotion decided that Detroit may have been forgiven.

"We were constantly trying to plot out a path forward, from this fight to the next one, to the next one," Isaacs says. "And who are stars were going to be and how we'd position them against each other. Ken was always part of that discussion, but it wasn't always easy to figure out how to plan on Ken. We never knew which Ken was going to show up or how long he was going to be able to fight."

UFC booked a tournament that featured a nice mix of new stars like Don Frye and Mark Coleman and returning stalwarts from what were already being considered the good old days, men like Shamrock and Kimo. Fighting for the first time without Funaki as his main trainer and guru, Shamrock looked to make a change, hoping to escape the distractions that plagued him in Northern California.

He'd met Cincinnati Bengals long snapper Greg Truitt at a charity event and gotten connected to the team's strength and conditioning coach Kim Wood, a legend in that world. Wood was more than happy

---

[155] This hypothetical deal would have included both real fights and pro wrestling bouts, including a match in the Tokyo Dome where Shamrock would win the IWGP championship from the company's top star Shinya Hashimoto. When he turned it down, it went to Japanese Judo star Naoya Ogawa and changed the course of puroresu history.

to help Shamrock train, even housing him in his own daughter's bedroom. The fighting star woke up every morning in a room covered with pink.

"Quite frankly, pro football has changed," Wood told the *Dayton Daily News*. "There are very few James Brookses or Anthony Munozes or Tim Krumries any more. My business is to train people and teach people how to get the most out of themselves. Anytime you can work with a world class talent—not somebody who's complaining or whining—it's an honor.

"When you really get to know people in pro sports, you usually get a little disappointed because you find out they're not quite as advertised. Ken is every bit as advertised. You're talking about a tough, focused, and intelligent guy."

While Ken flew into Cincinnati to spend his days at Wood's Hammer Strength gym, his team drove out in Ken's truck packed with training equipment and, according to one team member, a cooler containing human growth hormone.

Shamrock left Cincinnati looking huge and strong, packing on size especially around his waist and back. His team rented a U-Haul and left with a bunch of new Hammer Strength equipment for the Lion's Den.

The UFC's court battles had forced them out of most major markets and into the Deep South. Even this card, as stacked as they come, was relegated to the Fair Park Arena in Birmingham, Alabama. Before Shamrock's last UFC tournament, the martial arts world was waiting with baited breath for a single fight—his return match with Royce Gracie. This was similar, as the fight world was collectively praying for a showdown with the notorious David "Tank" Abbott.

Bad blood between the two men had been brewing since Abbott arrived on the scene. Prior to that, the Lion's Den had been the swaggering bullies on the block. Abbott's crew had an even more dangerous air about them, even assaulting other fighters and crews when the mood struck. It was a combustible situation.

"I used to describe to people what it was like at a UFC event," Isaacs says. "There were like these packs of dogs. And each pack had a lead dog. Ken was the big dog from the Lion's Den. There was no doubt about it. And when two big dogs were in the same room, something was going to happen. That was the nature of it. They could identify each other and it always triggered something…they're roaming, they're juiced up. It's high energy. At times it's a dangerous mix.

"I would see Abbott's guys and the Lion's Den guys come really close. They were all ready for that. But Ken had his guys under control. They were very protective of each other."

While their barks were loud, it wasn't clear to everyone that either intended to bite. Abbott was game to fight just about anyone, but something about Shamrock irked him. Ken, he felt, had been handed everything on a silver platter, given opportunity after opportunity despite rarely delivering as expected. Meanwhile, he had lit a fire under the entire fight world and spent months on the shelf after some back-and-forth with John McCarthy and his wife Elaine. Both men had a lot invested in the idea of a bout and a loss would have dealt a serious psychic blow.

"Tank Abbott really knew how to get under Shamrock's skin," Art Davie says. "He used to say 'he's the world's biggest 170 pound man.' Tank said to me, 'hey Art, you used to measure our wrists to see how big our frames were. How big are Shamrock's wrists?' I said 'seven and a half.' He said 'I rest my case. The guy's a middleweight.' Shamrock always used to say he wanted to face Tank. But I was never completely convinced that that was the case."

The trouble all started back at UFC 6 in Casper, Wyoming. Bob Shamrock had rented a gym for the Lion's Den to use during fight week and at one point, Abbott's crew descended upon it.

"Tank Abbott and his crew were always somewhat confrontational with us but we always were under restraint," Mezger says. "I'd sit there and listen to these jackasses call us names. And it's not like we couldn't beat the shit out of them. We'd have to take it, and have to take it, and have to take it."

At the next event, in Buffalo, Abbott had made a scene at hotel bar wrestling around with Frank Shamrock and security had to come and break it up.

"I was there with my then girlfriend Tiffany," Frank told me in a *Bloody Elbow* interview. "Tank was hanging out at the bar there and wraps his arm around my shoulder. He said 'Hey cowboy, if she doesn't get down tonight, I'll take you home and suck your dick.' At this point, him and I get in a little bit of a wrestling match."

Every time Shamrock hit the cage, Abbott was there with something to say, always goading him with his trademark witticisms. The fans loved it, but it made Ken's blood boil. Abbott was at his best and worst in the UFC 9 aftermath, hitting Shamrock when he was down, after the worst performance of his, or anyone's, UFC career.

"You saw Glamrock and you saw a Freddie Mercury-look-alike or whatever," Abbott said with a smirk. "They didn't go out there to fight. When I go in there, I'm not going in there to win—I'm going out there to fight!"

Tempers cooled eventually, but things escalated again in September, 1996, at UFC 11. While Shamrock wasn't scheduled to fight, he almost went toe-to-toe with a returning Tank.[156] Bohlander was in the tournament that night and dispatched the highly touted jiu jitsu ace Fabio Gurgel, the latest in a long line of Gracie replacements that seemed to fall on their collective faces again and again.

"He was the best Brazilian jiu jitsu competitor in the world at the time," Bohlander says. "If you were to look at every metric that you could, I shouldn't have been able to beat him. But because of Ken's hard-headed training style, I was able to."

Bohlander and Abbott were supposed to meet in the semi-finals, but Shamrock insisted Bohlander go to the hospital to get checked out instead.

"I broke my hand, but that wasn't why I couldn't continue," Bohlander says. "The hand was never x-rayed. It was the concussion that prevented any more fighting that night. I was dealing with a massive headache I gave myself head butting Gurgel so many times. I ended the night joking around with Frank at the hospital while they went through a concussion protocol. I learned my lesson after that."

Not knowing, or caring, about any of this an enraged Abbott screamed at Shamrock "you're a pussy and your fighter is a pussy[157]," and Ken got right in his face until the two were separated. The situation, already tense, was getting downright dangerous.

"I knew what Tank was about. I knew what his agenda was and it

---

[156] Abbott had been briefly suspended by the UFC after a confrontation with John McCarthy's wife Elaine. He eventually wrote a letter apologizing for his rascally ways and was invited back into the fold.

[157] Abbott declined to be interviewed for this book. "Let Ken have his memories," he said.

This anecdote is from Clyde Gentry's excellent *No Holds Barred* and has been confirmed by multiple people on the scene.

didn't bother me. Everybody has to do their own thing. I just basically let him do it," Shamrock said in a 1997 interview. "What I don't respect is when he downplays other fighters. To me, that's the worst thing you can do to another person. He made comments about Jerry Bohlander that really pissed me off.

"I didn't appreciate that. I came unglued...If he would have come up to me and made it right later on, things would have been okay. But he made no bones about it. He didn't care. So I figured, if he didn't really care, I don't care."

With that kind of tension in the air, it seemed like nothing could possibly contain the two camps as they all descended on Birmingham for Ultimate Ultimate 96. Abbott was certainly doing his best to instigate trouble, signing his name over the top of Shamrock's face on the event poster and generally talking loud trash.

Violence finally erupted, although neither of the principals was present, when the Lion's Den arrived at the Sheraton Hotel in a group of taxi cabs while Team Abbott was lolly-gagging outside. Words were exchanged and "Big Al," an enormous biker who ran with Tank, threw a hamburger at Frank Shamrock. It might have been comical if Frank hadn't been dressed to the nines and at the end of night drinking.

"He grabbed my sweater and I freaked out," Frank remembers. "I hit him like five times, and every time I hit him, he got shorter and shorter. And then when he got really short, my shirt came off, and all of a sudden I'm like Bruce Lee and I'm standing there with my shirt off and they're all like, 'woo.'

"He's on the ground and I have these nice boots and I boot him in the face like three times and then everything gets really quiet and weird and then we all leave. The next day, he shows up and he's got all these butterfly (bandages) holding his face together. I remember he was like, 'Hey guys, I'm really sorry about that guys.'"

Like UFC 3, there was no satisfaction to be found in the second "Ultimate." Despite all the hype and pent up hostilities, the two men never laid hands on each other. Abbott knocked Cal Worsham silly in his first bout and Shamrock advanced to the second round easily, making an example of fellow NorCal fighter Brian Johnston in a one-sided fight.

"When I fought him, I was so psyched out by his larger than life persona that I didn't execute the game plan," Johnston says. "Hell, I didn't even fight back when he took me down. He had already won. He deserved a way better fight."

But the dream fight just wasn't meant to be. Shamrock, who had already banged up his right hand on Frank's head in training, injured it further in his extended ground-and-pound shellacking of Johnston. He dropped out of the tournament almost immediately with a broken hand.

His semi-final opponent would have been Abbott, who ended up dropping alternate Steve Nelmark with a brutal right hand that folded him up like the proverbial accordion, head holding his limp body up on the mat at an inhuman angle. He went on to lose to Don Frye in a classic final to close the show.

For Shamrock, it was just another example showing why the tournament system no longer made sense for the sport.

"In my opinion guys like myself, Coleman, Frye, even Tank, don't necessarily have to fight in tournaments," he told *Fight Sports Newsletter* shortly after the show. "Once you have an established name or are a fighter that people like to see fight. Why would you put them in a tournament and have them fight people that people don't know and then maybe that person tires him out. Then, when it's the fight they want to see, one guy's wore out and one guy's not, so you don't get to see them really get after each other.

"You match up the guys that people want to see fight. Personally, my opinion on the Tank Abbott-Ken Shamrock fight, why have him go through a tournament and why have me go through a tournament? Why not match us up? Because that's what the people want to see."

Despite Shamrock's frustration, in some ways, just like the delay prior to a second Gracie bout, the outcome just built anticipation for an eventual match. Shamrock had looked like a new man before his injury and Tank had lost nothing in the eyes of the fans after giving Frye a whooping before finally running out of steam.

UFC had an option for Shamrock to return in 1997, but the sides couldn't agree to terms. He was due a substantial raise for his work, which included promotional appearances in addition to fights, but UFC offered a substantial pay decrease instead.

"Ken Wayne Shamrock sold a lot of tickets for us," Art Davie says. "But he was a very complicated guy. I always went with kid gloves with him. I wouldn't say he was a prima donna but you had to respect Ken and you couldn't take him lightly. You had to treat him with a certain deference and I did."

The two sides were having a hard time coming to terms, but the fight being offered was intriguing—Shamrock versus Abbott.

"We didn't have television then, only pay-per-view," Isaacs says. "So we had limited air time to make guys famous. We had done that with Ken and we had done that with Abbott. Even better, they didn't like each other. Captain America against the Bad Guy. I was excited to make that fight. "

In January, Pete Williams traveled to Hawaii for SuperBrawl 3 and beat John Renfroe with an armbar in the main event to win his second consecutive tournament. But before Pete took his time in the spotlight, Shamrock got into the ring and cut a blistering promo on Abbott, who responded in an ill-fated appearance on commentary at UFC 12.

"He's appropriately named Sham-rock," Abbott said, putting the emphasis on sham. "He's a fake. He's a fraud. He's a sham."

That event, scheduled for New York, ended up in Dothan, Alabama, after a desperate political struggle saw the state ban the event, then enact a 114-page rulebook when it looked like the show might go on despite their best efforts.

"I think extreme fighting is disgusting, it's horrible," New York Mayor Rudy Giuliani told *The New York Times*. "I happen to be a boxing fan, have been all my life. And I know there are issues regarding boxing, and they are serious ones. But this is way beyond boxing. This is people brutalizing each other."

The rules banned submissions on the ground and required amateur boxing headgears among many other absurd restrictions, essentially making a proper UFC bout impossible. In a single day the entire show, including Shamrock, two of his fighters[158] and even the Octagon itself, was packed onto a leased jet and shipped to Alabama[159].

"The really dramatic moment for me was standing there with one of our production guys and literally throwing the fighters luggage off the plane," Isaacs said. "Because the plane was overweight because the Octagon was so heavy. This is Thursday night and it was a Friday event. We never told the fighters. The airport closed at midnight and we took off at 11:55 PM."

---

[158] Jerry Bohlander won the first lightweight tournament at this show, beating alternate Nick Sanzo with a neck crank in just 39 seconds. The weight class would eventually be called middleweight before the UFC finally settled on light heavyweight as the appropriate nomenclature.

[159] Isaacs had actually scouted the location in Dothan a week before the move. Because of continued legal trouble, the UFC had backup plans in place for every event. That's how fraught the entire sport was.

It was a remarkable logistical accomplishment. But it was hard to celebrate considering it looked like the sport was dying a slow, painful death.

"We felt like observers at our own funeral," former UFC executive Campbell McLaren told me in *Total MMA*. "...Everyone really jumped on the bandwagon and they quickly passed legislation banning us. We later found out...that it was done in a very illegal and bogus manner...we were still fucked. It didn't matter."

Shamrock began training, even without a contract in hand, as the rumor mill pegged him for an eventual fight with Abbott, Marco Ruas or another tournament appearance. But the experience in Dothan lingered in his mind. Not only was the UFC cutting his pay, but things only seemed likely to get worse rather than better.

The announcement in Dave Meltzer's *Wrestling Observer* that Shamrock had signed a three-year deal with the WWF, coming as it did less than three weeks after the Dothan debacle, sent shockwaves through the entire sport:

> The signing ends a pressure-cooker of a week for Shamrock, who was torn between offers from UFC, New Japan, WWF and a potential meeting with WCW.[160] It starts another pressure-cooker, going into the world of pro wrestling and on the road with the natural resentment of wrestlers who have paid more dues and because of experience are for the most part at this point better performers that won't be making as much money or getting as much of a push. Nevertheless, these are the risks a promotion has to take from time-to-time.
>
> ...WCW took it with Hulk Hogan, paying him more than any wrestler in history has ever earned, and gave him the world title despite its most loyal fans resenting it because he was the outsider being put over the home team's superstar and basically telling the most loyal fans the product they love was really not the best. In this case, it'll cause resentment originally by some fans as it portrays a UFC star as

---

[160] Then WCW President Eric Bischoff tells me that he never had any conversations with Shamrock or a proxy.

being equal to the top WWF wrestlers on their turf. He also gives WWF a chance to give its product a level of credibility and believability it is sorely lacking and is the foundation of those record-breaking houses in Japan.

Shamrock's departure from mixed martial arts represented more than just one man's business decision. It was a clarion call to everyone else in the sport—now is the time to go.[161]

"It was a total surprise. I had been negotiating with Bob for him to fight Abbott right up until the minute he told us he was leaving," Isaacs says. "My first inclination was that he was scared to fight Abbott. I wanted to see that fight personally. I wanted to see that question answered.

"But when I thought about it, for Ken, it was a good move. We were so on the edge. We thought at any moment that this whole thing could go away. I understood why he felt he needed to go."

For Shamrock, the decision wasn't easy. Between the loss of his Pancrase salary and the UFC's cutbacks which would only increase over the next few years, his income was going to be cut in half. He had devoted his life to building the sport from the ground up for four years and 30 fights. He'd also created the first successful fight team, a group of young men that seemed poised to take the industry by the throat. They were at the forefront of his mind as he decided to sacrifice his career for theirs.

"I was taking care of 11 fighters," Shamrock says. "Three houses. Three buildings for a gym. I had to do something just to keep my empire up and going. I was responsible for so many lives. I was taking care of my wife's family. The Boys home. My dad. I had all of this that

---

[161] Shamrock's decision to choose WWF over New Japan left the door open for another UFC star to fill that need. It ended up going to Don Frye, who made a dramatic turn from likable UFC superstar to snarling, mustachioed villian. Abbott too would soon make his way into the world of wrestling with WCW. There was a market for the UFC's biggest stars—but the company itself had no platform on which to showcase them widely.

I was responsible for.[162] All that responsibility.[163]

"When I went and did pro wrestling, I did pro wrestling out of necessity, not because I wanted to do it. I did it because I couldn't make enough money to support what I built. And so I had to make a move out of something I love doing. Because I did it for 20 grand before. It wasn't the money that I left for. It was the comfort and the security I had built for everyone else that I wouldn't be able to continue if I didn't make a move."

---

[162] The Shamrocks would welcome daughter Fallon to the growing family on July 12, 1996.

[163] Shamrock estimates his monthly overhead was around $30,000. That number was workable when his Pancrase and UFC careers were thriving. When they went away, it became unsustainable quickly.

CHAPTER TWELVE
Getting RAW

Shamrock came into the WWF at an interesting time in wrestling history. After a decade spent chasing all of the opposition out of the business, a single significant promotion remained to challenge Vince McMahon for American wrestling supremacy. Unlike other territorial rivals across the country, World Championship Wrestling wasn't particularly easy prey. The promotion was owned by Turner Broadcasting,[164] had national television on cable networks like TBS and TNT and a loyal audience, especially in the South[165].

Attempts to expand out of the South and compete with the WWF across the country were met with mixed success. Signing former McMahon stars like Hulk Hogan and Randy Savage helped raise awareness but were costly and left the promotion looking very much like a copycat—worse, one using WWF's leftovers.

In 1995, a young executive named Eric Bischoff proposed grabbing the tiger by the tale and challenging McMahon directly, launching WCW Monday Nitro to compete head-to-head on Monday nights with WWF RAW. Nitro launched with a surprise defection by WWF star Lex Luger and prompted brutal bidding wars between the two companies for any available, high profile talent, each looking for an edge in what soon became a fierce competition. The result was a boom —both in wrestler salaries and interest across the board in what became known colloquially as "the Monday Night Wars."

WCW's introduction of Kevin Nash and Scott Hall the previous year had raised the stakes, with the resulting super group called the NWO leading to the promotion's first extended ratings victories over the WWF behemoth. WWF, used to being the biggest dog in any fight with fellow wrestling promoters, suddenly found itself on the back foot, desperate to find the magic ingredient to propel them back to the front of the pack.

---

[164] In the spirit of full disclosure, the author is currently employed by Turner Sports.

[165] The promotion was an offshoot of the old Mid-Atlantic territory. Turner bought the floundering Jim Crockett Promotions after an attempted national expansion nearly bankrupted the group. It was important programming for his cable empire and he didn't want to see it disappear.

For a talent like Shamrock, it was an environment that led to a big offer of guaranteed money, something previously unthinkable for wrestlers, who traditionally had gotten paid based primarily on their placement on the card. His deal promised multiple six-figures every year, rescuing his fighter gyms and preserving his family's increasingly lavish lifestyle.

It didn't take long for WWF to integrate Shamrock into their regular programming. McMahon himself called Shamrock at home with an invitation to get started immediately. Just one day after officially signing a three-year contract, he made his first appearance on RAW. Presented as just another celebrity in the crowd, he was interviewed by announcer Jerry Lawler and ended the segment in a confrontation with Farooq.

It was a disjointed couple of minutes, ultimately a reflection of his entire tenure there. Because of his enormous guarantee, there was pressure on the company's creative team to use him in a prominent spot—but no one was entirely sure what that would look like.

"When I first heard they were bringing Ken in, I was really excited," wrestling legend Jim Cornette, who was part of the WWF's creative team at the time, remembers. "I'm old school wrestling, so I immediately thought about ways they could do it as an interpromotional angle. This MMA fighter from UFC coming to challenge our guys. We could make a shoot out of it. But they ended up just making him another pro wrestler. They took a guy who had sold 300,000 fucking pay-per-views and turned him into one more wrestler.

"Vince[166] never got the MMA thing. He'd never seen it. You couldn't even get him to watch someone else's wrestling, let alone something else from the sports world. I thought we missed a big opportunity to create Brock Lesnar[167] before there was a Brock Lesnar."

While Shamrock had trained for wrestling in North Carolina, and even performed on the independent circuit for several years, it had been nearly a decade since he had been a regular performer. WWF was hesitant to put him immediately into high profile matches, especially since his contract and push would require him to work with top stars

---

[166] WWE owner Vince McMahon had the final call on all creative decisions.

[167] Lesnar, a monstrous former NCAA wrestling titlist, became both a WWE superstar and UFC champion and remains a special attraction for the company into his 40s.

right away. Instead, he was shipped to Calgary to work with the Hart family and trainer.

"He had already established a certain level of fundamental soundness as far as the physicality is concerned," Jim Ross[168], then head of WWE's talent relations department, says. "He had an amazing look, too. He turned heads kind of like The Rock did at the same time. So the key with Kenny was just getting him to understand and feel comfortable in the psychology of wrestling. Sometimes these tough guys, amateur wrestlers and MMA guys, are reluctant to sell or question how much they should sell. We need the light to come on before we can really use them, so they realize that selling is essential—it's not an option, it's a requirement."

In Calgary, Shamrock worked mostly with Leo Burke, a journeyman wrestler who had been instrumental in teaching Hart himself the ropes almost two decades earlier when Bret was launching his own wrestling career in his father's Stampede Wrestling. By then 50 years old and retired from the ring, Burke was too worn down for the physicality of wrestling. But his mind was sharp, and WWF used him a lot to help get new wrestlers ready for the big show.

"Leo Burke was a polish guy," Sean Dunster, who wrestles as Massive Damage and was in camp with Shamrock, says. "He's there to help get you ready for the fed. Leo was a genius at the psychology side of the business. He wasn't teaching people how to bump and things like that. He was teaching us how to put a match together, how to put a sequence of moves together in a way that makes sense."

Shamrock had a hard time, even as he transitioned to wrestling, leaving fighting completely behind. He was wired for confrontation and, if not exactly seeking it out, never backing down from it either, even as he prepped for his new job.

"I was at Cowboys in Calgary before my first wrestling match," he says. "I'm heading out to the parking lot and this guy I'd had a beef with at the club comes out and starts banging on the car. I jumped out and decked the dude. Dropped him.

"I get in my car to take off because there were a lot of kids coming out of the club, his friends, and they were coming towards my car. I remember just peeling out and might have run over one of them. I don't know if I killed him. I was afraid, so I was getting out of there."

---

[168] Also a Hall of Fame announcer, Ross currently calls the action for WWE competitor All Elite Wrestling and hosts a popular podcast.

The Hart family took Shamrock in, even as he and Bret were antagonists on WWF television where Ken was assigned referee duties for Hart's WrestleMania 13 co-main event with rising star "Stone Cold" Steve Austin. It was a feud so fierce that only the "World's Most Dangerous Man" could share the ring with the two competitors[169], offering WWF fans a glimpse of Shamrock in the promotion's highest profile bout while he worked with the Harts to hone his own skills in the ring.

"I was Stu Hart[170]'s birthday present," Shamrock says. "He put me in all these holds and stuff. I was like 'that hurt. Yes, that hurts too.' He was a tough old shooter and really liked legitimate fighters like me being part of wrestling.

"Even though I already knew how to wrestle, being there helped me a bunch. Bret helped me understand who I was as a pro wrestler. I didn't understand how to be me. He explained that I could say and do the things I would really do, I just had to control it. It's like practice. You're not going out there to knock somebody out or submit them—but you'll put them in the hold."

The WrestleMania main event was an instant classic, a paradigm shifting match that saw the villainous Austin become the company's biggest babyface overnight after his courageous loss[171] and Hart, previously the WWF's leading good guy, booed for his cruelty as he attacked his fallen foe after the match. The match, Hart wrote in his biography, wowed both fans and the promotion's newest wrestler:

> The cheering was so loud I couldn't hear a thing. My

---

[169] From Jack Dempsey to Joe Frazier, former boxing champions had long been used in the role of referee in major wrestling matches. Shamrock's inclusion on this list of real life tough guys shows how quickly the UFC had invaded the public's consciousness.

[170] Stu Hart, the patriarch of the Hart wrestling dynasty, was famous for torturing prospective wrestlers with submission holds in the basement of his home. Everyday life at the Hart home was often accompanied by the screams of football players and weight lifters who wanted to give wrestling a try and the basement was soon referred to as "the Dungeon."

[171] Rather than quit to Hart's infamous "Sharpshooter" submission hold, Austin, blood streaming down his face, passed out from the pain.

fists bounced perfectly off Steve's head and he never stopped fighting back. Ken Shamrock, wearing a sleeveless zebra-striped referee shirt, looked amazed at how close our work was, and how totally believable.

Shamrock only got physically involved after the match was over when he had to defend a prone Austin after the match and ended up suplexing Hart, who backed off rather than confront the former UFC star, earning jeers from the audience. It was a master class in wrestling booking, making three stars in a single match.

"Those guys were putting on a show," Shamrock says. "I was like 'this is impressive.' I was into it like a fan. It really set a high standard and it was good for me to see what it took at the highest level.

"I took Bret up for that suplex after the match and I remember in the locker room he told me 'I was getting ready to go up and help you, but before I knew it, I was up and in the air. Dude, remind me not to piss you off.' A lot of that was adrenaline. It felt real. It was a great match."

Introducing Shamrock into WWF programming presented the creative team with a significant challenge. Had Cornette and others gotten their way, Shamrock would have entered the company across the ring from Hart, much the way New Japan planned to use him in a title program with their own superstar champion Shinya Hashimoto. Instead, he spent months in a limbo of sorts, appearing on house shows as a referee, continuing his WrestleMania role on the mid card.

Although now commonplace in wrestling, in 1997 basic concepts that were central to Shamrock's character had to be introduced to an audience unfamiliar with MMA submissions or tapping out to concede defeat. The holds that devastated opponents in legitimate matches simply didn't appear devastating in a pro wrestling context, where even submissions required complex setups and were much showier than a basic armbar or heel hook. It was Hart, training with Shamrock in Calgary, who helped refine what would become his signature submission hold, the ankle lock.

"I was really good at rolling into those toeholds and always thought it looked pretty sweet," Shamrock says. "And I could get a toehold anywhere on the mat, in any position. So I could roll into it from anywhere.

"I wanted to do the toehold like we did it in Pancrase, but Bret helped me make it better. He said 'You need a move where people can see your face. Because if you're up and people can see you, it's easier for them to buy into you.' I let all my anger and frustration come out in my face."

With educating the audience a priority, WWF reached out to UFC for rights to use highlights from Shamrock's fights in the Octagon and had Ken confront heels like Billy Gunn in brief battles that ended with submission holds.[172]

"We traded footage for promotion from them," then UFC President David Isaacs says. "It was a straight up deal. It was just business. They had just signed Ken and building us up built up Ken too.

"It was actually a difficult decision for us. We did not want to be confused with professional wrestling. This was our first acknowledgement that there was a crossover audience and that people would know the difference between the two. We were able to get in front of their much larger audience and they got some of UFC's credibility and our top star."

His first match in the ring was billed as an exhibition—with Lion's Den fighter Vernon White serving as the unlucky guinea pig, ending his night with several stitches in a bout that was panned by critics like Dave Meltzer who spared no feelings calling the two-minute match a step in the wrong direction for Shamrock:

> Shamrock has great charisma walking to the ring but they have no clue how to book him and this was a major step backwards. There is nothing that looks worse than a fake UFC match. Crowd didn't react and booed the tap out from punches since wrestling fans see that in almost every match as nothing but a transition spot. This needed a submission finish. White needed nine stitches since the glove punches, even with Shamrock holding back, actually opened

---

[172] Dan Severn was the guest color commentator for Shamrock's match on RAW with Gunn. The WWF was negotiating with him for a program with his former UFC foe but weren't able to strike when the iron was hot.

his head up badly and they went to the finish before doing a lot of planned spots.

"They tried to get some other guys like Paul Varelans[173]," White says. "They said no, so Ken came to me. 'They'll give you $5,000, but you have to get juiced[174].' I didn't know what juicing was. Next thing you know, we're in the match and he's really hitting me. We're taking each other down, rolling, and I'm like, "I thought this is supposed to be an exhibition match?' Ken gets me on the ground and he screamed. Next thing you know, I'm getting punched. I don't remember exactly where he had the razor, but I got cut by a razor. I got juiced.

"The sad part was that I was in the hospital getting stitches, so I didn't even get to go out and meet any fans. I didn't get to hang out with anybody or anything. Ken was gone. He was out partying, so I really didn't even get to hang out with Ken. I got my $5,000, a 'Raw is War' hat, a 'Raw is War' shirt and a 'good job.'"

Shamrock's first actual match in the WWF ring was against a fellow veteran of the Japanese shoot style scene, former WCW champion Leon "Vader" White[175]. Like Shamrock, Vader had signed a huge contract to jump ship from Atlanta to New York.[176] His WWF tenure, however, was a disappointment. McMahon lost faith in him as his weight inched ever up, turning him over time from an athletic big man into an obese big man. Beyond his aesthetic failures, in McMahon's eyes at least, he'd run into locker room trouble after the reigning WWF

---

[173] Paul Varelans was an oversized UFC fighter most famous as a foil for more skilled, smaller fighters like Marco Ruas. He had made an earlier appearance for Extreme Championship Wrestling that didn't end well, perhaps explaining his hesitance to get back into wrestling. As the story goes, Varelans was offered oral sex in exchange for losing a match to an ECW wrestler. When he got back from doing the job, the valet allegedly told him "Sorry, I don't blow jobbers."

[174] Wrestling matches used to be made more exciting with the introduction of blood. The old maxim in wrestling is that "red makes green," meaning blood in matches is a good method of increasing box office. While many fans believe this involves the use of Hollywood-style blood packs, it's often created with a small sliver of a razor blade that the wrestler or his opponent scrapes across his forehead.

[175] Vader's three matches with UWF-International star Nobuhiko Takada are among the best the genre has to offer.

[176] In professional wrestling in the 1980s and 1990s, Atlanta was shorthand for Turner's WCW and New York referred to McMahon's WWF.

champion Shawn Michaels accused him of being too rough in the ring. A match with Shamrock, on paper at least, would be right up his alley.

The promotion for the match was one of the best builds WWF had done in some time. Vader, who had been arrested in Kuwait after bullying a television host during a WWF tour, continued in that role on WWF Raw, roughing up announcer Jim Ross before Shamrock finally made the save. Meanwhile, making the most of their new relationship with UFC, the WWF aired several excellent personality profiles helping further introduce their latest acquisition to wrestling fans around the world.

"It was a match made in heaven," Shamrock says. "He was out of the perfect mold for me. Because I didn't have to worry about going 'oops' because he could take it. He had done all the stiff matches in Japan. When we went in there, we both agreed that we were going to rough each other up. No hard feelings. If it had been anyone else it might not have worked out. They would have gone to the office and complained. He didn't get pissy about it."

Though he was walking with a limp afterwards and had to take some time off after the ordeal, it was a match that Vader also enjoyed. It reminded everyone in the locker room who he was and what he could do in the right circumstances—perhaps most importantly himself. The two men had spent time together in Calgary working through the specifics of the bout with Bret Hart in the week before the match and it mostly went according to plan.

"That was my style match," Vader remembered. "It allowed me to be me, without someone complaining that I was going too hard in there. Ken was trying so hard to get over and he might have gotten carried away. It was his first match and he was green for our style. He was trying to do his best and he really beat the crap out of me. He was reverting back to a shoot and hit me right in the nose with a knee. He broke my nose. That was okay. He wasn't trying to hurt me. And I got some time off to get it fixed, which was nice."

Vader did spend some time on the shelf after the match[177], leaving the WWF a little unsure about how to proceed. What might have been a feud that cycled through several pay-per-view events turned into a one-off, and Shamrock was sent out on the road as a referee with the hope that he would continue to soak in knowledge.

---

[177] I mention this in part because wrestler's recollections and the historical record don't always match up nicely. Here it did.

It was more than a month before they put him in the ring again, in a dark match after RAW on June 12, 1997, teaming with the Undertaker and Mankind against the Hart Foundation. It was a matchup that allowed Shamrock to work with two of the company's most experienced wrestlers against the team that was helping train him.

"Shamrock is a competitor," Ross says, comparing him to other combat sports athletes the company has signed over the years. "They want to excel. They're just these competitive animals that don't want to be embarrassed. They want to look good. They want to look good, they want to perform well, they want to be the star of the show. It's not good enough to just be there and pick up a pay check. A guy like that wants to win, no matter what the competition is. In this case, it's having good matches and being a top performer."

Shamrock was a fast learner, quickly developing into a solid, conventional American-style worker. Soon he was wrestling competitive back-and-forth matches with undercard guys like Billy Gunn that resembled everything else on a standard WWF card. Had you not known about his UFC and martial arts background, you'd have never guessed he was a different kind of animal than the average wrestler. That, Cornette thought, was both a testament to Shamrock's quick development, and a huge mistake by the company.

"Ken was an excellent pro wrestler," he says. "Ken became one of the boys, and he was a top star as one of the boys, but he could have been really set apart and made the world's most dangerous man in a serious way.

"He got over very well, but not as good as he could have if anybody in the company at the time was in any way interested in presenting guys as real and legitimate."

While Shamrock was making his mark and learning how to navigate life in the WWF, his decision to leave the UFC in his rearview mirror proved prescient. In May, cable giant TCI confirmed their decision not to offer no-holds-barred fighting to its customers, writing Bob Meyrowitz a terse letter explaining their rationale:

> Thanks for the constructive effort you and your colleagues have made to meet some of our objections to carriage by TCI of Ultimate Fighting Championship events. However, we have decided to maintain our current position regarding carriage of the telecasts.

A primary reason for our decision is that states in which TCI has millions of customers do not allow the events to be held within their jurisdictions. This is a clear indication that regulatory authorities in these states consider the events inappropriate, given their current format.

The long-term solution obviously is to seek the type of widespread state sanctioning that is common for other athletic events of this type. Please keep us informed if you make progress in this regard.

In July, Shamrock teamed with Austin, Goldust and the Legion of Doom to battle the Hart Foundation on their home turf in Calgary.[178] It was one of the most memorable bouts of the era, with a raucous, partisan crowd cheering the Canadian villains and booing the good guys. The electricity in the air between Bret Hart and Austin all but sizzled and Shamrock's inclusion in the match was a clear indication to the fans that he was an important player.

"It was very important to me to be seen with wrestlers of that caliber," Shamrock says. "To be seen as a top star, you had to be associated with the top stars and move with that crowd. I was able to stand with some of the greatest wrestlers ever in a match I don't think people will ever forget. Being in that ring with those superstars showed the fans and even the wrestlers that I belonged.

"That match was awesome. We got to be the heels. At the same time, we didn't have to change anything. We just did what we did and the crowd went crazy. That was a testament, really, to Bret Hart and Stone Cold and the rivalry they had built. Bret was able to create this Canada versus the World story and they bought into it big time. That was a great time because no matter what we did, it got over."

As Shamrock continued to advance in the ring[179], he was also settling into life on the road with the WWF, a fast ride full of constant travel and nightly partying. Showing up to the matches, he found out,

---

[178] A real life confrontation between Hart and Shawn Michaels led to Shamrock's inclusion in the match despite his relative inexperience.

[179] His next feud was with Davey Boy Smith and included Shamrock being covered in dog food and his first WWF losses, by disqualification and countout. Shamrock, no longer the outsider from UFC, was firmly just another wrestler involved in standard wrestling shenanigans.

was just part of the gig. Getting from town to town, keeping yourself in shape and maintaining your diet were a daily challenge. And then there were the unofficial responsibilities after the show was over that often lasted until the bar closed, the sun came up or it was time to drive to the next city.

"Pro wrestling, especially in that era when he first came to us, the boys kind of had a social club," Ross says. "It was somewhat obligated. There were sometimes you'd hear guys kidding a guy for going up to his room after the show and getting on his computer or calling his family. The guys would get kidded for not going partying, and Kenny was going to go party. And God forbid they got a strip club that comps them their booze because they're stars and they're there. That's the kiss of death right there. He was going to be there early and stay late."

No stranger to the night club scene himself, Shamrock was still shocked by the way his new co-workers hit the strip clubs in each town, their notoriety and fame leading to almost endless opportunities for dalliances with the opposite sex.

"The parties, the girls, everything is free," Shamrock says. "It was like being a rock and roll star on tour, except we were on tour year round. There was no going home and resting for a week. It was like being on a roller coaster but you couldn't' get off. You don't have the ability to stop the ride. Only Vince does. And he isn't stopping it for anybody."

Problems popped up for Shamrock almost immediately. On August 24, 1997, the WWF had a house show in Albuquerque, New Mexico. The night before they had been in Chicago. The day before that it was Houston, Texas, where they'd flown from a show in Hyannis, Massachusetts. It was a dizzying, nonsensical schedule that crisscrossed the nation and Shamrock was having trouble adjusting.

The days were spent traveling, looking for a place to work out, maybe catching a nap. The nights were packed with wrestling and then the endless party that was life on the road with WWF. After a particularly raucous time in Chicago, Shamrock didn't make his flight the next morning.

"We banged on his door and he just wouldn't come out," one

wrestler says[180]. "He had a girl in there and I think he must have passed out. He wouldn't get up. Eventually we just had to leave for the airport and wish him the best you know?"

For most cities, you could possibly get away with that. There are a lot of flights to places like New York or Atlanta. But there was just one that would have gotten him to New Mexico for the show that night—and he missed it. It was the second show he hadn't shown up for and that wasn't going to work in the tightly regimented world of the WWF.

Four days later, Shamrock and Ross had it out on the loading dock of an arena in Tacoma, Washington. Ross had to fine Shamrock a week's pay, over $5000, and wasn't sure how the fighter was going to respond.

"We don't do that," Ross remembers. "You can get away with a lot in wrestling, but we don't do no-shows. It's fucking intolerable. The biggest trait I always looked for in hiring talent was reliability. And when you no-show because you got messed up or drunk and you don't want to get out of bed and go to work, you're not reliable. I can't use you.

"I remember telling Jerry Brisco 'I'm going to take Kenny out to the loading dock because I want to talk to Shamrock about no-showing. If I'm not back in 10 minutes, come find me and make sure I'm not dead.' It was a joke, kind of. I remember thinking I might be on the ground. Because I had no idea what he'd do when I tell him what's going on."

"We advertised you," Ross told him. The fans were counting on seeing you. You have to be there. Burning the candle on both ends would end your career before it ever really begins. Worse, you could end up dead.

Shamrock took it all in and surprised Ross with his response.

"He apologized," Ross says. "Kenny had the right instincts. Kenny's got a good heart. I think sometimes in that area he was very easily distracted and there were a lot of distractions. A good looking guy, you know we're on television, girls were flocking to him.

"No matter how good you look, or what you can do in the gym, or how much weight you can lift, or how much cardio you can withstand that lifestyle is a fait accompli. You can't stay in the fast lane and not expect to ever wreck or get a ticket. It's going to happen."

---

[180] There is a very firm "no snitches" mentality in the wrestling community. Some of Shamrock's contemporaries would only discuss him if promised anonymity.

The grind of life in the WWF started to wear on Shamrock early. In September, about half a year into his run, he was injured after a match with Farooq in Muncie, Indiana, and ended up coughing up blood. While the Observer reported it was a lung infection, Shamrock says it was a legitimate injury.

"That was real," he says. "I had a tear in my lung and I didn't realize it until I went to the doctors after I had worked for a couple of shows. I would get slammed and after I got slammed one or two times, I would start coughing up blood again. The impact pulls the lung and it is like what they call a micro tear. But it closes back up. When you get slammed again, it opens back up and it bleeds a little bit more.

"That's why I was coughing up blood. They went and did all these sonograms and everything and put me through some lung stress stuff. They ended up saying 'hey, you got to stop. Otherwise it's going to tear and stay open and you're going to drown.' It was good to know because, you know, it could have been one of those times it could have just ripped and then I might have literally died in the ring."

It was an inopportune time for an injury. Frontier Martial Wrestling, a hardcore promotion in Japan, had paid a reported $100,000 to use Shamrock and Vader in a match at Kawasaki Stadium. Both had made their names in Japan and the thought was they would help the promotion draw the biggest crowd in company history.[181]

The match was short and extraordinarily violent. Primarily consisting of punches that blackened Vader's eyes and left Shamrock woozy, it ended abruptly after just over seven minutes when Shamrock began coughing up blood following a Vader powerbomb.

"He dropped to one knee and blood was pouring out of him," Vader said. "He looked at me and just kind of shook his head and we stopped the match. That was not the scheduled finish but he was scared he was going to choke on his own blood. It was pouring out just like a faucet. I was scared, and I was yelling for a doctor. I read in the Observer that this was a work and I was acting scared. There was no work about that[182]."

* * *

---

[181] FMW drew more than 50,000 people to the venue, a former baseball stadium whose team had abandoned it for new digs in Yokohama.

[182] Bruce Pritchard, who joined the two in Japan to represent WWF's interests, says that this was the planned finish but that Shamrock's injury was real, which is why they kept the match short.

While Shamrock was struggling adjusting to life in pro wrestling, his Lion's Den fighters were continuing to make their marks on the no-holds-barred world in his absence. Frank Shamrock and Jerry Bohlander took over as the new leaders of the team, and in June they broke ground on a new facility in Lodi, California, open to the public with hopes of funding the fighting team in the face of continued cutbacks across the sport.

With bridges to Pancrase burned for most of the team, they found a refuge in the competing RINGS organization, another shoot style promotion that was considering a move towards more legitimate fighting. Frank went there twice to fight the company's top native competitors Kiyoshi Tamura and Tsyoshi Kohsaka.[183] Pete Williams joined him for the second bout, taking on Joop Kasteel on the undercard.

While Williams won the fight, Ken was not happy with his performance. A poor result was one thing—it could happen to anyone. But a poor result that was due to poor preparation and a lack of training was unforgivable. And that's what Ken believed he saw on the tape when he finally got a chance to view the fights.

"He was very right to be angry," Vernon White says. "When the cat's away, the mice play. People were smoking weed at the gym, not working hard. Nobody wanted to train as hard as Ken wanted us to train. We wanted to show that we could be just as lazy as everybody else in the sport and still win."

When Ken finally arrived to have it out with Frank, Tsyoshi Kohsaka was training at the gym, another Lion's Den opponent seeking wisdom from the fight team that had given him fits in the ring. Shamrock saw him out of the corner of his eye as he entered his facility, but his attention was squarely on his brother.

Yes, Bohlander was equally in charge in theory, but Bohlander wasn't family. Bohlander, Ken decided, was a great follower, Frank a leader. Shamrock put the blame squarely on Frank's shoulders and arrived at the gym expressly to give him a talking to.

"Look at him," Ken told his brother, pointing at Williams. "He was

---

[183] There are rumors that both of these fights were works. If so, they were extraordinarily well done.

not in shape. That was your responsibility. To make sure he stepped in the ring in shape. You were in charge of that. You only took care of yourself."

Brian Espinoza, who helped out in the office, quickly saw himself out when the computer monitor went flying.

"Ken called Pete in and said 'Dude, you're a fat piece of shit. You're slow,'" Espinoza says. "And Pete said, 'Yeah, but Ken I won.'"

That's when Frank laughed, not a guffaw but almost a giggle. Ken, never much for keeping his emotions under wraps, lost what little composure he had left. What was meant as a motivational speech turned into a full on tirade.

"He started to chuckle," Ken says. "I flipped up the table on him and said 'what the fuck is so funny?' He stopped and looked like I just shocked him. I was pissed off. He wanted the responsibility to run the gym. And I gave it to him. Then he pissed all over it by caring only about himself."

The computer monitor was an old school one, heavy and substantial, from the days before flat screens. It went flying by, inches from Frank's head and into the wall. Whether it was meant to hit Frank or not is a matter of interpretation.

"I think that was more of a dramatic point than trying to hurt anyone," Bohlander says. "If Ken wanted to fuck Frank up, Ken wouldn't have needed a computer to fuck Frank up. I trained with Ken, I trained with Frank. Frank made me tap out one time. Ken could make me tap out at will. If Ken wanted to whoop Frank's ass and he wanted to make a point, Ken was going to whoop Frank's ass and make a point. He wouldn't have needed to throw a computer at him."

Everyone around the Den had seen plenty of tense, violent moments. But this was something beyond the usual Ken Shamrock mind games. He was, some onlookers say, completely unhinged and taking out some of his own regrets with leaving the fight game behind on his team.

"I was there that day. He can say whatever he wants, that was Ken's fault," Lion's Den fighter Mikey Burnett said. "Ken fucking flipped out on him. That goes back to being on the road with WWF. I don't know what all he was on, but he was crazy. He blamed everything on Frank, but I don't think that's what it was. These guys were staying in the limelight and fighting and Ken was battling with doing pro wrestling. And I think he took it out on Frank."

Once things boiled over, a lot of grievances came to the surface.

Frank, according to onlookers, felt disrespected and overlooked. Ken, for his part, felt like Frank wasn't living up to his end of their agreement and taking advantage of Ken's absence in a number of ways big and small.

"He took my truck out boogie bouncing," Ken remembers. "Underneath there was dirt clods and weeds, all these scratches on it. Tina had told him not to. And it smelled like pot on the inside of it. The gym was like Sodom and Gomorrah. I was no angel. But I kept all of that away from the training and separate from my life as an athlete. That's not how I raised those guys or what I wanted the gym to be like."

The next day, Frank was in the wind, years of friendship and even his adopted family now firmly resigned to the past.

"Frank was probably the best of all of us, he had the most potential," Burnett said. "Very strong, very athletic, very strong mind. But no one would have ever known that if he hadn't left. Ken would have never let him do it— fight in the UFC.

"It was an ego thing. Ken had problems with everybody that was doing well with their career if it got to a point where they might be doing better than he was with his career at the time. He was weird about it. He wanted everybody to do good, but not better than him."

Bohlander and some others knew he was frustrated and considering making a break from the Lion's Den. No one understood it would be so awful and so permanent.

"Frank just up and left," Ken says. "My dad tried to talk to him 'Make sure you pay Ken what you owe him.' I should have done something to stop him. When I look back on it, I handled it wrong. No question. I was pissed off."

Frank wasn't sure what would happen when he drew a line in the sand. He always suspected that Bob favored Ken. But he didn't realize that his own relationship with his foster father was contingent on his arrangement with Ken.

"They kicked me out because I wouldn't run the gyms for Ken and follow his lackey lead and be a mindless idiot," Frank says. "Bob's response to the whole thing was 'make it right with Ken. Do what Ken says and you're back in the family.' That's what my Dad told me.

"Ken was fucking crazier than I am. I was like 'what are you talking about? We're lowering people out of fucking windows. He's having us have his urine replaced by a fucking doctor. What the fuck! Everything is a fucking lie and a fraud and fucking bullshit and you want me to go lead that? What are you talking about?' Nope, 'you gotta make up with Ken and do what he says or you can't be in the family.' I was like this guy loves me but he don't really know what love truly is."

Frank ended up in San Jose, forming American Kickboxing Academy with Javier Mendes, and solidifying his relationship with Maurice Smith and Kohsaka. He would become a legend in his own right, one of the best fighters of the UFC's lost years, the time between the initial period Ken helped pioneer and the mega-promotion that would emerge in the late 2000s. But he would do it without the fighting family that had helped make him who he was.

"I felt really bad for Frank," Burnett said. "Because for the first time in his life he had a family, us. The Lion's Den, the way it was. Frank was about to wrestle Dan Henderson in The Contender and I was going to go with him. Ken said 'Fuck no, you're not going with him.'

"When he left I know he went through some hard times and I know he went through some bad situations. He asked me to leave with him, but I was just in a position where I couldn't. I was fixing to have a kid, fixing to have a UFC fight."

The gap between Frank and the rest of the Den became unbridgeable when he took a fight with Kevin Jackson to become the UFC's first middleweight champion. It was long expected that a Lion's Den fighter would be the first champion—but that it would be either Bohlander or Mezger, who had both won tournaments in the new weight class and believed they had established themselves at the top of the pecking order.

UFC had cleared it with the fighters and with Ken that teammates could meet for a championship prize and both Mezger and Bohlander were game. Instead, because the fight was scheduled for Japan and he was a name there, Frank swooped in and earned the title with an armbar in just seconds.[184] Bohlander, who had been Frank's roommate and close friend, hadn't known his former training partner had taken what he thought was his title shot until the fight was actually announced. An already fragile relationship between Frank and the team was broken beyond repair.

"I was pissed off at Frank because we were like best of friends, we were super close," Bohlander says. "We did everything together. Everything from going out and drinking to picking up on girls to

---

[184] He'd first dispatched Enson Inoue in Japan to earn the opportunity at a Vale Tudo Japan event.

frigging training with one another.

"I knew that he was thinking about leaving. What I didn't know was that he was negotiating behind my back. You know what, you gotta look out for number one. He looked out for number one, I can't blame him at this point in my life.

"But, back then, it was catastrophic. Because he was one of my best friends, if not my very best friend at the time, and my understanding was it was going to be me and Guy fighting for the title."

When Frank won the title, it was Maurice Smith who was there to greet him in the ring, not his foster brother. While it was never mentioned on television, his Lion's Den days were firmly in his past.

Shamrock's tumultuous visits back to the Lion's Den were few and far between. The WWF had an aggressive road schedule and Ken was booked almost nightly for most of the year. He took two weeks off after the Vader match before stepping back into the ring for a string of house show main events for Bret Hart's world championship.

It was a somber time for the locker room. On October 5, Brian Pillman, one of Shamrock's early travel partners, was found dead in a hotel room. Ross' fears that led him to lecture Ken earlier that year had been realized—only it wasn't Shamrock in the casket, or his young kids who were left fatherless.

The death shook Shamrock, who had spent a lot of time with Pillman, who for better or worse was one of the wrestlers who indoctrinated him into life on the road.

"On one of my early trips, Brian was riding with me because he couldn't rent a car," Shamrock says. "He didn't talk a whole lot and was drinking these Diet Cokes, one after another. There were four of them on the ground. He seemed a little bit off.

"We get out to eat at this diner where all the boys had gone and he can't walk. I thought he was dying. I went in and I grabbed Stone Cold. I was really worried. Steve came out just to laugh at him. I thought he was dying but they told me he had just taken some gimmicks. That's what they called somas[185].

"He was literally drooling all over himself. Everyone was laughing at him and I thought it was so cruel. I dropped him off in his room and thought 'these people are wacked.'

"But just a couple of months into it, I was right there with everybody else. Later that night, I went down to get some water because I couldn't sleep. And I see Brian Pillman walking around just blitzed. I remember thinking he'd be sleeping it off all night, but he was right back at it. Two or three weeks after that, he overdosed. I was introduced very early to how ugly it could be."

Not even death could slow the WWF freight train. A little more than two weeks later, Shamrock was in the ring for a title bout with Hart. This was not only Shamrock's first title bout on RAW (and Hart's last), it was a match that suddenly took on added importance behind the scenes.

Unbeknownst to the viewing audience, Hart had accepted a deal with WCW and would soon be departing WWF for its bitter rival down south. This kind of talent exchange was becoming the norm, but this departure had an added wrinkle—Hart was the reigning WWF champion and wasn't keen on losing the belt to his real life nemesis Shawn Michaels.

Shamrock was on a short list of the wrestlers Hart was willing to do the job for on his way out—but WWF boss Vince McMahon was just as insistent that it be Michaels as Hart was that he absolutely would *not* lose to the Heartbreak Kid, especially in Canada which just happened to be the home of the next WWF pay-per-view, Survivor Series.

The two had reached an impasse with no real clear solution. Hart had creative control built into his contract and refused to do the favor for Michaels, who had turned their storyline feud increasingly personal over the year. The whole thing was a complete mess, all documented by a film crew there to tell the story of Hart's life.

While consideration was given to dropping the title temporarily to Shamrock[186]— and Hart even tapped out to the ankle lock after the

---

[185] Somas are a powerful muscle relaxer. They work well to help mask the pain associated with the wrestling business but can be deadly when abused or combined with recreational drugs and alcohol.

[186] The *Wrestling Observer* reported: "There would be a non-finish in Montreal, and on the next PPV, there would be a four-way with Michaels, Hart, Undertaker and Ken Shamrock. It would be an elimination match, so Hart

referee was knocked down, ultimately the match ended in a cluster of bodies and chaos when Michaels and DX interfered. Shamrock got a chance at revenge the next week when he faced Michaels one-on-one. The WWF was devolving into complete madness and Shamrock found himself right in the middle of it all.

Survivor Series 1997 will go down in the history books as one of the most controversial, amazing nights in professional wrestling history. Unhappy with Hart's reluctance to drop the title on command to Michaels, McMahon decided he'd just take the belt back, arranging a heist that was broadcast live to the world on pay-per-view. Hart believed the bout would end in a disqualification after interference from the two men's factions. Instead, once they had worked out the details of the match, Michaels and McMahon's closest confidantes devised a scheme for him to win the match in the middle of the ring without Hart ever having a clue about what was transpiring until it was too late.

"It was probably the most uncomfortable day I've ever had in the wrestling business," Michaels told ESPN. "By the time the day comes, the decision has been made. But no one knows how it's going to get done until Bret and I sit down to start discussing the match—none of this can actually go into play until we do that. And so it was just an uncomfortable day knowing what you know, how others assume it's going to happen, and then you having to be the one to orchestrate it all."

Ultimately, Michaels locked Hart into his own trademark submission hold called the Sharpshooter. The planned spot was for Hart to reverse it and take control before the two teams eventually brawled to end the show. Instead, referee Earl Hebner immediately called for the bell, signaling that Hart had conceded the match.

Afterwards, in the locker room, sides were drawn up. Shamrock ended up with Bret and the Hart Foundation, suddenly feeling they were in unfriendly territory.

"Bret came up to me and said 'hey man, you got my back?' Because

---

would lose cleanly in his last night in, to either Undertaker or Shamrock. Hart had great respect for Undertaker, and Hart personally recruited Shamrock to WWF. The point being is that Hart considered Shamrock almost a protégé, since Shamrock even trained in Calgary for his WWF debut in Hart's camp under Leo Burke and he'd have had no problems losing to either one on the way out."

he thought something was going to happen," Shamrock says. "I said 'Absolutely.' He told me 'I'm going to kick Vince's ass and I don't want anybody jumping in.' What am I going to say? I was in the locker room with Bret. There was Davey Boy, Anvil, myself and Owen. Vince came in with Pat Patterson, Shane and few of the agents. And they said 'everybody out.' Nobody moved. And Bret ended up flooring Vince."

It was the end of a legendary road for Bret in the WWF in some ways. Despite his physical absence, however, Hart remained the focal point of the show even after he was gone. McMahon cut a famous promo, telling the wrestling world "Bret screwed Bret," using the controversy to become the biggest bad guy in all of professional wrestling.

This was bad news for Shamrock, who despite being Michaels' next opponent, ended up being an afterthought. The first night after the Montreal Screwjob, Michaels devoted much of his attention to running down Hart, even as Shamrock confronted him directly. In the subsequent main event against Triple H, Shamrock ended up pinning Michaels, who wasn't even in the match, only after the show had gone off the air.

"I think a lot of times Shawn got heat when he was just being his character," Shamrock says. "He's funny, he does things to hurt people. He pushed the edge of what was real and what was not. If you take that personal, that's on you. He's being him. You have to be you. If I had bought into what everyone was saying about him, it might not have turned out so well. Because I might have taken some things personally."

There were concerns in Michaels' circle that things could get ugly. It had gotten physical between Hart and McMahon and if that could happen, anything could. Shamrock was a Hart guy—Bret, in fact, had pushed for Vince to pursue him after talking with Ken and Bob about it. That connection, perhaps unfairly, made what remained of HBK's Kliq[187] a little nervous.

"It got to the point where Shawn and I had hand signals worked out in case someone tried to turn one of Shawn's matches into a real shoot," Triple H said in *The Unauthorized History of DX*. "If things turned into a shoot, he'd flash a hand signal and I'd hit the ring and

---

[187] An unofficial group of friends, the Kliq at one point included Michaels, Kevin Nash, Scott Hall, Triple H and X-Pac. It was a powerful group behind-the-scenes in WWF.

start kicking ass. They might beat us up, but they'd get a hell of a fight with both of us. That's the point we had reached after Montreal.

"The first time we did it was when Shawn wrestled Ken Shamrock at the DX Pay-Per-View in December. I remember talking about it. Shamrock may be the world's most dangerous man, but he can't take both of us. Shawn would give me the hand sign, and I'd come running to the ring and clobber him.

"Shamrock was real good friends with Bret. And even though he had come to us and said, 'What you guys did was business, and I got no problem with you,' how did we know that this wasn't the setup?"

Unfortunately for Shamrock, the Montreal Screwjob continued to dominate WWF programming for the remainder of the month. The next week Shamrock didn't even appear on RAW and the week after that, Michaels did an extended skit teasing a final battle with Hart, only to end up in the ring with a midget dressed up like the "Hitman." It was fairly entertaining television but did nothing at all to build up his bout with Shamrock.

This was the build for what would end up being the only pay-per-view main event of his career. The two were overshadowed by an entertaining back and forth between the Rock and "Stone Cold" Steve Austin, in what would become one of the defining rivalries of the era. It underscores the issues Shamrock faced during his entire tenure in the WWF—as good as he was, as over as he was, he was in direct competition with some of the most memorable, genre-defining wrestlers in the history of the business.

In the end, the two men had a solid match in an otherwise forgettable show, the last gasp before WWF programming would be dominated by the endless feud between Austin and McMahon.

"I remember Owen saying 'You have to get yours. Because he'll eat you up if you let him.' Going into that match, Shawn was really cool to me, but that was kind of his m.o. in the locker room," Shamrock says. "He's cool to your face but can make a match look like he's the only one in there. But he sold for me, which was a question whether or not he would. We had a good match.

"He's not a guy who's a fraidy cat. He's not scared. I think he respected me and that I could work. He wasn't worried that I was going to punch him in the face. I never had a problem with him. He was always professional. He was a superstar and I was in with him. I was really happy about the match."

At the end of the bout, Shamrock looked strong. He had Michaels trapped in his patented ankle lock submission, forcing DX to interfere to save the title for their leader. But after the match, attention turned to Owen Hart, who came from out of the audience to finally seek revenge for HBK's betrayal of his brother at Survivor Series.[188] Shamrock, by design, faded into the backdrop. He'd made a decision five days before the match that would impact his WWF career forever.

---

[188] To make it look good, and to get around WWF's policy not to allow wrestlers to cut their own foreheads to get blood flowing, Hart had taken a razor blade to his own fingers to make it look like he had bloodied Michaels' nose.

CHAPTER THIRTEEN

World's Most Dangerous Man

Shamrock's match with Michaels, the best in-ring worker of a generation, *should* have had his complete attention. It was his first main event on pay-per-view and a chance to establish his ability to compete with the top stars in the business. But, despite the stakes, his mind wasn't entirely on what he was doing.

The timing couldn't have been worse.

With Hart leaving, Michaels hurting to the point retirement[189] was imminent and Austin barely holding on after a traumatic neck injury in the summer of 1997, WWF officials were considering what the future of the promotion would look like. It was the time for Shamrock, and every high profile wrestler on the roster, to make his case for a top spot.

Instead, Shamrock showed McMahon, his heart wasn't fully in his work.

"I thought Kenny had a great performance (against Michaels) and it spotlighted Kenny and what he did really well," WWE executive Bruce Prichard said. "However, Ken's heart was in MMA. You're not going to invest your money in a guy who isn't 100 percent invested in it. We

---

[189] Michaels was breaking down after years of crazy bumps and physical abuse. He exacerbated a pre-existing back injury against the Undertaker in January and his match with Austin at WrestleMania 14 would be his last for several years.

kept him strong with the DQ, didn't beat him. Then let him go pursue his MMA career."

There was a part of Shamrock that was still obsessed with the sport he had just walked away from, still feeling he had things to prove. He had pitched WWF several times on joint promotions for MMA fights, tried to secure a position as the UFC color commentator and generally kept a very close eye on the entire MMA world[190].

Despite rapid-fire advances inside the cage, no-holds-barred fighting continued to decline in the United States as a business enterprise. As WWF was about to enter a golden age, UFC struggled just to survive. Facing political pressure everywhere they attempted to host a show in the United States, they took their event on the road to places where the sport had a demonstrable fanbase and more popular support.[191]

In December of 1997 they scheduled a show for Japan, hoping to ride the coattails of Pride's early success. They partnered with the Kingdom[192] promotion and hoped to steal the Japanese formula of using professional wrestlers to supercharge fan interest in the new sport. It worked well enough to score a television spot on channel 4, albeit on tape delay in the middle of the night. But, for the UFC at the time, any win was a big win.

The successor of UWF-International, Kingdom included a number of wrestlers who came up in the same martial system that had produced Shamrock and the Pancrase founders. Most important of these wrestlers by far was Nobuhiko Takada, the wrestler who had tested Rickson Gracie at the first Pride just two months earlier and was found wanting.

According to reports, he was in serious discussions with UFC—but wanted a fellow professional wrestler as his opponent. UFC reached

---

[190] While Shamrock was out of the cage, Lion's Den competitors Jerry Bohlander and Guy Mezger won the first two UFC "lightweight" tournaments for fighters under 200 pounds.

[191] UFC went to Puerto Rico in 1996, Japan in 1997 and Brazil in 1998. These trips were both a chance to break ground in new areas but also intended as a respite from the regular cycle of court and media battles they fought prior to every event in the continental United States.

[192] Kingdom took the shoot style wrestling of the UWF revolution to new heights, often becoming all but indistinguishable from actual MMA competition.

out to WWF to see about using Shamrock, offering more than $100,000 to use him for a single bout. But the company had plans for Ken in December and beyond, with Jim Ross beginning to talk him up both on commentary and behind-the-scenes as a potential main event player.

Talks turned to using Vader, a former Takada rival in the role, but ultimately went nowhere. When they couldn't announce the star wrestler for the main event, ticket sales lagged and the UFC and its Japanese partners got desperate, making an offer that *Pro Wrestling Torch* reported the WWF simply couldn't ignore:

> The Japanese promoters made several offers to the WWF, since the WWF has rights to Shamrock's bookings. The WWF turned them down initially, understandable considering their streak of bad luck with injuries. Putting Shamrock in a position to get injured and miss extended ring time at a period when their roster was depleted didn't make sense. The Japanese, though, eventually upped their offer to the WWF to a reported $300,000-plus for the rights to Shamrock for one night. After talking it over with Shamrock, the WWF agreed to the deal. Obviously Shamrock will get a sizable chunk of that booking fee for participating in the match, a match he feels comfortable he can handily win.

The agreement between WWF and UFC included a provision that saw the wrestling company agree to plug the fight on its programming in exchange for the rights to air the bout later, likely part of a mini-documentary that would include footage of Shamrock's preparation for the contest and behind-the-scenes footage in Japan.

Shamrock missed the RAW in Portland, Maine, following his pay-per-view main event with Michaels and the television taping the next night in Durham, New Hampshire, leaving immediately to train with Guy Mezger in Dallas. He would have less than two weeks to train for what would be the highest profile bout of his career.

"Even when Takada was at his very best, let's say a 28-year-old Takada, I could beat him as this broken up 50-year-old right now," Mezger says. "That's what a little puss that guy is. So Ken's like, 'Oh, hell yeah.' I mean it's not even like that fight is going to be even remotely close."

"Ken was like, 'I'm going to train for this, but I don't think he's going to do it.' And I go, 'Why's that?' He says, 'He's going to want me to throw the fight.' And sure enough, I think that's what happened."

By the time the news was being revealed in the wrestling media, Shamrock was already back on the road with WWF, taking on D-Lo Brown in a match taped for the December 22 edition of RAW and then wrestling Rocky Maivia, Hunter Hearst Helmsley and Phinneas Godwin on a three-night tour of Tennessee between December 11 and December 14.[193]

Takada, as Shamrock expected, had balked at taking the fight and the Japanese promoters paying the freight on the big-ticket main event weren't interested in bringing Shamrock over to fight anyone other than Takada at that price. Shamrock continued to train, hoping to get a spot on the UFC's card in March of 1998, but that was too close to WrestleMania for WWF's comfort.

The brief flirtation with returning to fighting was never mentioned on WWF television and he only missed a handful of dates. But his obvious preference for real life combat cost him big time in what was a furious contest behind the scenes for position in the pecking order. While rivals like Helmsley and Cactus Jack clearly lived and breathed for the business, Shamrock now had an asterisk attached to his name. He was still over and still performing well—but there was suspicion he wasn't in it for the long haul.

"Kenny was a man's man," one WWF executive says. "We liked him, he was good to be around, he was tough, he worked banged and beat up and he kept getting better and better and better. And then, as I recall, he decided he wanted to go back to fighting more than he wanted to be a top athlete for us. So that kind of curtailed that situation."

* * *

---

[193] He was also on the road in Little Rock on December 15 and expected to present the legendary Danny Hodge with a Living Legend plaque shooter to shooter. Then Hodge would be in his corner in the main event. Instead, Michaels insisted on making the presentation, despite being a heel, and fans let him have it. Eventually the show was called off when the DX crew was pelted with garbage on the way to the ring. There was no main event and someone set off a smoke bomb in the arena. Just another night for a pro wrestler in the WWF.

As he started his second year with WWF, Shamrock was placed in the defining feud of his short career, taking on the Nation of Domination as the faction entered its last days. It was a program that allowed Shamrock to play to his strengths and minimized his weaknesses.

"Ken just couldn't figure out how to deliver the long promos you needed to be a top star in those days," one WWF contemporary said. "He was, frankly, really bad (on the microphone). In the ring he could hang with anyone. But if you gave the Rock or Stone Cold a mic, it wasn't a fair fight. Ken was about as articulate as a tree stump."

That made his pairing with the Nation perfect. Ken could focus on wrestling Rocky Maivia while most of the work crafting the broader narrative was handled by Nation members as they worked through an internal drama focused on Rock's attempts to usurp leadership of the group from Farooq. It was a very entertaining months-long soap opera —but one that left Shamrock as sort of a supporting player despite, ostensibly, being the lead babyface.

"He's the ultimate badass, the toughest guy in the company and yet by the end of (1998) he'd become a dork," Arnold Furious writes in *The RAW Files: 1998*. "Mainly because he couldn't talk. In any other era Shamrock would have been a world champion. He was legitimate, he learned the main event game at a decent speed, but his promos were lousy so Attitude was a terrible time for him to be a top guy."

The focus here was on Maivia. The previous year he'd been the target of fans' ire as an ever-smiling generic babyface they didn't think deserved his push. As a heel, he was a revelation, stealing scene after scene weekly on RAW and basically forcing his way up the card by making himself undeniable. By early 1998, he and Shamrock were a hot enough pairing to main event smaller house shows in tag team action and his future seemed almost impossibly bright.

"I watched the Rock[194] happen right in front of my eyes," Shamrock says. "The minute they gave him the mic and stop trying to choreograph his personality, he was like a rocket. They took the reigns off him and he just ran. He was this funny character in real life and started being himself. Once that happened, nothing was going to stop him."

---

[194] "Ken Shamrock helped build "The Rock" character. Huge Attitude Era influence," Rock wrote on Twitter. "We tore the houses down together. I'll always be grateful and respectful. He's a fucking machine. They don't make em like that anymore."

Shamrock

The two feuded all the way through WrestleMania[195] and beyond, though like everything else, they played second fiddle to the ongoing serial drama that was Mike Tyson. His high profile appearances leading into Austin's title win over Michaels reminded the mainstream of WWF's existence and introduced the wider world to Stone Cold for the first time.[196] While Shamrock had actually challenged the boxer the previous year in an early appearance, by this point the company was fully committed to Austin as the next big babyface star.

Helping launch the Rock to stardom isn't bad as consolation prizes go, and Shamrock was fully committed to the task. Rock had already established himself as a funny and entertaining guy. But that was the path to becoming a babyface, especially during the Attitude Era where fans were more than willing to cheer on vile behavior that would have once immediately marked a wrestler as a villain.

Instead, WWF was looking to build a rival for Austin. So, they needed the Rock to be seen as a little more menacing and a little less amusing. Shamrock had an idea to help make that happen. The February 9 match on RAW between the Nation and Ken and DOA member Chainz was booked to end after the Rock nailed Shamrock with a chair shot. Par for the course in those days—until Shamrock suggested that Rock hit him right in the face.

"I said 'you going to hit me in the back?' And he said 'I want it to be a headshot,'" Shamrock says. "I said 'Dude, I would rather take it in the front than the back of the head. Just swing at my face.'"

"What?" Rock replied.

"Just swing at my face," Shamrock said. "I'll look up at you and as I start getting up, just hit me right in the face. Make sure it's the flat part

---

[195] Many of their matches ended with questionable finishes. At the Royal Rumble, for example, Rock hit Shamrock with a foreign object and then placed it in Ken's incredibly tiny trunks. When Shamrock eventually turned the tables on him, Rock showed the referee the object and Shamrock was disqualified. This kind of goofiness was typical even on house shows, allowing Rock to keep the Intercontinental title without really ever beating Shamrock in the ring.

[196] Austin shoving Tyson in the middle of the ring became national news. According to the Torch "besides coverage in newspapers everywhere the next morning including USA Today, that night ESPN's SportsCenter, Fox Sports Net Primetime, NBC's Today Show, and various other news and sports shows showed clips and talked about the incident. It was treated as tongue-in-cheek at the end of the programs, not as a legitimate news story, but the publicity was there that the WWF was looking for."

of the chair.'"

"'What are you talking about?'" Rock sensibly asked. "Hit you in the face?"

"'Don't worry about it,' Shamrock said. "I promise I'll take care of myself. From that angle you can't actually possibly hit me in the face unless you're doing a golf swing. But it will look like you did. So swing it like a bat."

"Are you sure?" Rock asked, giving him a chance to change his mind.

"Just bring it," Shamrock said. "I'd rather get hit in the forehead than the back of the head. I've got a big old skull. You lay it in there. I mean it. I don't want anyone saying it looked fake."

The result was an epic shot, one that they would repeat even in low stakes situations like house shows. Four days after Shamrock's Lion's Den fighters wowed fight fans at UFC 16[197], he and Rock took it even further, upping the violence a notch during the March 17 RAW.

Shamrock was on the receiving end one of the most brutal chair shots in WWF history in a match with D-Lo Brown[198] after begging the Rock to hit him a second time. While it couldn't have done him any good long term, Shamrock preferred what he felt was a little bit of control over the situation that didn't exist with the typical chair shot delivered from behind.

"I'd taken some bad chairshots before," he says. "I'd take 100 of those to the forehead before I took one on the back of the head. I couldn't get people to believe I was fine. It popped the boys. These are *workers* and they totally bought it.[199] Mankind copied me[200] but took it to a different level. He didn't take one, he took five."

---

[197] Bohlander beat former Olympic gold medalist Kevin Jackson with an armbar while Ken was busy making Rock tap to an ankle lock in Anaheim. He had asked for the night off but he and Rock had become staples of the show and WWF didn't want to disappoint fans at a major arena.

[198] Before the match Shamrock told Rock to "shut your monkey ass up" and to not bother sending D-Lo down to the ring because "I don't care about this little monkey." Pretty shocking to 2020 ears but routine for the truly shocking Attitude era.

[199] The extra dose of violence helped the feud become a legitimate drawing card for the company. The two set a record gross for wrestling in Tacoma, Washington, in a main event that February.

[200] In a famously brutal match, the Rock devastated Foley in front of his family with a series of chairshots.

Shamrock survived another brutal unprotected chairshot from Rock in what would end up being his only high profile singles match at WrestleMania—then had the rug pulled out from beneath him when the referee reversed the decision after he refused to break his patented ankle lock submission.

It was a decisive win that somehow resulted in a loss when Shamrock couldn't maintain his cool. He ended up tossing three referees and a random man in a suit before order was briefly restored. When the decision was announced, Shamrock snapped a second time, attacking the Rock who was being removed from the ring via an explicably slow-moving stretcher.[201] With Rock's blood dotting his left arm, Shamrock lifted the Intercontinental championship to a huge response. But it was Rock who left the arena with the strap.

The story WWF was telling of Shamrock slowly losing control was a matter of art imitating life. His marriage and life in California were crumbling. The new Lion's Den he had invested so much in wouldn't survive the year and his marriage was hanging by a thread. When he was home, he and Tina spent most of their time fighting. And, on the road, it was like he wasn't married at all.

"Joining WWE was like being let out of the military," Shamrock says. "The doors are open. You can go to the clubs, go out every night. And you have the money to do it or everything is given to you because they want you to be a part of what they are doing. It's like going to Disney World and all the rides are free. I was being paid to play. All of the sudden the gates were open and it's all open now. If you're not ready for it, it will eat you up."

What had seemed like a good time at first soon became a grind. Drug use went from recreational to a matter of surviving from day to day.

"When I first started doing it I was tired from constantly traveling from one place to another," Shamrock says. "So, I'd do some cocaine to get going. Then, after the show, we'd go out and party, drinking and having a great time. Maybe you need some somas to go to sleep. Then you wake up the next morning and have to travel again. So you'd hit an energy drink, or some coffee, or more cocaine to get you going.

"It's this never ending wheel. Pretty soon, the body starts to wear

---

[201] After the match, Dave Meltzer reported "the only funny part was with the cameras off, Maivia, who was stretchered and then took more of a beating, got up and walked to the dressing room."

down. You get a tear here, or a dislocated joint there. So, you go to the doctor and they give you pain pills. Now you're taking those all the time. Because you couldn't stop or someone would take your spot. So you work through all this."

Veterans of this game could weather the whirlwinds they created for themselves with a storm of poor choices. Shamrock, thrown in the deep end, sometimes found himself struggling to keep his head above water. He would miss shows occasionally, his body crashing from the never ending onslaught of partying and drugs. Occasionally, Tina would call WWF officials to let them know he was too sick to make a town.

"He could've been the champ if he didn't get as fucked up as he did," one former opponent who was close to decision makers in the WWF office says. "Absolutely, one hundred percent. A lot of stuff was overlooked just because he was Ken Shamrock. That was true of every star back then.

"You could show up not in the best condition, as long as you can perform, as long as you still did your job, they would overlook it. But showing up is a huge part of any job. You can't just miss shows and have the missus calling in for you.

"Once that got around, there's all the politics backstage. People whispering that he wasn't dependable. That was stuff that he wasn't probably the best at. And that's just a fact of life everywhere in this business. There's more to it than just in-ring skills. I'm not sure Ken ever fully understood that."

Shamrock says he knew he was making mistakes, knew that he couldn't go on the way he was living. But, at some point, it's like you're watching the water circle the drain and you don't know how to reverse the momentum.

"You have to be disciplined in your training, disciplined in your travel and disciplined in your eating habits," he says. "And I got off track. I started paying more attention to where I could go play in the next town we were going to. Do the show, go play.

"I just went off the track. It will eat you up. Pretty soon you don't know which way is up. It is a very dangerous game, pro wrestling. And that's out of the ring. People couldn't see it in the ring. I was always professional enough to deliver my matches. But when the match was over, I was out of control, out there endangering my career — and my life really."

***

For much of 1997, WWF was in negotiations with Shamrock's former UFC rival Dan Severn, now the NWA champion as a pro wrestler as well as a cage fighter at events around the world[202]. He had been considered a potential opponent for Shamrock at WrestleMania but ended up debuting the next night at RAW instead.

As The New Midnight Express wrestled The Headbangers in a forgettable tag team match, the NWA's defect mouthpiece Jim Cornette joined the commentary team to introduce Severn to millions of wrestling fans.

"I may not be supposed to say this," Cornette drawled, "but he beat your precious Ken Shamrock in a no holds barred fight.[203]"

After the bout Severn, wearing a suit, strolled into the ring to lay waste to the Headbangers in trademark Dan Severn style, tossing them like rag dolls and making them squirm on the mat. The crowd, no dummies, chanted for Shamrock. They were ready for what would have been the rubber match between two of the most prominent cage fighters on the planet.

"I gave Vince (McMahon) and (WWF head writer) Vince Russo ten pages of notes on what Dan Severn was strong at and what he's weak at," Cornette says. "What he could do and what he couldn't do. How to feature him and get the most out of the fact that here's the UFC's only triple crown winner. You could do a lot with him— but don't make him one of the boys.

"They had Ken Shamrock and Dan Severn in the same company at the same time. It's not rocket science. But they didn't understand the whole UFC thing even though they were selling hundreds of thousands of pay per views."

Two weeks later they teased moving forward with the match, having Severn and Shamrock go nose-to-nose before a tag bout in Philadelphia. Moving forward as fast as possible seemed the expedient thing, especially with the crowd reacting big to the potential bout at the slightest provocation.

"You've got to do the match with Dan quickly," one former WWF

---

[202] Severn's refusal to sign an exclusive deal with WWF delayed his debut with the promotion and likely prevented what could have been a major WrestleMania moment with Shamrock.

[203] Ross pointed out that the two were actually 1-1. It seemed clear that this was building to a big match—one that somehow never materialized.

creative team member said. "Because otherwise Dan gets exposed as a bad worker and people lose interest. He was not a natural talent like Shamrock and didn't seem to have an interest in developing into anything other than exactly what he was."

Unfortunately, for his bank account more than anything else, Shamrock's never-ending feud with the Nation was also ongoing, even as WWF teased a Severn match, and ultimately cost him the opportunity to settle his score with "The Beast." Because of the nature of the Nation, matches often devolved into gang style warfare, with up to a dozen men going toe-to-toe right up until it was time for a commercial break.

That's how Shamrock found himself side-by-side with Steve Blackman, rushing out to defend Farooq in a brawl with his former comrades at arms. It was a wild scene, though kind of just another day at the office on a show that routinely bordered on pure chaos. For Shamrock, it was disastrous, costing him a month and a half of prime dates when WWF's business was picking up steam[204].

"Mark Henry, the big strong guy, was outside the ring," Shamrock says. "We weren't even in the ring. We were pushing on each other. It was a big run in and he was pushing into me and I stepped in to pick him up. And those mats, they're soft. I picked him up to turn him and put him against the side of the ring. As I did, my foot stuck in the mat and I heard my foot pop, snapped. So then they actually had me do a match a few weeks later even with a broken foot[205] and they put my foot in a chair and Owen Hart jumped on it like they broke my leg.[206]"

After missing all of May[207] recovering from his injured foot, Shamrock returned for an extended feud with Hart. Before that could

---

[204] That same night, Austin squared off with his boss Vince McMahon in the main event. The most iconic feud of the Attitude Era was fully underway. Not coincidentally, WWF beat WCW in the ratings for the first time in 83 Weeks.

[205] Reported at the time as torn ligaments in either his foot or his ankle in the Wrestling Observer depending on the issue.

[206] Hart was the second tag team partner (after Mark Henry) to betray Shamrock and join the Nation. Perhaps he didn't have particularly good instincts when it came to choosing friends?

[207] Shamrock made his first on-camera appearance since leaving for WWF at UFC 17. He did an interview in a wheelchair, selling the foot injury. But when Pete Williams knocked Mark Coleman out with a head kick, Shamrock was hilariously and miraculously "cured" and celebrated with his team in the cage.

fully commence, there was the King of the Ring, expected, at long last, to be the rubber match between Shamrock and Severn. Instead, Severn lost in the semi-finals to the Rock, who then fell short to Shamrock in the finals in a really good match[208]. The chance for Severn and Shamrock to draw real money, the Observer's Dave Meltzer believed, had already come and gone:

> WWF realistically only had one chance, and it wasn't foolproof, to turn Dan Severn into a money player and that would be to have him destroy people and not be a pro wrestler but an outsider, and even at that, the only guy he'd draw money against would be Shamrock if it was made clear that it wasn't a pro wrestling match but a UFC grudge match in WWF rings due to contract legalities.
>
> The odds were against it even if it was done right, but unlike Shamrock, who survived and has done well even though not booked well for the most part with a few flashes of exceptions, Severn doesn't have the charisma to overcome this. Unfortunately for WWF, they botch up that outsider angle every time they get the chance and it's hard to fathom why because it's one of the easiest to pull off and as long as it isn't done too often, almost always draws big money (all the New Japan stuff, Savage in Tennessee, NWO in WCW all come to mind).

Severn went into the event believing he was going to the finals to put over Shamrock—something, he writes in his autobiography *The Toughest Guy in the Room*, he wouldn't have had an issue with:

* * *

---

[208] The match was overshadowed by what followed—Mankind's legendary Hell in a Cell match with Undertaker that saw the hardcore legend take two insane bumps off the top of the cage.

It was the most polarizing moment in modern wrestling history, somehow managing to both establish Mick Foley's place in wrestling history *and* lead Pro Wrestling Torch critic Bruce Mitchell to coin the phrase "meat puppets" to describe the way promoters look at interchangeable wrestlers.

> For the record, if I'd made it to the finals of the King of the Ring and they'd asked me to do the honors for Ken Shamrock, I wouldn't have minded... there are plenty of creative ways to end a pro wrestling match—through interference, or referee manipulation, or through the use of a foreign object like a steel chair—to keep both wrestlers strong. It's not a matter of whether you win or lose, but how you win or lose.

Shamrock survived a potentially scary moment in the semi-finals earlier in the night, landing right on his face after a hurricanrana attempt against Jeff Jarrett.

"The funny thing about Ken is you can never tell if he got his bell rung or not because he would never sell it," WWF executive Bruce Prichard said. "And he always kind of had that crazy look in his eye anyway. It looked absolutely brutal and you would have thought he was hurt. But he came back saying 'no, I'm fine. No, everything's good. What's next?' Just kind of bobbing his head, ready to go eat somebody."

The next night several more bells were rung as WWF unveiled the Brawl for All, a series of mixed rules bouts[209], mostly between undercard wrestlers, that were unscripted shoot contests. The real fights, designed to eventually put over legendary tough guy wrestler Steve "Doctor Death" Williams as a future opponent for Austin, went over like a lead balloon.

Originally intended for Williams to win[210], Shamrock and Severn were not even invited to compete[211]. But as the tournament rolled on, fans talked of little else—so both were eventually extended an offer.

"When they first announced the concept they said 'Ken and Dan, you're not going to be a part of this.' A few weeks later, they gave me a

---

[209] Five points were awarded for scoring the most punches in a one-minute round and for each takedown. A knockdown was worth ten points. This scoring system, to put it gently, was poorly implemented and incoherent by the end of the tournament.

[210] Williams, then 38 years old and long past his tough guy prime, was brutally knocked out by the unheralded Bart Gunn

[211] The Pro Wrestling Torch reported the initial brackets, which included Stan Stasiak in the slot eventually occupied by Severn.

call," Severn recalled. "I asked 'how much.' They gave me a figure and I said 'sure.' It was a no-brainer."

His one appearance, it turned out, was anything but. Severn squeaked by The Godfather in a takedown heavy fight that saw the former UFC champion fail to live up to his fearsome reputation. Shamrock, smartly, steered clear of the mess, focusing instead on defending his status as "King of the Ring" against former winners like Hart, Triple H[212] and even a returning Mabel.

On the road, Shamrock and Hart perfected a short submission match but had to make significant changes when WWF decided to film the match beforehand in the famous Hart family "Dungeon" in Calgary, Alberta. In reality, the Dungeon was a well-worn, makeshift basement gym, part schoolhouse and part torture chamber.

The space, in truth, wasn't especially well suited for a wrestling match. That's part of why it was so interesting. It's fascinating to see a piece of established art like a pro wrestling match moved onto an unfamiliar canvas. It created unique challenges that made it compelling even if it didn't exactly work perfectly.[213] In the tight quarters, with cameras too close for any sleight of hand or chicanery, the two pounded each other hard in a match that was more brutal than technical, as Severn watched on as the special referee.

"Owen was a tremendous worker," Shamrock says. "I'll never forget that Dungeon match. He threw me into the wall seven times and put my head through the ceiling. It was crazy. But I suplexed him on the floor and the floor was *hard*. So, I guess we were even. To do a match like that, you needed a special kind of individual who was willing to take a little extra beating."

Shamrock had won 20 consecutive matches against Hart on the house show circuit, reversing his sharpshooter into an ankle lock for the finish. Here, Hart survived that false finish and eventually knocked

---

[212] "When it comes to you, I catch on a little quicker. Well, sometimes I'm a little slow, but now that you're trying to step on my turf, something that I accomplished last night and try to take away from me. Well, I'm gonna catch on pretty quick. So, what you're saying is right here tonight, if you got the time, this is the place, and you, both of you, enter into my zone. Let's get it on," Shamrock, addressing Hart and Triple H on RAW. His struggles with the microphone played a big role in hindering his progress.

[213] Wrestling journalist Wade Keller was especially offended by Hart bouncing off the walls of the basement like they were ring ropes.

Shamrock silly with a dumbbell while Severn was down after an inadvertent kick from Ken.

Once again, Shamrock managed to lose a major match while looking strong in defeat.

To keep things interesting, Severn was further inserted into the Hart feud to keep the story moving forward and the hope of a match with Shamrock alive. That was how wrestling worked at the time, with storylines constructed on the fly, momentum and shock value trumping logic and consistency at every turn. Severn was a perfect example of the schizophrenic nature of the narrative, one night challenging Hart and other times choking Shamrock unconscious. He was also occasionally allied with Ken and Blackman despite simmering tension both on-screen and off.[214]

It didn't make much sense, but there was an effort by some in the WWF office to keep Severn and Shamrock in close proximity. To many, it was a match that simply had to be made. For Ken, Severn was like an albatross weighing him down and dragging him slowly down the card.

"It wasn't that I didn't like him, although I didn't," he says. "It's that he just didn't have it. He was about as exciting in the ring as he had been in the Octagon. And that's not very exciting. The fans never really got into him and I didn't really want to work with him. It was hurting me."

Like it or not, Severn remained part of the program. After all the teases and internal discussions, the two met for the first time in a triple threat match with Hart on the August 17, 1998, RAW. A week later, the first and only Ken Shamrock vs. Dan Severn pro wrestling singles match was given away on an episode of Monday Night RAW and ended in a disqualification after Hart attacked Shamrock and left with Severn as his new "trainer."[215]

The match was part of both a hard push towards SummerSlam that

---

[214] "Ken and I had the bare minimum interaction with one another," Severn wrote. "There was never much of an exchange between us other than a nod of the head to acknowledge the other's presence. It was standard alpha male behavior."

[215] In addition to the poor, abused officials, Shamrock also "snapped" and attacked his friend Blackman. At some point, Shamrock stopped seeming like a highly competitive, out-of-control athlete and started looking like a garden variety psychopath.

included a Hell in the Cell bout between Mankind and Kane and the Brawl for All finals[216]. There was a fierce battle for ratings supremacy with Nitro, as the Monday Night War was in full swing. WCW countered with a Warrior interview and a tag team match between Kevin Nash and Goldberg against Hulk Hogan and the Giant that WWF couldn't match.

It was an exciting time for fans as both companies attempted to outdo the other, experimenting with form and violating every established norm promoters had been insisting was the "right way to do business" for years.

Going into SummerSlam, WWF was hot enough to attempt more than a mere sellout of the historic Madison Square Garden. The company also sold tickets to the neighboring Paramount Theater where the Hart-Shamrock match would take place live. The audience there would watch the rest of the show on a giant screen broadcasting all the way from the arena next door.[217]

"For years the theater had been used in the Garden for closed circuit TV," one former WWF executive said. "When we would sell out the Garden, they would put the event up on those big screens in there and people would pay to go see it. That hadn't been the case in a long time. Being popular enough to have that overflow again was pretty cool. We didn't think people would pay just to see the show, so we wanted to offer a unique experience. It had to have one of the most intriguing matches on the show, something worth a premium. And this match was pretty unique."

WWF constructed a special "Lion's Den" cage for the rematch, 15-feet wide and nine-feet high. It had an odd slant and a catwalk above where the referee kept a careful watch on the proceedings. There simply wasn't enough room for him to officiate inside the weird structure. The company reached out to UFC celebrity official John McCarthy to work the match and give it a little more MMA flair, only to receive a furious call from an irate UFC owner Bob Meyrowitz in

---

[216] WWF advertised this show in the sports section of the national edition of USA Today, something unheard of for a Vince McMahon television wrestling show in this era.

[217] According to the Wrestling Observer, the closed circuit theater "was almost a bomb, with 2,522 fans, of that 1,816 paid, in the 4,500-seat building, paying $32,688. Considering the hype for this show and the state of the business, that theater figure just exemplifies…that closed-circuit is dead."

reply.

The referee would be WWF mainstay Jack Doane instead.

The match itself was exciting and innovative, a combination of submission holds on the mat and a fast-paced, traditional pro wrestling cage match. The tiny area forced the work to be crisp and clean— and it was. Shamrock, in particular, used the cage to his advantage, springing off the fencing to nail Hart with several high risk moves before finishing the bout with his patented ankle lock as "trainer" Severn walked away in disgust..[218]

The win propelled Shamrock into the final high-profile push of his short career before settling in as a permanent fixture on the middle of the card.

In September, Vince McMahon, still in the midst of his epic feud with Steve Austin, punished Stone Cold by making him face Shamrock in the main event of RAW. The battle in the ring, lasting more than 12 minutes, was fierce.[219] Behind the scenes, it was even more brutal, as WCW counter-programmed with the first ever match between Sting and Bill Goldberg. Shamrock and Austin drew WWF's peak rating— but even the box office power of Austin couldn't compete with the ultra-hot Goldberg.[220]

The next week Shamrock, Rock and Mankind had a three-way match to crown an official number one contender only to see a newly villainous Undertaker and Kane interfere and leave all three laying.[221] They ran it back on pay-per-view at WWE Breakdown, one of the better matches of Shamrock's career but also one that helped WWF

---

[218] Years later, cage fighter Anthony Pettis would become a cult figure after a clip of him springing off the cage to kick Benson Henderson in the hit went viral. But Shamrock was there first.

[219] The match ended, of course, with Undertaker and Kane running in to interfere. WWF storytelling, at the time, didn't often include the concept of the "clean finish."

[220] While Meltzer has reported that Goldberg was WCW's answer to Shamrock, Eric Bischoff tells me that's not the case at all.

[221] Both promotions had begun giving fans marquee matches on free television as the ratings war raged on. According to the Pro Wrestling Torch RAW had a 5-4-1 record against Nitro in the ten weeks leading into the fall of 1998. The competition between the two brands was fierce.

make the tough decision regarding which of their hot acts they were going to elevate and which they would shuffle backwards in the scheme of things.

Since his debut, the Rock had been plagued by shouts of "Rocky sucks." Here, the fans were chanting his name instead and a loud "Shamrock Sucks" rang out despite Ken being a pretty clear babyface throughout his WWF tenure.

Mankind jumped off the top of the cage with an elbow drop and Shamrock was the man's man babyface who came within inches of winning. But the loudest reaction of the night went to the Rock's "People's Elbow[222]."

Wrestling was changing. And it was starting to look like there wasn't room for a performer like Ken Shamrock at the top of the card in 1998.

"Rock was supposed to be the heel and the crowd was behind him the entire way," one WWF decision maker said. "We knew two things right then—one, that Rocky had an eventual run as a top babyface in him if Austin faded and two, that Shamrock, as quickly as he had developed in the ring, wasn't going to be able to become a top level babyface in our business. There were so many larger than life personalities that I don't think Ken's personality was going to resonate with the audience at that time."

While the office was downshifting the Shamrock Express in favor of Triple H and the Rock, he actually won his first ever WWF title belt on October, 12, 1998, in Uniondale, New York. Shamrock beat Blackman, Val Venis and X-Pac in a one-night tournament for the vacant Intercontinental title, playing into the now regular boos and leaning further and further towards the dark side.

He attacked Mankind with a chair[223] during his semi-final match with X-Pac then destroyed a valiant Pac to win the belt. The tournament was indicative of just how little wrestling there was in the professional wrestling of the era. The three bouts took a combined 11:12, each of them like a snippet of a wrestling match designed mostly to move the story along. The Torch's Wade Keller thought it was a sign

---

[222] The next week on RAW, Foley would say "in the one hundred plus years of pro wrestling, the People's Elbow is the single worst move I've seen."

[223] Foley had inexplicably confronted Shamrock backstage to tell him that he had never been hit by a weaker chairshot than Ken's. I don't believe in karma, but he was kind of begging for it.

of things to come:

> The WWF did a great job booking the IC tournament—not in terms of having great matches, since they were all short, but in terms of getting across Shamrock as a killer heel. Shamrock is probably ready for a run at the WWF title whenever the WWF wants to go there.

The extracurricular shenanigans led to a pay-per-view match with Mankind the next week at Judgement Day. It was a relatively straight forward wrestling match by the standards of the time, with the two exchanging holds and some UFC-style strikes before an amusing finish that saw Mankind, trapped in Shamrock's ankle lock, applying his own Mandible Claw to himself so he could pass out and escape the pain.

"I liked working with Ken," Foley says. "It was an aerobic workout for sure. He was intense and he worked at a fast pace. I think it was a real credit to Ken that he was so much better than he needed to be. I think there was a tendency for people with a shoot wrestling background to lose a little bit of the skills as a professional wrestler because everything MMA is the antithesis to what we do. You don't give people your body in MMA. Ken not only came back from MMA to be the wrestler he was but he actually improved a great deal. I gave him high marks not only for effort but for accomplishment."

The two would go on to have more than a dozen matches for the newly created "Hardcore Championship" at house shows around the country, often brutal street fights with Foley taking bumps his body could no longer afford and Shamrock trying to prove his head was somehow tougher than a steel chair.

At this point, Shamrock was less a distinct character in the world of WWF programming and more an established set piece to be maneuvered around to serve the purposes of others on the main stage. One week on RAW, McMahon put him in a submission match with Stone Cold to punish his disobedient champion. A few weeks later, he was again trotted out as a foil for the Rock, not to advance his own agenda, but as an obstacle in the babyface's path before they got to the real villain.[224]

By November he was just another guy in the ring as part of Vince McMahon's "Corporation[225]." It was a prominent heel faction and meant a lot of television time—but Shamrock wasn't one of the key players. His former rival the Rock was the group's top wrestler and had clearly distanced himself from Shamrock (and just about everyone else in the business) in the WWF pecking order. The group soon added Shawn Michaels as a corporate commissioner, pushing Shamrock even further down the ladder.[226]

It seemed like, despite still getting a star's response from the live audience, the WWF had determined that he was going to slot somewhere in the middle of the pack. That can be a comforting position for someone looking to kind of drift through a lucrative, middling career. For someone with grander aspirations like Ken, it was very frustrating.

"If Ken and I had better mic skills, we would have made three times the money," Shamrock's occasional partner, opponent and running buddy Steve Blackman says. "Instead of making $500,000 to a million a year, you could make two to five million a year, like Austin and the Rock. I just never had it in me to get on the microphone and just point at somebody standing 10 feet from me and yell at them."

One day Blackman and Shamrock were called into the office to meet with agents and writers.

"I'll never forget, they said they wanted to push me and Ken more, but they needed to see more mic skills. Which I understand in that business. They're like, 'If there's a guy standing right there beside you, and he was pissing you off, what would you say to him?'

"I said, 'I wouldn't say anything. I would just walk over and hit him!' And they kind of got angry at me, but I wasn't being silly. They said, 'Go send Ken in here.'

---

[224] Both matches ended with Shamrock on the receiving end of a brutal chair shot, something becoming far too common in his matches.

[225] "I could use a man like you," Vince told Shamrock, then proceeded to say they had a lot in common, as both came from nothing. Ken was a foster kid who lived on the streets. McMahon's father was the owner of the WWF. Perhaps the similarities are more obvious to someone else.

[226] The resulting feud with HBK's former DX comrades was a bright spot in this period, with Shamrock often teamed with Big Bossman in a team that eventually won gold.

"I walked out and all I said, 'Ken, they want to see you.' They asked him the same question, you're not gonna believe it. He gave them the same answer I did!"

The WWF during the Attitude Era may have been called professional wrestling. But, in many ways, it barely resembled the decades of wrestling television that preceded it. The focus was on storylines, sensical or not, and endless trash talk and banter. The top wrestlers, like Rock, Austin and an emerging Triple H, could deliver with a microphone in their hands *or* in the ring. Someone like Shamrock, however, was exposed every time he was asked to deliver a talking point on television.

"Interviews were his obvious Achilles heel and the thing that held him back in Titan land," wrestling critic James Dixon wrote. "Shouty and robotic, Shamrock was a disaster behind the stick throughout his entire tenure."

His time in WWF, though no one knew it yet, was coming quickly to an end.

CHAPTER FOURTEEN

Working Into a Shoot

While Shamrock was spending 20 days a month on the road[227] with WWF, his grip on the Lion's Den and the sport of MMA was slipping. After investing a bundle in a new facility in Lodi, he ended up shuttering it quickly and moving to San Diego where he built a new gym in Chula Vista that opened for training purposes in December, 1998, and to the public early the next year.

His wife Tina and her family were there, and though their relationship was more distant than ever, Shamrock wanted to make her comfortable, especially considering how often he was on the road. The two had a relationship that was basically non-existent when he was traveling then punctuated by fierce arguments on the few days Ken was at home.

"As soon as I got home, it was fighting," he says. "I want to go into the gym and train and I'd been home a short time and she's like, 'you're gonna go?' Or there was something where I cheated on her or something. I was getting accused all the time of stuff. Even when I wasn't doing stuff. It didn't matter. After awhile, I just didn't care anymore. It was just always something. It was constant fighting and I'd go there and be angry all the time."

---

[227] He wrestled in 17 different cities in November, 1998. That was a standard workload for a WWF wrestler at the time. As you might imagine, between the travel and the matches, the grind was very real.

As an attempt to create a more peaceful home life, the move was an epic failure. He was becoming almost a stranger in his own family. There were some occasional nice moments when the kids would join him at a WWF event, hanging out backstage and playing video games with Mark Henry and D-Lo Brown.

"One time "Road Dog" Jesse James lost his voice," Shamrock's son Connor remembers. "My dad was really good friends with him and Billy Gunn and they asked me, 'hey, do you want to come say our intro in the middle of the ring?'

"I was like 'Dad, can I swear?' Because you have to say ass.' I remember I was so happy but it turned immediately to disgust because Billy Gunn gave me a hug and he was oiled up for the match and I was like 'ugh, that's so nasty.'"

Then he'd be alone again, his wife and kids living their own lives in San Diego. When he did make his occasional appearance, it wasn't always cause for celebration. The kids would take turns going on "adventures" with dad that often went awry and took them out of their normal routines. It was more of a duty than a pleasure at times and put a strain on their relationships.

Just as frustrating, in some ways, were his experiences in the gym. It's not that he was struggling against top professionals in sparring—although Pete Williams did easily out fight him standing in one eye-opening session, making it clear there was some catching up to do. He was still among the very best in the world but couldn't prove it. Many believed the sport was passing him by. He believed otherwise and longed to show the world.

In December, 1998, former Olympic wrestler Mark Coleman came to train at the new gym in an attempt to escape a rut. Coleman, a dominant ground-and-pound artist, had become champion after Shamrock departed the UFC. But after looking unstoppable in early bouts, he had lost his title to Lion's Den-affiliated fighter Maurice Smith and had been brutally knocked out by a headkick from Shamrock's protege Williams.

Logically, he was interested to see what he could learn from the men who had conquered him—and especially from the man who held such sway over them. Coleman was still considered a top fighter. He'd prove it a couple of years later by winning the first Pride Grand Prix in Japan. But, in the gym training for an upcoming fight with Pedro

Rizzo[228], Coleman was dominated by a Shamrock who was almost 35 and a year-and-a-half removed from regular competition.

"I was there and there was no competition," Jerry Bohlander says. "Zero. I mean, Ken owned him.[229]"

Had his pro wrestling career been thriving, it would have been an easier pill to swallow. But the window was closing on competitive athletics for Shamrock just as his WWF career seemed stuck in neutral[230]. But walking away from wrestling was going to be difficult for the same reasons walking away from fighting made so much sense in the first place.

"It wasn't like my skills had diminished. It was that this business couldn't pay me," Shamrock says. "I couldn't stay with them because I couldn't pay my bills. My first year in WWF, I made $750,000. My second year I made over a million. I wanted to fight again and suggested ideas to Vince and people in the office to try to make it happen. But that was a lot of money to just walk away from.

"But I wouldn't walk away from fighting either. I wasn't going to. I enjoyed pro wrestling when I was there. I didn't think I would. I thought it was just a way to make money. But I liked it. But I wasn't going to walk away from my past, from the thing that created me."

Opening the Lion's Den in San Diego added to Ken's social circle in some important ways. At the public unveiling of the new gym, Shamrock met Courtney Ford[231] and Craig "Bullet" Levy[232], who managed a strip club in town called Deja Vu.

"Ken got special treatment because of who he was but we didn't always get the same treatment because we didn't have the name," Veron White remembers. "We'd get discounted drinks. Sometimes

---

[228] With Shamrock in his corner, Coleman dropped a close decision to Rizzo. At the same event, Bohlander was beaten by a brash up-and-comer named Tito Ortiz, who then fired two virtual pistols at the Lion's Den corner.

[229] Ken is more diplomatic but made it clear, in his own way, that the sessions gave him confidence he could still compete at a top level.

[230] WWF, meanwhile, was peaking. The year 1998 closed with nine consecutive ratings wins for RAW over WCW Nitro, with the WWF winning by more than a ratings point each week. The Monday Night War, though it would continue for a time, was essentially won.

[231] This is an alias. Courtney has left the strip clubs for civilian life and doesn't want her kids to know about her past.

[232] Levy passed away in 2004 after a battle with skin cancer.

discounted lap dances and stuff like that but we never really got the rockstar treatment that Ken got. When the club would close, he'd still be in there doing who knows what. His nights would continue on to the next day and the following day and the following day. I remember one time he told me he had been up for six days in a row."

Ken and his entourage became regulars there, hanging out almost nightly[233], sometimes continuing to party at Ford's apartment after the club closed. She normally had the day shift but would work Saturday nights. Clubs had to stop serving at 2 AM at the time, but Deja Vu was open until four in the morning. Then the party would move to her place and no one would come up for air until Monday morning.

"I was the other woman in his life," Ford says. "That's what he called me. He brought Tina over to meet me and was like 'I need her to meet you because she needs to meet the other woman in my life. With you and me being friends, she needs to know there is nothing like that going on.'

"I was the only one he wasn't having sex with which is probably why him and I are still friends after so long. The fact that I had an open line to hot strippers was part of the appeal of our friendship, I'm sure.

"We constantly had the parade of girls and of course, he's Ken and he's incredibly good looking and he's famous and he's a wrestler so had no shortage from just the women I brought around. Many, many times Ken banged a stripper in my house, in my bed. I remember him breaking my water bed.

"Then going to the clubs with Bullet[234] every Saturday night, and Bullet is also very good looking, very charismatic, so the two of them together were just ridiculous babe magnet central."

The drugs of choice at the time were ecstasy and GHB[235]. Shamrock couldn't get enough, especially of ecstasy which he took almost every weekend. He and his crew would hit the raves, high out of their minds, and just blend into the scene—as much as a muscle-bound pro

---

[233] "That's how we rolled," Kevin Woo, who helped manage the Lion's Den for a time, says. "We hung out at strip clubs everyday. Ken was the king of access. I got to judge the Deja Vu Girl of the Year. He was a pro wrestler on TV, so when you were with him you got treated like a big deal."

[234] Craig was known as "Bullet" because of the vial of cocaine he kept on a chain around his neck.

[235] "It was in liquid form and we would call it 'the sauce,'" an associate said. "As in 'Bullet and Ken were tossing out shots of the sauce.'"

wrestler can blend anywhere.

"He took a lot of it. Because he was so big—I think that was part of it," Ford says. "I would take one and it would hit me really crazy. Him, he would have to take two to feel it.

"He was at the raves in his loud clubbing shirt and his colored glasses. We didn't really like dance or anything, but we'd all hang out. Vernon was the ham. He'd be the guy with the glowstick necklaces dancing. We broke open a bunch of glowsticks in my apartment one night and splattered the place. When you're on like four hits of ecstasy, it's pretty cool. Not as much when you have to clean it up and try to get your security deposit back."

Eventually using drugs turned to something darker. Like many who dabble in the world of narcotics, Shamrock became convinced he could make some money dealing them too.

"I was going through some hard times in my life, got hooked up with some bad people," Shamrock says. "The popularity I had attracted them. And I ended up with an opportunity to really control the drug scene with ecstasy. It made me feel so good and I had the ability to buy so much and everyone around me seemed to want it. So, I just started selling it. Ecstasy, I was supplying a lot of that in San Diego. I was one of the main guys."

Today it's hard for Shamrock to articulate why exactly he did it[236]. The thrill was a big part of it—plus it just seemed so *easy*.

"I didn't just know the cops," he says. "They were friends of mine. I knew everything that was coming my way.

"It was really stupid. Here, I accomplished so much and I was going back to that life? I didn't need to. It wasn't that I needed the money. I wasn't rich by any means, but I didn't need to put myself in that position, where, if I got caught, I'd lose everything. I was just living. It was fun, exciting. Irresponsible fun."

Even as he delved deeper into the world of illicit drugs, Shamrock was also rubbing shoulders with the political elite. San Diego entrepreneur Tom Casey had made a fortune with his home I.V. business and retired by 30. At the time he was working with the Department of Defense to help automate a process to convert paper

---

[236] "He was just a gangster having fun running a city," one Lion's Den associate says. "He was living his dream. He was what he wanted to be and he was loved and feared by everyone. Even the cops loved him. He pretty much was king of San Diego."

maps for use in modern 3D modeling programs. As a result, he knew most of the powerful men who had helped crush the UFC—and thought he might be able to help mixed martial arts make a comeback.

"I knew John McCain and had dealt with him quite a bit," Casey says. "So, when I saw on the news one day that Ken Shamrock was coming back to San Diego to open up the Lion's Den in Chula Vista, I said, 'I might be able to help.' Ken was wrestling at the time so I met with Tina and (her father) Bob Ramirez and they talked to Ken. My basic plan was for Ken to be the spokesman for ultimate fighting. He had such a good personality and charisma. I told him, 'I can set up all the meetings with politicians you need to turn around.'"

Shamrock started joining Casey at fundraisers and political gatherings around California. He hit it off especially well with Duncan Hunter and his son and was eventually social friends with an entirely different kind of person than he was used to.

"We started becoming frick and frack on the political circuit," Casey says. "He always did such a great job. With Duncan Hunter, Ken became a regular up on the dais. He'd be up there with Chuck Yeager and Charlton Heston. It started working really well, and it was fun for me to bring Ken there and change things up a bit."

Eventually, Casey and Shamrock finally arranged the long sought after meeting with the man who had all but killed the sport—and they hoped could revive it. John McCain, the chair of the powerful Commerce Committee, had the power to make MMA the same way he'd broken it. Casey knew McCain had been a boxer at Annapolis, knew he saw himself as a scrapper and thought he could be made to see reason.

"I explained to John that what he'd written had really stopped the sport and sent it out to these Indian reservations," Casey says. "We were able to show him, in person, that Ken's the personification of a professional athlete. This isn't a bar room brawl by any means.

"The real truth was, the boxing promoters had gotten to him and told him all these bad things. But, as he met Ken and started hearing about it, he says 'you know what, I really don't have a problem with the sport. I sent out that letter, but I'd be prepared to make amends and step back from my opposition to this. You're a professional athlete. It's different than what I'd been told.' He had thought of it more as amateurs going out and just beating each other up.

"As we were leaving, McCain tapped Ken on the shoulder and said 'you know, my children are fans of you as a professional wrestler, so I knew who you were.' Ken had one of his Lion's Den books and autographed it and gave it to McCain. It was such a success that it became the opening we needed to work other politicians."

On the road, Shamrock sunk further and further into a life of drugs, alcohol and infidelity. Soon it just became what you did. There was no real pleasure in it, just a crushing sense of ennui and fatigue.

"We'd be at hotels downtown and it was just debauchery," one WWF wrestler says. "It's amazing what the body can take. Unbelievable. The mind goes way before the body does. The first few times it's exciting and fun. Then it's just how you pass the time and it takes more and more to be interesting. Eventually extreme amounts of drugs or orgies are the only thing that you can enjoy after a while. And then, even that can't make you feel anything."

Shamrock's regular traveling partner was the straight-laced Steve Blackman. Both men had martial arts backgrounds and similar no-nonsense personalities. They were good travel partners and gym buddies—and not opposed to having a little fun on the road.

"I was driving the car one time, and we get up to the toll booth," Blackman says. "He's laying in the backseat with some girl going at it. I put down his window to the booth instead of mine and she was back there laying on top of him. There was some old lady at the booth, and I said, 'Look at the crap I have to put up with!' And this lady's eyes were as big as saucers.

"Ken looked up and just burst out laughing, and the girl buried her face in embarrassment. I paid the toll and we drove off. But I mean, on the road, everybody turns into a crazy person."

Blackman remembers one time they were particularly exhausted and decided to stay in the little motel right across the street from the arena. The two talked about how nice it would feel to finally get good a night of sleep before getting up early the next morning to fly to the next town.

"I hear a car door about midnight, and I look out the window, and there's Ken in a cab, heading out again," Blackman says. "I couldn't believe it. So much for a good night's sleep! I could barely even think. I could barely stand. And he's doing everything I'm doing when it comes to working out and wrestling and traveling—and he's out there partying, doing all kinds of stuff too. It wears you down. If you don't rest properly whenever you can, and eat properly, you'll never survive. You'd see guys crashed on the locker room floor for an hour. I mean, you gotta get it where you can, or you just won't make it."

While he struggled to hold it together, both at home and on the road, Shamrock found himself slipping further and further down the card. In January 1999, the WWF introduced the character of Ryan Shamrock, supposedly Ken's little sister[237] and the albatross that would sink both his personal and professional lives.

It began when Val Venis[238] made a pass at an attractive young lady in the front row, a very Val Venis thing to do. Shamrock came racing down the aisle to put a beating on Val, only for Billy Gunn, who was already feuding with Shamrock, to saunter down and moon the woman on camera. The pretty extra was revealed to be Shamrock's sister Ryan and she soon became a regular part of WWF's increasingly raunchy programming.

For weeks, Venis courted Ryan, unveiling his new movie "Saving Ryan's Privates" and causing an angry Shamrock to announce his sister "has no right" to make her own decisions because he's there to make her decisions for her. But the heart wants what it wants and Ryan was smitten with Val, even getting caught in flagrante in a hotel room at the Skydome as part of a memorable RAW.

Shamrock's intensity was unnerving and not completely compatible with a brother looking out for his little sister. At one point he destroyed so many referees who were attempting to restore calm between him and Venis that head official Earl Hebner threatened a boycott[239].

Shamrock kept simultaneous beefs going with both Venis and Billy Gunn, leading to Gunn as the special referee for Shamrock's pay-per-view match with Venis, delivering a fast count that allowed his sister's

---

[237] Real name: Alicia Webb.

[238] Played by Canadian Sean Morley, Venis was a male porn star who came to the ring with a towel wrapped provocatively around his waist. As a provocateur, he was no Rick Rude in this writer's humble opinion.

[239] This being WWF, Hebner forgot all about his vow, not weeks later, but a few segments later on the same episode of RAW.

new beau to take Ken's Intercontinental title[240].

It was a disappointing match, thanks in part to Shamrock's serious illness that kept him out of the clubs for a week afterwards and in part due to the fact he had spent the weeks since the Royal Rumble wrestling Gunn, and not Venis, at every house show in the lead up to the match. He hadn't been in the ring with Venis a single time in 1999 prior to their pay-per-view match.

"Ken Shamrock, he was a wild one," Venis said. "He had cardio coming out the wazoo. I'd run him and run him and run him and he still wouldn't blow up. I'd blow up trying to make him blow up.

"He was constantly learning. The day you stop learning is the day you should get out of the business. And Ken Shamrock always had that open mind and he did learn. Every day he'd learn something new. He had a good attitude."

WWF continued to push this angle hard for weeks on television, to some level of crowd interest.[241] After Venis publicly broke up with her[242] in the ring after winning the title, Ryan was passed around by his various foes. [243] While it wasn't clear exactly where it was going, it *was* clear that WWF had significant interest in the story, often devoting multiple segments of precious television real estate to it each week.

Then, in a blink of an eye it was gone. Gunn was replaced in the storyline with Road Dogg and Goldust, the sexually ambiguous artist formerly known as Dustin Rhodes, and his sidekick the Blue Meanie. Both, at different points, put the moves on Ryan, confusing not just Venis but the fans as well. [244]

---

[240] The two broke up the next night on RAW. WWF programming at the time was all over the place, whatever it needed to be from week to week with no concern for consistency or logic.

[241] A Cleveland crowd chanting "Shamrock's Sister" was both a testament to Webb's good looks and a lack of enthusiasm for the male wrestlers in the ring.

[242] At one point he told her ""I told you it was real, I told you it was good, but I also told you it was never real good."

That just seemed mean.

[243] "Unfortunately, she didn't even seem like she cared a bit in the ring," Dave Meltzer wrote in the Wrestling Observer. "Guess she went to the WCW skit school of acting."

[244] "Why is Ryan Shamrock with Goldust now?" Arnold Furious writes in The RAW Files: 1999. "It seems like the louder the crowd gets, the more convoluted the booking becomes."

In partial defense of the terrible and inconsistent writing, the story WWF wanted to tell was explicitly rejected by a furious Shamrock and Gunn was reportedly removed from the angle due to problem behavior behind the scenes. Of course, on paper, the original idea was much, much worse than what actually occurred. The story as it played out was merely confusing and forgettable—the initial concept, courtesy of WWE's head writer Vince Russo, was downright awful.

"They wanted the angle to be that instead of me wanting to protect her, which is what they initially said it would be, that I really wanted to be with her," Shamrock says. "Like, sexually be with her. They want me to actually pretend like I'm having sex with my sister. And I've got a son named Ryan Shamrock too.

"I'm like, 'um, this doesn't feel right.' I said 'I can't do that. I have kids and they got to go to school with their daddy wanting to have sex with his sister.' Really?"

Across the board, WWF wrestlers were being pushed into territory they weren't wholly comfortable occupying[245]. Some, afraid of losing a steady paycheck, went along to get along. Others, like Shamrock's former MMA rival Dan "The Beast" Severn, weren't willing to do anything they weren't entirely on board with. Severn tells his own version of this common tale in his book *The Realest Guy in the Room*:

> When a member of the creative team finally approached me for a heel turn, their idea was so outlandish and stupid, I really didn't know how to respond.
>
> "We want to put '666' across your forehead," they explained. "It's the mark of the beast."
>
> "Not gonna happen," I said, shaking my head.

Owen Hart was put in a similar spot, rejecting a handful of ideas he found embarrassing before eventually being talked into a reprise of the Blue Blazer. This time, despite his roots as a serious wrestler, his personal integrity and general decency were recast as out-of-touch,

---

[245] The company came under regular fire from mainstream outlets that didn't understand that wrestling wasn't necessarily programming directed at children. McMahon had over-the-top interviews with Bob Costas and Inside Edition in this era, often doing seemingly more harm than good to the company's public image.

comedic and worthy of scorn.[246]

Shamrock's punishment was more typical of wrestling promoters upset with a talent—he was made to look bad and lose matches. He was even knocked unconscious by comedy sidekick the Blue Meanie on an episode of RAW in March.

"I think they probably realized that they weren't going to trap me into something, so they just started beating me," Shamrock says. "I don't have a problem with that either. You know, I went in, I did what I needed to do. But, because I felt I was going the wrong way as opposed to the first year and a half I was there when things were going well, after that I went to my agent and said, 'dude, we gotta find a way out.'"

By WrestleMania, or RyanMania for the select few obsessed with Ken's sister, he was reduced to a forgettable four-way match[247] with Road Dogg, Val Venis and Goldust, his goal of main event glory feeling further and further away as his former rival the Rock headlined the mega-event against Stone Cold.

His declining status in the wrestling world did nothing to damage Shamrock's enduring popularity in the world of no-holds-barred. In April of 1999, a few weeks before WrestleMania, the UFC ran a pay-per-view special called Ultimate Ken Shamrock made up entirely of Ken's bouts.

Despite a lengthy absence, his possible return was one of the most consistent topics of conversation among both hardcore fans and fellow fighters.

"I was a different kind of popular," Shamrock says. "Before, I was popular in karate magazines and what MMA industry existed at the time. But when I got on Monday Night RAW, I was popular in the

---

[246] A few months later, on May 23, 1999, Hart plummeted to his death during a pay-per-view skit while playing the Blue Blazer.

[247] Keller said the match was a mess and that "they had no chemistry and put on merely an average TV match," while Meltzer gave the match just *1/2, saying "the lack of heat made it seem dead and the weak finishes hurt as well."

mainstream[248]. People who didn't even follow sports knew who I was. It was another level of being famous."

Because of his celebrity, there was persistent interest from UFC brass, which still interacted with Shamrock semi-regularly since several of his fighters competed for the promotion. Interesting new possibilities emerged in Japan too, as Pride Fighting Championships became the worldwide industry leader. Don Frye, like Ken a fellow UFC refugee now immersed in the world of pro wrestling, was challenging Shamrock in a series of scathing interviews with the press.

But, as personal as Frye made things, he soon took a backseat on Ken's no-holds-barred hitlist to Tito Ortiz, a brash young wrestler on his way to being the biggest star in a shrinking sport. Ortiz, who had beaten Lion's Den fighter Jerry Bohlander earlier in the year, stole the top spot, not just by beating a second Shamrock training partner but by shaming and disrespecting him after the fight too.

Ortiz was a former college wrestler who had caught the NHB bug after spending some time sparring wrestling with Tank Abbott during the big man's UFC prime. He'd made easy work of Bohlander, surprising many who had seen the Lion's Den fighter dispatch Kevin Jackson, a much more accomplished amateur wrestler.

But unlike Jackson, Ortiz had a gift for fighting. More importantly, he had a gift for self-promotion. He printed up trading cards of himself to give out to fans before they even knew who he was and had one of the first sponsored t-shirts —one he donned immediately after the Bohlander fight.

"I worked at a porno novelty store called Xtreme Associates," Ortiz says. "That was my part time job. They told me they'd give me $5000 to wear their shirt after the fight. Shit, $5000? I was only getting paid seven grand to fight! Of course I said yes.

"The shirt said 'I Just Fucked Your Ass.' And I probably wouldn't wear it today. But it got a lot of people talking. 'What are you going to do for the next shirt?' I started having to think about it. Some of them we wouldn't do today. It was surreal. I was the first person doing these things."

While a t-shirt was enough to earn entry into the conversation, it was his fighting that kept him there. Bohlander had won four

---

[248] In February, Ken and some fellow WWF wrestlers, most notably The Rock, appeared on the sitcom "That 70's Show." It was the highest rated episode of the season.

consecutive UFC bouts and was a legitimate contender in the newly formed middleweight division. Mezger was considered a step up even from that, one of the first fighters to combine striking and grappling into something that resembled what would eventually become modern MMA.

Ortiz, young and hungry, didn't care at all about Mezger's credentials or the fact that he'd lost a previous fight to the Lion's Den stalwart. He was entering that stage of a top fighter's career where he believed he was unstoppable—and he wasn't about to let Mezger derail his hype train.

After almost ten minutes of back-and-forth fighting, an exhausted Mezger, who had relinquished his King of Pancrase title to take the fight, was too tired to intelligently defend himself. Referee "Big" John McCarthy stopped the bout with Mezger on all fours and seemingly incapable of doing much more than survive.

But, at the same time, Ortiz wasn't doing much to make Mezger think about quitting either, mostly delivering patty-cake blows with minimal impact. Suffice it to say, no one in the Lion's Den camp, least of all Ken, was happy with the stoppage.

"I wasn't hurt in the fight at all. I was tired. There's a difference," Mezger says.[249] "They should never have stopped that fight. I was telling John, 'John don't stop it. This is nothing.' It wasn't like I was taking hard shots. I'm not even taking hard slaps. I think they did because they were getting a lot of heat politically. It had to look a little safer.

"I'll be honest—I thought I'd be able to handle Tito a lot easier. Give him credit, he came out in shape, ready to fight. He gave me more than I could handle at the time."

While Shamrock argued with McCarthy after the fight, telling him he had a towel and would have thrown it in if he thought Mezger was in trouble, Ortiz fired two virtual finger guns at the Lion's Den corner, then shot them the double bird.

Ortiz, grinning like a banshee the whole time, went back to his corner and donned a t-shirt that read "Gay Mezger is My Bitch." That's when things got a little out of control. On commentary, UFC matchmaker John Perretti almost whispered "look at the shirt," before

---

[249] Mezger says he was sick throughout that training camp and probably should have pulled out of the fight. Instead, he took Ortiz lightly and paid a price.

the official cameras cut away from the action. But the microphones were picking up everything, as Shamrock screamed at Ortiz to show some courtesy to a fallen opponent.

"I thought you had more respect than that. I thought you had balls," Shamrock, now leaning over the Octagon wall yelled. "Hey, Tito. If I catch you with that shirt on, I'll rip your head off."

McCarthy eventually had to separate the two and pull Ortiz back to his corner. The Octagon door was locked to keep Shamrock from coming in. Very little of the footage made television[250], but enough that Dave Meltzer in the *Wrestling Observer* knew there was the potential for something special to come out of it:

> The show will probably be best remembered for an incident that didn't even take place on camera aside for a split second and was never really acknowledged to the home viewing audience between Ortiz and Ken Shamrock...as far as hyping future business, what would at one time have been considered bad sportsmanship, and whether that is good or bad is another issue, does work today to getting someone over with an attitude, as even a casual observer of today's sports scene, let alone pro wrestling, can see.

"I wore that shirt because Guy Mezger said crazy things about me before the fight. I stood up to the bullies. And that's what those guys were. Bullies," Ortiz says. "Lion's Den was like the Cobra Kai in *Karate Kid*. They would walk around with their chests puffed out like their shit don't stink. Like they were the best thing on Earth. They weren't respectful towards fans. They were like movie villains. It was unbelievable."

A furious Shamrock continued his tirade backstage after the show, yelling and throwing things in the locker room and generally creating a scene. Ortiz[251], without the entourage that followed Ken anywhere he went, was asked to stay in his locker room until Ken calmed down.

---

[250] Jeff Osborne was there shooting for the Fight World video magazine and compiled some great footage of the entire incident. Hardcore fans chased after the hard to find tape like catnip.

[251] A born troll, Ortiz told reporters backstage that he'd be happy to fight Ken at heavyweight—provided Shamrock took a drug test.

Eventually, he was joined by fired up fellow wrestlers Kevin Randleman and Mark Coleman who told him they had his back if any trouble came his way.

"I was by myself. That's why Coleman and Randleman came back there to help," Ortiz says. "I just wanted to slip out of the arena to the hotel. My bags were already packed. I was going on tour with Limp Bizkit. I got in the limo, got my bags and I was on tour for a week. I got out of there."

In the following weeks, Shamrock would become a cog in the convoluted battle between Vince McMahon and the Undertaker's "Ministry." On one episode of RAW, he was featured throughout the broadcast searching for a kidnapped Stephanie McMahon in his trademark deadpan style, suddenly a detective in tiny red Speedos.

Eventually, covered in blood and having gone through the ringer, he seemingly earned the boss's loyalty by finding his precious daughter and returning her unharmed[252]. It was campy fun in isolation but the lack of coherency was starting to wear on regular viewers and journalists used to a more serious presentation.

"When Ken Shamrock began asking people backstage if they had seen Stephanie, were we as viewers supposed to believe that the people backstage weren't already aware that the boss's daughter had been kidnapped?" Wade Keller asked in the *Pro Wrestling Torch*. "Then when Ken Shamrock found out where Stephanie was, he was the only one to go looking for her in the basement? You would think Vince would have sent dozens of people down there immediately. Come on, the TV writing can be better than this. There are so many unnatural actions by so many parties that it's almost impossible to suspend disbelief and just enjoy the show."

Just a few weeks later, McMahon himself was revealed as the "higher power" behind the Undertaker's operation, causing discerning viewers to wonder what the kidnapping and threats had been about in the first place. None of it made a bit of sense, but it was fast-moving crash television that was hard to look away from.

The storyline, such as it was, eventually led to a pay-per-view match between Shamrock and the Undertaker. Opinions vary wildly. To

---

[252] Two weeks later, Ryan Shamrock was also kidnapped and crucified in a very similar angle with predictably diminishing returns.

Shamrock and fans of the shoot style classics, it's one of the most interesting matches of his entire tenure, a change of pace from the typical WWF match of the time. To others, it was a boring, confusing mess.[253]

Whatever your opinion on its artistic merits, the match left the audience sitting on their hands before Bradshaw came down with a bat to signal the finish, an Undertaker win via his patented Tombstone Piledriver.

This set up a match with Bradshaw the next night on RAW. The two had previous behind-the-scenes encounter that made the match kind of interesting to Ken, but it ended up being a one-off that didn't really go anywhere.

"I'm in the ring working out with Steve Blackman, rolling around and tapping him out left and right," Shamrock says. "Someone goes 'get in there Bradshaw, you could take them.' So I go, 'okay, I'll lay down, I'll let you grab your best hold and I'll submit you in less than a minute.' And so everybody goes 'oh, come on Bradshaw, do it.' So Bradshaw goes to the ring and he grabs a hold on me, and in 15 seconds I tapped him out."

It was unusual for someone in WWF to test Shamrock's credentials, which made the Bradshaw incident memorable to him. Another challenge came his way from Paul Wight, better known as the Big Show, a monstrous specimen of a man who had recently been signed away from WCW and given a massive main event push.

"Big Show comes up behind me, we're in this green room, some of the families are there," Shamrock says. "Vince was in there along with his wife and he grabs me. He grabbed me, he goes, 'what are you gonna do now?' And so I just kind of dropped and I fell through his arms and rolled up into a knee bar. And I tapped him. I did a heel hook on him on the ground as he was standing. He goes, 'aargh.' And everybody turned and looked just as I was tapping him out."

Those rare bouts of excitement were far from the norm when it came

---

[253] In the Torch, Keller gave the match just 3/4* saying it "should have been ten minutes shorter since they should have known no one would buy the possibility of 'Taker submitting."

Meltzer said "The crowd was dead. This was actually a really great match had it been held in another place" before giving it just *3/4.

to life on the road with WWF. Mostly it was a blur of arenas, interstates, airports, drugs and girls. Lots of girls.

"There were girls everywhere," one Attitude Era wrestler says. "We always used to say, 'You know how good business is by how good-looking the ring rats are.' And the girls back then were pretty cute. So business had to be good."

While it seems like a dream life for many men, to Shamrock it was little more than a way to pass the lonely days that come with the nightly bursts of excitement in the ring.

"I had pretty much fallen out of love with her (his wife Tina) and started doing my own thing," Shamrock says. "By the last few years, we were just together for the children. But that kind of thing can't last."

Eventually, Shamrock found the companionship he was looking for with Alicia Webb, the young wrestler who played the role of his sister Ryan on television. It was an instance of art almost imitating life. Shamrock wasn't willing to let his character have the hots for his sister. In real life, however, the two became an item.

"I saw her walking down the hall when she first came in," Shamrock says. "She had this long blonde hair and features that just jumped out at you. She approached me and we started talking. We hooked up.

"Needless to say, traveling on the road four or five days a week, that was a lot of time to connect with Alicia. We drove together, we partied. It was probably the worst thing for me, to hook up with someone who was fun, a party girl. I was going through a tough time and I wanted to feel young. You want to feel vibrant and exciting. And Alicia was all that. She made life fun. But the problem with that was, I wasn't young. I was 35 years old and she was 19. We had a relationship, but after a couple of years, I was worn out."

If Shamrock was already living his life at 85 miles-per-hour, being with Alicia was like jamming the accelerator to the floor and shooting for 150. Shamrock had a seemingly insatiable appetite for young women, preferring strippers and Hooters waitresses above all else. And Webb was game for anything.

"She was young and hot and wild," one Lion's Den fighter says. "And I remember her introducing me to some other young and hot women. You know what? Ken was a good-looking guy on TV who had a shit ton of money. What are you going to do?

"I mean, you're going to fuck the hottest women. You are not going to sleep. You are not going to rest. You are just going to keep fucking and fucking and fucking."

Shamrock's drug habit, too, had gotten out of control. His tolerance level was so high that he'd take enough drugs to put another man on the floor and still be operating at full steam.

"Let me tell you, those wrestling guys party like maniacs," Kevin Woo, who helped run the Lion's Den at the time, says. "They're already full of steroids, so then they do all these drugs and then they think they're invincible. Ecstasy pills. Ken would pop them like they were nothing, like a jelly bean. A whole pack of them like M&M's. I mean, I might take one. I don't even think I'd take two. Motherfucker was just chomping 'em down like candy."

Through it all, Shamrock made all the towns, adapting to the wrestling life and, essentially, becoming a functioning addict.

"I was so much better than everyone else," he says. "The natural ability that was probably a curse because I was still able to go out and have fun and party. I'd still go in there and be much better than 90 percent of them in the ring. And people will go 'that's good right?'

"But it's a curse, because if I would have slipped, if my performance had been going down, it might've made me wake up a little sooner. Like 'whoa, I'm ruining myself here.' But because I was able to maintain such a high caliber in the ring and still be able to still do all that partying, it just meant I was able to do it for a longer period of time."

On RAW, Shamrock remained a major part of the show, joining a two-by-four carrying "Union[254]" with Mankind, Test and Big Show to confront the Corporate Ministry. For a time, the Union was cheered on by Vince McMahon, part of an onscreen battle with his son Shane for WWF primacy, causing many behind-the-scenes to roll their eyes as the notoriously anti-Union McMahon spouted pro-worker platitudes.

The unit were babyfaces just below the top level, where Stone Cold continued to reign. WWF decision makers wanted Shamrock to work a program with Chyna, Triple H's hulking female bodyguard, but once again, Shamrock shot down the idea.

"They wanted me to fight Chyna," Shamrock says. "And they were going to have Chyna go over on me. I had no problem with that. Have her come in and punch me and cover me. But they wanted me to have

---

[254] Full name: The Union of People You Oughta Respect, Son. UPYOURS for short. No, I'm not making this up.

a match.

"I said 'I can't do that. I've taught my kids never to hit a girl.' And they kind of laughed. But I couldn't punch her and then go and tell my kids they shouldn't hit a girl."

Shamrock actually got a chance to tell his side of the story on RAW[255], and true to his word, he didn't hit Chyna when she came out to have a match. But he did choke her and toss her with a belly-to-belly suplex, walking away "before he does something he'll regret," announcer Jim Ross explained.

It all felt very real, perhaps because it echoed the real life drama going on backstage. Wrestling trade journals like the *Pro Wrestling Torch*, seemingly unaware of the behind-the-scenes drama, were still envisioning a bright future for him:

> The best interview Ken Shamrock has given in the WWF to date may have been his interview backstage with Michael Cole saying he didn't know whether he could go through with hitting a woman. It was a little "too Tommy Dreamer" in its earnestness, but Shamrock's best chance to move to the next level as a singles star is being an "everyday talker" and dropping the "Let me tell you something!" wrestling interview schtick. He can still exhibit a temper as part of his gimmick, but toning down the over–the–top screams and the hitting of his own head would be good.

According to Ken, refusing to work with Chyna made him an important enemy backstage in Triple H, one of the top stars in the company who already had the ear of top brass long before he married McMahon's daughter Stephanie in 2003. Shamrock believes the beef was long-standing—when he first came into WWF, Shamrock was booked to beat Triple H routinely, at one point winning 11 straight matches as the two both attempted to work their way up the card.

"I was told that he put shit in Mark Henry's sandwich," Shamrock says. "Mark Henry was going to eat it. There's ribbing and having fun,

---

[255] Running unopposed with Nitro off the air that week, the May 10, 1999, episode of RAW set a new cable industry standard for wrestling with an 8.1 rating.

which is fine. But that was too far and I spoke up. He didn't like that.

"I think he also really had a real hard time with putting me over when I first came in, even though I put him over later. He had a hard time with putting me over and with the push I was getting despite being so new and green. We just never got along."

Even when not booked like a wrestler who *mattered*, Shamrock had a connection with the crowd that seemed unbreakable. He wrestled and beat Jeff Jarrett while wearing a strait-jacket at a June RAW in Worcester, Massachusetts, and maintained a credibility with the audience that even the silliness of the Attitude Era couldn't quite diminish.

"Shamrock is over big, and on this evidence, really could have been a top star for the WWF," James Dixon wrote in *Raw Files: 1999*. "Far bigger than he was. They just didn't know what to do with him long-term. The anti-authority role was already Austin's, and that would have suited Shamrock to a tee. He definitely worked best in the Attitude Era as an unhinged renegade babyface vigilante."

By the end of that month, whether it was Triple H's influence or not, Shamrock was downgraded to working with Blackman in an extended program, a match that could barely be described as "midcard."[256] Turning down an idea from WWF creative was always risky—and Shamrock had nixed two high profile ideas in a row.

"Most of the guys didn't want to go against what the office was doing, because nobody wants to lose their spot," one WWF wrestler from the era explains. "Before you know it, you're out of an angle, and now you're not getting your pay-per-view money, now you're not in big angles, stuff like that.

"So a lot of the guys don't like to go against what the office has planned for you, and most try to be grateful for the position you have. But, you know, you're still grown men. If something's bothering you and it doesn't seem right, you gotta speak your mind."

Shamrock's focus was far from the WWF ring by this point, as his

---

[256] The two pulled out all the stops in an "Iron Circle" match performed inside a circle of cars in a parking lot and then in a "Lion's Den" weapons match. Blackman even hit Shamrock with a car at one point, though the audience wasn't particularly enthused by any of it.

Lion's Den struggled a bit in the UFC without his steadying presence. He had turned the gym over to his brother Robbie Kilpatrick, fresh from another stint in prison, but that didn't last long.

"Robbie wasn't taking care of business so Ken made me the number one guy," White says. "He smarted off to me one day. Ken had me whoop his butt, and I did. I whooped him so bad he had to go to the chiropractor for a while. Then Robbie got in trouble again. Someone tried to kill him. His next-door neighbors found him tied up with a plastic bag around his head after somebody beat his ass. It was always an adventure with Robbie."

In July 1999, the UFC took its traveling circus to Cedar Points, Iowa, for UFC 21. To hardcore fans still watching on pay-per-view, the stars of the show were Maurice Smith and Pat Miletich. Behind-the-scenes, the talk of the industry was Shamrock. Not only did he all but announce on the broadcast that he'd be returning to fighting, he was a terror throughout the weekend, bordering on out-of-control.

"Ken confronted me in the lobby of the hotel, saying that I was afraid to fight Mikey (Lion's Den fighter Mikey Burnett) and all that sort of stuff, and screaming and yelling at me," Miletich, who defended his middleweight title the next night against the tough Brazilian Andre Pedernairis, says. "And I just said to Ken, 'Look, I'm not afraid of Mikey one bit. I'm not the guy that frigging makes the fights. I'm not the matchmaker, so go talk to (John) Perretti if you want the fight. I have no problem fighting you.'

"And he calmed down after that. I think he realized that I was just like, 'Fuck it. I'm not here to fucking argue with you. I got no time for this. Go talk to Perretti and make it happen.' Otherwise, just fucking leave me alone."

Shamrock proceeded to track Perretti down and an ugly scene unfolded in front of an audience that continued to grow as Shamrock's voice got louder and louder.

"He just charged over, completely took me by surprise," Perretti says. "There was a bunch of guys around. There 40 or 50 people there. It was ugly. It was belligerent. It was personal. Up close and personal with a 240-pound man and I was way past my prime..

"He was mad about Mikey Burnett being treated unfairly.[257] He's

---

[257] "Perretti started going off with his excuses, and that's why I blew up," Shamrock says. "I was like, 'You're a punk. You're taking away a guy's opportunity to win a belt because of your politics, because you guys don't

screaming at the top of his lungs. We were nose to nose. I told him, 'You're taking way too much Anadrol[258], pal. You're out of your fucking mind.' That's what I kept saying to him. "You're out of your mind." I said, "Take a fucking step back.'"

Shamrock eventually followed Perretti to a restaurant where the screaming continued until the manager was forced to call the police.

"He was picking another fight with me. He was so Anadroled out, he was purple. Chairs were getting tossed around," Perretti says. "He was scary. He wasn't Tank Abbott scary, but he was fucking scary.[259] Listen, he wasn't going to out punch me, that's for sure[260]. He was not fast enough to even figure out where I would be. He was going to take me down and bust my fucking leg and take it home with him. That's what I thought.

"He was out of his mind. He was purple with rage. I had never had that kind of relationship with him before. You can see pictures of us, friendly. And then he just took too many drugs, man. I know what that looks like. It was roid rage. Ken Shamrock was as big as a 180-pound man could get."

The next day Shamrock announced on-air that he would be returning to fighting[261] and Burnett cut a wrestling style promo designed to hype a Miletich fight that suddenly seemed much more

---

want Lion's Den to be in control of the belts.' And that's what it was. They just didn't want us to have all the belts. Mikey ended up quitting. He said, 'I'm not gonna fight for these guys anymore.' It ruined him, it did. They literally crushed his career over politics."

[258] Anadrol is an anabolic steroid often used by bodybuilders to add bulk. Shamrock, according to sources, was using it regularly in the WWF to maintain the size and look he needed as a professional wrestler.

[259] "Ken was in WWF mode and fucking jumped in his face and Perretti about pissed himself," one fighter who was there says. "He's holding this grudge from that, all this time? He acts like Ken beat the shit out of him. Ken didn't touch him."

[260] Perretti was, himself, a notable martial artist and a student of legendary grappler "Judo" Gene LeBell.

[261] "Sometimes you have to make noise in order to be seen," Ken told Mike Goldberg during the broadcast. "And Mikey is the number one contender...and he was promised after the Towsend Saunders fight that he would get a shot at Miletich and hasn't got to fight him yet."

interesting to UFC officials[262]. A week later, Jim Ross acknowledged in his column on the WWF website that Shamrock would be taking a step back from his wrestling career to focus on MMA:

> Ken Shamrock will be decreasing his WWF schedule in 2000 to return to the martial arts and fighting world. Shamrock wants to compete in a few fights next year and will then possibly return to an active WWF schedule. WWF officials are fully supporting Ken's efforts and may even explore the possibility of helping promote the World's Most Dangerous Man in these pending fights.

"I learned a lot of my philosophy from Vince," Ross says. "If a guy's heart's not in it and they want to invest their passion and their time into something else, you're not doing yourself, your company, your locker room, or them any favors by keeping them against their will. We would not have released him to go to work for another wrestling company, obviously, but to go live his dream again only shows that we had respect for him, we liked him, and we wanted to help him take his life to where he thought it needed to be.

"If we had been a hard ass, if Vince had been a hard ass, we would have made him stay the extra (option) year. But by then, all those opportunities in MMA would not have been as prominent. I don't know if that would have been fair to do to him. We did the right thing by letting him go when he wanted to go."

Shamrock's final WWF program was with a newly arrived Chris Jericho, a clear case of oil meeting water. Jericho, complete with an entourage that included Howard Finkel in a comedic performance reminiscent of Ralphus and Mr. Hughes as a bodyguard, hadn't quite figured out his WWF character and felt like someone trying to reprise a past role, in this case the cowardly WCW version of Chris Jericho.

The two spent several weeks involved in various shenanigans, from Finkel in disguise and Jericho trying to protect himself by wearing a suit of armor or a hockey goalie's safety equipment. They also engaged in what felt like a constant foot race, with Shamrock chasing either Jericho or Finkel around the arena everywhere they went. Shamrock,

---

[262] The rematch with Miletich never happened, causing a dejected Burnett to leave MMA behind for years.

as Jericho remembered in his book *Undisputed*, didn't do anything half speed:

> In his mind, if he was supposed to chase me, he was going to chase me at full speed—and he did. I ran down the aisle and when he spotted me he charged as fast as he could. I knew if he caught me he would hurt me, so I took off down the aisle like Ben Johnson post water bottle swig.
>
> When we raced through the curtain out of the audience's view, I slowed down but he didn't and he tackled me as hard as he could in the hallway.
>
> "Ken, did you really need to tackle me? Nobody can even see you!"
>
> "I knew I could catch you," he replied laconically.
>
> I have a feeling he would've chased me all the way to Yonkers until he did.

Shamrock, never a savant on the microphone, was the worst possible opponent for Jericho, who needs that kind of back-and-forth repartee to build interest[263]. He was also mentally checked out, antsy to return to his MMA roots. But, though WWF had tentatively agreed to allow him out of his contract early to pursue fighting, actually removing yourself from the wrestling hamster wheel is easier said than done.

On September 13, at a house show in Anaheim, Shamrock took a hard kick from Mr. Hughes that aggravated neck issues that went back to high school and made him a little nervous about getting injured in a wrestling match before he could escape back to fighting. He delivered a hard receipt and then confronted Hughes backstage before begging off that weekend's house shows and eventually the scheduled pay-per-view match with Jericho.

His final WWF appearance was a two-minute first blood match on SmackDown where Jericho, in full hockey regalia, caused him to cough up blood with a hockey stick to the gut and a splash off the top rope.

---

[263] The two also struggled in the ring. Once, after chopping Shamrock across the chest, Jericho found himself getting stretched on the mat.

"I don't like those chops," Shamrock said. "They're bullshit and they don't hurt and I'm not going to sell them."

Rumors circulated that his neck injury might cause him to retire from the ring for good. Then what was supposed to be career-ending neck surgery quietly turned into an injury that could be treated with rehab and rest. WWF, perhaps sensing a rat, asked Shamrock, who still had six months on his contract, to get a second opinion about the severity of his injury.

A series of closed door meetings then occurred and, instead of WWF co-promoting MMA events with Shamrock and him returning to the ring when he got fighting out of his system, he instead disappeared from the promotion never to return.

"My agent Barry Bloom looked through my contract and found some loopholes," Shamrock says. "I had certain rights carved out in my contract. One was the nicknames 'The World's Most Dangerous Man' and Ken 'The Rock' Shamrock, which is what I went by early in my UFC career. The other was the 'Lion's Den.'

"Those belonged to me. Well, they had made a doll with the 'Lion's Den' on it. They weren't allowed to use that. They had the Lion's Den match on TV without my consent. I owned that. They had 'The Rock' who was one of their biggest stars. We believed I had the rights to that too. So, we went to them and basically leveraged all that for my release.[264]

"They weren't interested in me anymore. They were just going to kill me off. And so I said, 'You know what? I just want out. I don't want anything. I don't want to try to run you guys into court but I want out. That's my deal.' And Vince did it. So we ended up using it as leverage in a negotiation to get me out of the contract so they couldn't kill my character."

For the rest of the year, the wrestling press would occasionally report that Shamrock would start back with the company at any moment. Reports on his neck injury seemed to shift as well, though it was soon apparent that his demise had been greatly exaggerated. It certainly didn't stop him from doing seminars or hosting a Pankration event with his wife Tina in San Diego.

To this day, despite almost every major name from the era making appearances for nostalgia pops at events like the Royal Rumble, Shamrock has never returned to WWE television in any capacity.

By challenging McMahon this way, he may have burned that bridge

---

[264] I wasn't able to independently verify this with anyone in the WWE.

to the ground—but that just lit the path more clearly for his return to the world of professional fighting.

CHAPTER FIFTEEN
Fighting for Pride

* * *

Shamrock had been teasing a return to mixed martial arts for so long that it came as no surprise when he announced he was officially coming back to the sport. What did shock some was the choice of promotion-instead of a return to the Octagon, Shamrock made his way back overseas to Japan, signing a two-fight deal for a reported $700,000 with Dream Stage Entertainment and Pride Fighting Championships.[265]

While UFC was devoting its scant resources to fighting legal and political firestorms everywhere they went and wearing down after years of battle, Japan had embraced the new style of martial arts with Pride FC leading the way. Pride, primed by years of very serious shoot style pro wrestling and fans obsessed with reality combat, had exploded onto the national scene and promoters dreamed of international expansion.

While some of the big names they'd signed like Mark Kerr were intriguing to hardcore fight fans, Pride executives knew they didn't have any mainstream cache in the wider world. But Royce Gracie and Ken Shamrock did. And both had their first professional fights, after years on the sidelines, under the Pride flag.

"When I made the move back to the MMA world, I was the first guy to bring pro wrestling fans back with me," Shamrock says. "I put feelers out with UFC, I talked to Vince about promoting MMA shows. It seemed like Pride was willing to accept me before the UFC was. UFC was going through a transition and were trying to sell the company. I don't know if they were ready. Pride offered me the best deal so I went there. It's really that simple. They were struggling with the United States market and they needed help promoting here."

Pride FC started as a promotional mechanism to showcase wrestler Nobuhiko Takada who headlined the Tokyo Dome twice in fights with the great Rickson Gracie, but promoters soon saw the potential to be something bigger. Pride wasn't just about a single athlete. It was a new form of martial arts competition.

Working closely with Kunio Kiyohara from Fuji TV[266], Pride

---

[265] Initial speculation centered around Bas Rutten, Kazushi Sakuraba and his brother Frank as Shamrock's potential opponents.

[266] Fuji TV is one of just seven nationwide stations available free over the air in Japan. It opened up the potential of a huge audience. At its peak, Pride corralled a 27.7 rating for a New Year's Eve fight. More than a quarter of all homes in Japan watching television that evening were watching Pride.

adopted a two-pronged approach. In addition to highlighting the best fighters in the world, they sought out new Japanese stars from the world of combat sports and challenged them with intriguing opponents.

The shows were an interesting mix of pro wrestling spectacle and a hodgepodge collection of some of the very best martial artists on the planet. Sometimes, in the case of men like Kazushi Sakuraba, Don Frye and Ken Shamrock, those two things were one and the same.

These weren't the underground, gritty cage fights Shamrock had gotten used to in his days with UFC. His final prizefight in the Octagon took place at the state fairgrounds in Birmingham, Alabama. His first fight upon his return was in the Tokyo Dome.

"It's hard for American audiences to understand because UFC is so big here now, but at that time, Pride was the organization," former heavyweight contender Heath Herring says. "UFC was around, but it wasn't anything compared to Pride when it came to pay days or how many people were watching. Pride was the big show, the epitome of the sport at that time."

Pride, in many ways, was more like a WWF event than anything MMA had ever seen. The shows took place on the grandest stages imaginable, often in front of tens of thousands of fans inside giant stadiums that usually housed baseball games. Filmed for national television in Japan and fueled by money both clean and dirty[267], the production values were out of this world, setting a standard that arguably still hasn't been topped 20 years later.

"Pride was a date night—the cool thing to do at the time—so people were dressed to the nines, and they got quite an experience, visually and otherwise," announcer Mauro Ranallo says. "It was Cirque du Soleil meets the Super Bowl meets WrestleMania meets your favorite rock 'n' roll concert.

"It was a hybrid of everything I really loved. I was immediately taken by the spectacle. From the moment you enter the building, it was an attack on the senses."

Shamrock got to see the glitz and glamour for himself right away. DSE

---

[267] Pride FC eventually collapsed after a magazine report linked the promotion to the Japanese mafia.

wasn't the kind of company to send out a press release to announce a big signing. They wanted Shamrock live and in the flesh, so immediately after signing the contract he was on his way to Japan, both to corner Guy Mezger in the opening round of Pride's Grand Prix 2000 on January 30, 2000, an epic sixteen-fighter, multi-night tournament to crown the world's best fighter *and* to announce his own impending bouts.

Mezger's opponent was Sakuraba, Takada's understudy who was beginning to make a name for himself on the undercards, where he had beaten a succession of top fighters like Carlos Newton, Vitor Belfort and the Lion's Den's own Vernon White.[268] While he would become a genre-defining icon, at the time he was still a work in progress, a quiet, undersized wrestler who didn't look like anything special—until the bell rang.

"He was a very unlikely star," original Pride play-by-play man Stephen Quadros says. "Before Sakuraba emerged as the leading man, the shows had really been a mishmash. They had karate guys fighting sumo guys and a lot of freak show elements led by Takada. Sometimes it was hitting, sometimes it was missing. But underneath that, even if they didn't know it at the time, they were building Sakuraba as a future Japanese icon capable of winning legit fights."

Sakuraba's original opponent was to be American wrestler Kevin Randleman but, considering Randleman had just won the UFC heavyweight championship, that announcement seemed dubious.[269] Sure enough, just two weeks before fight night, Randleman was out and Mezger was in. It was a trick Pride would become famous for, putting their favored fighters in the best position to win while limiting the chances of foreign imports like Mezger.

Because of the short lead time and an issue with his kidneys he was still working through, Mezger was willing to take the fight only if it was limited to a single 15-minute round. The Japanese agreed and the stipulation even appeared in the pre-fight media releases about the bout. But Shamrock, who seemed to have a special understanding of

---

[268] Sakuraba was familiar to hardcore MMA fans thanks to his bizarre tournament win at a UFC event in Japan. He'd staged a sit-in after a bad referee decision cost him a match, essentially getting a do-over and walking away with a win.

[269] Sakuraba and Randleman would eventually meet in the Pride ring almost three years later. Sakuraba won the fight by armbar.

the Japanese fight promoter psyche, sensed there was trouble coming.

"He knew it was going to happen before it happened," Mezger says. "He told me 'You're going to beat Sakuraba and they're going to pull something on you.' He had that way of making you believe in yourself. He said it like there was no doubt. Of course I was going to beat Sakuraba.

"But he knew they would try something. Before the fight he goes, 'Whatever I tell you to do, you do. Because they're going to pull some kind of BS on you.'"

After 15 minutes, despite what appeared to be a clear Mezger win, the fight was declared a draw. The referee sent both men back to their corners and prepared to send them back into the fray for an overtime round when a furious Shamrock, hair cut high and tight like a Marine, charged into the ring and started yelling at officials.

"He knew the arrangement. He knew there was only supposed to be one round," Shamrock says. "Of course, he acted like the whole thing was a misunderstanding. That's what they say when they know they've been caught in a lie. Guy wanted to fight but I sent him to the back."

Sakuraba was declared the winner in abstentia and went on to make MMA history a few months later in a 90-minute fight with Royce Gracie that launched him to superstardom. Mezger? He went home with the biggest check he'd ever made as a professional fighter.

"I have no idea what would have happened if I went out for that second round," Mezger says. "Would I have won? Would I have lost?

"I'll tell you why I made the right decision. Because the Japanese were embarrassed by their lying. They got caught and it became very apparent that they were pulling the wool over everyone's eyes. They got embarrassed by that. And the way that they handle embarrassment is by giving you more money. So I made a considerable amount of money."

It was a nice night for Mezger's bank account. But the Ken Shamrock era in Pride was off to an inauspicious beginning.

Shamrock's return to the ring featured a new cast of characters to replace the stalwarts who, like Ken, hadn't been able to stick with fighting as a way to make a living. Many of the original team members who had done so well in the early days of mixed martial arts had moved on, either to other trainers or from the sport entirely.[270] Others were based out of Dallas where Guy Mezger lived and only occasionally journeyed to San Diego to train at the home station.

In their place was a new generation, who while not reaching the same levels of success, maintained the same ethos as the originals, even as the sport itself slowly took on corporate airs.

Just as he'd been to the first gen Lion's Den fighters, Shamrock was mostly a mystery to this new blood, coming and going from the gym on a whim, disappearing for days or even weeks before showing up to crack the whip.

"He never trained me," Lion's Den fighter Tony Galindo says. "Vernon and I trained each other. Ken was like Don Corleone. He just came to have everyone kiss his ring and he would watch. If he got dressed to train with us, it meant someone was about to get punished. For something stupid most likely."

Kevin Woo helped run the gym while living in a small storage shed on his property. Manolo Hernandez came in as the Lion's Den's first jiu-jitsu coach. In many ways, nothing much had changed from the old days. Prospective fighters would still show up and, eventually, Ken would be there to find out what they were made of.

"These young fighters were a bunch of prima donna bitches," Woo says. "They hadn't even had a fucking fight yet but they strut around with a big ole fucking head. And the Lion's Den popped those heads.

"Ken always did that to anybody. It was tighter than a gang, almost. If you can't cut the mustard, we needed to know now. No use training you for three months and doing all this shit to make you into a fighter only to find out you're this big pussy.

"You gotta go through the pain. You're gonna get beat down. Ken would beat you down so bad that you'll never get beat down like that ever again. 'Cause nobody can do a beat down like that. That way, no matter what happened in a fight, if you get beat up, it's not going to be as bad as that."

Shamrock's first fight for Pride was scheduled for May 1, 2000, at the

---

[270] Mikey Burnett and Jerry Bohlander had both stopped fighting entirely, while Pete Williams was on his last legs as a professional and mostly based in Texas. The stalwart was Vernon "Tiger" White, a Lion's Den lifer.

Tokyo Dome, a featured match supporting the Grand Prix finals. But his first *actual* fight was months prior in San Jacinta, California, just before the second King of the Cage event at the Soboba Casino.

Mark Hall, a journeyman MMA fighter[271], had caused much commotion in the Shamrock household in 1999. Shamrock had done a few radio spots for Hall's independent event and hit it off with his sponsor, Simmons Mattress Company. When Shamrock received a new mattress set from the company in exchange for an appearance, Hall accused him of trying to steal his deal.[272]

While the stories diverge here, everyone agrees on the basic details—Hall didn't believe Shamrock had lived up to his end of the bargain to promote his fight show and ended up calling his house and cursing at Tina, calling her a "lying bitch" and a "cunt" and threatening to come down to the Lion's Den to settle the score with Ken.

For a man like Ken, that kind of disrespect just wasn't going to fly, even with his marriage on its last legs. When Shamrock saw Hall in the casino lobby, it didn't take much to get his motor running.

"He said something like, 'What are you calling my house for?'... Then he goes, 'Come over here,' like he was going to talk to me," Hall told *Full Contact Fighter* at the time. "...Then he kind of gets in front of me and my back was towards everyone else. As far as I can remember, he hit me so hard, just about that time he unloaded his whole right hand right in my face as we were walking over to where he wanted to talk to me.

"I took the whole thing, all his power and everything right in my face, my tooth went through my lip, all the way through my lip, I had stitches on the outside, stitches on the inside, my nose was all busted up, my eye. I've had eight fights in the Octagon and I never lost a drop of blood, and I didn't fight no slouches.[273]"

According to one Lion's Den fighter, Shamrock had them block the

---

[271] Hall was perhaps most famous in MMA circles for allegedly throwing a fight with Don Frye, under the same promotional management, at the Ultimate Ultimate 96. The easy win made it smooth sailing for Frye in the tournament final against Tank Abbott.

[272] This is the fact set as I can best figure it out. No one involved in this story is a reliable narrator here.

[273] The dispute was settled in a lawsuit that ended up with Shamrock agreeing to fight Hall in a Pride bout. When that fight fell through, the legal battle continued with Ken emerging victorious.

cameras and keep people away so he could deliver an extended lesson about disrespect, stomping and elbowing the fallen fighter in brutal fashion. Eventually security made its way to the scene. Because witnesses told police Hall had struck first with a headbutt, Shamrock wasn't taken into custody.

Hall, meanwhile, was taken away to the hospital.

The actual fight in the Pride ring with pro wrestler Alexander Otsuka was nearly as one-sided as the Hall drubbing. The two had done a pro wrestling angle at a King of the Cage[274] event in April, and Otsuka had relocated to Atlanta for almost a month to bulk up under the watchful eye of Tim Catalfo, but no one really gave Otsuka much of a chance.

The outcome seemed pretty clear to those with a discerning eye—Otsuka was a great pro wrestler with the BattlArts promotion, but not much of a fighter. But he'd won a 1998 fight with pioneer Marco Ruas[275] and rode that shocking upset to 12 fights in the Pride ring, compiling a 3-9 record.

For Shamrock, it was the perfect tuneup fight. The only thing that made it remotely interesting was his years on the shelf. What kind of fighter would emerge from the WWF grind? It was obviously a question he'd spent a lot of time thinking about and answering in the weeks before the bout.

"I haven't fought in four years in reality combat," Shamrock said before the bout. "Training with some of my boys in Dallas and the Lion's Den in San Diego—I used to be their teacher. I used to be their instructor. Now I find myself being taught. Because the game has changed so much in four years. I've been out of it for so long, there were a lot of things I needed to improve. It's been a long three months transitioning from the entertainment world into the NHB or the mixed martial arts, whatever they call it now."

In truth, besides a few weeks in Dallas with Mezger, Shamrock hadn't trained much at all for the fight. He felt untouchable according to those who worked with him at the time—a feeling justified when he

---

[274] Lion's Den fighter Vernon White knocked out Todd Medina in the main event in just nine seconds. The new California promotion became the defecto home for the Den fighters in the early 2000s and Shamrock seemed to have free reign there.

[275] Ruas was allegedly out of sorts due to his hepatitis medication and a knee injury, a double whammy that perhaps could only happen in MMA.

used an improved stand-up game to decimate Otsuka.

"He's probably one of the most natural fighters I've ever met," coach Manolo Hernandez says. "Like, he can go without training and still go in and break everyone's spirit that's been in camp for months.

"I remember the first time I got on the mat with him. I was in his guard and we're working on some techniques and the strength of his legs was so ridiculous that you'd give him your arm. Just to relieve the pressure of the squeeze."

It took a couple of minutes to knock the ring rust off, but there was little doubt Shamrock, even after the long absence, was on an entirely different level. Otsuka had managed to take both jiu jitsu ace Renzo Gracie and Ukrainian slugger Igor Vovchancyn to the final bell before losing by decision—but Shamrock was a different matter. He was, to borrow a phrase from his WWF days, in the zone, looking not just to win but to make an impact.

Otsuka played to the crowd and ran the ring ropes, attempting to sucker Shamrock into some pro wrestling shenanigans. But Ken stayed focused and finished the fight with a left hook, pausing to allow the referee to intervene before eventually following up with a right hand on his grounded opponent.

After the fight, rock legend Eric Clapton gave him ceremonial flowers to commemorate the occasion. He was carried around the ring on the shoulders of the Lion's Den fighters in attendance while Tina hugged commentator Bas Rutten ringside, relief as much as joy evident on everyone's faces.[276] It was perhaps the last happy moment the two would spend together before their relationship was completely and irreparably fractured.

Shamrock's in-laws had joined the family business when Ken and Tina had arrived in the San Diego area, working at the Lion's Den alongside Woo. Bob Shamrock had once filled these roles and more, but Bob hadn't joined the caravan down to San Diego. Ken's decision to leave fighting behind and then to bring Tina's family into the business had

---

[276] The goodwill dissipated when Shamrock took the microphone and delivered a rambling, endless speech in English. It had been a long night of fights and the usually polite Japanese fans gently booed him until he finally departed the ring.

created a rift that was slow in closing. Ken's time was limited when he had days off from the WWF grind and Bob was the odd man out between his wife, his kids, his fighters and the siren song of the night life.

For a time Bob attempted to run his own team called Shamrock 2000, looking to take advantage of the skillsets he'd mastered with Ken. He was also looking for a fighter to help get revenge on UFC middleweight champion Frank, his estranged son who, in his mind, had abandoned his family[277].

Without his father looking over his shoulder, Shamrock offered little or no oversight or accountability. The specifics of the business, any business, quickly bored him and he was happy passing the detail work onto others.

Things at work quickly got very ugly when Ken returned full time to fighting. Ken and Tina had a hard time keeping the business and their personal life separate and her parents being around all the time was surely awkward.

While he barely did anything to hide his infidelities, he held her to a different standard. He wasn't going to dig into her outside romantic life too hard—but he didn't want it shoved in his face either.

"I did mine away from business, not in business," Shamrock says. "I told her and her family that this isn't gonna work if you don't keep everything out of the business. You want to do what you do, then do what you do. But don't do it in here at work. This is off limits.

"And what does she do? She hooks up with one of the young boys. She was already hooking up, but that was like in my face. She took that guy in my room, in my bed, in my house. The brand new house I just had built with this $30,000 bathroom she wanted.

"She brought it right out in front of everybody and put it right in my face. And I just said, 'okay,' and I let them all go. I said, 'you've got to go.' They were like, 'well, you were doing it.' Well, I don't do it at the gym. Nobody does it here."

They had been together for the kids, though being around such a toxic relationship certainly wasn't doing them any favors either.

---

[277] While Val Ignatov, the sambo specialist he was grooming for Frank, wasn't up to the task, another fighter eventually got the job done, albeit years later. Nick Diaz, who had worked out with Shamrock 2000 before most of the operation moved across town to become Cesar Gracie Jiu Jitsu, eventually plastered Frank in a StrikeForce fight.

"You hear it behind closed doors, through the walls, when you're in the house with somebody and they're yelling," Shamrock's son Connor says. "I know from my Mom's point of view she pretty much gave up everything so he could go pursue his dreams. He went off and did all the stuff he did and left her there, and she's like 'I didn't give up everything so you could just go and throw it all away.'

"I don't know exactly what happened. We all would have chose my mom at that time. I mean, my dad, the way we perceive it, it's his fault. He's always leaving all the time. My mom's always been there. She raised us. My dad, I love him, but back then it's like 'I don't know you, dude.'"

As the two laid their various infidelities bare, the marriage reached a critical state it could not survive. For Shamrock, the pain ran deep. Because of his background, growing up without a stable home, he wanted the picket-fence life he had only seen on television. But he'd never seen a successful, functional relationship in his life and didn't know how to be the man he wanted to be.

"It was some fucking dysfunctional shit," Woo says. "One day we were at his house and found a note he had left for the police saying, 'If I'm found dead, Tina did it.' He was scared, man."

Fights with Tina would drive him out of the house in a fury, sometimes not to return for days. Without the responsibility of the WWF schedule to keep him at least partially sober, Shamrock lost himself almost completely to drugs and alcohol[278].

"I wanted that tight knit family," Shamrock says. "I wanted it so badly, I overlooked a lot of stuff. I always had this idea that somewhere along the line we'd fix it. But it kept getting worse. We just weren't willing to do the work. Both sides.

"And that was hard for me to accept—that I had a broken family. Especially where I came from. I knew what happened to kids in a broken family. I knew what was coming for my kids because of the divorce. It just ate at me. How could I do that to them? But I couldn't fix it."

Shaken by Tina's relationship with one Lion's Den fighter, he was convinced that the other guys at the gym either knew about what was

---

[278] "After 30 minutes in a club or bar he wouldn't even know his name," one Lion's Den fighter says. "Partying was seasonal and then it became constant. Coke, ecstasy, Nubain, GHB. He had a legendary tolerance for drugs, but that was because he was high probably 90 percent of the time."

going on or were part of it. The result was a confrontation with White and Galindo at a San Diego bar that ended with both of his students outside on the ground and Shamrock surrounded by local police.

"Ken had me and Vernon meet him at a bar in downtown San Diego," Galindo says. "I got there first and he beat the fuck out of me in public in the middle of the bar. The bouncers came over politely and told Ken to please take me to the alley in the back because people were calling the cops. I was like 'fucking pussy bouncers.'

"As he dragged me outside to keep beating me, I could see Vernon from the distance and yelled 'thank God Vernon is here.' I knew he was going to go after him and leave me alone."

Soon, White was also on the ground. A knee to his hip hampered him for months after, but in the moment, his concern was the kicks Shamrock continued to deliver.

"He actually thought that I had sex with Tina," White says. "I was thinking to myself, 'I hate your wife. There's nothing about having sex with her that appeals to me in any way.' He actually attacked us.

"He was on drugs and had been up for six days. Reality and fantasy were intertwined. He had no idea what was real and what wasn't."

Police showed up and Shamrock refused to back down. Both fighters told the cops they had fallen down. That Shamrock's knuckles got bloody trying to help them back up. No one was buying it but the testosterone was thick at this point and things were threatening to get even uglier.

"Ken started yelling at the cops," Galindo says. "'My wife was fucking one of my students and they were covering for him!' We were like 'bro, dude let's go.' The cops reached for their guns and Ken is like 'what you going to shoot me, huh?'

"The guy actually believed his most loyal dudes were covering for his wife banging some student. I was like 'this guy doesn't fucking know us.' And Vernon, man—he was there before there was a Lion's Den. That dude has been there for Ken more than the entire team its entire existence. And never got the love."

Ken eventually called Courtney Ford from Deja Vu, one of his best friends, looking for a lifeline, hoping she could calm him down. When her roommate handed her the phone she could hear Ken screaming at the cops and knew things were bad.

"He's screaming 'Do you know who I am? I'm the World's Most Dangerous Man. I trained these fuckers. You back off. This is personal business.' And I'm like 'Ken, Ken, Ken, where are you?' I hopped in the car and just came and got them. He called me and that was probably the smartest thing to do. I am not another guy that he's gonna want to pick a fight with. Ken would never lay a finger on me or another woman in anger. I think it was a good thing that he had the foresight, as mad as he was, to call me.

"I just said, 'get your ass in the car. Let's go to my house.' Clearly, the cop didn't want to arrest him, but he was also afraid about what Ken was going to do because Ken was beating the ever-loving shit out of Tony and Vern. He was roid raging, for sure."

They all eventually piled in her car and went back to her place, scene of many wild nights past, to work it all out.

"I remember him pacing in my living room as they sat on my couch and I got ice and wet towels to clean up blood," Ford says. "Ken just yelled. He needed to get it off his chest. He was very angry. The divorce was messy. The fact that she was banging one of his fighters kind of sucks. It wasn't Tony or Vern. It was guilt by association. I think Ken was just roaring to kick the crap out of somebody and they were the ones that were there."

Shamrock eventually moved out of his house and into an apartment with Alicia Webb. As his relationship with Tina deteriorated, Alicia became a more open presence in his life. She had moved down to San Diego when he was still in the WWF and the two had continued their whirlwind romance. Now, he was slowly trying to integrate her into his daytime world and it wasn't always easy.

"I never really liked her," Shamrock's daughter Fallon says. "I felt like as soon as she came into the picture she tried to take over my mom's position. I have this one memory ingrained in my mind where we were stopped somewhere and she took me to go to the bathroom and I remember her saying 'you can call me mom if you want.' That kind of stuck with me because I was like 'why would I call you mom, you're just dating my dad.'

"Until I was five or six years old, and I know this sounds kind of harsh, but I didn't really know him. I talked to him on the phone sometimes and that was really hard sometimes. Asking like when are you coming home and him not really knowing, not really knowing the next time I was going to see him. We didn't have a close relationship. It wasn't like a typical father-daughter relationship. It was very strained and we saw each other once in a blue moon.

"It is difficult growing up like that. You see other girls with their dads at father-daughter dances and bring your dad to school day and I never really had that when I was younger. Everyone finds it unbelievable that I remember anything but the things I can remember I remember a lot of yelling and a lot of fighting. Those are the vague memories I have. I remember lots of fighting and it was never really a happy marriage. I only have snippets here and there because I was really, really young."

Meanwhile, in the midst of all this, he was supposed to be preparing for a high level prizefight against another Japanese pro wrestler—Kazuyuki "Ironhead[279]" Fujita. On paper, this might have seemed like a repeat of the Otsuka bout, but Fujita was a different kind of animal, more fighter playing pro wrestler than pro wrestler playing fighter. Though trained in the New Japan dojo, he had petitioned his mentor Antonio Inoki to let him participate in real fights, interested in testing his wrestling prowess[280] against the best in the world.

Otsuka, at his best, was a tough guy capable of taking a beating and surviving against the top fighters in the world. Fujita had the skillset to beat them under the right circumstances. It was a different task, but Shamrock wasn't preparing like it.

"He tried to keep this a secret as best he could, but when he came back from professional wrestling, he was pretty busted up," Casey says. "His shoulders, his knees, everything was really shot, and he didn't have any money to go get it fixed. So he constantly tried to compensate. Initially he did it by juicing up to make himself strong to cover up for the parts that were weak. It fundamentally changed his entire fighting style. He went from a takedown grappler to a standup boxer. He just couldn't get people down anymore because his knees couldn't take it. He kept trying to fight through it.

"For a lot of years, when I first knew him, he didn't really train very much. He didn't have the motivation. He was never really challenged. He was out coking it up and doing the night life at the strip clubs. I'd go down to the gym because I knew Pete and Vernon and Tony. Ken

---

[279] According to Dave Meltzer in the Wrestling Observer "apparently they've tested him as his bones throughout his body are unusually large and his skull is too thick for a human being."

[280] A former Japanese national champion, he was a top level competitor in both freestyle and Greco-Roman wrestling.

would never be there. Or, if he was, he'd just pass through."

While Casey and a few others occasionally attempted to be the voice of reason, Shamrock was too deep into this new world to easily crawl out of the hole he was digging.

"I was going through the divorce, possibly losing my kids, struggling with declining in my abilities," Shamrock says. "There was so much going on and everything seemed so hard. I was just trying to push my problems away or cover them up with drugs. Trying to mask it so I didn't have to deal with it.

"It was almost like I had so much anger, so much pain, and so much responsibility, was taking care of so many people, so many people depending on me including the fans, including promotions, including my family, including my fighters. It seemed like I was taking care of everything. I just wanted it to be dead. I wanted to eat all this stuff, take as much as I can, so for however long it lasted, I'm not thinking about anything."

When friends would attempt to address these things with him, to talk about the huge shift going on in his personal life, he would immediately close up.

"He would just completely cut it off," Mezger says. "I tried to make sense of what was going on with his girlfriend at the time and all the crazy shit that was going on. I'm like, 'What's going on with you? This is crazy.' It was just, Ken was not open for conversations back then like he is today, you know what I mean?"

Shamrock's plan was to test himself one more time in a tune up, this time against Fujita, and then take on one of the top fighters in the world in early 2001. But this, unlike his first bout, was a fight Shamrock could lose if he didn't take it seriously. And he certainly didn't.

"He wasn't living healthy right then. He was living like a maniac," Woo says. "We were partying big time."

Between drugs and drama, he simply couldn't find much time to work on his craft. Tina, he believed out of spite, had left the kids in his care for weeks when he should have been in the heart of training camp with Mezger in Dallas. Instead, he was in a small apartment with a load of additional responsibilities.

"I had some issues that were really weighing on me heavy," he said in a 2009 interview. "I was going through a divorce and my kids were basically dropped off on me two or three weeks before the fight. I had a two bedroom apartment and suddenly four children living there.

"They just got dropped off and left there. I was scrambling to try and provide for them. I completely lost focus on everything I was doing. I had some health issues, like high blood pressure and everything that comes along with that. It was a bad time for me."

While it didn't entirely keep him out of the gym, it did create a burden for some of his staff at the Lion's Den.

"I remember he would do stuff like, 'Hey man, meet me for a lesson.' And then I'd show up and he'd leave me with the kids," Hernandez says. "He did that a couple times. I was like, 'You motherfucker.'

"These kids were fucking maniacs too. And we had a pro-wrestling ring, and they're trying to do flips off it. They're doing all kinds of crazy shit. I was always afraid one of them was going to get hurt bad. Can you imagine what he'd do?"

When he did get some time for himself, Shamrock was as likely to be found in the club as at the gym.

"I was either with my kids or, when I didn't have them, it was party time. I wanted to be free. I didn't want to think about stuff," Shamrock says. "When I went out to party it was my time to forget everything. And I would. It pretty much ended up being all the time."

He had lingering neck and knee problems from his wrestling days and it didn't always seem worth the effort to push through it. Cockily, he believed he could win against opponents he didn't really respect even without putting in the work that once seemed so important.

"Dude was in an alternate reality," one Lion's Den fighter says. "He believed his own hype. Ken was 98 percent ego and two percent emotional little kid. You can't tell the emperor he is not wearing any clothes. He will kill the messenger."

The standard eight-week fight camp that would become the norm in mixed martial arts never really existed at the Lion's Den. In the early days, the fighters would train non-stop, not in a traditional "camp" for the purposes of a particular opponent. Later, as age, injuries and lethargy took over, time in the gym became sporadic rather than obsessive.

"His training was never really top notch to begin with. It was so-so," Pete Williams says. "He wouldn't show up to training a lot of times when we were in Lodi either. But, after WWF, his training—let's just say if it was us training like that and he was there to see it, that would be totally fucking unacceptable. That'd be ass-beating worthy. If it was *us*.

"There was a definite lack of commitment to preparation and probably doing a lot of drugs and who knows what else. You're not in the right state to be training at the level you need to."

It was hard to tell anything was awry early in the fight at the Seibu Dome, an outdoor stadium shaped like a flying saucer where more than 30,000 fans had come mostly to see the three final fights, all featuring Japanese pro wrestlers.[281]

Shamrock had sweated profusely on the long two-hour bus ride from the Tokyo Hilton to the event site, perhaps thinking about his encounter with Don Frye two days earlier at the rules meeting where the two had nearly come to blows. Lion's Den fighter Tre Telligman had stepped between them and Shamrock stormed off rather than lose his cool.

The verbal battles with Frye had gotten intensely personal as the former UFC tournament winner had done everything he could to get under Shamrock's skin and get him to agree to what would be a big money fight. Frye was friends with former UFC fighter Cal Worsham who was training fighters with Bob Shamrock and had the inside scoop on Ken's personal issues, dropping them into interviews in a way Ken felt was beyond the pale.

"Ken and Bob just happened to be mad at each other at that time, and I knew about it. I took advantage of it like a dirty rat, you know," Frye says. "I crossed a line. Ken didn't. Ken was a pro, but I crossed a line and attacked the family[282] and I ended up paying for it when we fought. I haven't said anything about anybody's family since then."

There would be time to settle the score with Frye later. For now, the focus was on Fujita, a much bigger wrestler with a strong takedown game. Shamrock, just two bouts into his comeback, had his work cut out for him.

With wrestling legend Inoki looking on and his nemesis Frye in

---

[281] The American pay-per-view broadcast on DirecTV, airing 12 days after the Japanese event, was built around Shamrock as the main draw.

[282] At one point, Frye even talked to Bob about being in his corner for a fight with Ken.

"I want the whole world to know that he treats his dad like crap," Frye told Full Contact Fighter. "Somebody who did so much for him."

Fujita's corner[283], Shamrock dominated the open minutes. Shamrock easily stuffed Fujita's takedown attempts and made him pay with strong punches, at one point wobbling his foe with a powerful left hand. When it did look like Shamrock would go to the mat, he savvily grabbed the ropes several times, earning a yellow card for violating the rules but not losing position and ending up on his back.

After dropping Fujita with punches, Shamrock caught him in a guillotine, making the wrestler's face turn purple. But Fujita survived the attempt and Shamrock seemed to have expended all he had in the attempt. Five minutes into the fight he was gasping for breaths.

It was hot that evening. Some say temperatures exceeded 100 degrees. Underneath the television lights, certainly, it was more than a little noticeable. But that didn't explain Shamrock's sudden collapse. Just over six minutes into the fight, he was barely standing, holding onto the ropes in the corner to steady himself, asking his corner to stop the fight.

"He seemed to be saying to throw in the towel," Williams remembers. "And I was like, 'What? No fucking way.' The one thing you've taught us, if you've taught us nothing else, is you fucking don't give up."

Almost fifteen seconds passed with Shamrock asking his corner to end the fight, his students reluctant to do so. He was winning the fight, and easily. Even in the clinch, where Fujita theoretically had an advantage as a Greco-Roman wrestling standout, Shamrock was destroying him with hard uppercuts and knees. Stopping the fight didn't make sense.

"Suddenly he's wanting us to throw in the towel," Mezger says. "But he's winning the fight so nobody's throwing in the towel. We're like, 'Why would we throw in the towel?' We're like, 'We can't be hearing him right.' And then he kept saying the same thing. I couldn't really hear it, but other people said he was saying something about his heart."

In the *Wrestling Observer*, Dave Meltzer was as shocked as anyone:

> Fujita bulled Shamrock into the corner, where Shamrock hooked the rope again to steady himself.

---

[283] Shamrock's main cornerman, Guy Mezger, was present for the fight but had been absent for a portion of the pre-fight process. He'd fought Wanderlei Silva earlier in the night and been knocked out.

At this point you could see something was wrong in his face as he looked exhausted and said "towel" and motioned as if to throw it to his corner. His corner didn't respond at first, because it almost seemed surreal, and he kept motioning and finally they threw it in...He just appeared to run out of gas. This may be a tough one for Shamrock to mentally handle because I'm sure this isn't how he wants his last fighting memory to be, although he is under contract for more fights, it's not the kind of finish that the Japanese (or for that matter the North Americans who do see it on PPV) will be forgiving of.

"The first couple times, I was like, 'No, man. Just fucking just do nothing. Just defend. Just hang in there.' He beat the shit out of this guy from fucking ring post to ring post," Williams says. "But, he just had this look in his eyes— like he was worried. I don't think I'd ever seen that.

"I told him to give me three more minutes. And he said 'I can't, my heart. Petey, my heart.' And he had had some trouble leading up to the fight and I was just like, 'Oh, fuck. Well, I don't wanna have this guy fucking die on me.'"

When the referee stopped the fight, the ring filled with Lion's Den fighters and concerned onlookers. Don Frye, despite being Shamrock's sworn enemy, went over to make sure Ken was okay.

"Everyone was worried he'd had a heart attack," Brian Johnston, who was in Fujita's corner says. "Don had been a volunteer firefighter and had some emergency medicine experience."

Shamrock ended up walking with Webb to the back on his own two feet. It had been a scary situation, but fortunately not a tragic one.

"He wasn't the Ken of old anymore," Mezger says. "He went and saw a doctor, the doctor there. We were all outside. They were in there a good 40 minutes. We were all concerned about what was going on. We thought he was having a heart attack, which I will attribute to the fact he was doing all those drugs at the time.

"Nobody was honest with me about it. I was like, 'Ken seems off. What's going on?' And everyone started talking about how Ken was doing all the drugs. I was like, 'Why didn't you guys kind of say something to me because I can talk to Ken man to man while you guys are all student to man.' I didn't know about it. I didn't find out about it, to let you know, until much later on."

While his career seemed fragile and the future bleak, Shamrock wasn't one to dwell on losses. A few months later, in an interview with *Full Contact Fighter*, he had put it all behind him and basically dismissed it as a factor going forward in his career.

"I couldn't see anything. It was blurry," he said. "Basically I was seeing white flashes, my heart was pumping through my chest and my body just shut down...I don't feel like I should get my head crushed in, or beat in, or die before I tap. Maybe at one time I did, but at this point it's not how I feel because I have kids to raise.

"By no means am I getting soft or not as good as I was, I just did not train properly....I've had three let downs[284] in my career, where I didn't do what I thought I was capable of doing and each time I've come back strong. This is going to be no different. I'm going to come back and come back strong."

---

[284] The other two let downs were his first fight with Royce Gracie and the second bout with Dan Severn.

CHAPTER SIXTEEN
Holding Grudges

Moving out of his house removed any semblance of normality from Shamrock's life. It became a blur, even when his father moved down to San Diego to take over the reins at the Lion's Den. The constant stream of women, drugs and partying that had begun in his WWF days extended right into his second act as a cage fighter.

"Once he showed me a handful of pills," Manolo Hernandez says. "And he goes, 'Hey, check it out.' And I looked at them and he goes, 'Here, open your hand.' I thought he was going to hand me a pill. But, instead, he handed me the car keys and he took all of them."

Webb was at the heart of the wild nights. Although Shamrock was 15 years her senior, those close to him say she was definitely the dominant member of their partnership, at least emotionally.

"Once he met Alicia he didn't care about Chula Vista. Or his life," one Lion's Den fighter says. "He was the happiest person in the planet. He did more drugs and banged more women with her than you could count. She was his everything.[285]"

Not only did Alicia occupy Ken's time, often in the company of another hot young lady she had found at a restaurant or club, she was

---

[285] Another family friend remembers it differently.

"Ken once told me that his time with Alicia was both the best time of his life and the worst."

legendary among Ken's friends for bringing other girls with her to party, turning many nights into wild Bacchanalian orgies.

"I remember one night, we had been partying all night," Vernon White says. "There were people in rooms all over the house, getting into all kinds of stuff. Alicia had passed out in their bedroom and I was going to hang out with some of the fighters.

"As I'm walking down the hallway, I see some movement in one of the rooms and I kind of like peek through and it's Ken banging this little stripper chick from the back with the door cracked, looking to make sure Alicia wasn't coming. He asked me, 'Is she still passed out?' and I'm like, 'yeah'. 'Ok, thanks.' And he went right back at it. I lightly closed the door and went down to the room and hung out with the guys. That was a normal Friday night if Alicia passed out."

While Ken played, his adopted father returned and got busy trying to make the Lion's Den a functional business. Tina and her family, according to sources, had not been the best stewards of the Shamrock empire and there was a lot of damage to repair, both financially and reputationally.

"I see myself taking the stress off of him so now he can concentrate on his fights whereas before he couldn't," Bob told journalist Josh Gross. "He couldn't concentrate on Fujita, there were too many things going on and he couldn't take care of business. I see myself as being able to take that pressure and he can focus on the training."

One of his first orders of business was reestablishing the Lion's Den as a destination for prospective fighters from around the world. He brought the tryout back and dozens of fighters braved the hazing and intense workouts for an opportunity to fight.

Journalist Jason Probst was in attendance for one tryout and was flabbergasted by the Herculean tasks required just to get your foot in the door. But, as he gave the fighters a pep talk, Ken Shamrock laid out exactly why it was worth the trouble:

> "What you're about to get into is a long-term deal," he says. "It's not like climbing a mountain or jumping out of an airplane. It's a life decision. Anybody that wants to bug out now, no hard feelings." Nobody budges.
>
> Shamrock continues, adding that every man who makes it through the tryout will be guaranteed the

opportunity to fight in a big-time show. This is the brass ring, and what separates dojo tough guys from real fighters with serious cred in the mixed martial arts community.

A fighter with a good record in the numerous fighting events - which are multiplying in virtually every state as the sport rides a snowball's effect of legitimacy into the public consciousness -- has a world of opportunities available to him. Besides the fight purses of tens of thousands of dollars for winning a UFC bout, successful fighters can teach courses, hold seminars, sell instructional videos, and have the kind of instant recognition that martial artists used to break boards and perform similar gimmickry for.

While it was arguably no longer a place to get world class training, Shamrock remained a force behind the scenes in the sport, able to place fighters in UFC, Pride and at King of the Cage.[286] It was the key to keeping fighters in the gym, even if they might have been better served elsewhere.

"The ones that stayed all needed something from him,"one Lion's Den fighter says. "Including us fighters. He was the connection to the UFC. And a pro card. It's that simple.

"We needed him and he needed us too. Because even when he didn't show up for months, he took 20 percent of everything."

In some ways, little had changed at the Lion's Den despite massive changes in the sport. The stories fighters from those days tell are echoes of the ones told by the original team, only without the success that presumably made it all worth it.

"He's like that really crazy fighter—that really good father," fighter Joe Hurley told journalist Loretta Hunt. "He made us what we are, all of us. He made us into a family. None of us were really good athletes, like world class or anything, before. We were high school wrestlers and shit like that and he made us into something else.

---

[286] At one point Tom Casey was helping Ken negotiate a deal to fight exclusively for King of the Cage that would have included a 25-percent ownership stake. The group would have been rebranded "Ken Shamrock's King of the Cage."

"He had that ability to turn us into fighters. He'd go in there and teach you and show you everything and say 'Do this.' And then, if you didn't do it, he'd make you pay for it. There were times he would walk in and point to one of the younger guys and say, 'I'm going to beat the shit out of you.' We'd think about it all day long and then he wouldn't even show up that night. Or sometimes he would show up—you never knew.

"But at the same time, he'd give you those words of encouragement. One time we fought and afterwards he said 'Joe, you're ready to fight. I'm impressed,' and that meant everything...He was the God of your fight world. He was just the right combination of mentor, father and drill instructor."

Despite the setback against Fujita, the year ended on a strong note. Ken was somehow named Black Belt Magazine fighter of the year, Vernon White was champion in two different organizations and the team had dominated the final King of the Cage show of 2000, including a devastating Galindo knockout that put a stamp on what the team stood for going into a new century.

The Fujita fight ended up being Shamrock's last bout for over a year. He was scheduled to fight the fearsome Igor Vovchancyn at Pride 13, a serious challenge with major consequences for the 37-year-old. Vovchanchyn, the runner-up in Pride's World Grand Prix, was the number two ranked heavyweight in the world. A win would have lined Shamrock up for a title fight against tournament winner Mark Coleman—a fight, based on time together in the gym, Shamrock was confident he could win.

But fate intervened and a perpetually snakebit Shamrock aggravated his now perpetually hurt neck a couple of weeks before the event. He sent his teammate and training partner Tre Telligman[287] instead and made the long flight to Japan solely to lend moral support to his squad.

An eight-to-one underdog, Telligman shocked the fight world with the best performance of his career, controlling the smaller striker at range and on the ground. After first refusing to accept the preflight

---

[287] Telligman, who lost his right pectoral muscle in a car crash as a kid, was one of the unsung heroes of the Lion's Den.

ceremonial bouquet of flowers from Lion's Den rival Tito Ortiz, he went out and made Vovchanchyn look utterly and completely normal. No one celebrated harder, with a more genuine smile, than Ken, who had almost not made the event at all.

"Ken's plane never showed up in Japan," Telligman remembers. "We were all freaking out and we're hearing the plane went down. Then we found out that it had caught fire, but landed in Alaska. It looked like he wasn't going to make the fight.

"It's hard the day of the fight. We're a very tight knit group and it was weird. Not having one of my brothers felt funny. Then, as Igor was making his entrance, I see Ken running through the crowd and coming towards the ring. I felt such a surge of energy. He had taken a car straight from the airport and come immediately to the ring. He hadn't slept for two days and just been through this ordeal. But it meant so much to him to be there for me. I never forgot that."

Afterwards, an overjoyed Shamrock couldn't help but gush over his teammates success and sing the praises of the revitalized Lion's Den.

"I don't know if any of you ever had a baby before," Shamrock told announcer Stephen Quadros after the fight. "But you know, when you first see the baby come out and you start crying and it's the most important thing that's ever happened to you in your life. Now, I've had four kids and those are four of the most important parts of my life. I'll tell you what, actually being there to watch Tre defeat Vovchanvyn, it ranks pretty damn close.

"I'm proud of these guys. I'm proud of all my boys back home. There's one thing that will never change and will always be here from the beginning to the end—and that's that we have been here with each other through the thick and thin. It's been real thin at times, when I had to go away. These guys were still training and we had our problems. But we're family and we stuck together. And we'll continue to stick together and become stronger and stronger."

The Lion's Den reestablished its place in the mixed martial arts world throughout 2001. As Shamrock rightly predicted, they had their losses to go along with the triumphs. But the team mattered again, even in defeat.

"We were drug-fueled gladiators," one Lion's Den fighter says. "Roids were the standard base. We did off-season cycles and fight cycles. Fight drugs and power drugs. Off-season drugs, you don't have to worry about cardio and showtime drugs for stamina."

The only ingredient missing was Ken himself, who after the neck injury, blew out his knee and was reportedly dropped from his Pride contract when the term expired.

As Shamrock spiraled, there was no one to help catch him and redirect him in a positive way. His father Bob had his own father Chuck's declining health to distract him and the relationship, newly repaired, perhaps couldn't have survived a confrontation. Even those closest to him, some onlookers say, were content not to confront him as long as the money continued to flow.

"They just spent his money like crazy," one fighter says. "He let them. He blindly gave them his checkbook and accounts. As the saying goes 'you can't rape the willing.' As long as Bob got to go eat at his favorite restaurants, buy new parts and have his Cadillacs detailed, he didn't get too much involved. It's actually kind of sad."

Not having much success securing a fight with Pride or the UFC, Shamrock set out to create his own luck. His next fight, in August, was one he set up for himself in Atlantic City, New Jersey, taking advantage of the UFC and others pushing the state to finally legalize the sport.

Ken Shamrock Productions was created, in part, to ease Ken's way into retirement[288] and to give his fighters a steady gig in a fight world that seemed uncertain at the best of times.

"It was brought to my attention when I decided to go ahead and do this that I worked for the UFC, Pride, and the WWF, and I made everybody else money," Shamrock told *MaxBoxing*'s Thomas Gerbasi. "I didn't realize the actual power or popularity that I had until I did a few things around the area and I got a real good response.

"I realized that I could go out and do my own show, fight on my own show, and I will make my own money. Sure, it's going to be hard and I've got to put up with all the little failures here and there but I did it in fighting. There were times when I failed, but I came back stronger. I believe that's what is going to happen with this promotion. There are times when I'm going to run into a wall and get knocked down. I've got to get back up and figure out how I'm going to get around that wall."

Instead of a glorious return to the fight scene, "MegaFight: Enter the Lion's Den" was a disaster. It was originally scheduled as a pay-per-view but time ran out before Shamrock could get the deal complete—and good thing too, because it would have immediately been one of

---

[288] He would end up fighting for more than another decade. The best laid plans so often go awry.

the legendary busts in MMA history.

Four of his fighters from California weren't cleared to compete, mostly because of issues with their medical paper work, regulation by the state athletic commission proving to be a double-edged sword for athletes used to operating in a more free-wheeling environment.

Shamrock spent most of his time worrying about running the event instead of preparing for his own fight, an easy win over journeyman Sam Adkins. The fight, comically said to be for a world championship despite Adkins having no wins of note, was over in just under a minute and a half courtesy of a pro wrestling style hammerlock.

In the end, only 1600 fans showed up. Most of the card was made up of Lion's Den fighters, in part because they would work at a discount. Across the way were mostly fighters from the local scene. It made for a combustible environment, according to Gerbasi, especially after fans didn't appreciate the referee stopping Vernon White's bout with local Joe Pirole in the semi-main event:

> Unfortunately the local fans didn't appreciate the stoppage, with one idiot sending a bottle into the ring, which when thrown, bounced over the cage and injured a young fan. And when the Lion's Den crew in attendance saw this, they ran through the crowd to exact a little justice. Fortunately for the bottle thrower, local security got to him first.

Things were just as combustible after the show as Shamrock and his team departed in a limousine on their way out for a night on the town. His partners in the show were hesitant to cut him a check, having lost a bundle on the failed venture. That wasn't, of course, what Shamrock wanted to hear.

"Something was going on between the owners, the casino and the promoter," Shamrock says. "I just told them, 'listen, I'm not leaving without my money and I'm going to run out of patience here real quick'.

"They had told us 'well, um, gate wasn't what we hoped it was going to be.' Your guys's job was to promote the fight. My job was to put the fights on. So I said,' It's not my problem. And you're not leaving and I'm not leaving til I get my money. We can take it or you can give it to us.' Because we knew he had the money."

It became kind of a tense scene, Lion's Den manager Kevin Woo remembers, and tempers were getting short.

"The promoter didn't really pay him because the event didn't really turn out that great. So we're riding back in the limo," Woo says. "I said 'pull over and walk him out in them woods.' Then talk to him and see if he'll sign a check. But Ken wouldn't do it."

The event was the breaking point with Bob Shamrock who had pushed for Ken to participate. Soon after, the two had one of their periodic splits over a disagreement about money. At the heart of it was Bob's disdain for Alicia. Like he'd done previously with Tina, he drew a line in the sand and made Ken choose between him and his significant other. Ken sided with Alicia and Bob left town.

"My dad was taking money and putting it into the cash box," Shamrock remembers. "And he was putting it in the trunk of his car and he was using it for going out to eat and filling his car with gas and fixing his car. It wasn't like he was stealing money[289], because he was supposed to get a paycheck. But he wasn't depositing it and it just wasn't good business. I just told him 'you can't do that.' And so he ended up leaving. He thought I was accusing him of stealing. He earned his money. But it just was the way he was doing business was bad."

As crazy as the fight business was, it paled in comparison to the nights at the new house Shamrock shared with Alicia Webb.

"He'd be walking around his house in just his underwear at a party and Alicia is in her underwear," Woo remembers. "Things were crazy. Pete North, the porn star, would come over. It was a crazy thing, dude. Alicia, she likes girls too. So it would be like a threesome every night. It wasn't really Ken's choice, it was Alicia's."

It wasn't unusual for a night to end with bodies strewn all over the place, people going at it hot and heavy in every nook and cranny and drugs and empty bottles strewn all over the place. Ecstasy was the drug of choice with GHB a close second. If you took too much, you'd end up knocked for a loop[290]. In the right amount, it would just make

---

[289] "Ken was made to fight. Not to balance a check book," one Lion's Den member says. "He trusted all the wrong people. All the wrong people. All the time. That's why he doesn't have any money."

[290] This side effect is why it's called the "date rape drug."

you loopy, making it a favorite of the strippers who descended on the house. Occasionally things got a little too out of control and there were a few scares when people were found initially unresponsive after partying a little too hard.

"I remember Alicia OD'ed in my hot tub," Shamrock says. "She went from the shower into the hot tub high. Luckily I was in the room or she would have died. She went into all these convulsions and slipped under the water.

"I grabbed her and pulled her out and put her on the floor. I took her to the hospital and luckily she was okay. I remember thinking, if she dies, I'm in deep, deep, deep trouble.[291]"

Eventually drugs touched every aspect of Shamrock's life. Even sleep didn't come without a fight.

"I could take a Patron Silver, the whole bottle, and chug half of it in one drink and pass out for an hour or two," he says. "Then I'd wake up, finish the bottle and pass out again. That's the only way I could sleep after all the drugs."

With money dwindling away, his own drug dealing took a turn. What had once seemed like easy money suddenly became every bit as difficult to navigate as the Byzantine fight world.

At some point Shamrock had come into contact with "Mikey" a gay porn star famous for both his large member and the copious amounts of ecstasy he moved. Looking for a big score, Ken made the biggest deal he'd ever made, escalating things to a different level.

"Ken spent his last $30,000 on ecstasy," Woo says. "We were selling them. We called 'em T-shirts. There's so much drama with all that. Even if you're making money, we were spending so much money so fast man."

With Shamrock's money in hand, Mikey suddenly got squirrelly. A furious Ken sent one of his fighters, Tony Galindo, to collect but he came up dry.

"They came up with this story that these two Mexican guys robbed them," Pete Williams says. "I think they really just stole the shit. When you're dealing with shady people, shady shit happens. They might have owed someone else. I don't know.

---

[291] "I didn't know what that meant," Shamrock's son Connor says. "I was in fifth grade. We got picked up. We had to go to the hospital. At the time, I just thought 'oh, she's in the hospital.' Now, I'm like she od'ed in the bathtub? That's not something cool to keep your kids around."

"What are you gonna do in that situation? Dealing in the underworld, you're not gonna call the cops. It's like, what are you gonna do? Are you gonna go hire someone to beat the shit out of these people? How are you gonna get your money back? So I think you just have to just take a loss on that one."

Shamrock's deteriorating mental state and dependence on drugs and alcohol was impacting more than just his life in the ring—his relationship with his own children, often present for things no child should see[292], was being irreparably damaged.

"I try to remember good times but there's not a lot to remember," his son Connor says. "He misses every birthday, forgets to call you. All the important things, he's not there for. The times you have are like 'oh, we went out to eat today' or 'he came home and we played laser tag for ten minutes.' I don't know if he remembers differently but there's only so much I remember as a kid.

"I love my dad and never want to hurt his feelings but I don't expect anything from him. When he promises you things and then never follows through you kind of steel yourself to the fact that you can't count on him."

His daughter Fallon has similar recollections, or lack thereof, of her childhood in the Shamrock households.

"I still had these like really vivid memories of good times I had with my brothers and my mom and my grandparents," she says. "It wasn't like that with my dad when I was younger. I had nothing that really stuck in my memory except the fighting with him and my mom. That's kind of the earliest memories I have of him. There weren't a whole lot of good memories."

With opportunities in Pride uncertain, Shamrock found himself in much the same place he'd been back in 1997. He wanted to continue in the fight game, but money wasn't as easy to come by and wrestling

---

[292] "Bringing them into the middle of some of that stuff was wrong," Shamrock says. "You tell yourself 'they're sleeping, they won't know. They're too young, they won't know.' But they did. But it's like you don't know how to stop it once it starts."

remained as hot as ever.[293] He sent feelers out to WWF[294] and there was some interest there—but the company was cautious having been burned by Shamrock before.

In October, UFC, now under new ownership, found itself in desperate straits. They had finally gotten the sport cleared in Nevada and subsequently on nationwide pay-per-view. But that good news was followed by a disastrous turn of events when half of their main event, Vitor Belfort, was forced to drop out of the fight on short notice.

Shamrock was one of the first names considered as a replacement. It was tempting—the man across the cage would be UFC light heavyweight champion Tito Ortiz and the bad blood between the two was very real. But when UFC offered Ken $160,000 to step into the Octagon and he countered with $500,000, the deal was dead and UFC looked elsewhere for a cheaper opponent.

Instead, his attention returned to the other grudge match he had brewing—a fight with fellow pro wrestling refugee Don Frye. It was a fight Frye had been building in the media for years, one Shamrock had told friends he would never accept to prevent Don from getting the pay day he wanted.

But, with his own bankroll looking perilously slim, Shamrock was suddenly willing to consider the fight. The personal nature of the beef was also a huge positive. Not much could get Shamrock's attention in the haze he was in at the time. Frye, however, was the kind of opponent that forced him to focus.

"He finally had an opportunity with Don Frye to have a big fight in Japan," Casey says. "And he tried. He juiced up, he worked out. Ken knew it was a real opportunity and Don Frye was a serious fighter. For the first time, he took it seriously. He really got jacked up, but his knees were so bad he couldn't train like he wanted to. He got these knee braces and got the Japanese to agree to let him use them even though they had these metal braces on the sides. That was his issue, his knees would go sideways on him."

---

[293] Shamrock was advertised around this time for a number of independent dates, a tour of Australia and a match for the straight-to-DVD promotion the UPW. None of them, for various opaque reasons, ended up happening.

[294] Dave Meltzer reported: Ken Shamrock has called WWF, as has agent Barry Bloom, about returning although at this point negotiations haven't started. There is some question from WWF whether at this stage of Shamrock's life he is willing to come back and work 200 days on the road.

His training for this one, unlike his first two Pride bouts, was serious, a throwback to the glory days of Pancrase and the UFC.

"He was ready for that fight," Mezger says. "We were all there to help him, both in Dallas and California. Everyone knew how important it was for him."

The bout was briefly considered for November at the Tokyo Dome but a quad-tear and torn cornea forced Frye to postpone the fight. Things had changed since Shamrock was let go from his contract earlier in the year, and Shamrock once again found himself in position for a big money deal.

UFC had opened the door for the sport to make a big splash on pay-per-view and Pride was very interested in expanding its own horizons. For the first time they planned to offer the event on the same day it took place in Japan, hiring famed boxing publicist Jackie Kallen to spread the world to an American audience that thought of MMA exclusively in terms of UFC. Shamrock, a legitimate draw in the early days of the sport and more famous than ever off his WWF run, was expected to be a difference maker.

"The UFC and all these other organizations have failed to realize that people still remember the original fighters," Shamrock told the press at the time. "They're trying to bring in new faces and trying to build new names without building them off the old names -- and that's the way most things happen. The UFC is a good example of that. They brought in Tito Ortiz, who had never really beaten anybody[295]. They're trying to build the name of someone who has been beaten by Frank Shamrock, who has been beaten by Guy [Mezger], but really has never faced a Royce Gracie or a Mark Coleman or a Dan Severn or a Ken Shamrock. I think Pride has the right idea."

Twenty days before the show, Shamrock and Frye embarked on a five-city press tour, designed to capitalize on the American fighters' notoriety in the States. They hit Detroit, New York, Dallas, Phoenix and Los Angeles to meet with the media and participate in autograph signings. Plenty of fans showed up, but media was scarce. The one mainstream story that came out of the appearance, according to Dave Meltzer's *Wrestling Observer*, was centered on Kallen, who had recently

---

[295] Shamrock was cleverly setting up his next big fight in the middle of promoting his current blood feud. He was already in tentative discussions to meet Ortiz for UFC and was delivering his comments as much to Dana White as to the press.

announced an upcoming movie on her life starring Meg Ryan:

> The week-long press conference tour Pride had with Ken Shamrock and Don Frye has to ultimately be considered a flop...With all the thought that Shamrock is going to mean something in the U.S., it's been too many years and even though he had WWF stardom, he's been off that TV for a few years now as well, plus, he was a star in the WWF at the beginning, but was never portrayed that much as a bad ass by the end...
>
> They saved the pro wrestling angle for the final stop of the tour, on 2/8 in Los Angeles at the Hard Rock Cafe at the West L.A. Beverly Center... Shamrock grabbed the mic and yelled, "I'm not going to sit here and listen to this punk ass bitch here talk crap." He said he would beat Frye's ass right there.
>
> Frye stood up and they did a staredown and Shamrock called Frye a chicken, but luckily there was a glass of water conveniently there for Frye to throw in Shamrock's face. Shamrock went after Frye, with Antonio Inoki trying to separate them. They rolled around with no punches thrown, although Shamrock's face was marked from a scratch.
>
> After it was broken up, Shamrock challenged Frye to take it outside. Kallen grabbed the mic at that point and said that now both fighters would be available for interviews. Apparently that was unintentionally hilarious. And just as funny, both Frye and Shamrock then sat down for lunch a few tables apart.

While the two pro wrestlers knew how to put on quite a show, the surface shenanigans covered up raging infernos just below the surface. Shamrock, who liked to manufacture animus with every opponent to get himself in the right place mentally to hurt them if the situation called for it, had worked himself up into a lather.

There was some water under the bridge since the worst of Frye's comments and even an appearance as a tag team in a pro wrestling match at the end of 2000[296]. But once the rhetoric fired back up again, it didn't take much to get Shamrock riled up all over again.

"I always try to find something in a fighter I dislike, dwell on it, and try to build some anger towards the person," Shamrock told me in a 2008 interview. "I was able to build up a lot of anger towards Don Frye from some of the things he said about my father and towards me. It was something I was really able to dig into and really create the anger I needed to fight him[297]."

Frye, likewise, came into the fight with serious bad blood. Sure, he was playing it up for the cameras, but the heart of the feud was real, on his end mostly on account of what he would later call petty jealousy.

"That was real, man," Frye says. "We didn't like each other. Shit, it was all we could do to keep from fucking going at each other. We had to keep an eye on the ball and realize, you don't get paid for fighting outside the ring.

"It was all me. I was just an asshole and I was jealous of his success. He was successful in the public relations market and in the WWF, and I felt slighted because I had won a real championship in UFC, won a tournament, and he hadn't. But he had all the notoriety anyway. It hurt my ego."

The staredown was as intense as any in the history of MMA, Frye and his notorious mustache going nose-to-nose with Shamrock's stylish new mutton chops[298]. Neither man blinked for what felt like an eternity, their noses eventually touching before referee Yuji Shimada separated them.

"It is on folks, it is on," commentator Stephen Quadros said, hardly able to contain his excitement. "The fight we have been waiting for, the grudge match of grudge matches."

There was no feeling out process as the two immediately charged across the ring and started the fight in style. Shamrock had prepared heavily for a battle in the clinch instead of working on his takedowns from range, no longer the Ken Shamrock of old.

---

[296] Frye and Shamrock teamed up to take on Nobuhiko Takada and the Great Muta in a match that set the all-time Osaka wrestling attendance record, packing the Osaka Dome with 42,756 fans.

[297] "He'll probably never fight again when I'm done," Shamrock said in the pre-fight hype interview. "If I get a hold of something, I will break it."

[298] "People said 'You look like Wolverine,'" Shamrock says. "So I decided to stick with it."

"A lot had to do with my health," Shamrock said. "I had some knee problems and it was tough for me to shoot and get to the ground. I really forced myself to study my standup so I could get to the clinch and get a takedown.

"Instead of shooting, I could use the clinch to get them down. I really had to get my hands busy so I could at least fight half way decent on the standup. So I wasn't forcing my shots or forcing a takedown."

The training paid off, as much of the bout was contested in that position, the two men destroying each other to the body with stinging punches and knees. Frye, who dismissed Shamrock's punching prowess before the bout, seemed to get the better of most exchanges, but Shamrock scored with plenty of his own strikes. It was a grueling bout, contested at close quarters, by two snarling animals.

"My back was bad, my shoulder was bad, and I took a Vicodin pill before that fight," Frye says. "I was in more pain than necessary, but not as bad as it got after that. And that's all I could do. That's all I brought to the fight. I couldn't rotate my shoulder and turn the punch over. I didn't have any lateral movement. I fought with what I had to fight with."

With three minutes left in the ten-minute first round, Shamrock dropped suddenly for a leglock,[299] eventually securing an inverted heel hook and twisting with all of his considerable might. Shamrock was a leg lock man—he had been for more than ten years at this point. But he couldn't quite get Frye to concede.

"I found out later he'd taped his ankles with the shoes on[300]," Shamrock says. "On anybody else's leg, the leg would have been broke. Anybody else, I had him. And it still hurt his knee.

"But because he had it taped like a cast, I couldn't turn it. I couldn't turn it over. I've broken four or five guys' ankles like that. And I hear his knee pop. But I couldn't turn it over. I'd like to know how they taped that thing. To me, that's cheating. You shouldn't be able to do that."

---

[299] In the bonus footage shot for the Pride 19 DVD set, there is an extended pre-fight training session with Shamrock and some of his teammates. You can see him practicing this very same takedown prior to the fight, then delivering a perfect version under the bright lights.

[300] Looking carefully at the footage, you can see tape applied around Frye's wrestling shoes, perhaps allowing him some measure of protection.

Frye limped back to his corner and remained standing rather than sit and have his injured knee lock up.

"Did I think about tapping? Hell no," he says. "They don't pay me to tap. They pay me to play. You know?"

But he'd played hard—and there were potentially ten long minutes left in the contest. Exhausted, his corner supplied him with oxygen out of a can, a rules violation in the United States but apparently allowed in the anything goes world of Pride.

Things slowed down in the second round—with both men closer to 40 than to 30, how could they not?—and Shamrock had his hands on his knees in the corner waiting for the third round to begin. His body language oozed defeat. But Mezger wouldn't allow him to quit on himself, taking charge and all but demanding his best effort.

Each went for broke in the third with a wild exchange of haymakers. It was an even trade right up until the second it wasn't. Shamrock eventually ate a solid left hand[301] and dropped hard to the mat, fighting on instinct only in a desperate battle for survival as Frye laid in some brutal ground and pound.

"I'm dazed there," Shamrock admits, watching the fight back 16 years later. "There's a part here I don't know. That I don't remember it. This is where he won the fight. I come to with Guy yelling at me. I'm just trying to recover my senses."

Frye, for his part, felt his confidence ebb a little as Shamrock simply refused to stop fighting. His energy level, drained by the tough fight and the extra muscle he'd packed on, had begun to dwindle with each concussive blow that Shamrock somehow weathered.

"I wondered, what the hell do I gotta do to put this guy down? I was looking for a foreign object to hit him with," Frye says. "But that guy's tough as nails. He came to fight and there was no quit in him at all."

Shamrock, somewhat miraculously, managed a hip escape and ended up in the top position, Frye hanging on for dear life, hoping for either a restart or to wind the clock down, confident he'd win a decision.

Instead, hearing his corner tell him he was running out of time, Shamrock dropped back for one more desperation heel hook, the two

---

[301] Frye had tried switching to the southpaw stance several times during the fight, usually losing those exchanges to Shamrock. This time, he landed a left on the button and it changed the complexion of the bout.

eventually ending up in a classic dueling leg locks position that Ken had helped popularize in Pancrase.

"I'm cranking that sucker and I just can't turn it," he says. "I could hear his knee pop. That guy is tough."

The bell rang and both collapsed back on the mat, completely spent. When they got to their feet, the two bitter enemies embraced in a fine display of sportsmanship.

"That was a great fight," Shamrock says. "We built it up and then we went out there and put on a heck of a fight. After it was over, we were good. There was no reason for us to hate each other. We settled it in the fight. No matter how it ends up, you had your shot."

Frye agrees.

"We fought for 20 minutes," he says. "If you can't get it out of your system in 20 minutes, you should go see a psychiatrist, you got real problems. Oh yeah, we were always real polite when we'd see each other after that. Since then, I've never said a bad thing about him. Every bad thing I said before that was just to hype the fight."

Both men raised their hands in victory, then waited for the judges to render a verdict. Unlike the UFC or boxing, Pride officials scored the bout in its entirety. It didn't matter at all who won individual rounds. They were looking at the fight as a whole—and ended up awarding Frye a split decision victory. But, though he had his hand raised, Frye paid a terrible price.

"As soon as I walked out of the arena and got back behind that curtain, boy, I fell like a stone," Frye says. "We got a picture of me and all my crew in the locker room, and I'm laying on a table with ice on both ankles[302].

"My wife and I, we flew to Hawaii the next day and by the time we got off the plane, my ankles were the size of a big woman's butt. Boy, I'll tell you, I could barely crawl off that airplane. If we'd gone to LA which is what we'd normally have done, they'd have had to wheel me off that sucker."

Shamrock, too, paid a heavy toll for his fighting spirit that night. He was staggering around the ring a bit after the fight and struggled for some time after the bout.

"He left a lot on the mat with Don Frye," Casey says. "He had a very

---

[302] The final tally for Frye: a hairline fracture of his right ankle, a sprained left ankle and a partially torn meniscus. He would later admit the fight led to his subsequent painkiller addiction.

serious concussion and they really had to take care of him after that fight. He could barely walk out of the ring. That really hurt him. He never really recovered."

Even his fighters, men who had seen and been on the wrong end of plenty of brutal beatings were growing concerned. There comes a time when a fighter's body can no longer support his aspirations, when the accumulated knowledge and skill of a lifetime is suddenly housed in a battered, imperfect vessel that can't execute what the brain is telling it to do. Shamrock, they feared, was fast reaching that point.

"He took some hard, hard punches, man," Mezger says. "You don't shake those off in your 30s, you know? My concern was how much damage he took. He had to have a major concussion from that. Multiple concussions. I looked at Ken and Ken wasn't focusing and he wasn't talking, I was like, 'Oh shit, dude. He's messed up.'

"It was a fucking hell of a fight. It was one of those fights you don't want to have because both guys walk away dying, going to the grave earlier because they took so much out of each other."

While the fight was an instant classic, it didn't do the box office[303] Pride had hoped for. It was also the last fight on Shamrock's contract, leaving the fighter, once again, searching for a home.

---

[303] The buy rate, despite being live for the first time and featuring two high profile American stars, only went up 50 percent.

CHAPTER SEVENTEEN
A Living Death

* * *

The Frye fight left Shamrock's career balancing perilously on a ledge, one false move from being over. If you ignore the Adkins bout, which most people did, he had lost two consecutive fights for the first time in his career and was starting to look every bit his 38 years of age.

He attempted, as he'd done in 1997, to start a bidding war on his services. With the losses, WWF was less keen to bring him in on a special deal that would allow him to work minimal dates and take time off for the occasional super fight. If we was going to return, it had to be with the standard, grueling WWE road schedule. Shamrock wasn't sure he'd survive the 20 matches a month they were asking and desperately sought some other options[304].

As luck would have it, Shamrock was making his availability known at the same time Jeff and Jerry Jarrett were launching a new and ambitious wrestling promotion called NWA-TNA. It was an interesting combination of Jerry's old-school sensibilities learned as a wrestling promoter in the territory days and his son's experiences at the right hand of the very modern Vince Russo, controversial architect of some the best and worst excesses of the 1990s. The idea was to produce a weekly pay-per-view at the cost of $10.00 and eliminate many of the travel expenses that made promoting wrestling such a daunting gamble.

Shamrock spoke with Jeff in March[305], about a month after the Frye fight, and shortly after, verbally agreed to terms to join the promotion for its August debut for 26 dates[306]. At $7500 an event[307], he and Scott Hall were the most expensive talent but expected to bring in mainstream attention. Shamrock had very few concerns, according to Jerry Jarrett and only one demand—he would not work with current NWA champion Dan Severn.

---

[304] The Observer would report that WWE later agreed to Shamrock working 12 dates a month but wouldn't agree to his money terms. Shamrock does not recall this.

[305] This was one time the dirt sheets didn't have the jump on a big story, possibly because Bob Shamrock, a perpetual leak in the Lion's Den camp, wasn't in the loop.

[306] The promotion's plan was to broadcast one PPV live, then tape the next week's show as a cost-cutting measure.

[307] The source for this is Jerry Jarrett's amazing book *The Story of the Development of the NWATNA*, essentially a reprinting of his diary from the time period. It's a fascinating, if occasionally dry, portrait of a wrestling startup, warts and all.

"Everybody wants me to have a match with him," Shamrock says. "I'm pretty good at carrying people. I tried with Dan and it's terrible. He wouldn't listen.

"It was strictly business. I knew that, going into TNA that I had to have good matches. I'm new. It's a different organization. I gotta go and be impressive. So when they wanted to bring in Dan, I was like, 'no.'"

For Shamrock, the risk posed by TNA's unsure position in the marketplace was one worth taking, particularly since he was using the wrestling income to supplement the big pay days he was lining up in the suddenly much more lively MMA scene. He was negotiating with King of the Cage to headline their first pay-per-view and with UFC for a fight with Ortiz.

Both had storyline elements that made sense—Ortiz had been feuding with the Lion's Den for years and Severn's history with Shamrock bridged his time in both MMA and pro wrestling. But, while Severn was hesitant to take the fight[308], Ortiz was gung ho, all but begging the promotion to make the match.

"Shamrock had become an even bigger name in WWF and then I saw him fight Don Frye in Pride," Ortiz says. "And I told Dana White 'I want to fight him. He has a huge name and it would be great for the company.'" And we were able to make it happen. He was the only person I fought as champion who wasn't really a top contender."

Shortly after he made his debut for TNA, the Tito fight was announced for November 22, 2002, at UFC 40, the first bout in a three-fight deal for the company. But his run with the upstart wrestling company was over before training for the fight could ever get started.

"I think that Jerry Jarrett had the right idea," Shamrock says. "But Jeff had other ideas, and he convinced his dad to go a different direction. But I believe if they would have stuck with the idea, put the belt on me, we could have done well."

He'd won the NWA title on the first pay-per-view event, but it was all down hill from there. He had indifferent matches on most of the shows and didn't seem to gel with the fans in the company's home base of Nashville. A disastrous ladder match against ECW veteran Sabu was the final straw. Less than a month into his run, he dropped

---

[308] He was demanding drug testing among other things. That would have been problematic at the time as Shamrock was battling through an assortment of injuries with plenty of chemical assistance.

the title to Ron Killings and was gone for good.

"The truth is, Shamrock wasn't as popular with our fans as we'd hoped he would be," one TNA executive says. "He was also one of the most expensive talents on our roster and we were losing a lot of money on every show at the time. When we discussed his future, he was a complete gentleman. He didn't seem upset at all and was very focused on his fighting career."

There was also the matter of Alicia. Jerry Jarrett was interested in bringing in Sean "X-Pac" Waltman, who seemed to connect better with the audience and was good behind the scenes when pitching potential investors. But there was a stumbling block—his heat with Shamrock over Alicia Webb. In his book, Jarrett mentioned stories floating around about sexual infidelity and swinging clubs. For once, the "telegraph, telephone, tell-a-wrestler" gossip circle wasn't far off.

"At three or four in the morning, with drugs everywhere, it's a different world when it comes to sex," Shamrock says. "I didn't fit well. Because I had boundaries with sex. And she had a lot of male gay friends that would come around and there was always this anticipation for something to happen with me. But my doors just didn't go that way. She was constantly trying to bring another man into the bedroom and I wouldn't do it. It ain't going to happen the other way."

The issue started to press on their relationship and eventually on Alicia's birthday in May, Shamrock compromised on a swinging scenario where they would be with other people in the same bed at the same time.

"Waltman was there with me, Alicia and his wife," Shamrock says. "There was a pile of cocaine, just out. In a pile on the shelf. I stuck my nose in there and sniffed almost all of it. I sat there while this was going on and I was checked out. Just staring at them. I don't know why I was angry. She was passed out and they wanted me to have sex with her."

Shamrock was almost a spectator in his own body at this point, lost in dark thoughts, thinking about how his life had come to this point. He didn't feel like himself—and despite the rock star life, he knew he wasn't happy.

"It was just unhealthy and we were doing a ton of drugs," Waltman says. "He didn't really want to be with my wife but he wanted to make Alicia happy. And it was fucked up because I wanted to be with her and that was *his* girl and it was fucked up of me.

"I remember waking up with Alicia in one arm and my wife in another and him standing over us. Pretty crazed look in his eyes. Alicia started going off, not going off on him but just like 'What are you doing?'"

The situation eventually devolved into a screaming match and Alicia leaving to be with Sean[309]. Shamrock says it was a breakup that was a long time coming.

"After a couple of years, I was worn out. I couldn't keep up with her," he says. "As much as I tried, I just couldn't. That put a strain on our relationship, whatever that relationship was. There was a point in time where I wasn't enough. She wanted more.

"I wasn't mad at Sean. I was mad at her because she was taking advantage of a situation. He had two kids. I knew what she was doing and Sean was blind[310]. I used her the same way she was using me. We both wanted to have fun."

The break wasn't as clean as it could have been. Waltman, who left his family to be with Alicia, experienced the same dull ache that Shamrock had been dealing with for years, missing his kids more than anything.

"She was going back and forth and still living in Ken's house and working at some strip club," Waltman says. "She went back there and they had sex. And she told me about it and it broke my heart to be honest with you. I shouldn't have really been that mad at her because that's how our relationship started by fucking around and shit. It wasn't long after that, that he had his fight with Tito and I felt like that might have negatively affected him. I had a lot of guilt about that."

His personal life might have been falling apart, but the show, always,

---

[309] "Like a week later Ken can't find Alicia," one Lion's Den fighter says. "So he calls X-Pac's wife and she can't find X-Pac either. Well guess what? They ran off together."

[310] Eventually, he would come to understand.

"Her and I are close to this day," Waltman says. "She was great with my kids, she was just fun, she was the life of the party. But you know at some point that's not what you want in a significant other."

must go on. And, for UFC, this was one of the most important shows in the promotion's history.

The new management team had succeeded in getting the sport back on pay-per-view and cleared in the state of Nevada, opening up Las Vegas to be their home base. For years it had been assumed by most people around the sport that this was all it would take for money to start flowing in. Instead, because of the lack of established names, fans weren't willing to buy into this new UFC.

"They were dying," Shamrock says. "They had the connections to get it legalized in Las Vegas, but they didn't know anything about promoting or putting on a show. They were close to shutting the doors before me and Tito saved them. Dana White begged me to come in and fight.

"He was begging me to come fight for them. They were doing 30,000 buys on pay-per-view and he told me 'we just want to break 100,000.' I said 'I can get that for you easy.'

"He goes 'a lot of people say that, but they haven't been able to do it.' I told him 'I can do it.' They couldn't afford what I was asking, so I made a bet on myself and would get paid based on hitting those numbers. We went forward and did 140,000 to 150,000 buys. That's a huge increase."

It was the biggest fight in the history of the modern UFC, a last ditch extravaganza before new owner Lorenzo Fertitta, who was losing money on the property, gave up on the concept for good. The owners and matchmakers were legitimate fight fans and wanted to help the sport move into a bright new future. They had pledged not to rehash the greats of yesteryear and focus on contemporary athletes. But lofty goals tend to disappear when the bottom line is written in red instead of black.

"Why'd we bring back Ken Shamrock?" a former UFC executive says. "Why the fuck did they bring back Tank Abbott after they specifically said, when Zuffa bought the UFC, that's not what they were about? Do you want to sell tickets? Well, what do we think is going to do that?

"It was never expressly said to me 'hey, we're doing shitty and here's why we are doing this thing we said we weren't gonna do.' But you just figure it out. I figure other businesses are like that. Even if things are not going well, it's not ever something you want to admit to. It would just depend on the day. 'We're doing awesome.' Really, can I have a raise then? 'No, actually we're doing terrible.'"

Fertitta wanted to see whether, with the right ingredients, MMA was a viable product on pay-per-view. It might have been better, sure, if Ortiz could talk or Shamrock could still fight. But considering the options, Shamrock versus Ortiz was the best possible test case, a story that no one had to think about too hard and would be difficult to mess up.

"It's nice for people to have something to lock onto and those two genuinely did not like each other," a UFC decision maker says. "It helped to have things like that.

"Tito was a very charismatic guy but the weird thing is, he can't talk at all. You kind of would assume if someone is charismatic that means they can speak, but no. He looked charismatic in pictures. I had a poster of him on my wall and my daughter was fascinated by it. That guy looks different. He had this aura about him but he quite often hurt it once he opened his mouth.

"It's hard to build a rivalry for him based on him telling a story. It had to be on a very simple level. You have the old legend and the brash newer guy and there will be people who want the up and comer to win and a lot of people who want the legend to shut this smartass punk up."

The promotion hired Fear Factor's Joe Rogan to be the color commentator and then arranged for both fighters in face-off in memorable segments on Fox Sports' *The Best Damn Sports Show Period*. It was their first attempt to sell this simple story—and it was a smashing success. The tension captured the mainstream in a way no fight had since the early days of the sport.

The two were perfect foils, though some critics thought the back-and-forth bordered on the absurd, more pro wrestling than serious sport. Dave Meltzer, in the *Wrestling Observer*, declared it was the best shot the group had at garnering any attention from casual sports fans:

> They did a great job of making it a match you want to see as opposed to two good fighters having a fight. Shamrock, who was never a good pro wrestling interview, was very good at using pro wrestling interview techniques here. All the hosts of the show when it was over were talking about wanting to go to Vegas and see the fight and how thick the tension was between the two.

* * *

"It was like a modern Muhammad Ali versus Joe Frazier," Ortiz says. "Ken came from WWE and he knew how to talk. He knew how to get people riled up. And then you had me—I was pretty much a smart ass. I was a brash kid from Huntington Beach and I just laughed at the guy. He was this tough legend and I just laughed in his face. People wanted to see what would happen. The baddest man on the planet versus the champ."

The promotion culminated in a press conference that was equal parts compelling and hilarious, as a deadpan Shamrock gave a heartfelt speech right out of an inspirational sports movie, attempting to stand up for honor and decency in a fight world suddenly ruled by the brash, unruly Ortiz:

> "This is really, really difficult for me to stand here right now. Since the first UFC, I have fought many different fighters and I've tried to carry myself with a professional attitude. I know at times, I've been difficult to deal with at times when times were necessary. I feel that for this sport to continue to move like it has now—Dana White and Zuffa has done a great job putting this thing together—is that we have to have some sort of control or some sort of respect between each other.
>
> "Whatever you want to do before the fight, during the fight—but when the bell rings and your hand is raised or not raised, you show a little respect. And if you don't want to show any respect at all, don't show any disrespect. To me, that's lowering our event to where it doesn't need to be. We're trying to elevate ourselves to a professional organization and in order to do that, we have to have professional athletes. I take nothing from Tito Ortiz's ability, but I do have a lot to say about his attitude and what he did to me and the Lion's Den—I did say I would not leave the mixed martial arts world until I got in there and got the opportunity to knuckle him up and since that day, Tito Ortiz has done nothing but open his mouth, disrespect me and the Lion's Den.
>
> "For whatever reason he has, I don't know and I don't care right now. All I care about is getting in the

ring and getting it on with Tito Ortiz. On Friday night, at the MGM Grand, right here, when the gate shuts and the bell rings, Tito Ortiz is going to find out what Ken Shamrock is all about. I guarantee that. So if I was you, I hope to God you come ready. Cause if you don't, I'm going to beat you into living death."

When Shamrock was done, Ortiz laughed out loud, causing Shamrock to kick a chair at him, deftly intercepted by UFC President Dana White. Shamrock and the Lion's Den then stormed out of the building, leaving media and other fighters dumbstruck.

"I might have overreacted by laughing hard, but it was all I could do," Ortiz said. "It was either I was going to get up and punch him in his face or I was going to laugh about it. I figured I'd be the bigger man and I'd laugh about it.

"...He flipped out like Ken Shamrock always does. He can't handle the pressure."

Things were calmer the next day at the weigh in and Shamrock weighed in at a shocking 201 pounds, a full four pounds under the light heavyweight limit[311].

After that, the hard work of promotion was done. The only thing left to do was step into the cage to see what he had left. Although he attempted to maintain a positive outlook, reality was, it wasn't much. Shamrock had a torn meniscus and ACL.[312] Though he had done his best to learn how to fight without the stability offered by two good knees, he knew it was going to be a struggle against an athlete like Ortiz. Despite the bad blood, he respected Tito as a fighter and knew that he could be in for a tough night.

"When they came to me to fight Tito, I wanted to get it fixed, but I didn't have time or the money," Shamrock says. "I had to wait. The fight was too close. I went in and fought on a bad knee.

"It was a second chance. I didn't have the physical skillsets

---

[311] "That was the first time I'd ever cut weight for a fight," Shamrock says. "The last time I'd been in the UFC, there were no weight classes. The sport had changed a lot."

[312] Knowing about the injury, White had Chuck Liddell waiting in the wings to fill in if one of the fighters had to drop out. The UFC, with so much invested, wasn't going to let this show fail.

anymore, but I knew how to build fights, how to market fights. I made more money in the second part of my career than in the first. Watching my skillsets diminish was frustrating. Because, mentally, I still had it. Mentally, I still had the desire and the want. The body wouldn't follow."

Early odds favored Shamrock but, by fight night, Ortiz was the clear favorite, certainly among smart fans and bettors who understood how far the sport had progressed and how limited Shamrock had become. Even in his own somber locker room, even in his own mind, he wasn't really expected to win.

"Kenny knew before the fight that his odds were against him," Kevin Lynch, a photographer documenting the UFC for the incredible book *Octagon*. "Kenny knew before the fight that he had no choice but had to do the fight, and he did it even though he knew he was going to get hurt. I mean, that's incredible courage. There's honor in that.

"Kenny was calm as he was sitting there. I got a picture of him where he was looking down and he was alone almost in that moment with himself. And I think he had already felt defeated before he went out there. He may not admit to that, but I could see this warrior, this wounded warrior, going out there because that's what men like him do. You know? He said 'I don't have a choice, I gotta stand up for what I believe in, and I'm going to go out there even if I'm going to get my ass kicked.' It was very powerful."

In truth, Shamrock was there for two reasons—to fill an empty bank account and help preserve the sport he had helped invent.

"The UFC, that's my legacy," Shamrock says. "I built that. Me, and Royce and Dan and Tank and all the original fighters. It's got to survive. So, I went and did it even though I had a bad knee. Because I knew, as bad as it was going, UFC wasn't going to be around much longer if I didn't. I fought a guy in his prime, much bigger than me."

Both men were limited to two cornermen due to Nevada Athletic Commission fears of a brawl. Ken entered the arena with Guy Mezger and Tra Telligman. Ortiz made the walk with UFC heavyweight champ Ricco Rodriguez and veteran fighter Fabiano Iha.

"The electricity in the room was just unbelievable," Shamrock says. "Loud, very loud for both me and Tito. It was just crazy. That was a memory I won't forget."

After a spirited introduction by Bruce Buffer, Shamrock took the center of the cage as the bell rang, securing double underhooks and pushing Ortiz into the fence. But Ortiz manhandled him, almost big brother style, reversing position and battering him with punches and a big knee.

Early in the first round, Shamrock landed a counter right hand in the pocket that briefly dropped Ortiz to one knee. But before he could capitalize, Ortiz was not only back up but on the offensive. Those moments of hope, as the time ticked away, were fewer and further between.

Ortiz was able to take Shamrock down with ease[313], where the older man could do little but weather the storm. And Ortiz was in shape to deliver a pounding for all 25 minutes if he needed to. Shamrock's best chance, in theory, was a to latch onto a submission on the ground the way he had against Frye earlier in the year. But Ortiz was an underrated grappler and too slick to fall for an old dog's old tricks[314].

"There were so many people saying how close the fight was gonna be and that Ken was really tough and strong," Ortiz told journalist Thomas Gerbasi in 2003. "They were just saying so much stuff and giving him so much credit that they didn't realize how hard I worked and how good I became. At UFC 40 people saw a whole different side of mixed martial arts. They said, 'man, you really dominated. You picked him apart.' If he wanted to be the champ, he had to earn it. That night he sure wasn't going to be the champ and he was not going to earn it because of all the work I put into it."

Despite the relatively one-sided nature of the fight, the arena buzzed throughout. The crowd chanted "Tito, Tito, Tito" at one-point, before eventually being drowned out by the roars of "Shamrock, Shamrock, Shamrock." On commentary, Rogan added a level of excitement that had never previously existed on a UFC broadcast. There really were no losers on the show—except Ken, who took a horrific beating that became difficult to watch.

After fifteen minutes, the bout no longer looked competitive and the third man in the Octagon, veteran referee John McCarthy, was growing concerned as Shamrock's face was beaten to the point he was hardly recognizable. McCarthy detailed the bout's finish in his autobiography *Let's Get it On*:

---

[313] "He wouldn't have been to take me down before the injuries," Shamrock insists. "Koslwaski, Dan Severn, Mark Coleman. None of those guys, Olympic level guys, could take me down."

[314] He had also trained for a time before the fight with Oleg Taktarov, a former Shamrock associate and leglock specialist.

* * *

At the end of the third round, Shamrock looked my direction. "I can't see anything John."

I walked him to his corner and told Tra Telligman, his lead cornerman, "Your fighter's having trouble seeing."

I wanted Shamrock's corner to have the chance to pull him out of the fight, but I had also told the ringside physician what he had said to me. It was time to get him out; the question was which way it was going to happen. Shamrock's corner called it, saving their man from any more damage. It was a great bout and an honorable ending.

The fight was an economic success, drawing the biggest crowd for a combat sports event in Las Vegas that year and the biggest gate in UFC history[315], almost doubling the next best effort.

"We saved MMA," Shamrock says. "He needed me and I needed him. MMA needed us. He was in his prime and trying to get where I was already at. I wouldn't have wanted to hear that either. 'Get out of here man, it's my time.' Now that he's been through it, he has a better understanding of what was going on."

Shamrock's face was already bruised and swollen before the fighters had cleared the ring. By the time he got back to the hotel, it was a frightening sight. Like the Frye fight, the price of his bravery was permanent.

"Ken never fully recovered," Casey says. "We had to walk him around because the doctor came up to the hotel room and told us 'don't let him go to sleep. You just keep him up, keep him on his feet.' So we were walking through old Las Vegas and he couldn't even see out of his eyes he was so beat up. He left it in the ring. He put up a good fight, but Ken's not a boxer. That was it for Ken's fight career as a serious fighter."

---

[315] 13,770 and $1,540,340,000.00 respectively according to a UFC press release that read almost like a victory lap.

The Ortiz fight had left Shamrock at a crossroads. Though not officially divorced, his marriage was a shambles. His relationship with Alicia, too, was all but over. And, he was quickly learning, his financial life was also in ruins.

"Ken was sending all his paychecks back home and Tina never paid any taxes on the money," Casey says. "This became a factor in Ken's career going forward. When he left wrestling and returned to fighting, the first one to have him in a chokehold was the IRS. He came out of professional wrestling owing the IRS $340,000.

"He wasn't able to pay that, so with their interest rate, they just continued to choke him to death. That kind of lasted through his whole career. Even when he had the big fight with Tito, the IRS was literally cageside to grab his check from him. So, Ken had a lifetime fiasco with taxes. He always had to fight for a paycheck but could never get ahead of the curve. He couldn't keep up with the continuing accumulation of interest and penalties."

The accumulated stress led to some drastic action. Shamrock moved out of his house and into an apartment with Jon "War Machine" Koppanhaver, taking over the rent and the master bedroom before eventually putting down a year's rent on a modest condo for both himself and Tina.

"I literally walked away from it," Shamrock says. "Left the house, left the furniture, stopped making payments on it. I went and got this condo and spent $17,000 to pay the rent for a year (2003). Furnished it and put my now ex-wife upstairs. I took the downstairs. And I told her 'I want to raise my children even if we're not together.'"

Although there was talk of retirement after the Ortiz fight, the money concerns made that almost impossible. He told the media the weight cut had drained him too much and he was confident he could compete at heavyweight. The truth was, he needed the money.

Despite the wrecked knee, he signed to fight Ian Freeman[316] at UFC 43, before eventually deciding he just wasn't up to the task when he simply couldn't train on the injury[317]. Like Tra Telligman had at Pride

---

[316] Vitor Belfort and Tank Abbott were considered before the UFC eventually settled on Freeman when those fights fell through. It was reported that both Shamrock and Abbott asked for a $100,000 advance to take the fight.

[317] He also worked a match at the Tokyo Dome for New Japan just a couple of weeks before dropping out of the fight. This seemed to go mostly unnoticed in the MMA community at the time.

13, Lion's Den fighter Vernon White agreed to fill in at the last minute, late enough in the process that Shamrock's face still appeared on the poster. White had less than two weeks to prepare for his UFC debut and was only a week removed from a grueling loss to Jeremy Horn when he signed the fight. But, with Shamrock watching from cageside, he acquitted himself well in a draw, his second close decision in a month's time.

Between rounds, Shamrock did an interview with Eddie Bravo, surprisingly receiving some boos from the crowd as he explained that his knee injury was preventing him from stepping into the cage as promised.

"It's progressively getting worse and worse so I gotta go in and get it fixed so I can come back in here and do what the original Ken Shamrock does," he said. "And that's take people down and beat the shit out of them. And beat the shit out of them standing up. So, when I come back I will be bigger better and stronger."

Ken's transformation didn't occur overnight[318]. But a realization that change was necessary did. Shamrock got in touch with his adopted father Bob, begging forgiveness and asking to be part of his world again. His life, once an endless wave of beautiful women and nights he couldn't remember, became simpler.

"I was sick of women. I didn't want to have anything to do with them," he says. "I didn't want a relationship. I was tired of sex. There was nothing there anymore. I would be with three girls, models, and I just didn't want it anymore. I was burned out from it. I was on the couch downstairs, raising my kids. I remember asking my dad if he knew how to get in touch with Tonya."

Don and Jerry Ann Mambourg had been two of Bob and Dee Dee Shamrock's closest friends in Susanville. Ken and their daughter Tonya had known each other for years, first meeting when he was 13 and she was 10[319].

Ken was immediately smitten but knew instinctively that the daughter of Bob's friends was off limits. But the two had kept an

---

[318] At one point a terrified Koppanhaver called Lion's Den fighters when he couldn't wake Ken up after he mixed a number of substances. When they told him to call 911, he explained he couldn't "there are drugs everywhere."

[319] Shamrock remembers telling the other kids at the Boy's Ranch "I'm going to marry that girl someday." It's not as romantic as it seems—at the time he used "marry" as slang for intercourse.

interested eye on each other throughout their school years, though nothing much ever came of it. At one point, as a swaggering high school senior, he'd given her a ride home in his Trans-Am and she had invited him inside. He'd politely declined, preferring to maintain an almost big brother role.

"That used to piss me off," Tonya remembers. "He would keep all the guys away from me. And whenever I would go to parties, I would be in trouble as soon as I got home. He would go home and narc on me.[320]"

On a return visit home from college, he'd finally decided to ask her on a date, calling Don for permission and asking him to have her call him back. Twenty years later, both coming off bad relationships, she finally did.

"I remember thinking 'Wow, I don't know what to say to her,'" Shamrock says. "I was embarrassed that she might find out who I was, who I'd become. What's she going to think of me? I didn't know how to talk to her. She's a woman. Not some girl out having fun. A grown woman."

At first Shamrock was unsure about moving too quickly. Tonya didn't feel like a fling and he was afraid he was too broken to be with anyone so soon after Tina and Alicia. He wasn't even sure if he could be in a real relationship.

"I didn't want to start something I couldn't finish. Especially with her. She was special," Shamrock says. "I told her, 'I don't know if I can be faithful. I don't know who I am.' And she said 'You're still you. Let's give it a try.'

"I was scared. This was something pure in my life. I just didn't believe in love. Everything I'd ever been a part of or known had fallen apart. I believe love just doesn't happen. But all the stars lined up. It was almost like divine intervention. All the sudden there was life."

Soon the pair was inseparable. With Tonya's help, Shamrock cancelled his appearance in New Japan's G-1 Climax and finally got the ACL repair he'd needed for years that September.

"He couldn't do any fighting, he couldn't do anything without a

---

[320] Ken would tell Bob, who would tell Tonya's parents in an old-fashioned game of telephone. He never knew he was getting Tonya in trouble—at least so he says with his wife glaring a hole through him 30 years later.

great deal of pain," Tonya says. "We got $5,000 from the UFC[321]. And then, the rest of it, I paid for. It was all out of pocket. Otherwise, he wouldn't have been able to fight.

"After the surgery, after we started dating he made amazing improvements[322]. He wasn't drinking, he was completely away from all drugs. His whole face, his skin coloring, everything changed."

Two days after the surgery, he started physical therapy and the swelling disappeared within a couple of weeks. Shamrock moved into Tonya's apartment in Reno to do his rehab, with Tonya and her family acting as nursemaids. Bob Shamrock, after the passing of his father Chuck, had joined them as well and was soon putting Ken to work getting his body and mind back in order.

"It was pretty amazing the way that my body has come back and recovered," Shamrock told journalist Ryan Bennett. "I'm ready to rock, right now. I'm doing weights, trying to strengthen the legs, the thighs, trying to get the nerves firing again. So, everything is coming around a lot faster than I expected and even faster than my doctors expected."

In November, Shamrock took a break from his rehab to attend UFC 45 where he and Royce Gracie were the first inductees into the UFC Hall of Fame. Their Hall of Fame plaques were awarded in front of the appreciative crowd at the Mohegan Sun, though both men would continue competing for more than another decade.

"There are certainly many current and former UFC athletes who deserve and will receive this recognition," UFC President Dana White said. "But, we feel that no two individuals are more deserving than Royce and Ken to be the charter members. Their contributions to our sport, both inside and outside the Octagon, may never be equaled."

The next few months were an exceptional challenge for Ken and Tonya as they attempted to bring their two broods together. Tonya had three children and Shamrock four of his own—plus an aggressive ex he was

---

[321] "That's the UFC 'paying for it'," Ken adds sarcastically. The Shamrocks believe, if they didn't want to continue using him as a headliner, UFC wouldn't have paid anything at all.
[322] "It was like I aged ten years in a year (2002-2003)," Shamrock says. "And then, within a year, I regressed ten."

technically still married to and his always difficult to manage father.

"They weren't always happy about it," Tonya remembers. "There was fighting amongst themselves and anger at Ken. My kids were angry at Ken's kids. Ken's kids were angry at me. We were trying to bring this whole dynamic together and trying to keep it as cohesive as we could. Plus, Bob was also living with us. So it was like this whole big Brady Bunch kind of trying to come together."

In February 2004, after Tonya helped Shamrock finally secure a divorce, the two made the decision to get married in a ceremony that still rankles many to this day. Afraid that Tina wouldn't allow the kids to attend if she knew about it, Ken and Tonya told everyone they were heading down to Fresno for one of Tonya's daughter's soccer games. No one knew they were actually going to a wedding until they were there, told the nice clothes they were provided were for a fancy dinner with friends of the family.

"Are you serious? You just snuck us down here and didn't tell us anything," Connor Shamrock says, still visibly upset 13 years later. "They said, 'Well, we knew you wouldn't have gone.' Of course, we wouldn't have gone! Because we don't agree with it. But it should have been our decision.

"I lost a lot of respect for my dad and Tonya that day. For the longest time, any respect I had built up for her, I just lost it. My dad, you literally lied to me, lied to me, just to get me up here so you guys could get married. That's messed up. You literally lied to your kids in order to get what you wanted from us. You could have forced us to do it anyways but at least told us. You're our dad, it's not like we're going to tell you no. It's not like they even told us on the way there.

"They just took us into this building and said 'hey, we're getting married right now.' I think they were afraid my mom would not have given us the choice. She would have. She would have said 'I'm not going to force them to go if they don't want to go.' No one would have. Her daughters wouldn't have gone, we wouldn't have gone."

For Shamrock's daughter Fallon, the wedding day was the first time she'd even met Tonya.

"My dad picked us up from our grandparents' house and we ended up going to their wedding," she says. "I didn't even know who she was. I didn't have any time to get to know her before they were married. For us kids, it wasn't really a happy celebration with them getting married, even her own kids. It was almost like we were thrown into it and we really didn't have time to get to know her and give our approval, so to speak, of our dad getting married again. It was just 'we're getting married.'"

A week before the wedding, just five months into a recovery process that was supposed to last nine months to a year, Shamrock was back in the wrestling ring[323] at the UPW fifth anniversary show in Anaheim. Before his match with Sylvester Terkay[324], Shamrock challenged Tank Abbott to a bout at UFC 48 in July, telling his longtime rival he was going to "slap him sober."

It took a dozen security guards to keep an enraged Abbott[325] from making his way to the ring to confront Shamrock, a perfect angle to promote a potential bout. But Tank, who had lost three consecutive fights in less than five minutes combined during his disastrous UFC return, didn't end up signing the contract[326]. Instead, Shamrock would knuckle up against another familiar face—Kimo Leopaldo, who he had beaten soundly at UFC 8.

Initially Shamrock had been offended when he heard Joe Rogan's call of UFC 40. The comedian suggested that, because he captained his own ship and worked with the same team he'd been training with since the early days of MMA, Shamrock hadn't evolved as a fighter as much as he might have otherwise.

With his father's help, Ken realized there was truth there, even if it wasn't a pleasant one. Bob Shamrock had known many of the fighters in the Lion's Den since the very beginning. Some had even lived with him. He loved and cared about them. But they weren't, in his opinion, what Ken needed to compete with the best in the world circa 2004.

In the months leading up to the bout, Shamrock took Bob's advice and, for the first time in his career, turned his training over completely

---

[323] Shamrock also wrestled future New Japan Pro Wrestling legend Shinsuke Nakamura in an exhibition bout in early March.

[324] Known as "The Predator," Terkay was the NCAA wrestling champion the year Shamrock helped launch the UFC. The previous year he had taken Kurt Angle to the limit in a second place finish.

[325] It was unclear just how real this confrontation was. Many in the building thought it was a shoot, as Abbott was apparently plastered. But a little birdie told Dave Meltzer that Abbott and Shamrock had talked on the phone the afternoon of the event before it all went down.

[326] "He wasn't in the mood to fight," is how UFC President Dana White described it. He promised the media the fight would happen eventually down the road. It, of course, didn't.

to someone else.

"I think I was training with my guys and I got too comfortable," Shamrock told *Boxing Insider*. "I think that (Rogan) hit the nail right on the head."

Erik Paulson, an MMA veteran who was competing in Shooto before UFC even existed, took over his overall preparation while three-time Olympic boxer Battalia Balamoundo[327] handled his boxing, diet and overall fitness. They traveled an hour each way three times a week to train Shamrock at his San Diego home base and found the 40-year-old fighter to be a willing and engaged pupil.

"I was surprised because he said to me that he would like me to teach him as well as train him," Paulson told journalist Josh Gross. "He was probably one of the best athletes I've ever trained for a fight because he just relinquished everything and let me do my thing."

For Shamrock, it was the most disciplined training camp of his career. With the exception of a highly profitable[328] trip to Japan to wrestle former UFC heavyweight champion Josh Barnett in the Tokyo Dome[329], Shamrock was focused intently on the business at hand. Paulson was able to make concessions to his broken down body that kept him relatively healthy while he rebuilt the Shamrock fighting engine.

"Paulson was a tremendous trainer," family friend Tom Casey says. "Ken's shoulder was shot again and his knee was still tricky. Paulson compensated for Ken's injuries and Ken took the fight seriously. He had the belief he could beat Kimo. In a way he got lucky that Kimo ducked into a knee, but he was prepared to take advantage of that luck —which is why you train."

Although the heavyweight championship was up for grabs in a fight

---

[327] Balamoundo was not impressed with Shamrock when he first started working with him. "He was too slow. He wasn't moving well, his condition was terrible...and he used to close his eyes sometimes when he punched." But by the time camp closed, he was gushing about his pupil's capacity to learn and overall boxing game.

[328] Shamrock made a reported $17,000 for the match.

[329] The two seemed to be setting up a sequel after the match, which ended in a disqualification. But it ended up being the last match of Shamrock's New Japan run. The match was a hard-hitting homage to the shoot style Barnett had watched as a fan and Shamrock had participated in back in the early 1990s. A lost banger for sure.

between Tim Sylvia and Frank Mir[330], UFC 48 was still headlined by Shamrock, a clear sign of his sustained box office prowess[331]. The staredown ahead of the fight was intense, lasting nearly as long as the bout itself. Shamrock tested his power (and his surgically repaired knee) in the clinch. Despite a 26 pound weight difference, Shamrock bullied the chemically-enhanced Kimo[332] around the cage before finishing the night early with a knee that knocked the Hawaiian silly.

"I was really content with his performance against Kimo," Paulson told *Boxing Insider*, a website that also launched KenShamrock.com. "...Ken totally changed his strike game. He's actually ten times better now. His right hand—at the end of training, nobody wanted to spar with him. He broke two noses and had three knockouts. And that was with 18-ounce gloves. And I had a bruised leg for two weeks after a leg kick."

After the fight, Dana White congratulated Shamrock on his victory and Ken gave a speech praising his father and encouraging fans never to give up on themselves. But the victory parade didn't last long, as a familiar bleached blonde fighter made an appearance in an attempt to gin up a little controversy.

"What's your decision partner?" Tito Ortiz[333], playing the role of journalist, asked Shamrock. "You say your knee's a lot better now. We can do it again.[334]"

This, as you might imagine, went over like a lead balloon on the dais and the two were eventually yelling back-and-forth as security stood between them, Ortiz not looking completely comfortable while Ken was in his element. He had one fight remaining on his contract and he wanted nothing more than another shot at Ortiz.

Unfortunately a torn rotator cuff would put that fight on hold while

---

[330] Mir broke Sylvia's arm with an armbar to win the title. Sylvia, and the crowd, protested the stoppage even after seeing a slow-motion replay that clearly saw his arm snap.

[331] The UFC 48 DVD became the first in company history to top the "Sports" category in retail sales, a section normally dominated by WWF.

[332] According to journalist Loretta Hunt, Leopoldo's Nevada State Athletic Commission drug test results "revealed traces of Stanzolol metabolite, phenylpropanolamine, ephedrine, and pseudoephedrine."

[333] Ortiz had lost consecutive fights after beating Shamrock at UFC 40 and was no doubt looking for a bounce back fight he was confident of winning.

[334] "Well Tito, I can go right now," Ken responded. "I've got plenty of energy."

Shamrock got surgery to repair it. That injury, exacerbated during the preparation for Kimo, left Ken with almost nothing at all to show for the bout, except a a much needed check in the win column.

"When we got together, there was a huge tax lien," Tonya says. "Hundreds of thousands of dollars. Ken's first fight after we got together was the Kimo fight and he didn't really make that much money. We had to pay half of that in regular taxes.

"And then with the offer and compromise, basically that whole purse was almost gone. And we still had to live. We couldn't pay all of the other taxes and still live. So it's like we were always playing catch up.

"He was never able to make enough to get completely caught up on taxes because when we first got together the tax lien was so large. You're always constantly paying penalties. The taxes have been a nightmare since the day I married him."

With his shoulder surgery scheduled for August in Reno, Shamrock had a month to bring in a little bit of cash, working with Larry Goldberg from *Boxing Insider* to book several appearances with TNA Wrestling, where he had been the inaugural champion two years prior.

"Dana wanted Ken exclusive but wouldn't pay him and Ken kept in his contract he could do (wrestling)," Goldberg says. "TNA was a shoestring budget. They would give him five grand and make him do two dates. They resented his asking for a second plane ticket for Tonya.[335] That was a rule for all events. Other wrestling stuff didn't interest him. He never did any of those conventions until recently.

"Generally speaking 5-10 grand and two airline tickets hotel and car service was what I responded with. But he did maybe two percent of the offers he got. An MMA promoter would have been better served booking Vernon White or one of the kids from the Lion's Den and get

---

[335] "I would kind of keep everything organized because he was all over the place," Tonya says. "Phone calls weren't getting returned. We'd gotten his knee taken care and people were trying to get into contact with him to get some fights organized. He needed to get some training organized. So, I just kind of stopped working and went to work helping him get everything taken care of."

Ken there as a coach in those days. He was like a a hot girl—he loved to be asked. But turned most down."

The two years between TNA appearances felt like a hundred for wrestling fans, who saw the promotion go through several seismic shifts in just a handful of months. Shamrock, fresh off a win in the UFC that shocked the industry with a strong showing on pay-per-view, wasn't utilized in a way that made sense to the Wrestling Observer's Dave Meltzer:

> The entire way Shamrock is used is totally stupid. First off, Shamrock is a successful character in UFC, and probably its biggest draw ever. He can do money promos. But when he comes into pro wrestling, he gets rid of his successful, believable character, and becomes a really bad cartoon character who is out of control, and does these fake promos that nobody can believe. The people who would be interested in Shamrock, are interested in the Shamrock character that gets over, not the cartoon character.

One benefit of the TNA run was the opportunity to bring all the kids down to Orlando for a television taping, one of the few bright spots in what was becoming a tense dynamic. Tonya and Ken were splitting custody with Tina and it wasn't an easy situation.

"Rebecca and Sara (Tonya's daughters) were living with us and they were able to do things on the weekend because all their homework was caught up," Tonya says. "But Ken's kids had to stay at home and get their work done because Tina wasn't having them do any of it. So, it was really hard.

"Tina was always telling them that I was just short term, like all the other women that had been in and out of his life. So the kids were thinking I was only gonna be here for a little bit. And even when we got married, you know, she was saying, 'oh, it's only gonna last for a short time.' So the kids were kind of leery of me for quite some time."

Tension was thick, especially between Ken's kids and Tonya's, a natural rivalry that was exacerbated by extenuating circumstances.

"He's living with her, now she's telling us what to do, she has kids and we don't like those kids," Shamrock's son Connor remembers. "They feel the same way, like 'we don't like you or your dad.' Well, we don't like you or you mom.

"I remember, my little brother, he was really good at playing basketball and Tonya's older daughter (Rebecca), she's four or five years older than me, was playing outside and she kept bumping into my little brother and it almost seemed to me like bullying. So I put her into the wall. I guess she had just had knee surgery or something so they got mad at me and I was like 'she was bullying my little brother.' I'm protecting my little brother."

Bob, meanwhile, was never easy for any of the women in Ken's life to handle. That hadn't changed, even as Ken began making a new life with an old family friend.

"He wanted Ken to basically go on dates with just him," Tonya says. "I'm like 'Bob, that's not normal.' When we go out with my parents, we go out together with my parents. If you want to go to dinner, you can go to dinner with us. You don't have to go with Ken alone. That's not normal."

While Shamrock recovered from his latest surgery[336] and helped his father Bob through a heart ailment, his Lion's Den fighters were getting a chance to shine in the UFC. Things, unfortunately, didn't go according to plan.

Vernon White lost a thrilling slugfest with Chuck Liddell at UFC 49, delivering solid strikes and his patented spinning kick in between getting knocked down by Liddell haymakers. He showed heart, but ultimately dropped to the mat one final time, courtesy of a hard right hand with just under a minute remaining in the first round.

At UFC 50, Guy Mezger was scheduled to fight Tito Ortiz in the main event, a rubber match to settle the score between the two. UFC decision makers expected Ortiz to dispatch Mezger again and help heat up a potential Ken Shamrock rematch to a boiling point.

Instead, Mezger pulled out of the fight with symptoms similar to a stroke[337]. He was staying with Shamrock while training in Los Angeles with his new team and banged his head on a bedside table after a tough night at the gym. On his way downstairs for breakfast, he had to dodge another obstacle.

"They have a kitten here and it plays ninja kitty and jumps out at

---

[336] Fights bandied about for Ken included the long-awaited Tank Abbott bout, a possible heavyweight title fight against Frank Mir and a rematch with Don Frye for a UFC event in Japan that fell through.

[337] Mezger would end up retiring even though he was eventually cleared to return to the ring.

you," Mezger told journalist Ken Pishna. "The kitty jumps out in front of me and instead of stepping on it, I kind of jumped over it about three or four stairs. When I landed, my knee buckled a bit and when I got back up Tonya asked me if I was all right. I said yes, but she said I seemed kind of woozy, that I wasn't responding correctly and seemed a little uncertain on my feet."

Booking a fight for Shamrock proved difficult. UFC executives were heavily influenced by the burgeoning internet culture surrounding the sport, where fans recognized Ken was no longer physically a top contender and heavily criticized his bookings, leading many to paradoxically claim that no one wanted to see his bouts—despite their demonstrable box office success.

With IRS agents all but circling, Shamrock was desperate for a fight —and just about any fight would do. Sometimes they were at home, with a new relationship that was still unsteady at times.

"If you got in an argument, he was used to just leaving and he would leave for days," Tonya says. "There was one time I was done. Done. He left for three days and I packed up everything and I was leaving. When he came home I was on the road and he called me and he asked me to come back and talk.

"And I told him that day, 'if you ever walk out of this house again when you're upset, we're done.' If we have an issue, we're talking it out. If you need space, that's fine. You get your own space in whatever part of the house you need. But you're not walking out of the house. And since that day, I don't think he ever has."

Settling his issues with UFC wasn't so cut and dry. He wanted a fight. UFC wanted to give him one. But this was before the era of mega-cards and UFC generally only booked one costly, high profile bout per event to control costs. Unfortunately for Ken, the early part of 2005 was already set in stone with matches featuring Ortiz[338] and Randy Couture, two of the promotion's high ticket fighters.

Dana White gave him permission to fight overseas if he could line

---

[338] Tito and Shamrock had another great confrontation here, immediately following Ortiz's win over Vitor Belfort. Ortiz ran Shamrock down in his post fight interview and Ken was given an opportunity to retort cageside.

"All I hear is talking," he said. "That's all I've heard him do so far is run his mouth about how he's going to do this, how he's going to do that. You want to fight me? I'm standing right here. I accept your challenge. What about you?"

something up, but the right opportunity never surfaced, even with the powerhouse Battle Management team now managing him. Instead, a seismic paradigm shift that rocked the entire sport gave Shamrock one last chance to cash in on the enterprise he'd helped build.

CHAPTER EIGHTEEN
TUF Enough

It's hard to overstate the importance of *The Ultimate Fighter* in transforming the UFC from a nice hobby for mega-rich casino moguls to a billion dollar business in its own right. The business had reached the heights possible with just the hardcore audience who had kept it alive while the government and cable companies did their level best to kill it. Without exposing the sport to a broader audience, the potential for growth was limited.

Television changed everything.

While UFC President Dana White wanted a weekly fight show, like the *Thursday Night Boxing* he had grown up with, reality television was the wave of the future. The Fertitta bothers had starred in the little seen *American Casino* and believed in the concept. The original idea was to focus on White—instead, someone came up with the brilliant idea to feature the fighters themselves and the sport was never the same again.

"People thought it was a bloodsport, that these guys were savages," Craig Piligian, the executive producer of the franchise, told journalist Chuck Mindenhall. "People just thought it was two men enter, one man leaves. That's what they all said. It's true—it just humanized the guys. Turns out they were normal guys. They were college grads, they had personality problems, they cried, they yelled, they were funny, they told jokes, and you thought, wow, this guy could be my next-door neighbor. This guy I could have for Thanksgiving dinner. This guy I could be buds with. It turned the fighters into relatable people."

The brilliance of *The Ultimate Fighter* was its ability to achieve multiple goals in a single hour of television—it simultaneously introduced a complicated new sport, humanized the next generation of young talent and served as a promotional vehicle for the coaches and their pay-per-view extravaganzas. It was an immediate ratings[339] hit, following WWE's Monday Night RAW and became a long-running staple of the sport.

"It worked," UFC announcer Joe Rogan says. "America got to know these guys. And they liked them. The success of the first season of *The Ultimate Fighter* legitimized a promising sport and let it blossom in front of us like no sport in my lifetime ever has."

The reality portion of the show culminated with a live fight event where winners would be crowned in the middleweight and light heavyweight classes. What the show was missing was a high profile main event.

Enter Ken Shamrock, paired off against rising middleweight prospect Rich "Ace" Franklin. It was a piece of matchmaking that left many, including the *Wrestling Observer*'s Dave Meltzer, shaking their heads:

> The plan for the main event of the 4/9 Spike TV special is Ken Shamrock vs. Rich Franklin. The reason this, which on paper appears to be nothing short of insanity, is happening is the idea they want Shamrock on the TV special because he's their biggest mainstream name and hopefully will help draw a rating. Spike TV itself pushed for Shamrock, because he's the biggest mainstream name and thus thought a fight with him would mean the most for ratings. The reason Shamrock is doing a fight where he has everything to lose and nothing to gain is it has been a long time since he's fought, and a long time (without a) six-figure pay day.
>
> ...The feeling is with Tank Abbott having no interest in fighting, the only match anyone wants to see Shamrock against is Ortiz, and there is no

---

[339] "Spike TV's The Ultimate Fighter got off to strong ratings start Monday," a press release read in January 2005. "Leading out of the network's WWE Raw stalwart, Ultimate Fighter grabbed a 1.4 household rating and some 1.7 million viewers from 11:07 p.m.-midnight Jan. 17, according to Nielsen Media Research data, a 36% jump from the year-ago period."

guarantee they'll even sign Ortiz[340], so that's the decision making behind it...The insanity is Franklin will be strongly favored, and if he wins, they've blown the Ortiz vs. Shamrock rematch, which would do roughly the same business the first one did. If they are going to put Shamrock on TV, they should find some buffed heavyweight who isn't a great fighter.

The bottomline, Shamrock's attorney Rod Donohoo says, is that UFC needed a ratings win to cap off what had been an amazing season on SPIKE TV. And, whether the hardcores liked it or not, the most marketable fighter in the entire sport was still Ken Shamrock.

"They wanted big fights," Donohoo says. "They wanted headline fights. That's what they were doing. They were looking to build some of these other guys. I don't think that they were looking to build Ken. But, I never got the impression they wanted to destroy Ken either. I just think they wanted to use him to the extent they could for the numbers. I think Ken knew that and Ken was okay with that, but Ken expected to be paid what he felt that he brought to the table.

"Ken thought he made the UFC. And the UFC thought they were making Ken at that time. I don't know—is the truth somewhere in the middle? I mean, this is me looking back now that I'm not in the battle. When you're in the middle of it you hate the other guy, right? But when you're out of it, you look at it differently."

The question wasn't whether to use Ken Shamrock—it was how. UFC could either attempt to find someone the aged, broken down fighter could beat, or they could accept that his days were numbered and do their best to transfer his gravitas and connection with the fans over to a promising younger man.

"If Ken pulled off the win, wow, an amazing story," a senior UFC executive says. "If he doesn't, which he's likely not to, then there's a good name on Rich's record. In that particular situation, there is almost no disaster risk because it would be such a good story. Ken was an expensive guy. He was not fighting for cheap so why are you paying him that money? Well, he might win and he has a name people

---

[340] Ortiz was asking for $300,000 a fight, more than anyone else in the company made at the time. That included Chuck Liddell and Randy Couture, who despite besting him in the cage, didn't have the same track record on pay-per-view.

give a shit about.

"Our attitude was always, as much as possible, to do no-lose matchmaking. We're not betting who's gonna win because MMA is crazy. I mean if Matt Serra can knock out GSP, there really are no safe matches to make. So we, really honestly, did not care who won because I couldn't control it. I don't worry about things I can't control."

Shamrock trained for a second time with Erik Paulson and team, but to some in his inner circle, his heart didn't seem to be in it the same way it had been with Kimo. Where some saw that as resignation and the recognition that UFC was throwing him to the wolves in the final fight of his contract, others saw arrogance. Franklin, supposedly smaller, certainly less experienced, was a fighter he could beat[341].

Franklin, a former teacher who was still working part time with at-risk students even as he fought his way to title contention, found himself competing against the athlete who had helped draw him onto the sport in the first place—and the only one any of his students were the least bit familiar with.

"Of course my students knew who Ken was and it had become common knowledge that I was competing," Franklin says. "They would always ask me 'do you think you could beat Ken Shamrock in a fight?' Because he had transitioned over to wrestling and was a bit more of a mainstream name for mixed martial arts at the time. And I was always like, 'Heck yeah, I could.' Just kind of talking a little bit of trash with my students, never thinking that I would be on a path for that to happen in my life.

"When I got the call from my management, I was like 'holy crap, we're going to sign this fight with Ken Shamrock.' Suddenly all this trash talk that I've done over the years —just playful trash talk with my students, I now have to back this up."

While Franklin drilled leg locks with the Miletich Fight team, Shamrock did what had become customary in the build to a big fight. That meant doing every media appearance necessary to help make the event a success, including an appearance on Fox Sports' *Best Damn*

---

[341] "He completely underestimated Rich Franklin and didn't train again," Tom Casey says. "Personal stuff. He just didn't train. They thought he was a smaller guy and looked like Jim Carrey's brother. Ken was actually doing pretty well, but that series of concussions he had gone through with Frye and Tito caught up with him…"

Sports Show Period[342]. Normally Shamrock tries to get himself in the zone, manufacturing reasons, real or imagined, to hate his opponent. Here, he spent plenty of time talking the clean cut Franklin up, almost sensing this was a changing of the guard moment. The World's Most Dangerous Man, the fighter who tried to get Tank Abbott to duke it out with him in the parking lot, was being, well, nice.

"I did radio interviews with him the week of the fight, the week I fought Stephan (Bonnar)," Forrest Griffin remembers. "He was real nice. It meant a lot. I knew who he was but he didn't know who the fuck I was. He was real nice anyways. We were sitting in the car and he said 'well, you're bigger than me, I'll let you sit up front.' He didn't have to do that. He was Ken Shamrock and I wasn't anybody."

Fight day was a weird one for Franklin. This was the biggest fight of his career and he wasn't sure what to make of the experience. Shamrock had weighed in well below the light heavyweight limit the day before and he realized he'd actually be the bigger man in the cage. Was there, Franklin wondered, a method to this madness, a competitive reason Shamrock might want to cede strength for speed? It puzzled and worried him a little.

Then, their two camps ended up standing out in the parking lot at the same time, awkwardly waiting for two different vans to take them over to the arena.

"It's like one of those things where for me, part of me wanted to walk up and be like, 'Oh my gosh, Ken Shamrock. Hey, it's nice to meet you' type of thing, and the other half is feeling awkward," he says. "… There was this 'You're going to punch me in the face in about two or three hours from now' type of feeling."

The Cox Pavilion, where the event was held on the campus of the University of Nevada Las Vegas, was a relatively small venue, usually home to the women's basketball and volleyball teams. The locker rooms are in the basement and the arena itself on the upper level. So, when it came time to fight, Franklin ended up riding up with Shamrock in a big freight elevator.

"Ken was in the elevator just looking like a Roman gladiator, and he locked eyes with me in the elevator and would not look away,"

---

[342] While mainstream sports sites now routinely cover MMA, at the time, Shamrock's ability to interact comfortably with the media was a big deal for the promotions that worked with him. People had a perception about the sport and he was well-suited to put them at ease.

Franklin says. "And I'm like 'he's got to be kidding me.'

"When we finally got in the cage and Bruce Buffer was doing the announcement, I locked eyes with Ken and I wanted to look away and I'm like, 'No, I'm not looking away. I'm not looking away.' He just looks mean and intimidating. He introduces us and then they cut to commercial break. Well, just because they cut to commercial break, I'm not going to break eye contact. So I'm trying to hype myself up in my head like 'I'm not looking away. I'm letting him know that he's not going to intimidate me.'

"So we end up staring at each other for about seven minutes because it was the whole introduction, then it cut to commercial break, then it came back and it was a recap introduction thing. And then walk out to the center of the cage. 'I want a good, clean fight. Blah, blah, blah.' Walk back to your side of the cage and then go. It was the longest stare down in my life."

The stare down, in fact, lasted longer than the fight itself. Franklin was the younger, and objectively, better fighter in the cage that night, landing the crisper, more effective strikes. At one point Shamrock appeared to either slip or fall to the mat for a takedown awkwardly depositing his posterior on the mat in front of a momentarily bewildered Franklin.

"I remember he went down and there was just a piece of me that paused for a second, like, 'Oh crap, what just happened to him?' I thought maybe his knee buckled or he tore it or something, something weird," Franklin says. "And there was a split-second pause in my mind thinking 'Is he okay?' I mean literally for a split second, and then it clicked in right away that, 'Oh, wait a minute, I'm fighting,' and then I followed up."

The awkward nature of the exchange created a buzz of the internet that Shamrock had thrown[343] the fight. Of course, the fact he ended up in top position and eventually went for his patented heel hook submission would seemingly invalidate that idea, but the clip was studied as closely as any video short of the Zapruder film, meticulously broken down and examined in minute details for any sign it wasn't on the up-and-up.

"At one point in that match, Ken had me in an ankle lock," Franklin

---

[343] "I've heard that several times," Shamrock said. "That's just ridiculous. Rich Franklin is a good fighter and you know what, man? He caught me and that's that."

says. "And I'll tell you what, if it was a worked fight, first of all I didn't know about it. And if it was a worked fight, he sure as hell made that ankle lock look good, because, let me tell you, it hurt."

Halfway through the first round, Shamrock threw a high kick and slipped, his knees simply not capable of the feats he once took for granted. Franklin pounced and a few seconds later, to borrow the iconic phrase from UFC announcer Mike Goldberg, it was all over.

UFC officials, who had signed Franklin to a new eight-fight contract just before the fight, no doubt breathed a sigh of relief. Shamrock himself seemed resigned to his fate, happy enough just to be there for a historical moment, collect his check and return home.

"It was great to be here on network TV," Shamrock said. "If I had won, I go on. If I lose, then you build another star off me. But I was happy to step in against Rich. He's got a great attitude."

While Shamrock was the headliner, it was the fight just before his that stole the show and ignited the new MMA golden age. Stephan Bonnar and Forrest Griffin weren't UFC Hall of Famers like Shamrock[344] They were merely fighting for an opportunity. But perhaps the desperate nature of their encounter, with a UFC contract at stake, made the magic possible.

The two went toe-to-toe for nearly 15 minutes in a jaw-dropping display of will power and courage. It was a fight so spectacular that UFC President Dana White ended up giving the UFC contract to both men, an instant American classic[345] that defined for a generation what fighting was supposed to look like.

"Bonnar-Griffin was the fight that started the explosion for mixed martial arts and the UFC," White said. "To say that those guys went in and delivered is the understatement of the century."

Before the reality show, there was no such thing as a casual MMA fan. There was nothing casual at all about following the sport. It required a significant commitment of time and resources just to find

---

[344] Franklin, too, would go into the Hall of Fame in 2019.

[345] "You have just witnessed three rounds of the greatest action seen inside the Octagon in the history of the UFC," Bruce Buffer told a rapt live audience. Judging by the 15 minutes they'd just spent screaming and stomping their feet on the bleachers, they already knew.

the best fights from all over the world. You had to work for it, locating Japanese grocery stores and shady bootleg VHS dealers to get your MMA fix.

Even after Zuffa cleared the hurdle and got the UFC back on pay-per-view around the country, there was no easy way for prospective fans to learn about and explore this new sport. Exposure on SPIKE TV allowed new fans to ease into the unknown while also getting to know both the current stars and the stars of tomorrow[346].

The change in UFC's entire business model was immediate and the resulting venue increase was astronomical. The UFC made $14.3 million in 2004, $48.3 million in 2005 and an incredible $180 million in 2006.[347] *Bloody Elbow* reporter John Nash delved further into the details using a previously confidential memo, intended to be seen only by potential lenders and not meant for public consumption:

> In only two years the UFC saw a 1258% increase in their revenue. This included approximately 1700% growth in pay-per-view revenue, a 5500% increase in money from sponsorships, and a more than 10,000% increase in revenue from live and taped television.

In 2004, before *The Ultimate Fighter*, the leading line item on their ledger was ticket sales. By 2006 it was third, behind pay-per-view and live television. Money was flowing in—and that meant Shamrock's $230,000 for the Franklin fight, at the time the highest payday in UFC history, would soon be eclipsed routinely, salaries slowly growing along with the overall revenue[348]. Although fighters still made a mere pittance, that nugget was getting bigger and bigger.

"There were guys who *were* making hundreds of thousands of dollars," Shamrock's powerhouse former agent Jeremy Lappen says. "The very top guys were around that range. That was sort of the peak of it. People started making a lot more money from pay-per-views after

---

[346] The show drew 2.6 million viewers and dominated the weekend with young male viewers. Both Griffin/Bonnar and Shamrock/Franklin had over three million fans tuning in.
[347] The data comes from a Deutsche Bank Confidential Information Memorandum.
[348] The UFC appeared to pay their athletes between 13-15 percent of their overall revenue, way below other major sports organizations.

the first *Ultimate Fighter* season with Randy and Chuck.

"That's when the business sort of changed. The pay-per-view dollars changed everything because they started selling a lot more buys. If you were a big name guy you could negotiate a participation in the pay-per-view."''

Shamrock was interested in re-signing with UFC, especially for a fight with Tito Ortiz, who had challenged Ken after his own fight at UFC 51. It was an epic pro wrestling style exchange and the fight, despite Shamrock's continued struggles in actual athletic competition, seemed viable. But negotiations with UFC stalled, as they couldn't reconcile Shamrock's record with his still considerable box office clout.

"We went around in circles," Lappen says. "They had a value that they thought Ken was worth, which I thought was much, much lower than he was actually worth. In our minds he had a much higher value. And they couldn't wrap their heads around it. I was explaining to them that his value is what somebody's willing to pay him, it's not where you would slot him in a top 20 list. And if he can get that money elsewhere, that's what he's worth. And they didn't really buy into that so we got the money elsewhere; we fought in Japan."

The *Wrestling Observer* reported that Shamrock was considered for the headline spot against Randy Couture at UFC 54:

> Shamrock's people turned down ridiculous money (for the same $230,000 range that he earned against Rich Franklin) for the proposed singles match with Randy Couture that would have taken place on the 8/20 show because as noted before, the management team of Couture, Shamrock and Quinton Jackson will not allow any of the three to face each other.

While Shamrock doesn't recall being offered that specific deal, what was "ridiculous money" at the beginning of 2005 was no longer so ridiculous in the new era that was emerging. As the negotiator for some of the top names in the sport, Lappen was on the front lines of what was reasonable for a top star. And, in his mind, Shamrock remained a marquee attraction.

"That's sort of how it went the first time I represented Ken with UFC," he says. "And I think that sort of opened their eyes a little bit about, he had other opportunities. He could fight elsewhere for the kind of money he wanted. They could either pay closer to the money that he wanted and have a fight for him, or he can fight somewhere else."

On the homefront, things remained rocky as Shamrock attempted to integrate his new relationship into his life. Alicia had returned[349] and attempted to reconnect with Ken and the custody arrangement with Tina was a constant source of discord.

"Tonya felt like we were a part of the problem with the kids," Shamrock says. "Every time they would come over, we were always checking on school. We had them in learning centers. We were pushing them in school. Like it was a focus and they were unhappy with us. We took Ryan out of football because he wasn't getting a C in each class.

"Tina went into court and had it overturned because they said we couldn't do that without her consent. When we asked her, 'why wouldn't you do that?' She says, 'well, that's all he's got. He loves it and he's having a hard time right now with the divorce and this and that.' And I was like, 'so you're going to let him play football after we pulled him out. You're going to put him back in, why won't you just make him get his grades up?' And she says 'it's not fair to him.' I felt like we were becoming a part of the problem, right? My issues with Tina were causing problems for the kids."

As tempers rose, the arguments would become more and more petty, until the fight was essentially just about previous fights. Shamrock and Tina couldn't spend even a few minutes together without a blowup, an untenable situation when you're trying to raise four children with joint custody.

"I remember my dad bought us all new clothes and we were not allowed to wear any of the new clothes over at my mom's house," Shamrock's son Connor says. "I was like 'these are our clothes why does it matter where we wear them?' He told us we couldn't wear any new clothes over at my mom's house because he wouldn't get to see them. Even as a kid that doesn't make sense. It was just making rules to spite each other. That was annoying as a kid, your parents always being angry at each other."

Tonya and Ken eventually decided to leave San Diego and all its

---

[349] "I said 'I am 36 years old, the mother of three. You need to realize that I am too old to play your games. You need to move on.' She is a piece of work," Tonya remembers. "To this day, if they are in the same town she will try to hit him up."

drama and potential bad influences behind and return to Susanville, California, where they both had grown up. They reopened the Lion's Den there, recruited a new crop of fighters and attempted to get a reality show of their own off the ground.

Shamrock saw *The Ultimate Fighter* as a relatively tame version of his own fighter's house, a fake version of something he felt was actually a very primal, powerful experience. With producer Scott Messick, he believed the time was right to give America the real deal. Over the fourth of July weekend, cameras rolled on tryouts for a new team.

"I don't want to compare what we're doing with the UFC," he said at the time. "The UFC has a different agenda and different aspects of the reality show which is not ours. Ours is going to be based around my lifestyle, the way I train fighters and live with my family being involved and then following the careers of the fighters as we lead up to a grand finale at the end of the show.[350]"

Ryan, Fallon and Connor stayed with Tina, living in their grandfather's house in Chula Vista. Sean moved with his father to start a new life where his dad had once lived in Bob Shamrock's foster home.

"It was hard to combine the families. Ryan and Connor you could put in front of a TV with their games. Sean was different. High energy," Tonya says. "And my daughters, they gave Ken all kinds of trouble."

Shamrock had never gotten close with his daughter Fallon. Suddenly being in a household with multiple young women was a real challenge for a fighter used to being around mostly male energy.

"(Tonya's daughter Sara) came in one day and told me she was having sex," Shamrock says. "I wasn't ready for that. I had my own girl who was five years old. Tonya and I got together and all of the sudden I have teenage girls. That was different, man."

As negotiations stalled out with UFC, Shamrock turned his attention back to Japan and a fight with Pride Fighting Championship. The promotion, still looking to break into the increasingly fertile American

---

[350] "I'm not sure why that didn't end up working out," Shamrock says. "They seemed really high on it."

market, had watched his success in UFC carefully and was interested in giving it another go, this time against their own fading legend Kazushi Sakuraba.

"UFC wasn't willing to go to where we thought Ken's value was and so we were talking to Pride as well," Lappen says. "We talked to Pride about the value of Ken's name and his marketability both in the US and Japan and really pitched them on the fight with Sakuraba. I thought that would be a great fight for everybody involved. With Ken's name recognition and Sakuraba's name recognition, it was a really compelling, interesting fight.

"We thought it would be a fight that Ken had a good chance of doing really well in. A good match-up for him. And a big money fight. Those two things weren't always easy to find in the same opponent."

Shamrock, sparring with a new collection of fighters he had brought to populate a new Lion's Den, seemed energized before the fight. Of course, he was getting increasingly good at talking about fighting even as his skills faded in the ring.

"Sakuraba, watching his tapes and studying him, he's a very sneaky character," Shamrock said before the fight. "He has a lot of personality and he brings that into the ring. He's a very good ring general. He likes to control the ring, he likes to control the pace of the fight. He wants to try to slow you down or speed you up. He wants to get you out of your comfort zone. When me and him get in there and fight, there is going to be a lot of experience in that ring. It's going to be an exciting fight."

As usual, Shamrock had a sixth sense about potential shenanigans, always a step ahead of where the narrative was likely going. He understood human psychology and storytelling—and where danger lurked in the ring.

"Obviously Sakuraba's their hero over there, so I've got to stay out of danger," he told *MMA Weekly* radio the day before flying to Japan. "I can't put myself in a situation where the referee might step in and call it. I've got to always be on top, always be in a dominate position. And that way there's no chance of them stopping it."

Sakuraba, despite being the biggest MMA star in Japan, wasn't immune to feeling a bit star struck as he stared across the ring at his opponent.

"There was a "star aura" emanating from the entire body of Shamrock," he wrote in his biography *Me*. "There he was, Ken Shamrock, built up from Pancrase and the UFC. Wow, he looks cool! I couldn't help but feel my heartbeat rise. 'Whoa, it's the real Ken Shamrock!' However, the opening bell forcedly tugged me back to reality."

Saku, bulked up and focused on his standup game after a training camp in Brazil with his former rivals at the famed Chute Boxe Academy[351], feinted a few takedowns but was clearly looking for a Muay Thai exchange. That was fine with Shamrock, whose knees and back no longer allowed him to train his wrestling game much at all.

The fight ended quickly, Shamrock falling into the ropes and turning his back on his opponent after the first significant blow, a hard left hand, landed cleanly. He protested vehemently afterwards[352], rightfully pointing out that referee Yuji Shimada routinely allowed Sakuraba to be beaten nearly to death before stopping the bout but was quick to leap in when the Japanese fighter was the one with the advantage. Sakuraba, celebrating with his new Brazilian friends, did his best to be gracious towards the angry American:

> In the ring, the scene was painted with a mood of celebration. In that air like a splash of water came Shamrock to complain to me about something. It seems he was saying he wasn't knocked out. The ref stopped it too early.
>
> As my left straight went through his face, his power switch definitely turned off. The thing is, as I continued hitting him, the second or maybe third punch woke him back up. I knew he was sleepy, and the ring is no place for that, so I used my punches to tap and wake up the sleepy Shamrock.
>
> Usually when an opponent comes to me with something like this, I just try to be respectful and accept it.
>
> "Okay, let's fight again. One more!"
>
> "One more? Okay!"
>
> Shamrock felt okay at that (did he?) and left the ring.

---

[351] Chute Boxe fighter Wanderlei Silva had beaten Sakuraba three times and replaced him as the top fighter in Pride's middleweight division.
[352] And to this day insists it was an early stoppage.

***

"He reached the point where he was physically strong, but his brain was damaged," family friend Casey says. "He just couldn't take a punch anymore. When I first met him, you could break a two-by-four over his head and he would just look at you. It started with Don Frye, but after the Tito fight, everything changed.

"Sakuraba barely hit him and Ken was out. Ken didn't know he was out. He jumps up and says 'I'm ready, I feel great.' You tell him he was knocked out and he doesn't believe it."

In the aftermath, Shamrock attempted to create some controversy, knowing every shred of doubt he planted could grow into another possible money bout. But nobody was really buying it—not even him some in his circle believed.

"Afterwards we're interviewing him and he's being honest," Pride announcer Mauro Ranallo says. "He's despondent, he's upset that this is where he finds himself in his career. It was kind of compelling. And then he was stopped by the producer and said, 'we need more Ken Shamrock.' And this is kind of where Pride was like pro wrestling. He said 'we need Ken Shamrock.'

"I'll tell you something, another person who was very good at doing this, was the late great Dusty Rhodes. But Ken Shamrock went from 0-100 real quick, just like that. He turned it on. His promos in MMA, I always found to be so much better than when he went to pro wrestling. He was incredible. We ended up with a vintage Shamrock melt down. It was vintage Ken Shamrock. It was amazing."

Less than a month after flaming out against Sakuraba, Shamrock appeared live on pay-per-view at UFC 56. Dana White stood between him and the UFC's other surprise signee—an unrepentant Tito Ortiz. The two were announced as the coaches for the third season of *The Ultimate Fighter*, the first without the prime WWE Monday Night Raw lead in.

Concerned about the loss of their powerful lead-in and moving the show from Monday to Thursday, Spike encouraged the UFC to put their best foot forward[353] and helped make that happen financially. In the Observer, Dave Meltzer opined that it was the most "pro wrestling" style segment UFC had ever aired:

> Shamrock acted like he wanted to go after Ortiz right there and people had to hold him back. Yes, they've even got the slogan for Ultimate Fighter 3, which may be a breakthrough season. Tito hates Ken. Ken hates Tito. Dana hates Tito. Tito hates Dana. And they'll all be on the show every week.
>
> ...there are those who think that match will set UFC records only because Shamrock and Ortiz both understand how to build up a fight and will have 13 weeks of reality TV to do so. I'm not as certain about a record, if only because they failed to protect Shamrock...Last year, before the losses to both Rich Franklin and Kazushi Sakuraba, there could have been considerable interest in a rematch.

"I didn't say yes right away," Shamrock said. "But when Dana called personally, I listened. He said 'you won't believe who the other coach is. Tito Ortiz.' I said, 'sign me up.'"

The deal came out of nowhere, just as Shamrock was focusing his attention on securing a Sakuraba rematch in Pride Fighting Championship and a potential coaching gig with the upstart International Fight League.

This new promotion, founded by real estate developer Kurt Otto and *Wizard Magazine* publisher Gareb Shamus, had the potential to be the first real domestic rival for the Zuffa-owned UFC. The league would look more like traditional sports, focusing on a team concept and offering fighters unheard of perks like monthly stipends, stock options and health insurance. The coaches were a big part of the initial marketing pitch to capture fans' attention—something Shamrock was a master of.

"I started the organization and I knew that in order for me to really get it off the ground the right way it would have to be with the right

---

[353] The show got preview coverage in both *Maxim* magazine and the *Boston Herald*, mainstream gets.

people," IFL President Kurt Otto says. "The most influential people ever in that sport. My concept of the IFL was having the legends being the coaches of these teams that would kind of cultivate the new talent coming up. No better place to do that would be through the gyms or academies of these legends.

"Certain names could give us credibility coming out of the gates. There was a handful of people that I felt were extremely crucial to have as my leading coaches coming out of the gate. Ken was one of them. It took some time, but eventually we did get Ken. He was one of the first two, three people on the list to get, just because of his status and him being a pioneer in the sport."

Some of the early coaches included Renzo Gracie, Bas Rutten, Maurice Smith and Pat Miletich, many of whom also competed in superfights for the promotion. UFC stalwarts Randy Couture and Shamrock were also on the short list of candidates.

"I was on a conference call with Ken," Miletich says. "And Ken agreed to jump on board and coach a team and made it very clear, and I'm quoting, 'Don't bail on me and go to the UFC as a coach on TUF and leave me hanging[354] and leave me on an island and get me blackballed by the UFC.' And I said, 'Look, dude, I'm a man of my word. When I say I'm gonna do something, I'm gonna do it.'

"And I committed to coaching in the IFL. Well, Ken went back on his word[355] and I was the one that ended up getting blackballed while he did TUF."

As great as the IFL deal sounded, nothing could compete with the deal UFC offered. It would be the biggest money fight of Shamrock's career, and, at 42 years old, he knew those opportunities were disappearing. Just as importantly, it brought Tito Ortiz back into his life. He'd spent almost four years dwelling on the loss at UFC 40. Now, however unlikely a win would be, he would have an opportunity to set things right.

"When I didn't have all the problems that I've had, I was an aggressive fighter," Shamrock told *MMA Weekly*. "I've kind of steered away from that a little bit because of some of the injuries that I've had,

---

[354] Miletich and Carlos Newton were initially going to coach TUF Season 3 until Ortiz and Shamrock signed on. They had even put together some marketing materials before everything changed.

[355] More than a decade later, it was very clear in conversation that this was still an issue that rankled Miletich.

trying to protect them and still get the win.

"When I fight Tito Ortiz, I ain't worrying about anything. I'm healthy. I'm going to get in good shape so that I can go three hard rounds throwing nothing but hands, feet, taking him down, smashing him with elbows, and then going for submissions. I will be very, very focused on this fight, and I will be in very good condition.

"It's all been about Tito for the past four of five years...It's hard to even think past that."

The show began filming in the third week of January for an April debut. Shamrock arrived in Las Vegas with his best friend, bodybuilder Dan Freeman, and boxing coach Roman Pollack, excited to be part of this new adventure and focused on building interest in the Ortiz fight.

The competitors, with an opportunity to fight in the UFC on the line, were decidedly less than impressed with Shamrock and his cadre as they essentially auditioned for each team. As Michael Bisping wrote in his book *Quitters Never Win: My Life in UFC*, Shamrock was like a dinosaur trying to operate in the computer age:

> A faded force as a fighter, out of touch as a trainer. "I don't do no BJJ stuff," he said, with the complacency of a man who'd decided there was nothing more to learn. "I am a brawler and a leg-lock guy."
>
> Team Shamrock's evaluation process consisted of a bunch of unstructured sparring that Ken watched dispassionately from afar, then 300 press-ups, 300 sit-ups, and 300 squats followed by "feats of strength" tests that had no relevance to the sport of MMA.
>
> The contrast with Tito's evaluation session the next day couldn't have been more pronounced...Anxious to get first-hand intel on our abilities, Tito rolled with each and every one of us....He used a great sweep on me and, after we'd finished, made sure to demonstrate it at half-pace.
>
> That was training with Tito Ortiz—no ego, just a guy with a ton of knowledge he clearly intended to share with whoever made it onto his team. And Ortiz's assistant coaches were also amazing to work with.
>
> ...After a day of training with each coach, there

was no doubt in my mind that I wanted to be picked for Tito's team.

"I felt like Ken was an alright guy. He tried his best as a coach," Shamrock team member Kalib Starnes says. "He was never really a very technical fighter and relied mostly on his athleticism and that showed through in the training. His athletic training, his weight circuits were great except for the lack of cardio training.

"He didn't bring a good jiu jitsu, Muay Thai or wrestling coach. There was no one good at holding pads there. Just two bodybuilders and a boxing coach.

"I just don't think he realized what we needed. Bodybuilding, protein shakes and sparring weren't enough anymore. You need well-rounded technical skills, proper psychological preparation, proper strategies, focused drilling. We didn't get any of that as a team."

The storyline going into the season seemed pretty clear—Ortiz was the cocky, brash younger fighter and Shamrock the respected veteran looking for one last moment in the sun. But the heavily edited program dumped that narrative right on its head, portraying Ortiz as a kind, thoughtful coach and Shamrock as out of touch and selfish.

Some of that was the truth. Shamrock and his team did clash, his old school approach rubbing them wrong and their refusal to buy into his system driving him nuts. But some of it was the fallout from the emergence of the IFL and Dana White's single-minded focus on this new enemy after they signed away UFC executive Keith Evans.

"Dana threw Keith Evans a party and gave him a replica belt back when replica belts weren't just lying around the office," one former UFC employee remembers. "He kept it quiet where he was going. Dana was like 'come on tell me, come on, tell me.'

"He goes 'I'm going to the IFL.'

"'Your going to the NFL? Oh cool, which team?'

"Keith says 'No, I'm going to the IFL.'

"He's like 'You motherfucker' and he immediately tossed him out of there. Dana and Lorenzo went upstairs with (UFC general counsel) Kirk Hendrick. They came back down and the party was still kind of milling around and made everybody sign a document saying they wouldn't go work anywhere else (in MMA). Because they thought the IFL would basically raid their town."

White declared virtual war on the new promotion, filing a temporary restraining order to stop them from using "Zuffa's

Confidential Information and Trade secrets." Then he went to battle with anyone and everyone even remotely associated with the new brand.

Pat Miletich, in a deposition for the lawsuit, says White was going scorched Earth on everyone—no one was safe, no matter how iconic:

> White further threatened me during the conversation, and implicitly the livelihoods of the fighters I train, stating that "when the dust settles, anyone associated with the IFL would not be associated with the UFC". I took this for what it was — a threat to me and to my fighters who count on me to represent them and obtain opportunities to for them to fight in the MMA industry. Because of the virtual monopoly that Zuffa has in the MMA industry, Mr. White clearly knew that cutting me and my fighters off from the UFC would have a devastating economic impact.
>
> Following my conversation with Mr. White, Ken Shamrock, another world-renowned MMA fighter, called me and told me that Mr. White had just "raised hell" with him about his being associated with the IFL. As I understand it, Mr. White had made similar threats to Mr. Shamrock whom I believe at the time had an agreement with the IFL to coach one of its teams. I further understand that Mr. White made the same or similar threats to Randy Couture, perhaps one of the most legendary MMA fighters in the world and a former UFC World Champion.

"Dana came unglued," Shamrock says. "I went, sat down and had lunch with him and told him, I was like, 'dude, I have a lot of fighters that have to play into this. They're not fighting in the UFC. Put them under contract[356]. But if not, they got to make money.' And he goes, 'but I'm not gonna let you be on (IFL shows).' And I say, 'I'm their coach.' He goes, 'if you do that, you're not fighting here anymore.' I

---

[356] "Ken was a lot of the problem between Dana and Ken," one close associate says. "If you know anything about Dana White, he's pretty direct. But Ken was always trying to angle him with other promotions because he was always under financial pressure and trying to get something going."

was like, 'dude, I'm under contract.' He goes, 'I don't care.'

"Suddenly, I became an enemy. They made me look like dog meat on that show. I didn't show up when he planned a meeting for me and then they showed guys training in the backyard, saying 'Ken Shamrock was a no show.' I told my coaches to be there because Dana had a meeting planned for me in the afternoon and then when I get to the meeting, they tell my coaches to stay home and then they filmed this thing in the backyard. 'Oh, Shamrock's a no show.'"

Whether it was a fair portrayal of events or not, the show was a ratings smash despite the move to Thursday and loss of the WWE audience. It was the highest-rated debut ever for an original series on SPIKE TV and did a fantastic job building personalities from the very beginning. The competitors were fun to watch and there was a crackling energy every time Ortiz and Shamrock shared the same space, even if onlookers never quite believed any of it was real.

"It seemed like pretty contrived," one fighter says. "TV bullshit. Like everything is chill, and then, when the cameras are rolling or they're setting up a particular scene, they would ham it up WWF style."

Ortiz, who picked eventual UFC champion Bisping and longtime promotional stalwarts Kendall Grove and Matt Hammill, dominated the competition, at one point winning five in a row. In the end, Shamrock's team only won three fights all season.

He tried everything he could, from tough love to outings at the golf course, to turn the tide. But he could never fully connect with his team[357], many of whom openly looked longingly at Ortiz's more modern style practices.

"Ken was a tired old fighter that was done, basically, and just trying to hang on for all he could," fighter Tait Fletcher said. "It's tough, he was a guy that taught me a lot of lessons. He taught me where I didn't want to end up. That desperate struggle for more and more."

Shamrock still believed his style of training, emphasizing toughness and valor, had merit. But he concedes that, in this case, it just didn't work out.

"At some point I lost it," he says. "I was just like, 'dude, if you guys don't want to train, you don't want to work. So be it, it's your career not mine. People pay me to spend a lot of time training you and you

---

[357] "I am the captain of the ship and I am going down with it," he told the team at one point to mostly silence. "...are you coming with me?"

guys want to act like this?'

"I couldn't do it. Not on that show. Too many primadonnas. There were some of them that wanted to work. But the ones who thought they were already there and knew it all got in the way. And the way I train people, you've got to earn it. You got to earn it. If you aint earning it, I'm not going to waste my time with you."

While Ortiz clearly won the coaching battle[358], the fight itself was up in the air. In a strange twist, this time it was Ortiz who had suffered a serious knee injury and was attempting to fight through it without surgery. The bout became questionable enough that UFC started floating a number of replacement opponents to Shamrock's team[359], just part of what his lawyer Rod Donohoo called the "fight before the fight."

"The incidentals were huge because they add up. Number of hotel rooms[360], number of fares, what class," Donohoo says. "You know, they offered business class but Ken wanted to go to first class. Everything was a huge fight. Everything.

"I remember being up with Ken until 1:00 or 2:00 AM both when we were fighting *and* when we would negotiate. The Tito fight, we had to negotiate different opponents before that, and it was always like that. It was this big battle. Always. I would negotiate directly with Dana because it was Ken. You know, he was the one that you negotiated with and then the lawyers would come in and you'd negotiate with them."

White was a straight forward, emotional bargainer. And while it wasn't always pleasant dealing with him, Shamrock's team never doubted his commitment to the product.

"He was all in," Donohoo says. "He wasn't a guy who was an empty suit. He was involved in every aspect of the show. They did one of those promotional pieces for the Tito fight. And Dana did not like the way the promotional video turned out.

---

[358] The lone bright spot for Team Shamrock was a pool contest where Ken, after pretending not to know how to play, dominated Ortiz and won $10,000.

[359] In the Observer, Meltzer reported that Ortiz had been pulled in favor of his UFC 59 opponent Forrest Griffin. But plans, clearly, changed when Ortiz was cleared by doctors to fight.

[360] "When he fought Tito Ortiz the second time he flew the whole family down to watch him fight," Shamrock's nephew Jeff Jorgenson says. "He put us all up in a hotel and took care of us. It was a whole family reunion."

"He flew somebody out, helicoptered them because there were fires going on, and he had the whole thing reshot. He insisted on it. He was perfectionist on that kind of stuff. He knew what he wanted. The reality is that he was heavily invested in these fights. There's no question about that. Emotionally and with his time."

The fight ended up going on as planned despite knee, back and leg issues that limited Ortiz in training. It didn't much matter[361]. Just like the previous pay-per-view saw Matt Hughes dominate and embarrass a returning Royce Gracie, the story of UFC 61 was in with the new and out with the old, as Ortiz ran through Shamrock in just 78 seconds.

After controlling Shamrock in the clinch, Ortiz picked him up for a high slam and then proceeded to slam an elbow into his temple that made Shamrock go momentarily limp. Referee Herb Dean lept in to protect the older fighter and all hell broke loose in the cage, to the point police eventually had to come in and restore order.

The crowd booed lustily as Shamrock protested the decision. Even if losing the fight seemed inevitable, it was important for his own peace of mind that he at least have the chance to succeed. *MMA Weekly* described the wild scene:

> Shamrock popped up very quickly and started to ask why the fight was stopped. The Octagon filled with security personnel, and the two rivals had to be kept apart as Tito celebrated his win and Shamrock appeared to be very upset with the stoppage.
>
> Multiple replays showed the elbows landed by Ortiz, and it did look like Shamrock was getting nailed pretty hard by all of the strikes. Anytime there is controversy like this about a referee's decision, there will always be debate about whether it was a good stoppage, but it did appear that Shamrock was not intelligently defending himself, and that is cause enough to stop the fight.
>
> While it's almost a forgone conclusion that Shamrock will scream to the high heavens about the stoppage, it was again Ortiz who dominated the fight

---

[361] Ortiz was a -500 favorite, meaning you'd have to bet $500 on Tito to earn back $100. That the odds were even this close is testament to Shamrock's ability to convince people he means serious business.

and walked out victorious.

In some ways it felt like a carbon copy of the Sakuraba fight. Once again, Ken took a heavy blow and seemed momentarily out of it. Then, his senses recovered, he jumped up and says 'I'm fine. Dean stopped the fight too soon.' It was like the same scene playing over and over again.

"It was an early stoppage," Shamrock says. "They stopped it. Nothing I can I do about it. I always believe I could win. Even when I got beat up, I still felt I could have won if they had just allowed it to continue because I think my strength is I never ever give up. I'll never quit. I find ways to win. I'll go farther than anybody else will.

"I believe that if it was a street fight, I would've won. I would've won eventually. Unfortunately it's in a ring and there's rules and there's somebody there saying that you've had enough. I'm not in control of that."

The show was a mixed bag—in the cage it was the worst major UFC show since Zuffa's first foray into pay-per-view at UFC 33. But at the box office, it set a new standard for pay-per-view buys, topping 775,000 while coming close to breaking the promotion's all-time gate record.

For the fighters, it was gratifying to be part of the most financially successful UFC event of all time—but also a little frustrating. They were drawing WrestleMania and De La Hoya numbers but not getting paid like it.

"The second fight, I made a lot," Ortiz says. "To me, in my mind, I wasn't making enough. I was still trying to make more. They were making 30 million dollars a pay per view, and we were only getting paid five percent.

"I remember Mike Tyson and the numbers he was getting, the money he was making. He was making $30-40 million a fight. I said, 'Dana, how come I'm not making that type of money?' He was all, 'you need to start getting those numbers and you'll make that type of money.'

"It never happened for me. They were doing those numbers. We're doing close to a million pay per view buys and I wasn't making no 30 million dollars. I wasn't making no 10 million dollars. I wasn't even making five million. I was getting held down, and that's why I started speaking up. The more I spoke up, the more I got pushed down."

The finish, though disastrous on the night, opened up the

opportunity to do one more event, this time a free television special on Spike TV called "The Final Chapter." By talking openly about the fight and how abysmal it was in basically every media interview that followed the bout, White both created the illusion of being a truth-teller and laid the groundwork for the rematch, positioning it as a gift to the fans. In truth, it was an offering to Spike TV and a demonstration of the brand's emerging power to draw a large audience.

"Dana White flew down and we met him in Anaheim," Donohoo remembers. "He slid a million dollar check across the table to Ken for the last Tito fight and they decided the third one would be on Spike. "

The event, at the Seminole Hard Rock in Hollywood, Florida, was the fastest sellout in UFC history. Despite criticism from the hardcore fanbase, Shamrock remained a compelling figure for casual fans and his return to the scene played a huge role in the company establishing a firm footing with executives at Spike TV. The UFC needed television to thrive. Spike needed young, male viewers. It, like the Ortiz and Shamrock matchup, was the perfect pairing.

The story was elegant in its simplicity. Two guys hate each other, clearly articulate why and then duke it out. After blood has been spilled, they embrace, satisfied they had their say. As a promotion, it was a fantastic success, but as an athletic contest, it was an absolute atrocity. Shamrock was good, at this point, at talking up a fight. He just couldn't, thanks to age, injury and technical advancements in the sport, hold up his end in the cage.

"Ken trained hard for him," new trainer Lance Foreman says. "By that time, Ken...all his fights and wear and tear were catching up to him. His low back was bad. I came in because I deal with boxing mostly and that's pretty much all Ken trained the last ten years was boxing because he could punch so hard, but his knees were gone and low back was gone.

"Tito was so much bigger than Ken. Going into the third fight, I was not liking it much. I was thinking, 'oh shit, I don't want this guy to hurt Ken.' He's just too big and strong."

The fight itself was a massacre. The only difference between the second and third fights were the additional minute and six seconds Ortiz spent pounding on Shamrock before the referee finally stopped the bout. It was as definitive and one-sided as fights get, the result never in question.

"The third Tito fight was the worst ever," family friend Tom Casey says. "Guy Mezger and I sat up in the bleacher section and looked at each other and agreed 'he shouldn't fight anymore.' I love Ken, but I couldn't do it anymore. I couldn't come to these fights because I didn't want to be one of the enablers. There were people around him saying 'yeah man, you can still do it.' Well, the fact is, you can't and you shouldn't. I wasn't going to be part of it."

Shamrock attempted to shake hands when it was all over, only to be initially rebuffed by Tito, who only conceded after Ken reminded him "we made a lot of money together." The UFC ran a nice montage as the show closed, sending the legendary warrior on his way, essentially wishing him well in his further endeavors.

His contract with UFC included an addendum stating he intended to retire after this final million dollar pay day[362]. White, in person, had insisted on including a second bout in the contract "in case anything crazy happens."

But the bout, as gloomily one-sided as it was, also rewrote the record book. Almost six million people[363] tuned in to see Ortiz's win, smashing the UFC's previous best.[364] That meant, despite losing six of his last seven fights, there were still going to be plenty of people[365] interested in being in the Ken Shamrock business.

Mezger, the closest thing Shamrock had to a peer in the fight game, tried to talk to him about stepping away but that just wasn't an option.

"The pro wrestling took a lot out of him. Ken was a beast. I fought a

---

[362] The specific language, which would become important in a later lawsuit, stated: "Fighter has determined the first Bout will be his final, after which he will retire, but has agreed to one additional Bout with ZUFFA in the event the fighter should either elect not to retire or come out of retirement to fight again."

[363] While different numbers have floated around, Spike TV eventually settled on 6,524,000.

[364] "(5.7 million viewers) shatters the UFC's previous record for the number of people watching a UFC fight at any given time," MMA Weekly's Ivan Trembow reported. "The previous record was 3.4 million viewers, despite repeated claims by Zuffa that the first fight between Forrest Griffin and Stephan Bonnar was watched live by ten million viewers."

[365] Shamrock and Ortiz did more than set records for UFC. As Dave Meltzer wrote in the *Wrestling Observer*, it was the beginning of a mini-MMA boom. "The fact is the success of the Ken Shamrock vs. Tito Ortiz program has not only put UFC on the sports map, but has resulted in making an entire industry."

lot of guys and I fought a lot of beasts, a lot of bad ass men in my day," Mezger says. "Ken Shamrock in his prime was one of the baddest guys out there. But the pro wrestling part of things I think just wore him out.

"I'm sitting there talking to him and I'm like, 'Dude, I'm concerned about this.' I became like this mother hen. It was hard for me to sit there and do that and Ken wasn't really receptive to hearing something other than, 'Continue to fight.'

"I just didn't want him to fight anymore. I mean, I didn't love Ken any less. If anything, more, because of wanting him to be healthy. I just think that he got between a rock and a hard place with some of this financial stuff and he didn't know how to get himself out of it outside of fighting."

CHAPTER NINETEEN
Miami Madness

Less than a month after Shamrock's third and final bout with Ortiz, the lights went out at an International Fight League event at Portland's Memorial Coliseum[366]. When they came back on, Ken was standing in the ring, introduced as the league's newest coach[367].

For the IFL, run by mega-fan Kurt Otto, it was another legendary fighter to add to its menagerie[368]. For Shamrock, it was an opportunity to rehabilitate his image as a trainer and a chance to provide a living to a group of young fighters willing to do what he believed necessary to earn it.

On November 26, 2006, Shamrock held an open tryout to any interested fighters, looking to field an eight-man squad for the

---

[366] The *Wrestling Observer* reported that the 7,362 in attendance included "only 1,000 paid and less than a $100,000 gate. It was very easy to get free tickets for this show." The league, in retrospect, was already in a death spiral before it had ever truly gotten started.

[367] Before he got started, Shamrock first needed to repair some relationships.

"Kurt Otto and Gareb Shamus said, 'What do you think about Ken coming back?' And they had a big meeting with all the coaches, and we all sat down," Miletich says. "When Ken spoke, he goes, 'Let me first start by apologizing to Pat.' Because he at least owned up to it, to what he had done, and so for what it was worth, he at least apologized."

[368] "Did our stock jump because he came on board? No," Otto says. "Was there a boost of excitement, internally within the media that covers MMA? Absolutely. We tried to promote and pump that up as much as possible. But at the end of the day it's a big deal when you're inside the world of MMA. Outside of the world of MMA, no one gives a shit."

upcoming 2007 season.

Although he had a small team of fighters training with him at the time, this was an opportunity to compete on national cable at a very high level. After an honest assessment, Shamrock concluded he needed to open up a wider aperture to have a chance at success. If his current fighters were going to make it, they'd have to earn it. He owed them an opportunity. It was up to them to capitalize on it.

"They weren't the brutal tryouts like for the Lion's Den team, but they were pretty tough," trainer Lance Foreman says. "We got applicants from all over the country. We probably had 70 or 80 guys[369] that showed up that one day. We spent two days going through them, and then when Ken picked his team, almost everybody he picked eventually made it into the UFC[370]."

The tryouts, however, were only the beginning. Just like in the original Lion's Den days, Ken wanted guys to fight their way onto the team. It no longer made sense for him to jump in there to test the fighters. Better, he thought, for them to prove it against each other. So, prior to picking his final squad, he had the fighters he'd tabbed as having the most potential come back to Reno to compete in an unsanctioned, closed-doors mini-tournament to earn their spot.

"It was me, Julio Gonzales, one of Ken's guys and then Dennis Hallman," Nevada Lions fighter Pat Healy says. "Us four were given the opportunity to come down to Reno for a closed door fight. I fought Hallman first. Then the two winners of those fights fought, and whoever won got the spot on the team.

"It was old Lion's Den style which meant Ken said he wouldn't stop the fight. It was up to you to tap out or quit. Obviously, it was over if someone got knocked out too. It was a pretty rough go. There was some beatings handed out and luckily I was able to get the spot."

Shamrock set his team up in the fighters' house at the Lion's Den in Susanville, working them hard three times a day, including long runs in the California mountains. The fighters who didn't make the team were in the same house with those that did and were used as fresh

---

[369] The IFL offered fighters a monthly stipend of $2000, a fight purse when they competed and health care. It was a fantastic opportunity for up-and-comers at a time when many UFC fighters were still making less than $10,000 a bout.

[370] Four of the five starters on the team made it to the UFC during the course of their careers, making it a pretty decent squad in the context of the time.

meat[371] to get the team ready for the first event—which just so happened to be a battle with his estranged brother Frank's San Jose Razorclaws.

"If we'd lost that fight, I would have taken some heat," Shamrock says. "Because of *The Ultimate Fighter*, the idea was already out there that I'm not a great trainer. I told them, they would take some heat too. Because the way I did it, I went outside the box. I did tryouts and really trained them. I didn't go get an established fighter from somebody else and use them. We built the team from the ground up."

The relationship between the foster brothers, always on shaky ground, was especially tenuous at the time because Frank was taking an aggressive posture in the media. When it came to the Lion's Den, in particular, he was typically dismissive of his older brother's intellect and accomplishments.

"Frank was really starting to take a stance about him being the main guy at the Lion's Den," Shamrock says. "That he was the one who did all the training. And that was completely the opposite. In fact, if anything, he looked out for himself when he was left in charge. And that's okay too. It's his life and he lives it how he wants. But don't go in and start trying to say that you were the one that made the Lion's Den run. Because that's just not true."

Although he playfully mushed Frank's face when they met in the ring after an impromptu battle of iron claws, the atmosphere was tense.

"Tonya and I were walking out of the locker room and Frank walked by," Larry Goldberg, who ran Shamrock's website, says. "She looked the other way and he shook my hand. She was not thrilled at me for that."

Despite losing Vernon White[372] to an athletic commission ruling, Shamrock's Nevada Lions picked up the win in their first contest, cause for celebration among the increasingly close-knit team. It was a

---

[371] "I kind of felt bad for the guys who were at the Lion's Den," Healy says. "They were kind of used as our training dummies. We kind of got the royal treatment and they were like our practice fodder. I remember some rounds where I had little gloves on and they had head gear and big gloves on. I mean, looking back on it, it seems a little bit unfair, but at the time I was like 24 or something, so I loved it."

[372] The California commission decided the veteran fighter with more than 50 career fights was too experienced to face the relative novice Frank put forward.

return, he hoped, to the simpler times of the original Lion's Den, something different than the group he'd assembled in San Diego that had been centered around night life as much as competition.

This team, living nearby the Shamrock family, came over several times a week for dinner, joining the already Brady Bunch-ish multi-generational clan. Bob, as generous and outgoing as ever, tried to hold the fragile family together.

"Sometimes we would go driving in his Caddie," Shamrock's daughter Fallon remembers. "There would be times where if I was bored or just sitting there with a sad look on my face, he would hop his car up on the sidewalk real quick and then drop down, like 'just checking to make sure you're awake.' That would always make me laugh.

"When he was living at my dad's in Susanville he had a whole setup going on in the garage and I would go in there and hang out with him and the dogs and we would talk about fixing up cars. I remember I told him I wanted a Cadillac just like his when I got older and he bought me a little model car and said I could have it until I'm old enough to get my own."

The fighters, too, got sucked into this new version of Shamrock Americana. As always, they were a collection of mostly misfits who might have otherwise struggled to figure out where they fit in. The Lion's Den was there to give them a purpose and a goal, with Ken and Tonya the center of an extended family.

"Ken was a father figure to my daughters and had to meet all the boyfriends," Tonya says. "Along with fighters at the house like John Gunderson and Pat Healy. One time my daughter didn't want to bring her boyfriend in to meet Ken. The fighters were all there for a barbecue. So he sent every single fighter out to the car to meet him. She was pissed. She was so mad at Ken.

"I'd known Ken since he was a punk kid. So the world of fighting wasn't really that strange to me. Ken was Ken. Plus, I'd been raised with group home kids my entire life. Our house was a fighter's house, basically. The boys are always fighting. I was probably eight or nine when a boy stripped another kid down completely naked and threw him outside in the cold weather. That's the lifestyle I grew up with."

The team, after some trouble in the local community[373], picked up

---

[373] "Susanville is kind of too small," Foreman says. "The cops were after us a lot."

camp and moved to Reno, Nevada, where the $30,000 Shamrock made a month went a long way towards building a top-level facility. Unlike *The Ultimate Fighter*, Shamrock brought in specialty coaches[374] to focus on striking and jiu-jitsu, while maintaining mostly a bird's eye view of the overall process—until it was time to work on leg locks when he happily lent his expertise.[375]

While he was an absentee trainer for much of the first half of the 2000s, with the IFL he remained actively engaged. Even when he did travel to an event or a signing, he seemed to the people around him to have eyes and ears everywhere, with very little escaping his notice.

"You can't ever get nothing by Ken, ever," Foreman, who ran the gym with his wife Heather, says. "The fighters, they'd be blown away. Ken could be gone for a week and we'd all be training without him. Somebody's got a fricking problem or done something screwy I don't even know about, and Ken would be like, 'Hey, did you know this happened?' And I'd be like, 'No, hell no. But how do you know? No one else even knows.'

"He just knows. It's flipping weird. It happened a lot of times. I would tell the fighters, because they wanted to be around Ken and he'd get real busy sometimes, 'Don't worry bro, he knows what's going on with you.'"

In April, Ken brought his oldest son Ryan with him on a trip to Moline, Illinois, where he broke the news to his dad that he wanted to drop out of culinary school and join the family business—fighting. His sons Connor and Sean also trained and his nephew Jeff Jorgenson[376] had his own aspirations to turn pro. After years of tension, for a time the sport that had once divided the family brought it back together.

---

[374] "We even had Kelly Davis and (former professional boxer) Kelvin Davis come in and they helped us out with boxing," Vernon White says. "I watched Roy Nelson go from a slugger to someone who was actually in there hitting people with real punches because of Kelvin and Kelly."

[375] "The one thing you have to respect about Ken is that he gets the whole entertainment side of the MMA business," Nevada Lions fighter Roy Nelson, who became the organization's heavyweight champion, says. "That's one thing he showed me. You don't have to be the greatest fighter out there to make money in this sport. Myself, I've got a double bonus. I can fight and I can also entertain."

[376] Jeff adopted the Shamrock last name when he signed with Strikeforce to fight but is actually the son of Shamrock's sister and not connected to Bob Shamrock directly.

An aging Bob[377] was part of this mix, returning to a role he knew well, counseling and listening to young men who sometimes had lacked love and discipline in their lives.

"Bob was just one of those people that was just so freaking nice that you want to go above and beyond to help that person, just to see them happy, too," Jorgenson says. "He would always give you sound advice. He's one of those people that would tell you, 'straighten up your shoulders, you're slouching a little bit.' And say it in such a manner that it didn't bother you. He was like our Master Splinter."

Ken, meanwhile, had martial aspirations of his own. The IFL was paying good money to coach—but many of the legends on the coaching roster were also stepping back into the ring. Shamrock was interested but owed UFC his next fight if he came out of retirement. So, in early June, he informed UFC of his intention to continue his active career.[378]

The promotion actually considered bringing him back for the additional bout. The day before a fight card in Belfast, Ireland, Dana White pitched the idea of a Shamrock fight at UFC 75 to *The Ultimate Fighter 3* winner Michael Bisping, who verbally agreed.

"Dana had come up with it on plane ride to Ireland," one former UFC employee says. "(UFC matchmaker) Joe Silva didn't know about it - when I told him an hour later he screamed 'That is fucking retarded!'"

With his team against bringing Shamrock back, White conceded the issue and, a week later, called Shamrock's lawyer to inform him that they were terminating Ken's contract[379], making him a free agent.

"The UFC cut my contract short," Shamrock told *MMA News* in a 2008 interview. "This threw me off a little because I had one fight left on my contract. I was expecting one more fight with them.

---

[377] In 2007, Bob and Ken appeared on the Speed Channel's "Payback" where Ken thanked his father for a lifetime of support with a custom Cadillac.

[378] "I have seven children, two grandchildren. I have to make a living. The UFC didn't offer me any fights and the IFL came along and offered me a job," he said at the time. "That's why I'm here, I make my living in the fight game."

[379] The next April Ken filed a lawsuit about this decision, saying the second fight on his contract was mandatory, not optional. He was asking for $230,000, the purse he was denied. Two years later, when it finally went to trial, the court sided with Zuffa and further required Ken to pay the promotion the $175,000 in legal fees they had accumulated.

"Basically Dana White decided to cut my contract short because I had chosen to be a coach in the IFL[380]...As far as I'm concerned if you have an agreement with someone you should honor that agreement. I think what they did was wrong and I want them to understand that you cannot do those things and not have repercussions."

While disappointed in that decision, Shamrock was ready to move forward with the IFL or another suitor instead. The success of UFC brought others to the table[381], chasing either the thrill of being around the fights or the allure of easy money. And all of them knew the name "Ken Shamrock."

There were a number of offers—but the one that made the most sense, on the surface, was the IFL. They had raised money with a public stock offering and already had national television on multiple networks. But putting that deal together proved difficult.

"They wanted to bring Ken in to do some fights but they weren't talking about anywhere near the same number he'd been making with UFC or even the ball park," Donohoo says. "We looked at fighting various people including Don Frye[382]. We were about to set that up and start building that fight when they made some management changes[383]. Ken wanted to fight. He did. But he wanted to be sure the money was there. There were plenty of opportunities but none for big money at the time because of what was happening with the economy[384]."

While Ken was negotiating his own return to the sport, his Lions were competing for an IFL playoff spot. The team was up 4-0 over the

---

[380] "He decided he wanted to go in the IFL. And he was permitted to do that in the agreement. He didn't breach his agreement," Donohoo says. "But they were furious. UFC was furious with Ken for going to the IFL. And it destroyed their relationship to the extent that it existed then."

[381] Including Ken, who promoted a couple of events at the Feather Falls Casino in California, including his son Ryan's debut.

[382] Another potential opponent was WWE Superstar and former Olympic gold medalist Kurt Angle. Those negotiations got fairly serious but fell apart when Angle wanted all of his pay in cash instead of a combination of cash and stock options.

[383] Former boxing executive Jay Larkin came in to run the company in October and brought sweeping changes, including huge cutbacks.

[384] A global financial crisis struck in 2007, creating several years of uncertainty for businesses in and out of the fight game.

Tucson Scorpions (coached by Ken's old rival Don Frye) in a match where they needed a clean sweep to make the postseason. Mike Whitehead of the Scorpions stopped Vernon White in :54 of the second round to play spoiler and end the team's chance at advancing. Shamrock never got the chance to coach in another IFL team competition.

The league had exploded on the scene and were quickly bleeding money, losing almost $14 million in the first six months of 2007[385]. It was an idea before its time in many ways, a new vision for what MMA could look like being presented before the original concept had fully sunk in with casual sports fans. With more than 150 fighters under contract, commitments to multiple coaches and the responsibility to create content for three different television networks, league officials quickly realized they were biting off more than they could chew.

"They were throwing the money away[386]," promoter Shannon Knapp, who worked for the fledgling league says. "IFL had an office in Manhattan and one in Vegas. Everything was very showy with the IFL. A lot of money got spent.

"There were a lot of executives making big money. Coaches that were making big money. They're paying these athletes every month. Everybody's getting paid.

"You have these people that have been in the sport for a long time that were in people's ears. They all had big ideas and if somebody's got a big checkbook, it's the time to let all your ideas flow...They all want in the pockets. That's what it's always about. The money. They go in for that money grab because nobody ever knows if it's going to stay around, or stick. It was always like that. You go and grab as much as you can."

Sensing the IFL was on its last legs, Shamrock began looking elsewhere. Unfortunately, as the IFL wound down, so did Ken's

---

[385] "I remember a speech (Otto) gave telling us how big of stars we were gonna be and how they had all this stuff in the works, like Topps Cards and all that stuff," Healy says. "He was kind of just hanging out and bragging about what it was gonna be like. I'll never forget that because I was looking around and there were probably six, seven hundred people in the crowd, and I was going, 'I don't know if we're on the same page here.'"

[386] "IFL CEO Kurt Otto was the biggest mark I've ever seen in the business," one insider says. "He loved hanging out with fighters, especially Bas Rutten. They had these special leather jackets made, giant rings. He was like a frat boy who stumbled on a blank check book."

interest in the Lions, continuing a pattern of walking out on students when it wasn't in his financial interest to keep them around.

"The gym went from where we'd have ten, fifteen guys at practice, to the end I remember I was the last one training there," Healy says. "I'd show up to practice and it'd be like two beginners and me. And I was getting ready to fight (future UFC mainstay) Jake Ellenberger in IFL."

While the Lions languished, Ken joined another new team concept called "Ring of Fire" for a show in the Philippines. His team, including former UFC heavyweight champion Ricco Rodriguez and future Invicta standout Tonya Evinger swept Royce Gracie's team and theoretically advanced to the finals to face an equally dominant team coached by Josh Barnett. But the show, like many MMA events of the era that began with grand plans, never returned for a second event.

"Ken was going with these organizations to try so that he would have some ownership in something," Donohoo says. "And there was a couple that we tried to do that, quite frankly, I personally didn't think they stood a snowball's chance in Hell. But Ken wanted to be a part of something and be an owner."

The next big idea sprang from the mind of Frank Shamrock. It was a concept that had been floated before, but never with such urgency and commitment. He wanted to fight his brother Ken—and he wanted to do it on pay-per-view.

Frank, who had returned to action full-time with a startup called Elite XC[387] in 2007, first dropped hints about the potential matchup shortly after the two brothers went head-to-head as coaches at an IFL event in January, telling CBS Sportsline "I have not talked to Ken about it, but I've talked to some of his representatives, and we got two thumbs up so I'm going to keep working on it."

The idea of two brothers competing in the cage was compelling. It was hard for the Lion's Den fighters who had come up with the two to

---

[387] The disastrous story of Elite XC, a partnership between Pro Elite and Showtime deserves its own book. But in 2007, they were an exciting new group with some financial backing and a TV slot on Showtime. With the IFL fading, they quickly became the UFC's top competitor.

imagine the fight, as Ken routinely and easily mauled Frank in training. But that was years earlier and the younger Shamrock had since developed into a legitimate MMA legend in his own right. And he wasn't opposed to punching Ken right in the nose if given the opportunity.

"I never had a relationship with Ken that wasn't about fighting," Frank said. "I've never had a serious conversation with him that didn't involve drugs or money or fighting. He trained me for a couple of years and was my mentor and will always be my mentor. I owe him my life in martial arts. But past that? I've never received a Christmas card, a Thank You card for anything I've done for him, or congratulations for anything I've ever done. We just don't have a relationship. I know my neighbor better than I know Ken Shamrock."

In early 2008, Ken and his son Ryan signed their own deals with Elite XC[388], whose CEO Gary Shaw was keen on the idea of seeing two brothers settle their differences in a cage. Frank even put up a website promoting the bout, which was briefly the talk of the hardcore community[389].

"I know how invested Frank was in it," announcer Mauro Ranallo, who is also a close personal friend of Frank's, says. "I believe even personally invested in this fight, which is saying something. He was really involved and really wanted to see this Blood Brothers pay-per-view come to fruition There's a lot of hurt, a lot of real deeply rooted pain between them. A lot of professional envy, but also a lot of personal enmity which is unfortunate, but you see it often."

Before the brothers could duke it out, both had prior fistic engagements in the Elite XC cage. Frank had a fight scheduled against san shou artist Cung Le in June, and Ken travelled to London in February to fight journeyman Robert "Buzz" Berry at Cage Rage 25[390].

---

[388] As part of the deal, Shamrock shuttered his own Ken Shamrock Productions after running five small shows in Northern California in 2007. The deal was arranged by his former business adviser Bill McFarlane who others in his circle believe was a less than honest broker.

[389] "It's going to be because this is the story that everyone can understand," Frank told *MMA Weekly*. "Even if you don't like fighting, you get the story. You get the storyline. You get the characters. You get the players. I think this is what breaks our sport open to the masses, for real."

[390] Elite XC's parent company, Pro Elite, inexplicably bought most of the leading independent MMA promotions, spending millions of dollars in

The bout with Frank, meanwhile, wasn't the only potential mega fight brewing. In early 2008, Elite XC announced it had signed a deal with CBS to put mixed martial arts on broadcast television for the first time in its history.[391] The promotion and its new partner were looking for fights that would connect with the mainstream and were keen to put Ken in the cage with street fighting sensation Kimbo Slice, a backyard brawler who had knocked out Shamrock's old rival Tank Abbott on Showtime.

"The groundwork has already been laid, and we talked about it," Shamrock told Fight Network's Jack Encarnacao. "I think he is a phenomenal puncher and a big, strong individual. He's got a lot of ability, man. But I also know he's very young in the sport, and there are a lot of things he doesn't know. Hopefully, I can exploit some of them."

But everyone's best laid plans[392] were blown to smithereens by a perfectly placed Berry jab, as the bigger man was simply too much for Shamrock. What was supposed to be a tune up was, instead, much more than a 44-year-old Shamrock could handle[393]. At his age and with his declining skillset, there simply weren't any fights left he could count on as sure things.

A furious Frank[394], watching financial backers he'd set up to fund the Blood Brothers pay-per-view walk away, lashed out at Ken in the press, accusing him of steroid use publicly and directly for the first time.

"My brother Ken did them his whole life," he told *MMA Madness*. "Why do you think that his mind is so fried? Why do you think he crumbles before the big fights? He's got no psyche. He let steroids give

---

exchange for little more than a collection of names. I can't understand or explain it.

[391] Technically "My Network TV" was an over-the-air channel too. But—come on!

[392] Slice ended up fighting James Thompson in Elite XC's CBS debut instead of Ken, setting a new record for MMA viewers in America with over 6.5 million tuning in for the main event.

[393] Gary Shaw claimed Ken was suffering from a stomach ailment and Shamrock later confirmed he was sick. It was a bad night overall for the Shamrocks, as Ryan broke his hand on the undercard and couldn't continue his bout.

[394] Frank would go on to lose his bout too, unable to answer the bell after Cung Le broke his arm with a kick.

him a false sense of security and the moment that stuff is gone he's no longer superman. He's just a regular man. But without all the hard work and without all the belief in himself that a regular man would have if he got up to that point. He's the only guy that I'll tell on, because he's always in trouble anyway."

The Berry loss was Shamrock's fifth in a row, all five first-round stoppages. It was an embarrassing run for a proud man who still struggled to reconcile his results with his self image as a winner and champion. Things had always come easily athletically. Suddenly, everything, even training for the fights, was hard. The MMA community was not always kind, disparaging the older fighter as he continued to compete well past his best days.

"I can handle the ones saying 'I don't want to see him fight anymore. He's not the same fighter anymore.' Because those are true," Shamrock says. "You know, I'm not the same fighter. I've tried to explain why I fight. It's because I enjoy it. It's my time to enjoy. But I also understand that it's hard for people who think I'm a superhero to see me in a place where I'm vulnerable. I get it. It's hard for me to be able to do what I want to do without disappointing people.

"I think the hardest time was when people were knocking my credibility. Saying that I was washed up and never any good. A lot of them never saw my original fights. They only saw the Tito fights and after and they're judging me on those fights. That right there bothers me."

But circumstances didn't allow him to walk away. Not only did he still enjoy the idea of fighting, the challenge of facing another man in the cage and the camaraderie of the gym— there was still a large IRS debt that lingered over everything. If he left the game, he would leave with nothing to show for his career except a collection of increasingly distant memories.

"It took me years," Shamrock says of his tax struggles. "Because not only are you paying the back charges on it, but now you're paying the interest on it as it collects. And they collect a whole lot when they start with $900,000 owed.

"It was around the same time where I started declining. I was still making money. I was still getting fights. But not as often and not for as much as I was when I was in my prime. That really hurt me in a sense of feeling insecure. I couldn't set up for retirement because every time I make money, it's gone."

Despite his struggles (and also, perhaps, because of them) Elite XC was still interested in matching Shamrock with Slice, a viral sensation on YouTube and bonafide ratings draw. With only three professional cage fights to his name, he was just beginning to understand how different MMA was from the street fighting that had made him famous.

"Street fighting is - well first of all you've got to have the respect from your homeboys and everybody on the street," Slice told me in 2010[395]. "They got to know and understand what's about to happen here, you know what I'm saying? If I knock your boy out, his crew got to know okay, now your nigga just got knocked out. You can't be pulling out pistols talking about 'another chance or this or that.' That has to be established and respected before the two guys even engage in combat.

"There's no comparison to the street fights and where I am at right now as a professional fighter. There's no comparison. Street fighting is one dimension. All you've got to worry about is guys throwing punches. In Mixed Martial Arts and being a professional fighter, you have to train to be prepared, man. Because these guys have skills and these guys are professionals. You can be hurt. You know, you could be hurt like with a punch, a choke, or something like that you know?"

In many ways, Slice was coming from the same place Ken had been 20 years earlier, fighting in a bar parking lot in a circle of cars in front of a group of men with money on the line. The only difference is that Kimbo's escapades came in the YouTube era and made him a superstar. Elite XC had something special—the issue now was sustaining it, a tricky prospect considering Slice's status as a neophyte in the MMA world. A Shamrock fight was a best case scenario for a promotion that needed a big night—a fight their attraction could conceivably win against a fighter with broad national recognition.

"I was super excited for that fight," Elite XC Head of Operations Jeremy Lappen says. "In my mind that was a great fight to promote. Kimbo was a big star at that time but wasn't necessarily the greatest fighter in the world. And we needed big marquee names to put him against, but names that would be a competitive fight for both of them. And Ken really fit that bill.

"I knew Ken could market the hell out of that fight. I knew he had a great name, a name from the top. He hadn't been super competitive in

---

[395] Kevin "Kimbo Slice" Ferguson died of heart failure on June 5, 2016. He was just 42-years-old.

recent years up to that point, but I thought that he potentially could beat Kimbo. But I also thought Kimbo could beat him.

"If Kimbo beat him it would help propel Kimbo even higher up in the public eye and make him an even bigger time star. And if Ken beat Kimbo it would resurrect Ken and be the great star to build around too. To me, it was a fight that made a ton of sense."

The promotion was in a death spiral, having lost more than $50 million in less than one year of operations.[396] While its first event on CBS was a massive success, more than half the audience disappeared when they ran the network using traditional MMA fighters without Slice or emerging women's MMA star Gina Carano. After borrowing several million dollars from Showtime just to have the capital to run the show, they needed a huge rating to justify their continued existence.

The stakes were high. Not only were they fighting for their network life and to prove MMA's viability in the true mainstream, but Elite XC was also in the final stages of selling the enterprise to CBS. As *Figure Four Weekly*'s Bryan Alvarez explained, a lot was all riding on this one night, making Shamrock versus Slice potentially one of the most important fights in the history of the sport:

> EliteXC's future is all coming down to the Kimbo Slice vs. Ken Shamrock CBS show on October 4th. If it does a good rating, CBS/Showtime will likely buy them and keep them afloat; if the show tanks, the company is probably history. This is one of the most important ratings in sports entertainment of the last decade.

It was a well promoted fight, advertised regularly during CBS football broadcasts and primed to potentially break records. Shamrock was in pure pro wrestling mode in the press conference before the fight, at one point breaking character to chastise a journalist about being too concerned with whether or not his various pieces of trash talk were

---

[396] "Pro Elite was really a tech play disguised as a fight promotion," one insider says. "They saw the real value in the website. MySpace was huge at the time and they wanted to build a community. The fights were just a way to get people there. They had Kelly Perdew, who had won The Apprentice, running it and were willing to spend money like crazy."

consistent and logical.

"Kimbo has gained a lot of notoriety, but, in my opinion, he doesn't deserve it," Shamrock said. "Snap, crackle, pop. I am going to walk across the ring, hit him on his ugly beard and break his leg."

On the day of the fight, all hell broke loose behind the scenes when Shamrock learned that Andrei Arlovski, an addition to the card after Elite XC decided to co-promote the show with Affliction as a cost-cutting move, was making more money than he was[397].

"There are things that you can have in a contract, a favored nations clause where you can say, 'nobody makes more than my fighter makes,' and there were things that you do to ensure that," Shamrock's attorney Rod Donohoo says. "Well, they brought in a different promotion, Affliction, that was throwing money at these guys. And they had a fighter making more than Ken. Was the letter of the contract violated? No, I don't think it was. I think the spirit was violated. These contracts are hard fought. Ken was very vocal and upset about this. No question about that."

Shamrock and Donohoo, on the morning of the fight, looked to renegotiate their deal with Elite XC and convince the promotion to live up to the spirit of their arrangement. They tracked down Lappen and Pro Elite CEO Chuck Champion and proceeded to lay their grievances out in a animated, but controlled manner.

"Ken was not happy and felt that he should get more money," Lappen, who was once Shamrock's agent, says. "So we had some meetings about that. And we actually did re-negotiate his deal to some extent to try and satisfy him. I think we gave him some commentary opportunities and things to placate him. We weren't paying anybody more money on the card—that was a fight that wasn't ours. We didn't have any control over that.

"He was upset. I don't think it was that crazy of a discussion. I had long history with Ken at that point. I had a lot of respect for him and I think he had respect for me. I dealt with him a lot and he's a good guy and there were no problems negotiating the deal. And I was sort of trying to get Ken to, I don't want to say calm down because he wasn't crazed or anything, but to sort of relax and take a look and try to see it from our perspective. And sort of, try to make him happy with the situation and we went back and forth and at the end of the day I

---

[397] Despite media reports that he was upset about Kimbo's pay, all parties agree it was Arlovski's hefty paycheck that prompted the discussion.

thought he was happy with it. It seemed like he was placated and was ready to fight."

Shamrock's head was in a bad place already. Bob Shamrock had slipped into a coma, slowly losing a long battle with diabetes. He'd suffered a massive heart attack in September and ended up having a six-way bypass surgery. Shamrock had spent much of his training camp at his adopted father's bedside, the fight not coming close to being at the top of his priorities list.

"From that time until the Kimbo fight we were living in the hospital," Tonya says. "The day of the fight, Ken got a phone call to make a decision about whether or not we wanted to pull him off life support or not. Ken's like 'I can't make that decision today. I'm going in to fight.' It was a terrible time."

Looking to burn off some steam, Shamrock grabbed longtime training partner Dan Freeman and went through what he called a "light workout' in his hotel room.

"We moved all the stuff out of the way in the hotel suite and started rolling around," Shamrock said. "Easy stuff like you'd do in the locker room to warm up. Just to get my mind back on the fight. As I had his back, my head came down just as he popped his head up. Boom. He caught my eye. It wasn't really that hard, and we even kept moving."

Shamrock thought nothing of it—until he saw the blood streaming down his face in his peripheral vision and was suddenly facing a worst case scenario. Shamrock rushed to the Cleveland Clinic with his personal doctor and ended up making a fateful decision that would do both himself and the promotion irrevocable harm. Eight sutures later, his night was over. There was no way he'd be able to fight.

"I'm not a fighter, but from what I've seen normally people aren't rolling hard in their hotel room the day of the fight where they could be banging heads with each other to get cut, so that's weird," Lappen says. "When something like that happens, if a person wants to fight they don't go to the hospital and get stitches and then have somebody in their camp call you and say they can't fight. Normally fighters would be so concerned about not being able to fight if they got a cut, they would glue it together or hide it from the commission to see if they could fight. To try and sneak it in.

"Instead, I got a call that they were already at the hospital, they had already gotten stitches and they were telling me they couldn't fight. Not asking the commission if they could fight, not anything. They told me they couldn't fight. His personal doctor called me from the hospital and said 'Ken got cut, we're here at the hospital. He already got stitches. He won't be able to fight.' This is before the commission even knew about it."

Things were tense as the Elite XC team waited at the loading docks for Shamrock's return to the arena, claiming he still wanted to fight. When they saw him, hope mostly vanished.

"Come on man," someone who was present that day says. "He's an O.G. of the fight game. And he handled this like a rookie. No one believed it was a coincidence. Some people are simple. Someone like Frank or Kimbo, they want money. If you give them what they want, they show up. It's simple.

"Someone like Ken is more complicated. Did he need the money badly? Yes. But would he throw that away over principle if he thought someone was screwing him over? I think he might. You have to remember that these are fighters. There are people in this game who don't think or act like regular people. Their clock ticks a little different."

Fury at Shamrock[398] would have to wait, though it would come, with accusations ranging from claims he cut himself open pro wrestling style to the allegation that he knew exactly what would happen when he got stitches and did it to hurt the show when he didn't get what he wanted. Eventually the commission would confirm Shamrock's doctor's intuition—the World's Most Dangerous Man wouldn't be able to fight.

In the immediate aftermath, chaos reigned.

"The panic level? It was at the highest level you could imagine," Ranallo says. "There were talks the show might be canceled. You don't know what was happening, but it was chaos. I felt bad, I felt bad for everybody involved. Selfishly, you're like 'gosh darn it, man.' You want to be a part of something like this knowing what people like the new CBS entertainment chief Kelly Kahl had risked to bring martial arts to major network television. Remember this is before Fox would deal with UFC.

"It was a catastrophe. I remember Chuck Champion trying to make everybody relax in the back. He's probably feeling it more than anybody but he had to devote time to making sure everyone else was okay. You look back knowing what you know now and, okay, life goes

---

[398] Afterwards, Frank Shamrock told people that he thought Ken may have bladed, cutting himself with a razor blade pro wrestling style.

on. But there was some high drama there in the arena. People were freaking out."

As bad as it was to lose Shamrock from the main event, Lappen knew that things could get worse. They needed a replacement fight, whatever it took to keep Kimbo on the card and the audience appeased, both at home on television and in the arena.

"We were gonna do a great rating," he says. "Kimbo was a huge star then and it was in Miami so everybody came to see Kimbo. It was terrible to lose Ken. But we were really worried about announcing that Kimbo wasn't fighting. If there would be riots. It was a big deal."

A lot of options were considered and an unlikely possibility emerged from behind the broadcast desk. Ken's estranged brother Frank was on the call as the color commentator, sitting at a production meeting a couple of days before the fight while Ken ran him down right to his face. But, for the purposes of telling an emotionally resonant story, he was willing to ride to his brother's rescue and take on Kimbo for the drama of the moment if nothing else.

"Frank Shamrock on that day tried to save the show," Ranallo says. "He knew that there were dollar signs and story lines. Frank was always about business. Frank always wanted the most compelling story line. Otherwise, why are we watching?

"He got it right away. This has gotta be entertainment as much as anything else. You've got to capture the imagination of the casual fan. What better story line than Ken Shamrock's brother there at the broadcast table, who's much smaller, unprepared, but willing to save the day and willing to represent the Shamrock name? It would have been a beautiful story."

But Frank, willing or not, was on a medical suspension in California, courtesy of a Cung Le kick that shattered his forearm. Officials were worried that he hadn't trained and that the fight would be ugly. Instead, they turned to Seth Petruzelli, a kick boxer on the undercard who was happy to step up into the main event.

"I was warming up for my undercard fight and I was about 45 minutes from going out for my match," Petruzelli said. "They told me Ken Shamrock was hurt and offered me the Kimbo fight and I accepted right away. I thought it would be awesome. The nerves actually kind of went away when they offered me that fight. I was nervous about my undercard fight, but the pressure kind of went away because there was nothing to lose. It was a win-win situation. I was taking it on short notice so if I went out there and lost, well, I did my best."

The entire spectacle lasted all of 14 seconds. With the world watching, the unheralded upstart crushed the King of the Streets in less time than it takes to read this paragraph, the entire MMA world changing in 14 blinks of the eye.

"All I remember is him rushing me. And I saw his chin stick out," Petruzelli said. "I was trying to throw a push kick and his chin stuck out and I threw kind of like a jab hook and caught him right on his chin. He went down to his knees and all I remember was seeing the blood on the ground and following up. I kept going and going and going. I knew if I just kept punching him the ref was going to have to jump in."

At ringside, Elite XC official Jared Shaw, son of deposed promoter Gary Shaw, screamed at the official for stopping the fight so soon. But there was nothing that could be done. Kimbo Slice, the biggest ratings attraction in mixed martial arts, had lost to a fighter no one had ever heard of.

"I was there cageside and watched the whole thing happen," Elite XC's T.J. Thompson told *MMA Weekly*. "I think (CBS) got cold feet watching. The way the Ken Shamrock pullout was handled, all the way from the beginning to the end with Seth Petruzelli. Watching Jared Shaw jumping up and down and screaming as a representative of the company, I think (it) was disgusting and embarrassing."

For a moment, as Lappen had hoped, things seemed like they might be okay. Even without Shamrock, the show had drawn more than 4.5 million viewers for CBS with the Slice fight exceeding six million. It didn't top their initial offering, but it was proof of concept that MMA could work on network television, even when things got weird.

Then Petruzelli started doing the media rounds and shook up the MMA world again, suggesting that Elite XC had tried to create an environment for Kimbo to succeed.

"The promoters kind of hinted to me, and they gave me the money to stand and trade with him," Seth Petruzelli told *The Monsters in the Morning* radio show in Orlando. "They didn't want me to take him down, let's just put it that way. It was worth my while to try to stand up and punch with him."

In some ways it was an allegation that didn't make sense. Shamrock was a ground specialist and would have surely attempted furiously to take Kimbo to the mat. Slice had been training with former Shamrock foe Bas Rutten with that expectation and would have been ready for Petruzelli to come at him with a similar gameplan.

"Dana White made a big deal about this alleged bribe," one Elite XC employee says. "That never happened. Someone told Seth 'hey, we need a good show. Go out and give them their money's worth and have an exciting fight.' It happens all the time at every boxing and MMA show to this day. Dana did the same thing. He offered a cash bonus for delivering a knockout. How is that any different? It's semantics."

But whether true or not, the mere hint of impropriety, combined with Shaw's antics cageside, caused the Florida State Athletic Commission to open an investigation into the claim, giving CBS a reason to walk away from buying Elite XC. The promotion may have been bleeding out long before they'd ever signed Ken Shamrock—but it died that night in Miami, killing the potential "Blood Brothers" pay-per-view between the Shamrock brothers right along with it.[399]

"It always blows my mind how things actually end up getting done in this world and for whatever reason, Ken and Frank never did put that fight together and so it goes," Ranallo says. "I really believe Frank has an amazing mind for business and I think it would have benefited both of them if it actually did happen.

"It would have been a spectacle fight. I think that it would have done well, I really do. I think at the time, just who they were and what they represented, and again the storyline, the background, it would have been a good fight and I think it would have been good for their pocketbooks. Which at the end of the day is what we do this for anyway."

Before the Kimbo debacle, Frank made the trip to see Bob for what ended up being the final time at the hospital in Reno. He appeared to be on the mend when he eventually had to be put on dialysis and had his leg amputated. As he got sicker, Bob asked for Frank often. Though the two had never truly reconciled after Frank's explosive departure from the Lion's Den, Bob talked about him often. He could be moved to tears discussing the circumstances of their separation and longed for something to bring both his adopted sons together again.

While many people dismissed the fight as a crass attempt at a

---

[399] Frank's contract was with Strikeforce, a promotion that ended up buying some of Elite XC's assets and inheriting its deal with Showtime and CBS. And Ken Shamrock was persona non grata at Showtime/CBS in the fallout of the Kimbo mess, making the fight all but impossible to stage.

money grab, it was deeply personal for the whole family.[400] Bob, in particular, told many people that his two sons could only bring peace to the family and come back together if they squared off in the cage. But the universe never quite aligned that way, though both brothers continued talking about it long after it seemed to be a distant memory to everyone else.

"Frank was the one that backed out every time," Ken says. "Every single time he backed out of it. That was personal. I wanted him bad. I wanted to beat on him. It's hard. I was in his head. I rented space in his head. I mean, I thumped on him for so long, I dominated him for so long. Even as I got older, that's still in his head.

"I couldn't stand how he treated our dad. Somebody who did so much for him. Now maybe there was a reason for it. I don't know. All I know is that my dad was dying and my dad asked for him and he wouldn't come."

---

[400] "Not only was there money—there were Hollywood players in the meeting that wanted to make a movie of the Shamrock story based around the fight," Lance Foreman wrote. "This was only a couple of months after Bob Shamrock died. I can assure you Ken wanted that fight more than any other. Bob Shamrock wanted the fight to take place as well and had hopes of the brothers making up after the contest no matter who won."

CHAPTER TWENTY
World Tour of Sadness

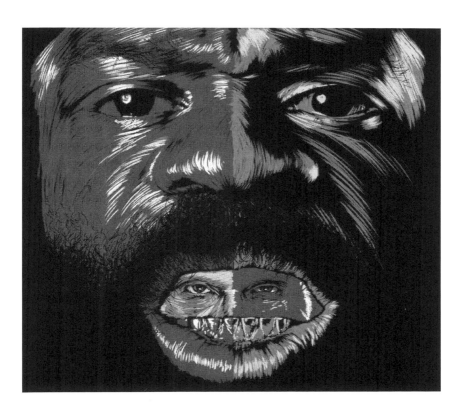

Nothing much had changed in Ken's world professionally after the Kimbo incident. Instead of convincing him it was time to hang up the gloves, the debacle actually hardened Shamrock's resolve. The tax burden wasn't going anywhere and he needed a payday to stay afloat. Physically, he could feel the sand passing through the hourglass every day, so he committed to the business of getting the most out of the fight game while he still could.

"Ken's one of those guys, man, he doesn't stress about adversity," his nephew Jeff says. "He just goes right through it. That actually taught me a lot on how to take on life, because I mean, no matter what, trouble is gonna be there. It's all about how you look at it, your perspective on it. You can choose to be stressed out about situations but what he taught me was that it's all about what you do with it. Your actions speak louder than words do, and if you want to do something about it, then do something about it."

Shamrock's relationship with religion helped inform his newly calm demeanor. His faith infused every part of his life and he shared his story so often at churches that his team formed the non-profit Lion's Den Ministries in 2009.

"Tough men," he would tell people, "submit to Jesus."

In the fallout from the Elite XC disaster Donohoo, who once had plenty of offers to sort through, had to go out in search of a fight. Miraculously, he found one, a bout with fellow WWE refugee Bobby Lashley for Roy Jones Junior's Square Ring Promotions in March 2009.

"Despite all that was going on, we were able to get Ken a very good agreement," Donohoo says. "We talked to Roy personally, and I talked to John Wirt who ran the company. We had a really good contract negotiated with the Lashley fight. I was very, very pleased with that. And then, Ken took a fight I didn't not want him to take. Ken felt he needed to do this for his family. He was trying to get something going. I wanted him with a bigger promotion. That's what *I* wanted."

Ken, however, had different ideas and was still looking to move into the promotional end of the game. Before the Lashley fight could go down, he made the fateful decision to partner with Wargods for a tuneup fight in February against an unknown patsy. The end goal was clear—a long-awaited match with Tank Abbott on pay-per-view with

Ken as the promoter.

"I get a call from Tank Abbott," trainer Lance Foreman says. "And I'm like, 'You want to fight Ken for Wargods?' He was like, 'Fuck yeah. Who doesn't want to fight Ken these days?' I'm thinking 'Good, Ken is going to whip your fat ass for saying that, dude.'"

The show, with both Ken and Tank fighting carefully chosen opponents, was a complete mess, with four of the 12 fights falling through at the last minute due to issues with the athletic commission and unhappy fighters. At one point they were threatening to shut the event down and Abbott simply picked up and went home.

"I get there and these guys are telling me, 'Tank, he left like two hours ago.' Because the commission told him they wouldn't sanction the show," Foreman says. "That's the freaking UFC behind that we thought. That was when they didn't like any other promotions doing anything.

"I called Tank 'hey bro, fuck the commission. Since when do you listen to them? Dude, we're on contract. Your opponent is here, bro. You got to get your ass back up here.' And he did. He was pissed because he had to drive.

"His corner was really bad. Some old dude that didn't even know how to put a boxing glove on. He had a towel and a damn container with orange juice and vodka in it. I told Tank, 'Like bro, do you need a corner, do you need some help? Get your hands wrapped?' He was like, 'No man, I'm fine.' He was just pacing back and forth in his room and I could smell the alcohol. I'm thinking 'this fucking guy is for real, man.' Then he goes out and knocks out that Mike Bourke in 30 seconds."

Shamrock's opponent Ross Clifton, an enormously overweight 395-pound heavyweight[401] the announcers cracked joke after joke about, went down with the first right hand and was quickly arm barred. The entire charade lasted exactly one minute and Ken earned $25,000—but paid a heavy price. After the fight, the now 45-year-old Shamrock was suspended for one year after testing positive for the steroid Stanazolol, as well as two other substances, 19-Norandrosterone and 19-Noretiocholanolone.

"Later in life, when I got older and had the neck injury, the shoulder problems, the back, the knee. Yeah, I had a hard time," Shamrock says.

---

[401] Clifton would die of a heart attack at 32 that September.

"I did some things to try to mask injuries. I loved what I did, and I didn't want to let it go. The competition, the fight, the fans, the attention. It's a drug. Don't let anybody tell you anything different. No one will ever be able to tell you you can't fight anymore. Until you have the belief it's over, it's never over. It has to be you. And I didn't believe it yet."

On January 14, 2010, Bob Shamrock passed away at Ken's home, family and friends there to hold his hand.

"He was on dialysis and ended up losing his leg," Tonya says. "We tried to get him into rehab after he lost his leg but he just lost the motivation to live. He told us 'I'm just done. I'm done fighting.' He asked us to take him off the dialysis machine and we brought him back to our house. He was gone within a week."

Bob, famous for his generous spirit and bad jokes, was playful to the very end, even when robbed of his voice.

"The night before he passed away I was actually at my dad's house when they brought him home," Shamrock's daughter Fallon says. "I remember we were sitting there and he couldn't really speak but everyone was around his bed and everyone was crying. He hit the button to lower his headrest and made one of my uncles kind of fall forward and he got a really big smile on his face. That was his sense of humor at the very end."

While he was most famous for his time guiding his adopted sons through the pitfalls and glories of the strange world of mixed martial arts, it was the Boys Ranch that was his true legacy. Over the years Bob helped hundreds of foster children find their path in life in Anza, Hemet, Susanville and Lockeford, California. While the media focused often on Ken and Frank, the Boys Ranch had dozens of success stories, kids who were one step away from prison or worse but just needed a helping hand to gently (or not so gently when the occasion warranted) guide them back onto the right path.

"We talked on the phone all the time," Dave Cranney, who spent time at Bob Shamrock's Boys Ranch says. "I called him 'pops.' All of us did that knew him. We called him 'pops.' He's sorely missed. I know Ken probably misses him because it wasn't until the end that they started making up fully...I think that gave Bob peace to go ahead and pass away because they did mend that fence."

About 200 people attended the funeral service, with more than 30 sharing stories of how Bob had touched their lives, including several former foster kids. A treacherous snowstorm kept many more away, closing the Donner Summit on Interstate 80.

From death, so often, springs life—and this was no different. Bob's illness and passing brought Dee Dee Barth, Bob's ex-wife and Ken's former foster mother back into the Shamrocks' lives. Ken hadn't seen her since she left in his teens and, for years, had held a grudge for her abrupt departure. But the two reconciled and today Dee Dee is the newest member of the Shamrock inner circle.

"I called Tonya and she said, 'You know, he's non-responsive right now, but let's put the phone up to his ear and you go ahead and talk to him.' So I did," Dee Dee says. "I said, 'Bob, you know, so sorry for all those years that we didn't contact each other. I'm sorry for everything,' and asked his forgiveness for leaving and, 'I know that caused pain for you and I'm so sorry.'

"I sang to him, because I'm a singer, and just talked to him about heaven and that he was about to go there and it was all right for him to go and that I would see him again one day. Tonya said that the whole time I was talking to him his face was moving and he was trying to respond. He died the next day. Ken was grateful, because he thinks that I played a very important role in Bob's death. I ushered him into heaven, I believe, and so I felt really good about that, that I had that opportunity."

While his death repaired one fractured relationship, it drove a wedge further between Ken and his foster brother. Frank didn't show up for the funeral, angering those closest to Bob, who say he asked often about seeing his son.

"Bob wanted to be able to say his piece to Frank," Tonya says. "And know that whatever conflict they had was over."

Instead, the two never truly reconnected—Frank called, but only after Bob had already slipped into a coma. The two brothers discussed it all publicly, on a mesmerizing Spike TV special called *Bound by Blood*.

"Frank had a choice about how he wanted to react or handle it," Ken said. "He left him laying there, not allowing him to go in peace. I just can't understand how somebody can just blow somebody off. What did he do to him to cause Frank to not go to his funeral? I mean, come on man."

A tearful Frank tried to explain why he didn't pay his respects to the man who had rescued him from the scrap heap of society and set him on the path to success.

"I didn't know what to do," Frank said. "I really regret not calling him because I still think about him all the time. Every time I see my name. He was my daddy.

"Bro, I was so damaged when dad passed, I couldn't even deal with that moment. I didn't even know what to do. And the hardest thing in the world was not to go. I did that out of respect. That's what I thought it was supposed to do.[402]"

Ken dealt with his father's passing the same way he'd dealt with almost any adversity in his life. He strapped on the gloves and fought. After serving a one-year suspension for his positive drug test, it was right back into the cage for a man who had literally been fighting since the sport was born.

Of course, as had become customary, there wasn't much choice. The couple still owed hundreds of thousands of dollars in back taxes and in February got the devastating news that he had lost his lawsuit against the UFC. Worse, based on the contract terms, that meant he was obligated to pay Zuffa's legal fees and court expenses, totalling $175,000.

"It was a tough time," his lawyer Rod Donohoo says. "He'd say, 'Look I got to make a living, Rod. This is what I do. It's all I can do.' It was just a really, really, really tough time for him and I hated to see that. It broke my heart to see that because you know, he was so much better than that.

"You look at their history of great, great, great fighters but in the end they ended up in fights in Tijuana towards the end of their career. But, they're not known for that. They're known for something else. They're known for the greatness of their heyday. But, it's not an uncommon thing to see. It is something that Ken kind of went through to try to do what he could to make a living for his family."

The first fight of what would become his 2010 world tour was in

---

[402] "You're a coward," was Ken's response. Though they've done an occasional appearance together since, the two are not close. After an initial interview, Frank declined further participation in this book.

July for Impact FC in Australia. The event struggled from the jump, overpromising and underdelivering. Just days before the show, they cancelled on several fighters, unable to afford their airfare then, after, had trouble paying the ones who did show up to compete in front of a mostly empty, quiet building.

It was a who's who of fighting—as it existed a decade earlier. At a normal event, Ken's opponent, a well-used former UFC contender named Pedro Rizzo, would have been the cautionary tale, a 36-year-old still out there grinding away far from the sport's limelight. But Ken had a decade on him, and though he got the best reaction from the crowd, it was nostalgia mixed with hints of sadness.

Shamrock came into the bout with a plan, looking to convince Rizzo that he'd be attempting to take him down and submit him. Instead, he was going to try to beat the Brazilian at his own game and win or lose on the power of his right hand.

"Ken's knees were bad," trainer Foreman says. "He couldn't do anything on the ground. So all the time we were doing combination punches. Ken couldn't kick nothing. He was not really healthy for that. But when the camera and other people were around we were pretending we were training nothing but grappling. But, the whole time we were saying 'Cannon.' All these combinations. Shamrock's got a two, three combination that would a knock out a fricking rhinoceros."

But once the fight started, the gig was up. Shamrock, after barely missing with a right hand, caught a leg kick early and didn't even really attempt a takedown. For the kickboxer, that was like getting the green light.

"His corner was telling him to pull up a chair because Ken is going to take him down," Foreman says. "But he threw a kick to keep Ken off of him and Ken didn't do anything to take him down.

"I was looking at Rizzo's corner, and I seen him like, 'he's not going to take you down, he's not going to take you down. Start kicking, start kicking.' Me and Dan Freeman were like 'oh shit.' He just started to turn Ken's leg into hamburger meat and Ken never got close to him again."

After several unchecked kicks, Shamrock dropped to one knee and grimaced. But referee "Big" John McCarthy, perhaps cautious not to get caught up in now patented "Ken Shamrock early stoppage drama," allowed Rizzo to drop a couple of punches before finally stepping in to stop the fight.

In the ring, announcer Elvis Sinosic, an Australian MMA pioneer who had once fought Shamrock's student Matt Rocca, asked the obvious question. Was this it for the legend? "As long as people want to see me," Shamrock said, "I'll continue to get beat up."

"It was strange, almost a pro wrestling vibe after a real beating," Sinosic says. "It was almost desperate like he didn't want to be left behind."

The next stop was in Lafayette, Louisiana, for a local promotion called USA MMA. They put more than 2000 fans into the Cajundome[403] but, aside from a fierce fight in the crowd during the first round, they didn't get a great show out of the main event.

Shamrock's opponent, a 5'9", 250-pound local journeyman named Johnathan Ivey was deferential to a fault, like many second generation MMA fighters a creation of the world that Ken helped build.

"I was a big Ken Shamrock fan," Ivey said. "At UFC 8 against Kimo he had worn wrestling shoes with the socks pulled all the way up to his knees for friction. For the first couple years of my career I wore wrestling shoes with the socks pulled all the way up, trying to be like Ken Shamrock. *Tapout* magazine called me the 'Leglock Master.' I was a big fan of who Ken Shamrock was and who he is."

The fight itself was a lackluster 15 minutes, with Shamrock looking mostly to counter and Ivey shell-shocked by the moment.[404] The most potent offense of the fight was a third-round Shamrock eye poke, though Ivey did manage to knock the legend down with an overhand left to close the second stanza. Much of the Shamrock entourage missed most of the fight altogether, petrified by what could happen.

"I showed up in Louisiana to watch him fight," family friend Tom Casey says. "It had been four years since I'd been to a fight because I'd vowed never to do it. He actually won, but only because that guy was so bad really. I spent the fight in the lobby holding Tonya's hand as she

---

[403] "Looking over the rowdy audience, it was clear that overly-printed t-shirts and sparkly jeans are to 2010 MMA as mullets were to UFC 1," Bloodycajunmma wrote. "One can always tell one's at an MMA show when it looks like an invasion from Jersey Shore."

[404] "I just had it in my head for whatever reason that he was going to shoot on me for sure," Ivey said. "This is Ken Shamrock, the guy I had gone to Blockbuster for, to rent all his tapes. I was expecting Ken to shoot on me and get me in a submission. So, I kept waiting for him to shoot. He never did. He never did."

cried her eyes out. He was getting ready to go in the ring and she knew he shouldn't be fighting. She cried because they were doing it for the money. It was just horrible. I told them 'I love you but I can't be part of it.'"

Ivey was the king of viral MMA and delivered a memorable moment at the end of the third round, doing two consecutive forward somersaults. Theoretically he was in search of a fight-stealing leg lock, but he didn't come anywhere near a confused Ken. While it might not have lived up to previous stunts like dropping a People's Elbow or landing a Karate Kid style crane kick in a real fight, it made certain the otherwise forgettable fight lived forever—at least as an internet meme.

Barely a month later on November 25, 2010, Shamrock was back in the cage for his third fight of the year, this time across the world in Durban, South Africa, at King of the Cage. For Ken, the opportunity was about more than fighting. It was a chance to share his redemption story, this time with his foster mother by his side.

"Ken loves to share his testimony and he has a story to tell when he goes into churches," Dee Dee says. "I had the privilege of ministering with him. I sang before he came up to speak. A mother/son team. That's my dream, that I can really minister with Ken and perhaps bring in my part of the story to share too, so that even older people will understand where he's come from, what makes him who he is today, and what God has done in his life."

The opponent couldn't have been *more* carefully chosen. The Shamrock team had seen Mike Bourke fall down against Tank Abbott on their own Wargods show in 2009 and he'd managed to put together a remarkable record of 2-12-1 in his last 15 fights.

But there was no opponent safe enough at this point in his career—the real rival in every Ken Shamrock fight since his return from WWE was his own body. Shamrock managed to knock Bourke down almost immediately but tore his hamstring in the scramble that followed as he looked for the kill.

"Thirty seconds in, Ken drops him...hits him with a straight right and drops him," Foreman says. "This fight was fixing to be over. He's on the mat and he grabs Ken's foot, and Ken turns to get out of it and his hamstring rips. Me and Dan Freeman were in the corner and we saw it. And we were like 'oh shit, man,' and Ken looked at us and he knew.

"I've never seen a leg so bruised up the next day. He went to the hospital. It got to where we don't want Ken to get hurt because when you're older it's really hard to heal up."

With pain overwhelming him, Shamrock ended up on his back with Bourke on top. Holding on for dear life, he attempted to push the bigger man off, only to grab his left leg in agony. The official had seen enough and, like that, the professional fall guy had the biggest win of his life and Ken Shamrock was, once again, struggling to make sense of a life where he was losing to the Mike Bourke's of the world.

When he got home and went to the doctor, the night, somehow, got even worse. Going into a fight hurt and mobility-impaired had become so normal, the pain such a regular feature in his life, that he'd barely even noticed a broken back.

"I tore my hamstring but my back was bothering me before the fight. I got it checked later on and they told me I'd fractured it," Shamrock says. "There's brackets in there from one to seven metal brackets that clamp my spine, my back. Same with my lower back. One, two, three."

With the Bourke fight, regular life began to descend on the Shamrocks. After years of essentially working in the family business as Ken's de facto business manager/personal assistant/consigliere, Tonya returned to the working world to make sure the Shamrocks had what they needed to survive—namely health insurance.

The $3000 they were paying a month for a poor plan was no longer going to cut it, especially as the wear on his body started catching up with Ken. The transition wasn't easy for anyone. At one point one of his kids was shoplifting sheets from Wal Mart to help Sean who lived occasionally out of his car. In San Diego, Tina sometimes struggled to keep afloat without money from fighting continuing to flow.

"There was a time when I couldn't even afford to get a yearbook because we were really tight on money," Shamrock's daughter Fallon says. "She was really upset she couldn't get that for me. We would struggle to get school pictures and new clothes for school. It was lot of hand-me-downs. I would wear some of my brothers' hand-me-down t-shirts and shoes. My mom would try to get us stuff when she could but it was struggle. There were days when we had a fridge full of food and days when we had to find what we could find."

Shamrock was so used to his wife's guiding hand on his back that simply making the towns for appearances and autograph signings became a struggle. Tonya, quite often, ends up doing double duty, a pillar of the Ken Shamrock business even as she deals with health problems of her own.

"Even though I'm working full time, I still have to stay in control of certain aspects of the business," Tonya says. "That's something we learned the hard way.[405] It was really hard on Ken because I controlled everything. I was the person they came to to book events, I scheduled the plane tickets. I ran everything.

"And when I couldn't travel with him, it was hard because he was used to me doing everything for him. There were times he was pissed. 'Why aren't you here with me?' I'm like 'you're a grown man. You need to figure this out.' I can't always be there."

Fighting was still there in the background, his name often attached to projects that never quite materialized. There was a potential legends tournament talent agent Rick Bassman was trying to put together, a hybrid rules fight with James Toney where he would only have 30 seconds to work on the ground against the boxing Hall of Famer, even a scheduled bout in Orlando that fell through when Ken got a bad staph infection—lots of smoke, but no fire.[406]

Another neck surgery followed the work he'd had done on his back, Tonya's solid new health plan paying serious dividends as Ken attempted to repair years of abuse. He sold the gym in Reno in March 2011, putting the Lion's Den to rest once and for all, and began to prepare for whatever life's next adventure turned out to be.[407] Unfortunately, it was heart trouble, as three separate incidents gave the family scares.

"It's a family issue. His brother has had four strokes," Tonya says.

---

[405] A series of bad investments including a failed foray into the gym business and a collection of even worse business advisors have all contributed to the Shamrocks' financial pain. They have lost hundreds of thousands of dollars thanks to unscrupulous or incompetent people in their circle.

[406] The closest he came to a fight was breaking up a slugfest between two women at the mall in 2012, inadvertently knocking one of them to the ground, which resulted in a slew of headlines from MMA websites looking for a few easy clicks.

[407] At 49, he pushed hard for another shot at WWE but there was no real interest from the promotion. Shamrock would eventually blame Triple H for blackballing him, telling the Mark Henry "shit sandwich" story publicly in a number of media appearances.

"I think Hunter had a real hard time dealing with that, especially with me being a real bad ass otherwise and there's nothing he could do about it," he told the Wrestling Glory Days podcast. "Then, opening my mouth to protect another human being, I think there is ribbing and there is having fun, there are things when you cross over the line, and so I said something."

"The first time he had water around the heart and he had a flutter. The top part of the heart is just fluttering. It's not beating correctly. That's why the fluid gathered around his heart, because it's just sitting there fluttering. So, they go in and do an electric shock type thing on your heart. It deadens the part of the heart that's continuously fluttering. They were able to go in and do an ablation.[408] The second time they were able to do another ablation because there was still the flutter.

"The third time he went in, he was in afib. That's the other part of the heart that is not beating correctly. It's a different chamber of the heart. Well, they went in and did an angiogram and found 98 percent blockage. So they had to put a stent[409] in."

Despite the heart issues and the creaking joints all over, giving up fighting turned out to be hard. He signed for a bout in Doncaster, England, against Ian Freeman, eventually walking away from the fight when the promoter didn't meet the payment schedule they'd set up to make sure he was taken care of.

Shamrock had learned the hard way that things can get dicey if you wait to get your money after the fight and wanted his purse put into escrow in increments to make sure he was covered if the event ended up not meeting the promoter's financial expectations. It was his practice to ask for a $5,000 retainer to enter serious conversations, something that infuriated some promoters used to fighters being less active in protecting their own interests.[410]

Scott Coker was a different kind of promoter. His Strikeforce brand, initially powered by Frank Shamrock's ability to draw a crowd in his hometown of San Jose, California, had eventually become so

---

[408] Catheter ablation is a procedure used to remove or terminate a faulty electrical pathway from sections of the hearts of those who are prone to developing cardiac arrhythmias such as atrial fibrillation, atrial flutter, supraventricular tachycardias and Wolff-Parkinson-White syndrome.

[409] A stent is a tiny wire mesh tube that is inserted into a narrowed or blocked coronary artery. The coronary arteries feed blood and oxygen to heart.

[410] The flip side to this according to one promoter: "In the industry, back in the day when you were about ready to go into the fight and the fighter wanted to renegotiate, they called it 'the Ken Shamrock move.'"

formidable that UFC chose to buy them out rather than compete. After a non-compete clause kept him out of the business for several years, he was back, running Bellator on Spike TV, and with UFC cornering the market on top contenders, he was looking for anything and anyone to spark an interest in the MMA community.

At an autograph signing, Shamrock[411] pointed at Royce Gracie and told Coker, "I want to fight that guy." Coker nearly fell out of his chair.

"I thought he was kidding," he says. "I asked, 'Wait, are you still interested in fighting?' The next thing I asked was 'Would you fight Kimbo Slice?' And he said 'I'd love that fight.'"

Coker had no intention of pushing either Shamrock or Slice into title contention. Instead, the two big names were intended to be a bridge—to connect lapsed fans to the promotion's crop of exciting young fighters the way Ken had done with Tito Ortiz in the UFC.

"We do some fights like this that I call fun fights for the general fan and other fights for the hardcore fan. We have something for everybody," Coker said. "The fun fights we do are designed to cast a net for the audience that used to be there.

"The beauty of all those eyeballs is that they'll get to see Pitbull [featherweight champion Patricio Freire] and they'll get to see Michael Chandler...We're going to build stars every time we have one of these fun fights. We're really going after it."

In the *Wrestling Observer*, Dave Meltzer spoke for many in the community,[412] drawing a hard line. This, he said, was not okay:

> Simply put, he has no business fighting. This is from somebody who personally likes him, understands that he probably will draw TV viewers one last time, and could use a nice payday.
>
> Fighting isn't fun and games. Taking punches to

---

[411] Shamrock, at this point, was working with a new business partner named Des Woodruff. Des, a "business leader and dynamic entrepreneur" from Indiana who Ken met when sharing his story at a church service there, had no experience in the fight business.

[412] "This was the bearded lady or the lobster boy," Jack Slack wrote at *FightLand*. "Just a freak show to get people in the door and to grab the ratings. Another Mickey Rourke versus homeless man...You have to respect Scott Coker for being the man willing to make a laughing stock of his product in the educated fan's eyes just to cater to that."

the head is never good for you. With each successive year, it gets worse and worse. Nearly ten years ago, when the much smaller Kazushi Sakuraba turned his lights out with one punch, he reached that point.

While fans and media seemed shocked every time Shamrock decided to step back into the cage[413], no one in his family was ever really surprised.

"He's going to be 80 years old and walking to the ring with an oxygen mask," his son Sean said. "He's gonna do it until he can't no more. It's exciting that he's getting back to what he loves to do. It's like things are back to normal."

Shamrock had reconciled himself to life without fighting, giving himself to the mercy of God. He went to Modesto, California, for an extended religious awakening, engulfing himself in the Word. Shamrock realized that he had squandered a gift that he'd been given and, once he fully appreciated what he had, held it too tight when every sign was telling him to move on.

"I took what God gave me and I put it above him," Shamrock says. "I was grasping on to what he gave me so hard that I forgot that he was the one who gave it to me."

It was only when willing to let go and submit himself to God's authority, he believes, that he was given another chance to pursue his passion.

While best known as a prize fighter, Ken's life encompassed so much more than that when he made his return to the cage in 2015. Shamrock was living a double life of sorts. He was a devoted husband and grandfather, with some of those grandkids spending time living with him and Tonya as their parents navigated troubled waters.

"Ken has this big, tender heart," his foster mother Dee Dee Barth says. "He can beat the living daylights out of a person in the ring, but you see him with his grandchildren, you see where his heart really is today. He's a loving man who'd do anything for those kids. I think also he's probably making up for a loss of a lot of things that he didn't do for his own children.

"He was apart from them a lot growing up, and so now he can do

---

[413] He had briefly been the talk of the fight world when he was seen at CES as rapper 50 Cent's bodyguard. But that was Ken kicking the tires on an investment opportunity, not a new vocation.

that for his grandchildren. He loves them dearly and he's so invested in their lives. It's a joy to see this big, old, muscular guy holding his grandbaby and loving on them."

At the same time, he was still *Ken Shamrock*. They'd all seen him struggle through his daily life, fully aware both that he wasn't the man he once was and that he was not fully willing to accept that. Even with every voice in his life telling him to walk away, Shamrock felt the call of the ring.

"He's had neck surgery, back surgery, he can't lift. He's had his shoulder filleted open," Tonya says. "If he gets taken down, he can't push up to get himself out. There's a lot of things that he's very limited on when he's fighting because of the surgeries he's had and the injuries. He knows that it's been harder for me to watch, because I know that the injuries can be more severe as he gets older. But he's not gonna stop until he wants to stop, you know?"

To escape the daily chaos of his regular life, Shamrock moved his training camp to his old stomping grounds in San Diego, where he lived out of the family's motor home while he prepared for yet another second chance[414]:

> Next to the bed in his Windsport motor home, parked behind a discount tire store in suburban San Diego, "The World's Most Dangerous Man" has a Bible and a Glock.
>
> "That's the American way," Ken Shamrock says, breaking into a smile with just enough malice to make you wonder. "Me and my Bible will beat the faith into you."
>
> There are no luxuries here.
>
> "Because of who I am and what I've accomplished, everything is pretty much given to me," Shamrock says. "People cater to me all the time. It's almost like I've lost that edge—lost the ability to want something and then put in the work necessary to get it.
>
> "I have to earn whatever it is I get from here on

---

[414] I traveled to San Diego to write a story about his latest comeback for *Bleacher Report*. It was the genesis of this book. He told me at the time "You know more about my career than I do," and we went from there, proving that wasn't quite true.

out. Right now I don't even have running water in that trailer. I have to go and shower at the gym. Shave at the gym. I have to bring in water in jugs in order to have water to boil for food. It's been rough."

Ken did the bulk of his training at the San Diego Combat Academy, really two repurposed bays in an automobile repair shop. Instead of rebuilding engines, they build fighters, even reclamation projects like Shamrock.

For Shamrock the camp, despite being miles from home, was a family affair. His new team was headed up by two familiar faces—former Lion's Den fighter Pete Williams and former coach Manolo Hernandez.

The grudge between the two fighters was an interesting mix of wrestling style theatrics and real resentments. Once, in the build up to the fight, the two passed each other in a hotel atrium. A television executive there says the violence in the air was thick enough to touch. When Shamrock fell out of the first fight between the two men, it really did set Kimbo's career back several years, costing him big money. When Slice suggested Shamrock was scared of him, it really did rankle the proud older fighter.

"When Kimbo said that, I thought, 'Are you kidding me? Who are you? Where did you come from?' I would never say that about another fighter. Because I don't know their situation. I would never do that," Shamrock said. "To me that's just a guy that's got no character, he's got no morals, he's got no respect for life or for people.

"I fought all over the world against everyone. I ain't afraid of nobody. Fighting in a ring is not scary. On the street, with guns and knives, where I came from? That's scary. Fighting in a ring? Please."

Almost 3 million people tuned into Spike TV to see Slice escape a choke attempt and knock Shamrock out with a powerful right hand. It was a record-setting fight for Bellator, though the weird circumstances surrounding the finish led many to smell a rat.

"I gotta tell you right now, that fight looked fake as fuck," Joe Rogan told his huge audience on the *Joe Rogan Experience* podcast. "There's a couple of things I don't like about that fight. I don't like that clinch, that long clinch that they had where they were mouth to ear. They were mouth to each other's ears for a long time.[415]

"How about the fact that when Ken did take him down he never hit him once? How about that? He never hit him! He had him down, he had him flattened out, he had his back and he's not crashing him. He's not blasting him with punches. He's got him flattened out and he's not hitting him. That doesn't make any sense to me.[416]"

It was a disappointing night for Shamrock, though, having flown his extended family to St. Louis to see the fight, he did his best to hide it. Worst of all it was going better than he could have possibly imagined before it all fell apart, building hope before callously pulling it away.

Slice, whose knees were also in terrible shape, couldn't defend Shamrock's takedown attempts and ended up caught in a rear naked choke. It was a best case scenario for an ancient fighter no longer used to being in good positions in the cage—and Shamrock didn't rise to the occasion.

"I was a rookie. It was like my first fight. I got into a position to win and I didn't take my time. I forced it," Shamrock said. "I was stronger than him, I manhandled him and I felt in complete control of that fight. But, when I got his back, instead of trying to use my technique and slide the choke in, I tried to choke him to death. I tried to use all my strength and power to muscle it in. Because I felt so much stronger and so much more dominant than him. And I overdid it, man. That's the bottom line. It was a rookie move. I had him dead to rights and I screwed up. I tried to force it instead of just letting it work. It got to a point I was squeezing it so hard that I turned it over and ended up sliding off his back.

"In training, I didn't work on finishing at all, other than some leglocks one day. I mostly worked on conditioning, movement on the ground and positioning," he continued. "I thought it was like riding a

---

[415] According to both fighters, they were talking trash to each other. Shamrock landed a knee and Slice asked him "that all you got?" Ken responded "No, I got something else for you."

[416] "When I first announced I was going to fight, people said I shouldn't be in the ring," Shamrock said. "They said 'He can't win that fight. He's 51. He's been out of the sport for years. There's no way.' The press was saying I was going to lose. The odds were saying I was going to lose. Now, after the fight, the same people are saying there's no way I should have lost.

"It had to be a work? I'm confused. Prior to the fight they were saying I couldn't win. Now they're saying I shouldn't have lost."

bike. When you do it, you just do it. I worked on getting the position, on taking the back. But never on finishing, on applying the move until the guy tapped out. I just worked until I had it and then let go. And I think that's where the mistake was made. In training I never actually made anybody tap out. It was all catch and release."

When Shamrock looked to readjust his hold, he slipped off Slice's back. Quick to seize on the opportunity, the street fighter proceeded to blast Shamrock with a flurry of hard right hands to the mush, forcing John McCarthy to jump in and stop the fight.

For all the criticism that followed, it was the most watched fight in the promotion's seven year history—a level of interest Bellator had a hard time recreating. In September, Bellator attempted to create a mega-event without any established outside stars, pouring serious money and production value into a Pride FC extravaganza called Dynamite.

It barely eked out an average rating, making it crystal clear that fans watch for personality and narrative, not the idea of seeing world class unknowns ply their trade. More than 21 years after he first stepped into the cage, Ken Shamrock still had something that people couldn't take their eyes off of.

"Kimbo was a popular fighter," Shamrock said. "I know that. But I had a huge part in making that happen. I was able to, during my time and even now at this point, break records nearly every time I walked into the ring. I think a lot of people miss what I've done in the MMA world.

"How I was able to market and control the industry so that people wanted to watch my fights. If you look at the fights I've been involved in—in the SEG UFC, in Japan, for Zuffa and today, they have been fights that have turned companies around.

"Promoters did bigger numbers when Ken Shamrock's name is on the card."

CHAPTER TWENTY-ONE
Final Fight (Redux)

For Shamrock, the loss wasn't a warning sign or an indication he could no longer handle the rigors of the cage. Instead, he believed it showed that five years on the sidelines were actually beneficial in some ways. His body responded reasonably well to hard training and he was still capable of getting himself ready for a fight in his fifties.

"I came back at 51, I gave up 30 pounds and I hadn't been in the ring in years," Shamrock said. "And yet, I missed winning because of a mistake. A simple mistake that was due to me having ring rust. Now that I've knocked the rust off, I'm going to get better.

"My timing, everything I do in the ring, is going to get better. Not worse. So why would I stop after a performance like I just had? I wasn't dominated. I dominated him. There's no way I'm stopping on that, man. I've got more. I've got a lot more to give."

Just as importantly, he could still deliver an audience—and a month after swinging and missing with Dynamite, Bellator's Scott Coker was able to coax Royce Gracie out of a nine-year retirement for the trilogy match Shamrock had literally spent 20 years trying to secure.

"It didn't take much to talk Royce into it[417]," Coker told the press. "He said 'What? I'll do it right now. I'll do it in a phone booth, I'll fight him on the street. Let's do it.'"

Shamrock spent the lead up to the event running down the greatest hits version of his list of MMA grievances in every media interview.

---

[417] It was later revealed that, like Shamrock years earlier, Gracie owed the IRS more than a million dollars in back taxes, penalties and fines. This likely played a key role in his decision to take the fight after rejecting the idea of a third match for years.

UFC 1 still rankled him—Shamrock had to give up his wrestling shoes and enter the cage barefoot having never trained or competed without footwear in his entire life. Gracie, meanwhile, was able to wear his judogi and actually won the first fight by choking Shamrock with the gi itself, making it a d efacto weapon as much as a fashion accessory.

UFC 5 was just as irksome. After training to slowly and methodically beat Gracie until the Brazilian simply didn't want to fight anymore, a strategy used effectively years later in Pride by Kazushi Sakuraba, Shamrock had a 30-minute time limit sprung on him at the last minute.

None of this, he believed, was fair, part of the Gracies manipulating their own fight show in their interest and the interest of the Brazilian jiu jitsu movement they were looking to spread around the world. Shamrock admitted it had worked and they had helped reshape the martial arts. But that didn't make it right.

Like he had for the Kimbo fight, Shamrock returned to his roots for what would turn out to be the final fight of his career, bringing Guy Mezger back as his head trainer, providing an old school feel for an old school fight.

"One of the reasons I wanted to train him before the Royce fight was because he told me it was going to be his last fight," Mezger says. "I said I'll do it. But I did it because I owed him. I owed him. He's got a good heart. I will not be one of the guys that asks, 'What has he done for me lately?' Even though I didn't really want to train him because I wanted him not to fight at all, I knew I could prepare him the best."

Also in his corner was a surprise face—Frank Shamrock, back in the fold to help provide strategy and advice after almost 19 years firmly entrenched in an enemy position.

"It seems crazy that you're 50 years old[418] and you want to go fight somebody. But Ken is a fighter," Frank said the day before the bout. "Thing is, he's not going to stop, so we might as well help him. I mean, I don't do it. I'm retired. I couldn't fathom it, but God bless him.

"We had a rough start, but once we got him going, he's just a monster. The beauty of Ken is, he was a street fighter before he was an athlete and before he was a fighter professionally and before he was a wrestler. So he knows how to fight. He's that guy that will knock you out."

---

[418] Ken actually turned 52 just a couple of days before the third Gracie fight on February 19, 2016.

At this point, the mixed martial arts media had almost given up on leveling criticism at these kinds of fights, all but accepting it as the new norm. Always a questionable venture, cage fighting was becoming big business. If there was an audience for it, promoters were going to put up the tents, the trapeze and have an old-fashioned circus fight. We all were, journalist Mike Chiappetta believed, partially responsible for the phenomenon, because no matter how much we knew we should, fans couldn't bear to look away:

> Every professional athlete has an expiration date, but expiration dates are easy to ignore when there is money to be made and eyeballs to draw. This is, after all, a business grown at least partially by a prurient interest in violence, and after having invested ourselves in these athletes' careers for so long, it's hard to look away, even for the final crash. That does not make it good, it just means we all hold some level of responsibility.

The fight itself, immediately following the comically bad co-main event between Kimbo Slice and Dada 5000, did little to make anyone in the audience forget that the two combatants were a combined 101 years old.[419]

A doughy, dad-bod version of Gracie, sporting a completely bald head and love handles, did little but circle for the first two minutes with Shamrock, equally wary, simply following around the cage. The first significant blow of the fight was a knee from Gracie—right to the cup.

It took a second to register before Gracie landed another knee to the head and Shamrock was taken to the mat as he grimaced in pain. Gracie, with no referee intervention, followed up with six unprotected strikes while Ken's hands were on the family jewels. The fight was stopped, and just like that, the feud that launched mixed martial arts was over.

---

[419] Not only did the the Texas Department of Licensing Regulations approve the fight, they allowed it to be an open weight bout so the two didn't need to be in the same weight class. They both weighed in as light heavyweights, with Royce hitting the scales at 190.8 pounds and a shrunken Ken weighing just 201.2 pounds.

"He hit me in the fucking nuts," Shamrock screamed as the referee was jumping in to stop the fight. "Fuck!"

A furious Shamrock exploded after the stoppage, screaming at Gracie, "You did it on purpose" multiple times as his corner tried to calm him down and commission members stepped between the two camps. It was recorded as the first knockout of Gracie's career.

"I was telling Ken, 'We come from an era of no time limit, no weight division, no gloves, no rules,'" a smiling Gracie said in the post-fight press conference. "Groin shots were allowed. But it did not catch his groin.[420]"

Shamrock eventually apologized to Gracie for his outburst after the fight. He had played this moment out in his head countless times, especially once he'd committed to it being the last fight of his career. But it had never played out quite like it did in the cage.

Winning and losing he could handle. He'd done plenty of both—but being stopped by a low blow that the referee somehow missed wasn't an ending Ken was ready to accept. He began advocating for a rematch almost immediately.

"In my opinion it's not over," Shamrock said. "I wouldn't want to win that way. If I hit somebody in the nuts and I knew I hit them in the nuts, I would say sorry and give him his time—his five minutes to recover. That's what I would have done."

Any momentum heading towards a potential fourth fight, mostly powered by the new television viewership record Bellator had just set[421], ground to a halt when Shamrock tested positive for prohibited substances in the standard post-fight drug screening.

"Texas had never tested, at least up to that point. We believed they weren't going to test,[422]" Shamrock says. "I was on some pain management and age management, the hormone replacement. I'm 52

---

[420] Video evidence disagrees. It was clearly a low blow. Also, groin strikes were not allowed in either previous Shamrock-Gracie fight. In fact, at the inaugural UFC event, a low blow was one of only three prohibited techniques. Biting and eye gouging were the others.

[421] Both Shamrock and Kimbo's fights came close to hitting three million viewers once coup was counted.

[422] Shamrock and Slice both tested positive for the steroid Nandrolone, giving credence to this claim as it's a steroid that stays in your body for a long period of time making it generally incompatible with drug testing sports. Ken also tested positive for methadone.

years old and I was under a doctor's care. Three weeks before the fight, I find out they are testing. So I stopped immediately and got on some alternative medicine. Well, it came up dirty.

"My quality of life goes way down without the treatment because I'm in so much pain. If I was to go off I would have a difficult time walking and even getting up and down."

The suspension cost Shamrock not just the opportunity at a Gracie rematch but also a chance to settle the score with another long time rival, Dan "The Beast" Severn. Like Gracie, it was a fight that had been brewing for years, a constant point of focus, if not for the fighters themselves, for the fans who had followed their story for more than a decade.

They were scheduled to square off a month after the Gracie fight for a new online promotion that was offering a mixed card that included a Roy Jones boxing match, Kurt Angle against Rey Misterio under pro wrestling rules and Severn and Shamrock in an MMA fight. The show was a complete bust, drawing just 280 people to a building scaled for ten times that number. The promotion lost a bundle and a furious Severn, whose replacement opponent fell out at the last minute, didn't get a chance to show the world how capable a 58-year-old man could be.

"They didn't want Dan. But I didn't want to fight a younger guy, so I said 'What about Dan?' I didn't mind fighting, so long as I'm fighting within my capabilities," Shamrock says. "Dan starts bashing me in the press. I text him 'Dan, I'm suspended. I'm going to court on it and can't talk about it. I can't talk about it publicly, dude.' He keeps bashing me, saying I'm afraid. After he *knows* why I can't fight because I told him. After that, I didn't want to do the fight at a later date or for someone else. I ain't going to put a dime in his pocket.[423] We had made peace. We were friendly. I went to bat for him and brought him in. And he bashed me. I was done with him. It pissed me off."

The death of the Severn trilogy served as the end of Shamrock's mixed martial arts career. At least as a fighter. He dabbled a bit with his new

---

[423] The two eventually reconciled, at least enough to do a pro wrestling match in Australia on August 31, 2019. Shamrock was 55 years old and Severn 61.

business manager Des Woodruff, associating his brand with a failed energy drink, a high-powered slingshot and a knockoff Apple-style watch, but never seemed to find anything he could truly sink his teeth into.

There were appearances, speaking engagements and opportunities to spread the gospel—but nothing that replaced fighting. And then there was the matter that had plagued Ken and Tonya since they first got married in 2004—the lingering tax debt they still owed despite years of chipping away at it where they could.

"Ken's not fighting, so there's really no big purses coming in," Tonya says. "So the amount of money that he brings in is just off of appearances and stuff. So our income level bracket is really low compared to what it used to be. So they need to reduce the amount of money or payments we owe. They are still asking us for money like Ken was making $500,000. And we don't make that kind of money.

"The finances stress me out at times. Whenever a chunk of money comes in, it has to be set aside and I have to make sure to adjust for the amount of taxes we're going to have to pay. It's a juggling act for me."

For Ken, once a creature of the night, life was now centered on the home, a small house in a solidly middle-class Reno neighborhood.[424] His wife went to work every day. He hit the gym with his father-in-law to help him get through some physical issues or stayed home with his grandkids while one of Tonya's daughters worked through some personal problems. On a fast night, they might go to the local casino to play slots. The church remained a constant.

"The only people I'm really close to and trust are my family," he says. "I don't have any friends that I hang out with. It's either my kids, who are grown now, or my grandkids or my wife. My wife and I do everything together. I don't have those buddy things where I go out and have a drink with the guys. That's not my life anymore."

In 2018, Shamrock started pushing a little harder in the gym, getting into top physical condition and surprising himself with how good it felt. He decided to dip his toes back into the combat sports pool, first in

---

[424] He is still Ken Shamrock, even in this domestic bliss. One day, with the entire family in the car, he left a road-raging man laying unconscious in the street after a dispute. It added to the list of lawsuits that have cost him an estimated $500,000 in his lifetime.

the shallow end with a two wrestling matches[425] for a small promotion in Australia, before fully diving off the high board the next year.

This, his family could live with. A fight, even an exhibition[426], would spark a full-on family riot, so he put those fears to rest by officially retiring in a Facebook post.[427] But everyone could stomach wrestling—so Shamrock started taking independent bookings at an extremely high rate[428], including a double-shot in Atlanta on Super Bowl weekend that included a bar fight with "Filthy" Tom Lawlor every bit as brutal as any of his hardcore matches in WWE.

The match, which included MMA-style striking, crashing around into furniture and even Shamrock dunking Lawlor's head in a toilet, also featured a spot gone awry where, as I wrote at Bleacher Report, Shamrock came inches away from accidentally smacking Lawlor's head off a raised wooden stage with a nasty powerbomb:

> Before the match, as promoter T.J. McAloon gave the small crew of wrestlers brief instructions—mostly to go out there and have fun in this unique environment —Shamrock apologized in advance for accidentally stiffing Lawlor, drawing laughs from the other wrestlers.
>
> In truth, his opponent's main concern was keeping Shamrock safe and sound in his first match back on the scene. At 35, Lawlor felt the aches and pains more than ever. He knew Shamrock, nearly 20 years his senior, would feel it even worse.
>
> "I didn't want to put him in a situation where he

---

[425] His last match before the return was a 2009 bout at Juggalo Championship Wrestling against Jimmie Jacobs. The crooked masked referee turned out to be Dan Severn, as the two were in the midst of ginning up interest in that third fight that never quite happened.

[426] Shamrock once casually brought up an exhibition boxing match with Vinny Pazienza after a family dinner and the looks from the other side of the table were scathing. He decided to pass.

[427] Although the end of the post put the sincerity of the sentiment in serious doubt, sounding less like a retirement and more like a challenge: "I do not have plans to fight again but if I get pushed too far well then I have to be me AGAIN I HAVE NO PLANS ON FIGHTING AGAIN"

[428] All in all, it cost almost $30,000 to bring Team Shamrock to Atlanta for two matches, an exorbitant rate that exceeded all other talent costs combined.

was uncomfortable," Lawlor said. "My job was to go out there and make sure neither one of us got hurt, while still giving the fans some good action. That was going to leave me taking the brunt of the beating. I knew that going in, and it ended up being pretty much what I figured."

The sight of Shamrock, resplendent in intricately embroidered Affliction jeans, throwing up into a trash can a few hours before doors opened gave no one any peace of mind. But as his body plummeted toward the hardwood floor, a different thought flashed through Lawlor's mind.

"As it was happening, I'm thinking, 'Holy shit. He's really just going to powerbomb me on the floor.' And in the split-second I'm thinking that, I hit the floor," Lawlor said. "Luckily, it's a spot I've done plenty of times in a wrestling ring if not a bar, so I was curling myself up for him to be able to lift me anyway.

"As I went down, I stayed curled up rather than taking a flat-backed bump, which probably would have killed me or broken my arm. It was close."

While the match didn't draw the big crowd the promoter had hoped for, it did establish that Shamrock still looked the part, could still move around pretty well and was willing to mix it up in some pretty unusual circumstances—and mix in as best he could with new generation of independent talent, many younger than his own children.

Shamrock lept into Impact Wrestling[429] with both feet, adding a degree of gravitas that most contemporary wrestlers lack. But that doesn't mean he isn't above a little fun. He even, much to the disgust of some traditionalists, took a bump for wrestler Joey Ryan's magical penis.[430]

---

[429] The promotion formerly known as TNA, where he was crowned NWA champion back in 2002, was amazingly still alive and kicking 17 years later after a rebranding and roughly one million changes of direction.

[430] Joey Ryan's penis has the unconquerable power to throw anyone who dares grab a hold. His member exudes power like none other before it. It's made some wrestling old-timers very angry, while managing to also make fans smile at arenas across the world.

After a couple more dates overseas, Shamrock ended up signing with Impact for a rumored $10,000 an event, joining fellow veteran Rob Van Dam to help bring some Attitude Era star power to a promotion mostly featuring independent talent.

He went viral in his first match, against a former NFL player nicknamed Moose, and, as Dave Meltzer wrote in the *Wrestling Observer*, was somehow more vascular at 55 than he'd been at 35. And he was pretty darn vascular then too:

> Shamrock showed up ripped to shreds at 55. He facially looked old and I don't know what he's doing, but the one thing he had that most older guys who train and even do drugs don't have is he still had the big cut legs. So he decided he was 30 and was going to fit into today's high flying style. But he's not 30. The first thing he did was a crazy dive, and he was falling at a really mad angle but Moose caught him and blocked the fall.

"I've never been one to use my words because I think words are cheap," Shamrock told *Yahoo Sports*. "I want to show that this is a competitive organization and I'm here to compete. My demeanor when I walk in that locker room is to prepare to do battle. I'm focused, I don't do a lot of playing around. I talk to people, sure, but there's an intensity that I bring to the locker room, to the organization, that wasn't there before."

Always careful to keep one foot in the realm of legitimate fighting, Shamrock continued his years-long pursuit of starting up his own promotion. But instead of mixed martial arts, a crowded space that barely even resembled the sport he'd helped build, he decided to take a chance on the burgeoning bare knuckle fighting movement, launching Valor BK in 2019.

"When you watch MMA, you always hear the crowd yelling 'stand them up, stand them up.' Well, we've stood them up and we're keeping them up. This is the ultimate combat sport," Shamrock says. "You can't get any higher than bare knuckle. It's pure. People didn't fall in love with what MMA is today. They fell in love with it when it was bare knuckle, no holds barred. That's the feeling we're trying to bring back."

The promotion held its first event at an Indian casino in North

Dakota on September 21, 2019, featuring gruesome, gloveless dust-em ups in a modified pit. It was visceral, brutal and a throwback to the no-holds-barred fighting of yesteryear.

"As a fighter all I had to do was make sure I made weight, train and step in there and fight. It was something I was used to. Now, being a promoter, I have a different vision of it. I see the whole picture," Shamrock says. "I just I want to share that love with all the fighters and fans. I fell in love with bare knuckle. That's what UFC was when I started and there's something special about that. When I look into the eyes of the fighters about to go out there, it gets me jacked up because I know that feeling. Being able to share it as a promoter is really exciting.[431]"

In 2020, Shamrock became a regular in Impact, appearing on AXS TV and mixing in with a collection of interesting talent, many of whom had watched him on WWE television as kids. He was announced as the newest member of their Hall of Fame[432] and seemed to be settling into his new role of older statesman.

It had been years since he'd last been a wrestling regular, but the abbreviated schedule felt sustainable even as 50 years old was further and further in the rearview mirror. It's likely Shamrock will continue adding these little addendums to his story as long as his body and spirit allow it. He was born with fighting in his blood—and nothing is going to change that.

---

[431] "The fighters came in and put on a great show," Shamrock says. "We saw big punching, we saw brawling, we saw dirty fighting, we saw clean fighting, we saw boxing. We saw everything tonight. By the end of the night, man, I was looking at people saying 'I'm not sure that this could have gone any better.'"

[432] WWE gave Impact permission to use footage of Ken from his time as a regular on Raw, perhaps opening the door for an eventual reconciliation.

Acknowledgements

Thanks first and foremost to Ken Shamrock. When he approached me in 2017 about working on a book project, I'll admit to being wary of the idea. After all, Shamrock already had two books about his life and had conducted thousands of media interviews over the course of a decades-long career in combat sports. I simply wasn't sure what I'd be able to add.

But I quickly discovered that he had barely scratched the surface when it came to telling the tale of his remarkable life and agreed to jump head first into the project. We had two ground rules—Ken wouldn't tell me what to write and he wouldn't try to prevent anyone in his life from talking with me.

He was clear at times that he wasn't going to, as he put it, "tell on himself," but when I came to him with topics from my other interviews and research, even painful ones, he'd talk about them openly and (mostly) honestly. He and his wife Tonya welcomed me into their Reno, Nevada, home twice and spent dozens of hours sorting through the often confusing and unclear timeline of his life. Many of the events depicted here are decades old and it's easy to lose track of whether something happened in 1987 or 1988 once enough time has passed to make the memory a little hazy.

Shamrock often gave interview subjects who were hesitant tacit permission to talk with me openly about their experiences together. This was particularly important when, as you've seen, the recollections placed Ken and people close to him on the wrong side of the law. Without his subtle thumbs up, I wouldn't have been able to write this book. He commands enough loyalty, respect and fear from many in his circle to have cut this book off at the knees had he chosen to.

To tell the story of his life, I conducted more than a hundred interviews with a wide-ranging cast of characters. These included everyone from fight promoters and wrestlers to roommates, friends and strippers. Some of them were an open book, while others would only agree to comment on background or anonymously. Occasionally, someone was both, depending on the subject being discussed.

In order to get as full a picture as possible, I allowed interview subjects to be off the record when they asked. All were immensely valuable in both telling Ken's story and confirming or refuting details others had offered.

I relied heavily on the MMA and wrestling media, both to compile a rough timeline and for details that might have otherwise escaped my notice. Though it is impossible to mention every source I read or watched, the works of Dave Meltzer, Wade Keller, Thomas Gerbasi, Josh Gross and Loretta Hunt were particularly valuable.

Most people were extraordinarily helpful and I appreciate everyone who reached out and shared their experiences with Ken or the stories and interviews they'd conducted over the years with members of the Lion's Den. David Bixenspan, Jason Cruz and Chris Tabar all came through in a major way with resources that were otherwise unavailable. Roxanne Modafferi, Chris Charlton and Hana Watanabe helped with Japanese translations and interviews.

James Frazier provided the drawings for the illustrated hardcover and Ryan Loco shot the amazing photograph for the front cover Kristina Snowden, as always, was a rock throughout the process. I couldn't do this without the support of all the people in my combat sports life and I appreciate all of you more than you know.

A special thank you to supporters on Indiegogo who helped fund this project:

Bruce Huckfeldt
  Ben Jensen
  Alaric Moore
  Michael Estepa
  Molly French
  Andrew Worth
  Wilton Bunn III
  Sam Hamer
  Larry Francis
  Susan Cingari
  Jason McClure

Shamrock

Jose Fernandez
Michael Sugarman
Rodney Miceli
Josh Mast
Joseph Corti
Paul Benson
Rickie Radosevich
Brandi Lutz
Michael Steczkowski
Reid Galbreath
John-Jo Carter
Philippe Lupien
Steven Crocker
Dominic Pecoraro
Matthew Alexander
Joe N Tippett
Kate Bowman
Alex Sovet
Matthias Plattner
Dave Walstra
Steven S. Paschall
John Pozarowski
Matthew Peter Phaedonos
Ryan Blackwell
Frank Kaestner
Lee Casebolt
Jonothan Whatley
Kyle Olson
Tomás Gleeson
Danny Kay
Michael Reisig
Pablo Garcia III
Ryan Hobbs
David Warren
Dom DaRocha
Ariel Goldberg
Shawn Stewart
Jason Thornton
Dustin Keener
David Mantey

Richard Bernal
Zandria Michaud
Matthew Towner
Thomas McCulloch
Danny Mitchell
Max Vessels
John Factor
John L MacArthur
Ryan Bowman
Dan Alban
Michael Kingston
Matt Callister
Brian Hemminger
Wesley Gorman
Matt Charlton
Randy Hubbard
Austin Grout
Amanda Earley
Derek Imm
Alex Orfanos
Jon Strosser
Theresa Kullander
Oliver Irons
Edward Holster Jr
Gerald Levinzon
Eddie Johnson
Gregg Gartside
Christopher Sharpe
Vicki Vance
Alexander Petzel-Gligorea
Shane Whitecloud
Larry Goldberg
Jason Williard
Mark Flores
William Suarez
Joe Charnish
Stephen Lynch
Chad Dundas
Michael Jarsulic
Kelsey and Rachel McCarson

Shamrock

Andrew Wallace
Riley Thiesen
Matthew Finnie
Shawn Stewart
Matthew Saccaro
Eric Stinton
Rich Hansen
Craig Grant

Made in the USA
Las Vegas, NV
06 December 2022

61284380R00234